Between One and Many

Between One and Many

THE ART AND SCIENCE OF PUBLIC SPEAKING

Third Edition

Steven R. Brydon

Michael D. Scott
California State University, Chico

Mayfield Publishing Company
Mountain View, California
London • Toronto

Library of Congress Cataloging-in-Publication Data
Brydon, Steven Robert.
  Between one and many: the art and science of public speaking /
Steven R. Brydon, Michael D. Scott.—3rd ed.
     p.   cm.
  Includes bibliographical references (p.) and index.
  ISBN 0-7674-0817-9
  1. Public speaking.   I. Scott, Michael D.   II. Title.
PN4121.B777   1999
  808.5' 1—dc21   99-29042
                                                                                         CIP

Manufactured in the United States of America
10 9 8 7 6 5 4 3 2 1

Mayfield Publishing Company
1280 Villa Street
Mountain View, CA 94041

Sponsoring editor, Holly J. Allen; production editor, Melissa Williams Kreischer; manuscript editor, Beverley J. DeWitt; design manager, Susan Breitbard; text and cover designer, Ellen Pettengell; art editor, Amy Folden; photo researcher, Brian J. Pecko; illustrators, Lotus Art; manufacturing manager, Randy Hurst. The text was set in 10.5/12 Goudy by Carlisle Communications, Ltd. and printed on acid-free 45# Somerset Matte by R. R. Donnelley and Sons Company.

Text and photo credits appear on pages 455–456, which constitute an extension of the copyright page.

Cover art, © Lauren Uram.

Preface

Public speaking is a dynamic transaction "between one and many"— between the one who is speaking and the many who are listening. The meaning of the message emerges from the relationship between speaker and audience. No speaker can succeed without knowing his or her audience, and no audience member can benefit by just passively receiving a message. Both speaker and audience—and the transaction between them—are essential to the process. As teachers and as authors, we focus on the transactional nature of successful public speaking.

Public speaking is also an art, a science, and a skill—one that can be learned, improved, and polished. We encourage students to think of public speaking as a learning experience—they don't have to be perfect at the outset!—and we offer them the tools to become the speakers they want to be. Public speakers can draw on a vast body of information, ranging from classical rhetorical theories to empirical communication research. In this book we include both traditional topics, such as logos, ethos, and pathos as the roots of persuasive speaking, and current ones, such as research on cultural diversity and the uses of technology in public speaking.

Today's students of public speaking will face many different rhetorical situations in their lives, and they will face audiences of increasing cultural, demographic, and individual diversity. Throughout this book, we focus on ways to adapt to audiences in order to have the best chance of being heard and understood. We stress the responsibilities and ethical issues involved in being a good public speaker. And we discuss how to be a good audience member: one who knows how to listen, to behave ethically, and to critically evaluate the message being presented. In sum, we attempt to provide students with a broad understanding of the nature of public speaking as well as the specific skills they need to become successful, effective public speakers, both as college students and throughout their lives.

Features of the Book

Integrated Text and Video   *Between One and Many* provides an integrated package of text and videotape for the students. This twelve-part videotape brings to life the theories and skills discussed in the text. Rather than simply reading examples of speeches and perhaps seeing them in class, students can view and study speeches and delivery styles on their own time and at their own pace. Text and video are coordinated so that students see examples of the type of speech they are studying throughout the course, along with a commentary and critique. This technique allows us to reinforce our points through modeling, which research has shown to be an excellent way to learn skills like public speaking.

The video can be bundled with the text for student use. Instructors can, of course, use *Between One and Many* without adopting the videotape for student use. The concepts and skills required for effective public speaking are fully described and illustrated in the text. Annotated outlines of student speeches are included to show students how to apply the principles discussed in the book to actual speech situations. The full texts of speeches by selected student and public figures are also included in the Appendixes.

Integrated Pedagogy   Throughout the text, boxes are used to focus attention on subjects of special interest. Five different types of boxes appear: Profile boxes offer examples of individuals who have used public speaking in their lives; In Their Own Words boxes provide examples of speeches by students and public figures, including several student speeches in outline form with marginal comments; Self-Assessment boxes allow students to assess their own skills and attributes (such as speech anxiety); Considering Diversity boxes show how the topic of a chapter applies to today's multicultural, multiracial, and multiethnic audiences. These boxes are a new feature that spreads the discussion of diversity throughout the book; Speaking of . . . boxes contain current, topical information that relates to the text discussion. Throughout the book, speechmaking skills are highlighted in special lists labeled Tips and Tactics. These lists make it easy for students to apply practical suggestions to their own speeches. Video File boxes in the margins call attention to corresponding video segments.

Help for Speech Anxiety   We recognize that most students come to a public speaking class with considerable trepidation. We devote a full chapter early in the text to speech anxiety, as well as a segment of the videotape. The text and video package offers many specific, concrete techniques that students can use to manage and even benefit from anxiety.

Emphasis on Adapting to Audience Diversity   We give significant attention to audience diversity based, in part, on Geert Hofstede's work on understanding cultural diversity. Using Hofstede's dimensions of collectivism and individualism, power distance, uncertainty avoidance, masculinity and femininity, and long-term versus short-term orientation, we offer ideas on how to analyze and adapt to audience diversity across cultures.

Full Chapter on Ethics   We feature a full chapter on ethics. Working from basic ethical principles, we provide and reinforce ethical guidelines for both public speakers and audience members.

Emphasis on Critical Thinking   Central to effective and ethical communication are the abilities to critically evaluate evidence, to present sound reasoning in one's speeches, and to detect fallacious reasoning in the speeches of others. *Between One and Many* continues to provide a strong critical thinking component, based on Toulmin's model of argument.

Highlights of the Third Edition

Based on the feedback from many instructors who used the second edition, we have incorporated a number of changes into this edition to strengthen the book.

Expanded Use of Computer Technology   We have increased and updated the discussion of the use of the Internet, including an extensive discussion of how to critically evaluate the reliability of materials found there, and stressing the inherent problems in overreliance on such materials. We also feature an expanded section on the use of PowerPoint to develop visual aids, including the pitfalls of letting the technology overpower the speech.

Addition of MLA Format   In a major change, we include examples of MLA as well as APA source citations in our discussion of documentation so that instructors may choose their preferred system of source citation.

Increased Use of Student Outlines   The third edition has replaced most manuscripts with outlines as examples of student speeches. Since few instructors require full manuscripts, this was done to allow for more examples that students could actually use. The outlines are fully annotated with marginal comments.

Updated Material   Examples have been updated throughout the book, including the replacing of Candy Lightner, founder of MADD, with Carolyn McCarthy, a leader of the victims' rights movement and a recently elected member of Congress. New student speeches have been included both in the text and on the videotape.

Expanded Treatment of Organizational Patterns and Styles of Delivery   The text now includes a greater diversity of types of organizational patterns, including nontraditional patterns often overlooked in Western societies.

Small Group Communication   A new section in Chapter 15 deals with speaking in small groups, with a specific focus on leadership responsibilities.

Organization of the Text

The basic chapter structure of the third edition remains unchanged, allowing an easy transition for teachers accustomed to the second edition. *Between One and Many* is organized to allow students to get up and speak early in the semester. As they learn more about the art and science of public speaking, they are also preparing for more demanding speaking assignments. We hope that our organizational scheme will suit the needs of most instructors, but we also know that different instructors have different preferences for how material is sequenced.

Therefore, we have designed each chapter to stand alone. Instructors can assign them in the order that best matches their own course plan.

Part One deals with the foundations of the art and science of public speaking. Chapter 1, re-titled "Everyday Speaking," focuses on the personal, professional, and public reasons for becoming a good public speaker, with specific examples of average people who use public speaking in their daily lives. We also introduce a revised model of public speaking and preview the remainder of the book. Chapter 2 provides an overview of the skills needed by public speakers and allows instructors to assign speeches early on without having to assign chapters out of order. Topic selection and writing purpose statements have been incorporated into this chapter to provide an early foundation for students in preparing their first speeches. Chapter 3 provides students with the tools they need to cope with the nearly universal experience of speech anxiety. Chapter 4 presents a revised treatment of listening, with a greater focus on listening to public speeches.

Part Two deals directly with adapting to the audience. We make explicit that the key to success in public speaking is focusing on the audience. Chapter 5 uses the rhetorical situation as an organizing principle, and introduces Hofstede's system for analyzing audience diversity. Material pertinent primarily to persuasion (such as latitudes of acceptance and rejection) are deferred to the persuasion chapter. Chapter 6 thoroughly discusses ethical communication behavior, both by speakers and by audience members.

Part Three is about putting theory into practice. Chapter 7 covers invention; the chapter greatly expands on our treatment of the Internet as a source, including how to test Internet information for reliability. Chapter 8 treats organization from an audience-focused perspective. We include a variety of organizational patterns, including Monroe's Motivated Sequence, the Extended Narrative, a Problem–Solution format based on a stock issues perspective, and discuss nontraditional patterns of organization and delivery such as the star, wave, spiral, and call and response. Material dealing with transitional statements is also relocated in this chapter. Chapter 9 addresses language use, with particular attention to adapting language to diverse audiences. We suggest ways to choose language that is inclusive rather than exclusive, nonsexist rather than sexist, and thoughtful rather than stereotypic. Chapter 10 deals with delivery skills, again focusing on audience adaptation. This chapter provides both a strong theoretical foundation based in nonverbal communication research and solid, practical advice for the public speaker. Chapter 11 presents a comprehensive discussion of visual, audio, and audiovisual materials that can be adapted to the audience and occasion to enhance most public speeches. A detailed discussion of the use of PowerPoint has been added for this edition.

Part Four addresses the most common contexts for public speaking that students are likely to face in the classroom and in their lives after college. Chapter 12 treats informative speaking. In this chapter we again stress audience adaptation, particularly in terms of diverse learning styles. Practical applications of learning principles are shown for speeches that explain, instruct, demonstrate, and describe. Chapter 13, dealing with persuasive speaking, has been significantly revised. We moved the discussion of Toulmin's Model of Reasoning to

Chapter 14. We increased the discussion of speaker credibility, and included opinion leadership in that context. Discussion of latitudes of acceptance has been incorporated into this chapter. Chapter 14 also provides a detailed treatment of critical thinking, with a special focus on recognizing and responding to fallacies of reasoning. A side-by-side comparison of pro- and con-arguments illustrates concepts of reasoning and identifies specific fallacies. Finally, Chapter 15 provides a discussion of speaking in everyday life. It includes helpful guidelines for impromptu speaking; speeches of acceptance, introduction, recognition, and commemoration; speeches to entertain; and speaking on television. A new section also has been added on speaking in small groups.

Teaching Support Package

The textbook is part of a comprehensive package designed to help you solve teaching problems in your public speaking course.

Instructor's Manual   Written by the authors and updated with the assistance of Rachel Holloway, an experienced college instructor, the Instructor's Manual includes a variety of useful resources. New sections of the manual include strategies for managing multi-section courses, a primer for graduate assistants and first-time teachers, and lists for quick reference of the speechmaking skills highlighted in each chapter. Revision of the manual has included new materials for the sections offering in-class activities, sample semester and quarter syllabi, sample evaluation forms, and transparency masters. The contents of the manual are based on the authors' collective four decades of teaching experience; many of the activities and materials have been class-tested with the thousands of students enrolled in the basic public speaking course at California State University, Chico, and Virginia Polytechnic Institute and State University.

Printed and Computerized Test Items   Approximately 1,300 test questions, including multiple choice, true-false, and essay questions, are included in the Instructor's Manual. As with other materials in the instructor's package, many of these test items have been class-tested. The complete test bank is also available in computerized format, allowing you to edit the questions from the test bank and to incorporate your own questions. The computerized test bank is available in both Windows and Macintosh formats.

Instructor's CD-ROM   This CD contains an Image Bank, PowerPoint slides, and other instructor's materials. Full-color images from the book, as well as the complete set of images from the transparency acetates and transparency masters, are included on the CD in a format suitable for classroom presentation, either with an LCD overhead projector or as part of a PowerPoint presentation. A complete set of PowerPoint slides, developed by Ulla Bunz, University of Kansas, provide a lecture outline for each chapter of the book. The Instructor's Manual can be downloaded from the CD and customized to fit any course organization. This complete package of presentation resources can be used with both IBM-compatible and Macintosh computers.

Transparencies   Overhead color transparencies are available free of charge to adopting instructors. The transparencies illustrate and review major concepts from the text.

Teaching Assistant Materials   Programs employing graduate teaching assistants or other first-time instructors will receive three additional package components, free upon request, subject to minimum adoption requirements. One is a book, *Between Teachers and Students: A Primer for Teaching Assistants and First-Time Instructors*. The second and third are videotapes, *Agents of Change: Graduate Teaching Assistants in the Basic Course* and *Models of Excellence*, focusing on the attributes of award-winning teachers. The guidebook and *Agents of Change* videotape answer many of the practical questions asked by first-time teachers— everything from what to do the first day of class to how to handle office-hour meetings with students. And the *Models of Excellence* tape shows what it means to be an effective teacher from teacher and student perspectives.

Web Site   A new feature of this edition is a Web site at www.mayfieldpub. com/brydon where both students and instructors will find additional supportive materials. Included in the Web site are a number of useful pedagogical aids for the professor, including PowerPoint slides, a syllabus generator, the Instructor's Manual, activities, a bulletin board, and guidelines for first-time teachers. For the student, the Web site will offer chapter quizzes and key terms, helpful aids for the first speech, assistance with speech outlining, e-mail addresses, and information regarding the video, as well as a number of useful links to other Web sites that can assist students in developing their speeches.

The Mayfield Quick Guide to the Internet   Students can receive free, shrink-wrapped with the text, *The Mayfield Quick Guide to the Internet for Communication Students*, by John A. Courtright and Elizabeth M. Perse. This useful supplement expands on our discussion in the textbook on using the Internet for research in preparing speeches. It explains the basics of the Internet, how to navigate the World Wide Web, and how to evaluate and cite information from the Internet. It also includes an appendix with literally hundreds of useful communication-related Web sites.

Videotape   The *Student Video Study Guide* that accompanies this book is available at minimal cost to students when the book and tape are adopted together. The major change in the video was to delete those segments that merely repeated material from the book. The emphasis on telling has been replaced with showing. We have expanded our treatment of delivery and visual aid, including a more extensive discussion of PowerPoint. We also added a segment taking students through the process of preparing and delivering an informative and persuasive speech. Speeches are generally the ones outlined in the corresponding chapters.

The videotape allows us to show what most texts only talk about. It also frees up valuable class time for the instructor and students to use in other productive ways. Each segment can be viewed independently of the others and is coordinated with a specific chapter in the text. Video File boxes in the margins of the book indicate where a particular video segment would be appropriate. The video not only reinforces the text but also previews material to be covered later in the class in more depth. We have found that the vast majority of students currently own or have ready access to VCRs. When the text is ordered without the video, instructors may still request a copy to show during class time.

Additional Videotaped Speeches   Also available to adopters is a videocassette of additional student speeches. Unedited and shown without commentary, these speeches can be a valuable tool in class when teaching students about the art and science of public speaking.

Acknowledgments

We gratefully acknowledge the support and assistance of many people at Mayfield Publishing Company who played a role in this book, including Holly Allen, sponsoring editor; Melissa Williams Kreischer, production editor; Beverley DeWitt, copyeditor; Susan Breitbard, design manager; Amy Folden, art editor; Brian Pecko, photo researcher; and Star MacKenzie, editorial assistant.

We are especially grateful to George Rogers, of Chico State, who produced the *Student Video Study Guide* that accompanies this text, and to the numerous students who consented to be videotaped for this project. Special thanks go to the speakers who shared their talents in providing sample speeches: Karen Shirk, Chalsey Phariss, Gloria Sobalvarro, Suzanne Mifsud, Josette Parker, David A. Sanders, Jonathan Studebaker, Kelli Wells, and Ryland Hill. We would also like to thank the individuals profiled in this book for generously consenting to contribute to our effort: Keith Hawkins, Jonathan Studebaker, Enrique "Rick" Rigsby, Tomoko Mukawa, Jeraline Singh, and Russ Woody. They are friends, colleagues, former students, and role models; they have all enriched our book and our lives.

A grateful thank you for the reviews and counsel of our peers in the classroom who graciously prepared careful critiques of our manuscript and videotape in various stages of development: Carol C. Bledsoe, University of Central Florida; Vincent L. Bloom, California State University, Fresno; Robert B. Bookwalter, Marshall University; Karen M. Borglum, Valencia Community College; Robert A. Brookey, University of Minnesota; Kerry Egdorf, Marquette University; Rachel L. Holloway, Virginia Polytechnic Institute and State University; Rebecca Mikesell, University of Scranton; Eric Moore, Fayetteville State University; Maggie Morrisson, Ohlone College; Deb Peterson, University of St. Thomas; and Gregory J. Shepherd, University of Kansas. We appreciate the help of all these individuals in preparing this book but we are, of course, ultimately responsible for its content. Any errors or omissions are solely our own.

And last, but certainly not least, we wish to thank our families, Pamela, Robert, Julie, Randi, and Colin, who not only showed great patience as we worked on this project but often provided assistance in more ways than we can possibly list.

Brief Contents

Contents

TO PAMELA AND RANDI—OUR WIVES AND BEST FRIENDS

Foundations

Actor and activist Edward James Olmos speaks frequently to high school students about issues of diversity and gang violence.

Everyday Speaking

OBJECTIVES

After reading this chapter, you should be able to:

- Describe the relationship between personal needs and the ability to speak publicly.
- Explain the role speaking plays in the professional promotion of self.
- Describe how speaking skills can make people better citizens.
- Demonstrate an understanding of the transactional and symbolic nature of the process of public speaking.

KEY CONCEPTS

In each chapter we will introduce you to some key terms you need to know. We place these at the beginning of each chapter to alert you to important terms you will encounter. In this chapter look for the following terms:

channel	interdependence
content (of messages)	message
decoding	perception
deficiency needs	relational component (of messages)
encoding	symbol
feedback	system
growth needs	transaction

If all my talents and powers were to be taken from me . . . and I had my choice of keeping but one, I would unhesitatingly ask to be allowed to keep the Power of Speaking, for through it, I would quickly recover all the rest.

—Daniel Webster

Cara Cupp, Randy Larsen, and Doug Peete.

Who are the people who commonly come to mind when you think about public speaking? What are the circumstances in which you imagine these people speaking?

Are the people famous—for example, a public figure like the president of the United States or a celebrity like Oprah Winfrey? Is the situation you imagine full of ceremony—for instance, a commencement address at a college graduation or a State of the Union Address before Congress? In reality, most public speeches are given by ordinary people in ordinary situations. The hundreds of thousands of speeches given each day are delivered by students in college classrooms, businesspeople hoping to win new clients, and public servants intent on helping ordinary citizens understand why they must, for example, sort their trash to promote recycling.

Most speeches are given, in other words, by people whose roles in life are probably similar to ones you now play or plan on playing in the near future. Consider the three people you see here. Cara Cupp is a first-year law student at Hastings School of Law in San Francisco. Randy Larsen is an environmental educator and environmental talk-show host whose program is carried nationally, including New York City, Los Angeles, and Chicago. Doug Peete is a systems consultant for PeopleSoft, a leading manufacturer of software solutions for business. Although they do not think of themselves as public speakers per se, each has been required not only to speak in public, but to do a good job of it.

Cara Cupp, for example, estimates she gave speeches in 75 percent of the undergraduate courses she took, even though the assignments were not specifically called speeches. She attributes her success in many of these courses, which helped her gain entrance to Hastings, to the skills she learned in her introductory public speaking class. Randy Larsen, who actually keeps a running record of his presentations, counts them in the hundreds since he graduated. In addition to his public speeches before live audiences, Randy's environmental radio talk show has been aired locally for several years. Now that it is being nationally syndicated, it will undoubtedly reach hundreds of thousands of listeners. Likewise, Doug Peete, whose degree is in computer engineering, tells us his contact with a client begins and ends with a presentation to an audience composed of people who do and do not share Doug's technical expertise.

Public speaking is an essential communication skill in today's world. Public speaking also is an extension and refinement of many of the skills you already practice in your one-on-one and group communication encounters. Our goal in this initial chapter is threefold. First, we demonstrate how common it is for people to use their speaking skills to satisfy their personal and professional needs, and to help empower others to satisfy theirs. Second, we make clear the connection between public speaking and the other forms of communicating you routinely practice, and we discuss public speaking as a specific kind of system of communication. Finally, we preview the chapters that follow this one.

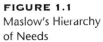

VIDEO FILE

If you have access to the videotape that accompanies this book, view segment 1, which provides an overview to a course in public speaking.

PERSONAL REASONS FOR DEVELOPING SPEAKING SKILLS

Although we may not consciously realize it, human communication is a need as basic to our well-being as the food we eat, water we drink, and air we breathe. Both clinical and case studies compellingly show that when we are deprived of this need, we are affected both physically and psychologically.

Satisfying Your Personal Needs

Abraham Maslow wrote that we experience two sets of personal needs: deficiency needs and growth needs.[1] **Deficiency needs** are basic human needs. **Growth needs** are higher-order human needs. Maslow arranged these two sets of needs in the form of a hierarchy to show that our deficiency needs must be satisfied routinely before our growth needs become important to us.

As Figure 1.1 indicates, there are four sets of deficiency needs: (1) *biological needs*, such as for food, water, and air; (2) *safety needs*, such as protection from

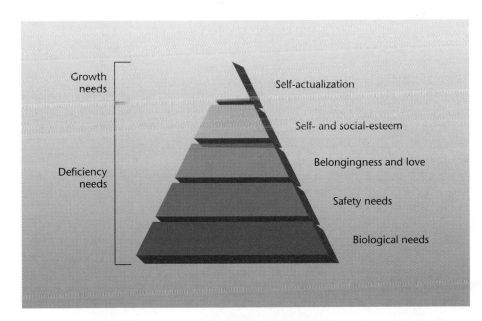

FIGURE 1.1
Maslow's Hierarchy of Needs

Accepting the Challenge: Keith Hawkins

Keith Hawkins's life reads like a scene from a movie about inner-city life. Born to a teenage mother in South-Central Los Angeles, abandoned by his father, and forced to live in a one-room shack in rural Florida by his mother's crack-addicted boyfriend, Keith was never in one school for more than 6 months until he was 13 years old. Passed from one grade to the next, even though he needed to be held back, he lacked basic skills in reading, writing, and math.

In the tenth grade, Keith had a life-changing experience. His best friend and football teammate was murdered. After the funeral, Keith's coach handed him his friend's jersey and issued him a challenge—to do something his friend had never done, despite being a star athlete: Stay out of trouble and make something of his life.

Not only did Keith accept the challenge, but his football coach became his mentor. In the process Keith became a better student, held office in his statewide student government association, and discovered a talent other than sports. Specifically, Keith learned not only that he enjoyed speaking before groups, but that he was pretty good at it. As a result, he took classes in speaking and received advanced training while he was serving as president of the California Association of Student Governments. He also began speaking to groups of kids with backgrounds similar to his own.

Today, Keith is a paid public speaker. He has traveled throughout the United States speaking to youth groups, schools, and even an assembly of the United Nations. Articles about Keith have appeared in the *New York Times* and *Time* magazine. Keith's long-term goal to become a professional speaker is being realized. He says this about his still-young life: "I feel you need three things in life: Something to do, something to hope for, and someone to love. Speaking gives me something to do, and the kids who come up to me afterwards to talk give me something to hope for, and someone to love."

physical harm; (3) *belongingness and love needs*, such as those experienced by a child for the love of a parent; and (4) *self- and social-esteem needs*, which involve believing in our self-worth and finding confirmation from others of that belief.

Growth needs are not as straightforward as deficiency needs. They include self-actualization, knowledge and understanding, and aesthetic needs. Self-actualization is the most commonly discussed growth need. According to Maslow, *self-actualization* is the process of fully realizing one's potential. Self-actualized people not only understand themselves but also accept themselves for who they are and what they have achieved.

The ability to skillfully present our thoughts and feelings publicly is increasingly important to the satisfaction of both our deficiency needs and our growth needs. Consider again the case of Randy Larsen. As an environmental educator and advocate, much of Randy Larsen's time is spent speaking to groups of all ages about protecting the air we breathe, water we drink, and food we eat.

Randy covers many topics in the process, ranging from the destruction of rain forests to the effects of agricultural pesticides on groundwater. Although Randy's public speaking skills are directly connected to his and other's deficiency needs, they also are connected to Randy's desire to self-actualize his own potential as a human being, a clear growth need.

As a first- or second-year college student, you may recall giving speeches in high school, whether you gave a class report, participated in a debate, or spoke to an assembly of your fellow students. Even if you have not had high school experience, it is likely you will use public speaking skills in the future. You may find yourself speaking after college, as a parent at a PTA meeting, a citizen speaking before your local planning agency about a development in your neighborhood, or as part of a nonprofit organization, such as the Red Cross, seeking to raise public awareness.

Meeting the Personal Needs of Others

As the case of Keith Hawkins, profiled for you in the box "Accepting the Challenge," shows, communication also is the primary medium through which we satisfy our needs and help others satisfy theirs. Public speaking skills also can empower others to satisfy their own deficiency and growth needs. Often people need someone who can bring their needs into better focus and enable them to act to meet those needs. Actor/activist Edward James Olmos, star of *Stand and Deliver* and *American Me*, spoke at the authors' campus on the topic "We Are All the Same Gang."[2] Having succeeded in meeting his personal and professional needs as a critically acclaimed actor, Olmos is now using his talents to speak out for the needs of others. He targets his message to those who are tempted to join gangs. His speeches promote peace, racial harmony, and the need for children to be vaccinated against violence. As he points out, "No child comes out of his mother's womb with a pistol."[3]

PROFESSIONAL REASONS FOR DEVELOPING SPEAKING SKILLS

Besides satisfying needs, there are many professional reasons for honing your public speaking skills. One major reason is to become an agent of influence in your career. As an agent of influence, you will be in a position to (1) promote your professional self, (2) better present your ideas to decision makers, (3) create positive change in the workplace, (4) become a functioning force in meetings, and (5) develop active listening skills.

Promoting Your Professional Self

The chance to speak in public frequently presents us with an ideal opportunity to enhance our professional credibility. Some time ago the authors of this text were treated to a presentation by Dr. Bonnie Johnson. She spoke about work she

How Much Experience Do You Have Speaking?

Most of us recognize that there is a high degree of correspondence between skill and training. Most of us also will admit that any skill suffers from lack of training and practice, whether it is shooting free throws or solving math problems. With this in mind, answer the following questions:

1. On a scale of 1 to 10, with 1 being little and 10 being considerable, what is your *training* in public speaking?
2. On a scale of 1 to 10, with 1 being little and 10 being considerable, what is your *practice and experience* with public speaking?
3. Given your score for numbers 1 and 2, how would you rate your *effectiveness* as a public speaker on a scale of 1 to 10, with 1 representing ineffective and 10 representing highly effective?
4. How well do you think the three scores you gave yourself correspond? We raise this question because students frequently think they are better speakers than their training and experience would predict.

Using your responses to these four questions as a guide, list 10 public speaking skills you could improve on—for example, listening more attentively, feeling more comfortable speaking, and thinking more critically about speeches you hear from others. Write down those skills or record them in a journal. At the end of the academic term, compare your goals with what you believe you have achieved in the class.

had done for Intel, the world's largest manufacturer of silicon chips. As someone trained in organizational communication, Dr. Johnson was given permission by Intel to study how well personnel were adapting to technological change in the workplace—for example, electronic workstations. When she had concluded her study, Intel offered her a position with the corporation.

Following her presentation, Dr. Johnson welcomed questions from the audience. One undergraduate asked her why she thought Intel had hired her. "Do you want to know candidly?" she asked. "Because initially they were more impressed with the public presentation I made to top management on the results of my study than the study itself. They hired me because I not only knew my subject but could effectively speak about it and its implications for Intel."

As exemplified by Dr. Johnson's anecdote about her experience with Intel, communication skills in general and public speaking skills specifically are both desired and rewarded in the workplace. Surveys of personnel managers at top companies consistently demonstrate that they look for college graduates who not only can communicate interpersonally and in writing but who also can deliver a speech well. Ask just about anyone who has climbed the corporate ladder, and you will learn that public speaking skills helped tremendously along the way.

Presenting Ideas to Decision Makers

Another reason organizations put such a high premium on speaking skills concerns the effective communication of ideas. Your success depends not only on your ideas, but also on how well you can present those ideas to people whose decisions will affect your career. When you think about it, every occupation and profession involves selling ideas to other people. For example, the life insurance salesperson who must persuade a client to increase coverage is unlikely to close the deal simply by dropping a brochure in the mail. On a larger scale, most corporations require managers to present reports or briefings describing their accomplishments and future plans and goals. Those individuals who seek to move beyond entry-level positions need to be able to convince others of the wisdom of their ideas. Thus, being able to speak to decision makers with confidence and authority is an indispensable tool for corporate success.

Dave Davies's experience at 3M is a good case in point. Although scientists by training, Davies and the people in his department have to justify resources they believe are necessary to their research. Thus, when Davies needed $20 million to advance his work on laser disks, he was required to publicly present his case to 3M's executive operations council, which included 3M's CEO. This was no sit-down presentation at a conference table. As is usually required in such cases, Davies made a stand-up presentation using both a lectern and visual aids.[4] The fact that Davies was successful in procuring the money reflected not only the promise of the product, but also the skill with which Davies presented its promise to 3M's executive council.

Creating Change in the Workplace

One of the most important tasks for any supervisor or manager is to be able to convince subordinates that proposed changes are desirable. To remain competitive, companies must implement new technologies and procedures. Yet many employees fear change. Often the best way to implement change is to sell employees on new ideas rather than to tell them to simply get used to those ideas. A willing and enthusiastic workforce is far more likely to accept change in the workplace than is a reluctant and suspicious one.

In addition, change need not always be initiated from the top. Many of the best ideas in industry come from employees who convince their managers that change is necessary. Consider the example of America's most successful retail store, Wal-Mart. Founder Sam Walton believed, "Our best ideas come from clerks and stock boys."[5] To prove the point Walton once rode 100 miles in a Wal-Mart truck just to listen and talk to the driver.

Lest you believe that this approach is unique, companies as diverse as Delta Airlines and Hewlett-Packard also listen to their employees. For example, "Delta spends a lot of time and money . . . checking out the employee's side of the story. Often the result is a substantial policy change," according to management consultants Tom Peters and Robert Waterman.[6] They report that senior management at Delta meet in an "open forum" at least once a year. Those in the lowest ranks of the organization have the opportunity to speak directly with those at the highest levels. And Hewlett-Packard has an "open lab stock" policy that allows workers to take equipment home for their personal use, in the hope that they might come up with an innovation.[7] Successful organizations don't just talk to their employees, they listen to them as well.

Becoming a Functioning Force in Meetings

Although small-group communication is not the principal focus of this book, many of the skills we discuss—ranging from active listening to critical thinking to making impromptu presentations—are directly applicable to functioning in group meetings. As communication professor Ronald Adler reports, the average business executive spends about 45 minutes out of every hour communicating, much of this time in meetings.[8] Further, surveys show that executives spend as many as 700 hours per year in meetings.[9] Your ability to speak effectively in meetings will be indispensable to your success in the workplace.

Developing Active Listening Skills

It is not enough to know how to present your ideas to others. You need to listen to the needs of others and to what they say in response to your ideas. On the average we spend up to 55 percent of our day in situations that involve the potential to listen.[10] Seldom, however, do we take full advantage of this potential. Active listening, which we discuss at length in Chapter 4, is essential to your development as a speaker. First, you won't have anything important to say unless you have listened actively to those around you. Second, listening will make you more effective in working with people. Study after study demonstrates that people who actually hear what is being communicated to them are much more responsive to others than those who listen with "only one ear." Responsiveness to one's audience, moreover, is one of the distinguishing characteristics of some of our nation's best public speakers.

Public speaking skills will help your development as a listener in several ways. For example, learning to give an effective speech requires the ability to analyze your audience, including what they think about you as a speaker and about the topic you plan to address. As part of their audience analysis, the best speakers listen to what audience members say well in advance of speaking. These speakers know that what they hear contains clues about what an audience is thinking. These speakers then use these clues in both the preparation and delivery of their speeches.

Learning to speak requires skill in organizing your thoughts and highlighting key points for listeners. As you learn to do this for your speeches, you will also learn how to organize the information you receive from speakers, separating the important ideas from the unimportant. Finally, speakers have to learn how to research and support their ideas. As a listener, you will need to evaluate the research and support other speakers provide to you. In fact, almost every public speaking skill we will discuss has a parallel skill for the listener.

PUBLIC REASONS FOR DEVELOPING SPEAKING SKILLS

Skilled public speakers serve as agents of change not only in the workplace but in the larger world as well. Were it not for those who spoke out publicly, the voting age would still be 21 and only White male property owners would be able to vote. All the progress of the past century has resulted from people coming up with new and sometimes controversial ideas and speaking out to persuade others of the wisdom of adopting them.

Becoming a Critical Thinker

As we discuss at length in Chapter 14, the ability to think critically about your own messages and those of others is essential to reaching sound conclusions about the issues of the day. Not only should speakers strive to base their persuasive efforts on sound reasoning, listeners need to take the responsibility to detect unsound reasoning. Some arguments that seem valid actually contain flaws that render them invalid. Becoming a critical thinker will make you less susceptible to phony arguments and less prone to engage in them yourself.

Functioning as an Informed Citizen

Our nation is a democratic republic based on the premise that for our country to thrive there must be a free exchange of ideas. Thus, it is no accident that the First Amendment to the Constitution guarantees freedom of speech, as well as freedom of the press, religion, and peaceable assembly. The fundamental premise of our Constitution is that the people must have the information necessary to make informed decisions. Even if you don't have an immediate need to speak out on an issue of public policy, you will be the consumer of countless speeches on every issue imaginable—from atmospheric warming to zero-tolerance policies in college dorms for drug possession. The ability to forcefully and publicly present your thoughts to others—whether as a speaker or as an audience member questioning a speaker—is more than a desirable skill. It is also a responsibility you owe to others and yourself.

Preserving Freedom of Speech

For some people, the way to deal with unpopular ideas is to invoke a quick fix: censorship. One of our goals in this book is to give you an appreciation for the importance of free speech in a democratic society. The empowerment of more and more citizens to express their views publicly should lead to vigorous debate about those ideas. Those who have confidence in the truth of their own views should welcome the opportunity to debate, rather than suppress, opposing views. Yet hardly a day goes by when we are not treated to an account of some person or some organization trying to suppress another's right to speak freely.

Raising the Level of Public Discourse

Regrettably, much of the public discourse of recent years in response to controversial issues has degenerated into name-calling and emotional appeals. Daytime

Justice Clarence Thomas Takes On Critics

It is often assumed that just because someone belongs to a particular racial group, one can infer what that person's political views are. Of course, that is not the case. Although criticized by many African Americans for his conservative views, Supreme Court Associate Justice Clarence Thomas decided to take them on directly. When invited to speak before close to a thousand African American lawyers and judges at the National Bar Association meeting in Memphis, Tennessee, in the summer of 1998, Justice Thomas took a strong position that he was entitled to think for himself. A few excerpts from his speech illustrate how he confronted this hostile audience, including many who had opposed even allowing him to speak before the group:

> I come here today not in anger or to anger . . . not to defend my views but to assert my right to think for myself.
>   I have few racial identification problems. . . . Nor do I need anyone telling me who I am . . . I am a man. A black man. An American.
>   Not one of us has the gospel. Not one of us can claim infallibility. . . . None of us has been appointed by God.

Although Thomas's views were not popular with the group, even those who oppose him credited him with the courage of his convictions. For example, the president of the National Bar Association, Randy Jones, said, "He spoke from the heart. He's a man who's not afraid to come into the lion's den and face his detractors and critics. I think we all have to respect him for that."

Source: Richard Cavelli, Associated Press, "Justice Thomas, Addressing Black Lawyers, Takes On Critics," *Chico Enterprise-Record,* 30 July 1998, A7.

TV is overrun with programming on which people verbally assault each other with messages that bear little to no semblance of reason. Geraldo Rivera quit his enormously profitable daytime talk show, for example, because he believed it was contributing to the erosion of reasoned speech in America. Even so-called current events shows such as *Crossfire* on CNN frequently break down into name-calling and emotional screeching.

We believe almost any topic—from abortion to religious zealotry—can be debated without the debaters personally attacking each other's pedigrees. Learning to focus one's public speaking skills on the substance of a controversy rather than the personality of an opponent is an important step in raising the level of public discourse. As more Americans learn how to make their views known rationally, and learn the critical thinking skills necessary to evaluate public discourse, the overall level of debate about issues in contemporary society is likely to improve.

Promoting Ethics

Finally, you cannot become a skilled public speaker without a corresponding commitment to becoming an ethical speaker as well. For example, in Chapter 6 we discuss the case of Senator Joseph Biden, who was caught plagiarizing the speech of a British politician. Biden's presidential campaign came to an abrupt halt. Both Biden and his advisors instinctively knew that his serious breach of ethical behavior was unacceptable to voters. So important is the subject of ethics to public speaking that Chapter 6 is dedicated to the topic. For now, suffice it to say that ethical speech is synonymous with effective speech.

THE PUBLIC SPEAKING TRANSACTION

Although this book deals with public speaking specifically, we recognize that public speaking is but one of many modes of human communication. We communicate one on one, in small groups, and through the mass media, as well as in public. Although each context in which we communicate has its own distinguishing features, certain principles of communication apply to all of them. Whether the focus is an intimate conversation between lovers, an informative speech before your class, or a speech at a political rally, the process of communication is best viewed as a transactional system.

A **transaction** involves a simultaneous exchange of messages between two or more people. A **system** is a collection of interdependent parts, parts arranged so that a change in one produces corresponding changes in the remaining parts. Consider a mechanical system such as a car. Its parts show varying degrees of interdependence. **Interdependence** exists when things have a reciprocal influence on one another. Changes in some of a car's parts will produce subtle changes in others. For example, even minor tire tread wear will affect a car's handling. The change is so subtle, though, most drivers don't notice it. In contrast, changes in other parts of the car can result in dramatic changes drivers cannot help noticing. Engine failure, for example, produces obvious changes throughout the hydraulic system of the car, including failure of the car's power steering and power brakes.

Perhaps this is why the public speaking transaction seems such a significant departure from the more familiar contexts of communication in which we engage. Whereas the changes that occur to the communication system when moving from an interpersonal to a small-group exchange are subtle, the changes that occur to the system when moving to an exchange between one and many can seem rather pronounced. Consider something as simple as the number of people communicating in a system and the number of lines of communication between or among them. As illustrated in Figure 1.2, the lines of communication increase

Dyad	Group of 4	Group of 6
(1 line of communication)	(6 lines of communication)	(15 lines of communication)

FIGURE 1.2 Lines of Communication. The lines of communication increase with the number of people. This may be one reason people are fond of the saying, "Too many cooks spoil the broth."

geometrically as the number of communicators increases. Whereas this change isn't especially dramatic as you move from two communicators to three or four, the change is staggering by the time you get to a group of even seven.

Figure 1.3 models the interdependent parts of the public speaking transaction as a system. Consider (1) the situation (context) in which the public speaking transaction takes place, (2) the speaker and the audience, (3) the messages they exchange, (4) the process of constructing and interpreting the symbols they use to convey their messages, (5) the channels through which the messages are sent, and (6) the role perception plays in the process.

The Situation

The situation (or context) in which any communication transaction takes place affects the nature of the transaction. This is especially true of the public speaking transaction. The situation includes the physical environment in which the speech is shared between speaker and listener. For example, is the speech shared in a classroom? An assembly hall? An outdoor amphitheater? It makes a critical difference.

Usually the situation also defines the purpose of the speech transaction. Are the people gathered to hear a speech eulogizing a beloved family member? To learn about a new policy that affects the amount of tuition charged students? Or to listen to a politician announcing her decision to seek higher office? Does the speaker want simply to pass on information to the audience? To motivate the audience to take some action? To persuade the audience to abandon old beliefs in favor of new ones? The purpose of the speech, too, makes a critical difference in the overall transaction.

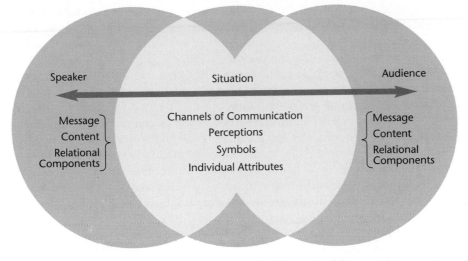

FIGURE 1.3 Public Speaking as a Transaction. In this model of the speech transaction, messages are simultaneously conveyed between speakers and listeners, with both parties functioning simultaneously as sources and receivers of messages. Communication is bound by the situation, and each person's perceptions are significant in interpreting the content and relational components of messages.

The Speaker and the Audience Members

In contrast to early models of speaking, which implied the speaker first talks and the audience then responds, the transactional model tells us speaker and audience exchange verbal and nonverbal messages simultaneously. That is, rather than taking discrete turns in this regard, speaker and audience members send and receive messages at the same time. Although the speaker typically is the dominant sender in the transaction, the audience is hardly passive. Even as the speaker talks and gestures, audience members provide **feedback**—they convey information back to the speaker with their eyes, seating posture, and voices. An audience leaning forward and staring intently at the speaker sends a far different message than one that is obviously fighting off sleep.

The sheer number of people in an audience also affects the overall speech transaction. It's one thing to speak with 25 other students in a traditional college classroom. It's quite another to speak to an assembly of the entire graduating class at commencement as people shift restlessly in their seats. Thus, you can no more afford to ignore the size of your audience than you can afford to ignore their feedback, the environment in which the transaction takes place, or the purpose for which you have gathered.

Messages: Content and Relational Components

The **message** is the meaning produced by the speaker and the audience members. In the transactional system modeled here, the message and the medium through which it travels are intentionally blurred. This is because the two are *interdependent*—not independent. What we would like to say to our audience is significantly affected by the manner in which we say it, and the way we convey the message is affected by what we want to say. This reciprocal process has a tremendous impact on how our message is perceived by our audience.

All messages are composed of two parts. The first part of the message is its **content,** the essential meaning, the gist or substance, of what a speaker wants to convey. For example, you might wish to convey your affection for another with the three words "I love you." The second part of a message, called its **relational component,** involves the collective impact of the verbal and nonverbal components of that message as it is conveyed. Consider how you might use your voice, face, and eyes to alter the impact of the words "I love you." You could make these three words an expression of sincere endearment, a plea, or even a statement of wanton desire.

Meaning is derived from both the content and the relational components of a message. Moreover, neither component is subordinate to the other in its contribution to meaning. What you say and how you say it, in other words, are roughly proportional in this regard.

Constructing and Interpreting Symbols

When we seek to convey our thinking to other people, there is no way to directly communicate our ideas. Our thoughts must be converted into words and gestures whose meaning can be interpreted by those receiving the message. These words and gestures are really **symbols,** things that stand for or suggest other things by reason of relationship or association. This process of converting our thoughts and ideas into meaningful symbols is called **encoding.** These symbols are then interpreted when received by audience members, a process known as **decoding.** This is simpler said than done. Whether an audience decodes a speaker's message as encoded depends on many factors, including but not limited to

- Language
- Culture
- Age
- Gender

On occasion, for example, some of our male students have referred to female audience members as "girls." When they used this label, we doubt these men meant adolescent and immature members of the opposite sex. Yet, that's exactly how most women in our classes decode the word. Thus, those males who have used the word *girl* in reference to women have "turned off" many, if not most, of the women in their audience.

Channels

A **channel** is the physical medium through which communication occurs. The transmission of the light and sound waves that make up the picture you see on your TV set requires a channel through which they can be signaled and received.

Words as Symbols

The following are examples of words and terms that describe the same things in the United States and Great Britain, illustrating that language is symbolic. As Henry Higgins points out in *My Fair Lady*, English (as the British know it) has not been spoken in America for years!

United States	Great Britain	United States	Great Britain
car trunk	boot	sausage	banger
pharmacist	chemist	washcloth	flannel
rude	cheeky	vacation	holiday
gasoline	petrol	French fries	chips
truck	lorry	chips	crisps
period (punctuation)	full stop	crackers	biscuits
worn out	knackered	subway	tube
elevator	lift	lawyer	barrister
crib	cot		

Picture and audio are encoded into electronic impulses, which must be decoded by your television receiver. In human communication, we primarily use our senses as channels for the messages we send and receive. We use our voice, eyes, and body, for example, to channel our speeches, conversations, and group discussions. On occasion, we also use our sense of touch, sense of smell, and even our sense of taste as channels of communication.

In the case of public speaking, we can also use supplementary channels of communication to augment the five senses. We can electronically amplify our voice so that it can be better heard or use visual media such as poster boards, overhead transparencies, and projected images stored in our computer to magnify what we want our audience to see.

Perceptions

The transactional system we've been describing for you demands that we both understand and appreciate the role of perception in public speaking. **Perception** is the process by which we give meaning to our experiences. It also is a highly selective process, as you are about to see.

Take a close look at the lithograph by M. C. Escher on the next page. Though it appears at first glance that the water is running downhill, a more careful examination tells you that this is impossible because the water is flowing continuously. Escher was able to create "impossible illusions" by taking advantage of our perceptual predispositions. We assume that the perspective in this print is an accurate representation of reality, when, of course, it cannot be so. When people look at an ambiguous stimulus such as this picture, they automatically look for something familiar . . . something for which they have preexisting meaning. This helps fool the eye, in this case, into seeing something that cannot exist.

This lithograph,
Waterfall (1961), by
M. C. Escher creates
an "impossible
illusion" by taking
advantage of our
perceptual
predispositions.

This tendency to perceive the familiar is both good and bad from the stand-
point of public speaking. It is good because it enables us to quickly establish a reference point from which we can plan our own speaking behavior as well as
interpret that of others. It's bad, on the other hand, because it can perceptually
blind us to other data that may be even more important to how we behave and
interpret the messages of others.

Consider a cross-cultural example. Direct eye contact is perceived as a sign
of attention and respect in most of North America. Thus, when we give a speech,
we use this knowledge to gauge how our audience is reacting to our message and

delivery. This North American norm, however, is not universal. Direct eye contact in some cultures, such as certain Asian societies, is perceived as an aggressive sign of disdain and disrespect.

It's common, then, for unaware North Americans who speak in one of these cultures to walk away from the experience with their confidence severely shaken. They mistakenly perceive their audience's lack of eye contact with them as a sign of disapproval. This mistaken perception, in turn, usually has a negative influence on their entire speaking performance.

As a public speaker, you can never assume that your perceptions of such things as the context, your audience, or the messages your audience feeds back to you are foolproof. Just because some person, some place, or some circumstance strikes you as familiar, that doesn't necessarily make it so.

Words and Things

Finally, public speaking, like other forms of communication, is symbolic.[11] Words are symbols that we use to describe persons, places, and things. Gestures, too, can be symbols, as is the case when we wave our hand to signal good-bye or shake our fist at someone to signal that we are angry.

Although we deal with the symbolic nature of public speaking at length in Chapter 9, we mention it here because you need to understand that the meaning you attach to the verbal and nonverbal symbols you use to express yourself may not correspond to the meaning others attach to them. What's more, this may be the case even when you share a common language, as the earlier box comparing American and British English illustrated.

As you prepare for your first speeches, you need to think about the degree to which you and your audience share meaning for symbols you commonly use to express yourself. This means, at a minimum, checking out the degree to which you and your audience share a common language, come from a similar culture, and share a similar socioeconomic background.

PREVIEW

The preceding discussion is a framework for the entire book. In the chapters to follow we flesh this framework out. This means the concepts just introduced will be refined and expanded to fit the primary topic of a specific chapter.

Because public speaking classes typically are taught in a limited period of time, you can expect to be up on your feet and speaking long before you have learned everything you need to know about the subject. We wrote Chapter 2—which overviews the process of developing, organizing, and delivering your first speech—with this fact clearly in mind.

If you are the least bit apprehensive about your first speech, then you can look forward to reading Chapter 3. This chapter clears up confusion about the common fear of speaking in public, explains the origins and consequences of this fear on speech performance, and provides you with easily understood and practiced skills to help you manage your fear. What's more, you will learn from reading Chapter 3 that these same skills can help to improve your performance even if you are completely confident about your speaking ability.

To reiterate, a major reason for learning about public speaking is the development of listening skills. Much as we need to listen, most of us are not as skilled at it as we need to be. Research shows most of us would benefit from listening training. Chapter 4 discusses the relationship between good listening habits and effective public speaking. In the process, it details for you the types of listening involved and suggests practices for improving each of these types.

The best prepared and delivered speeches are those that are developed with the audience in mind. Competent public speakers try to learn as much about their audience and the speaking situation as they possibly can. What they learn assists them in predicting what kind of speech will succeed with their audience. Chapter 5 details the process of analyzing your audience and speaking situation, and the necessity of adapting your speech to both.

Chapter 6 zeroes in on a topic of real significance to today's world: ethics. Reading Chapter 6, you will learn about varying ethical perspectives and their relationship to the speech transaction. You also will be called on to make a commitment to the ethical practices described there in your own speeches.

One of the toughest tasks for many beginning students is getting started. Aristotle called this process of getting started invention. In Chapter 7 you will learn not only about invention, but also about avenues for research you can travel to prepare your speech, including the Internet.

Just as there is more than one way to putt a golf ball, there is more than one way to organize a speech. This is especially true in light of the fact that today's multicultural audience may decode your message using different patterns of organization. You will learn about organizing your message using alternative patterns of speech organization in Chapter 8.

As we noted earlier, public speaking is a symbolic transaction. This fact is elaborated on in Chapter 9's treatment of the language of public speaking. You will learn that language is both complex and central to one's cultural heritage. You also will learn how to use this knowledge to your and your audience's advantage in your speeches.

Chapter 10 throws a realistic light on a subject fraught with misinformation: the role of nonverbal communication in the delivery of your message. How nonverbal communication functions in the delivery of your speech is explained and examples provided. Common misconceptions about this type of communication also are dispelled.

Using visual and audio means to enhance your speeches seems such a simple thing. Yet, as you will read in Chapter 11, nothing could be further from the truth. Presentation aids such as overheads or media projected from a laptop computer in combination with a projection machine require precise care in both their construction and execution. Public speakers routinely abuse these presentation aids in the classroom, in business, and in government.

Informative speaking is far and away the most common type of public speaking you are likely to encounter. Informative speeches are an essential component of most college classes, whether or not they are labeled as such. A lecture essentially is an informative speech. So too is a book report or an oral presentation based on a term paper. Chapter 12 outlines and discusses the types of informative speeches common in everyday life and details the elements that combine to make an effective informative speech.

Chapter 13 builds on the discussion about informative speaking. You will learn about the process of persuasion as well as the process of persuasive speaking. You also will be shown the perceptual characteristics that influence judgments about your credibility and will read about message variables that can enhance the persuasive effect of your speeches.

Chapter 14 extends what you learn about persuasion to thinking and speaking critically. You will be treated to information on deceptive communication practices that are commonly used by unscrupulous communicators, and you'll learn how to recognize the fallacies that frequently characterize their messages. In the process, you also will learn how to avoid using such fallacies in your own reasoning and speaking.

Finally, Chapter 15 introduces everyday circumstances in which you can expect to be called on to speak. Some of these circumstances, such as a wedding toast, are social. Others, such as being asked without warning at school or at work to make a progress report on a project, are task oriented.

All in all, we think these chapters combine to provide you with the introductory knowledge and skills necessary to see you through not only the speeches you will share in your class, but also the lifetime of public speaking all college graduates can expect. Good luck as you proceed.

SUMMARY

There are good reasons to study and practice public speaking. A personal reason for developing public speaking skills is to satisfy your own needs. *Deficiency needs* are basic human needs, which must be satisfied before higher-order needs can be met. They include needs for food, water, air, physical safety, belongingness and love, and self-esteem and social esteem. *Growth needs* are higher-order human needs, which can be satisfied only after deficiency needs have been met. They include self-actualization (the process of fully realizing one's potential), knowledge and understanding, and aesthetic needs. Public speaking can also help meet the needs of others by empowering them to satisfy their own deficiency and growth needs.

Professional reasons for developing public speaking skills include becoming an agent of influence, promoting your professional self, being able to present ideas to decision makers, creating change in the workplace, becoming a functioning force in meetings, and developing active listening skills. Public reasons for developing your public speaking skills include becoming a critical thinker, functioning as an informed citizen, preserving freedom of speech, raising the level of public discourse, and promoting ethical behavior.

The transactional model of public speaking views it as a *system of interdependent* components, all of which are capable of affecting one another simultaneously. The basic components of the speech *transaction* include the following elements: (1) situation, (2) speaker and audience, (3) *message*, (4) construction and interpretation of *symbols*, (5) *channels*, and (6) *perception*. In preparing or presenting a speech, it's important to realize that the meanings people attach to various symbolic representations may differ greatly.

Check Your Understanding: Exercises and Activities

1. This chapter introduces you to Maslow's hierarchy of needs. How can public speaking skills help you fulfill each of these needs? Write a short paper or give a brief speech explaining your answer and giving examples.

2. How important are public speaking skills in the profession for which you are preparing by attending college? If possible, interview either a practitioner of the profession or a professor in the appropriate department about the ways public speaking might be applicable in your field. Give a brief (1- to 2-minute) presentation to your classmates or write a short paper about your findings.

3. Attend a meeting of a local-government agency, such as a city council, planning commission, or board of supervisors, or attend a student government meeting on your campus. Chances are you will see several speakers present their views in a public forum. Write a short paper about one of the speakers. What impressed you most about the speaker, and what impressed you least? How did the ability to speak help this person achieve his or her goals?

Notes

1. Abraham H. Maslow, *Motivation and Personality*, 2nd ed. (New York: Harper & Row, 1970).

2. Elaine Gray, "Actor/Activist Brings His Message of Peace to a Packed Laxson," *Chico Enterprise Record*, 16 September 1995, A1.

3. Gray, "Actor/Activist Brings His Message," A8.

4. *In Search of Excellence* [video recording]. (Boston: Nathan/Tyler Productions, 1985.)

5. Thomas J. Peters and Robert H. Waterman, Jr., *In Search of Excellence: Lessons From America's Best Run Corporations* (New York: Harper & Row, 1982), 247.

6. Peters and Waterman, *In Search of Excellence*, 253.

7. Peters and Waterman, *In Search of Excellence*, 245.

8. Ronald B. Adler, *Communicating at Work: Principles and Practices for Business and the Professions*, 3rd ed. (New York: Random House, 1989), 4.

9. Adler, *Communicating at Work*, 216.

10. Anthony P. Carnevale, Leila J. Gainer, and Ann S. Meltzer, *Workplace Basics: The Skills Employers Want* (Washington, D.C.: U.S. Government Printing Office, 1988), 11.

11. W. Barnett Pearce and Vernon E. Cronen, *Communication, Action and Meaning: The Creation of Social Realities* (New York: Praeger, 1980).

CHAPTER 2

Your first speeches to your classmates will help you gain experience and confidence.

Your First Speech

OBJECTIVES

After reading this chapter, you should be able to:

- Analyze the basic features of the speech situation as it applies to your first speech.
- Identify the general purposes associated with public speaking.
- Select an appropriate topic for your first speech.
- Construct a specific purpose for your first speech.
- Develop a clear thesis statement for your first speech.
- Invent your first speech, utilizing appropriate sources for information.
- Organize your speech to (1) open with impact, (2) focus on your thesis statement, (3) connect with your audience, (4) preview your main points, (5) organize your ideas with three to five main points, (6) summarize your main points, and (7) close with impact.
- Present your speech in a conversational, extemporaneous manner.

KEY CONCEPTS

audience	manuscript delivery
brainstorming	memorized delivery
credibility	preview
extemporaneous delivery	signposts
general purpose	specific purpose
impromptu delivery	thesis statement
invention	

A journey of a thousand miles begins with a first step.

—Chinese proverb

25

The wisdom of the proverb "A journey of a thousand miles begins with a first step" rings true for anyone who has ever given a speech. Often the toughest part of a speaking assignment is deciding where to begin. For example, you may have a general idea of what you'd like to speak about but have no clue about where to begin your research. Or you may be like many students, uncertain about a topic that you find interesting. Will your audience also find it interesting? Is it appropriate for the classroom?

This chapter takes a general look at the individual steps you need to master to develop and deliver your first speech. This is not a substitute for the content to follow in later chapters, but a detailed preview of it. It's designed to assist you in developing an overall sense of what effective public speaking involves, starting with choosing the right topic and ending with identifying a style of delivery that best suits the situation. The steps we discuss are (1) analyzing the situation with which you are faced, (2) deciding on a purpose, (3) choosing a topic that is suitable to both the situation and chosen purpose, (4) constructing a specific purpose and developing a clear thesis statement for your speech, (5) inventing the substance of your speech, (6) organizing your speech, and (7) presenting your speech effectively.

FIRST THINGS FIRST

Analyzing the Situation

One of your first speech assignments may be to introduce a classmate or yourself, to share a brief story with the class, to prove a controversial point, or to illustrate your pet peeve. Whatever the assignment, you need to understand completely the situation in which you find yourself and the expectations that come with the situation. This is essential in order to effectively develop a speech that fits the situation and addresses those expectations.

For starters, you need to know who your audience is. **Audience** refers to the individuals who share and listen to a public speech. Typically, you will be speaking to your classmates, some of whom you may already have come to know in the first few days of class. But even if you have not, you can make certain assumptions about them based on their attendance at your university or college. Do you attend a small, rural, liberal arts college or a large, urban university? What are the common majors emphasized at your institution? Beyond knowing these general facts, you can also observe your classmates in the effort to discover things about them. Are most of them the same age as you, older, or younger? People of the same age tend to share many of the same experiences. For example, the authors of this text grew up in the '50s and '60s. For us, the assassination of President John F. Kennedy was a defining experience. Yet for most of today's younger college students, Kennedy is but a distant historical figure. Although Kennedy's death is still important in a historical sense, the O. J. Simpson trial, the deaths of Kurt Cobain and Princess Diana, or Kenneth Starr's investigation of the Clinton presidency may seem like defining experiences for you and your classmates.

Knowing the common experiences you share with your audience allows you to predict what topics are likely to elicit a favorable response. Factors such as the

Today's public speakers need to adapt to multicultural, multiethnic, and multiracial audiences.

age, sex, and social status of the people with whom you speak may also help you predict audience response. Depending on who they are and what experiences they share, audience members come to any speech situation with a variety of expectations. For example, your classmates probably expect you to speak to them as a peer. If you violate that expectation, taking on an air of superiority, for example, you may not get the response you desire. Regardless, only after you thoroughly understand your speech situation, your audience, and their expectations should you begin to consider the purpose for your speech.

Choosing a Topic

Once you've analyzed your audience and the situation you face, one of the hardest things for many beginning speakers is the selection of a topic. Sometimes your instructor will do this for you, but it's just as likely you'll have to decide on a topic yourself. (For one student's thoughts on topic selection, see the box "Speaking with Passion: Jonathan Studebaker.")

An obvious place to begin is with your own interests, experiences, and knowledge. Remember to look for topics as you go through your day. For example, you may see a television program, such as *20/20* or *60 Minutes*, that deals

VIDEO FILE

If you have access to the videotape that accompanies this book, view segment 12, which shows a speech by Jonathan Studebaker.

Speaking With Passion: Jonathan Studebaker

Born with osteogenesis imperfecta, or brittle bones, Jonathan Studebaker has conquered his disability while leading a full and productive life. From 1983 to 1992, he was the honorary head coach at the East-West Shrine Football Classic. He was the kicking coach for the Chico State football team for three years. After graduating from Chico State, he founded Project Speak Out as a forum to educate people on the challenges of having a disability while encouraging others to reach for the stars. Jonathan speaks to audiences ranging from service organizations to church, school, and sports groups.

Mike Bellotti, head football coach for the University of Oregon, states, "Jonathan is one of the best motivational speakers that I have had the pleasure of listening to in my coaching career." Mike Andrews, director of public relations for Shriners Hospitals, sums up the impact of Jonathan's public speaking: "Seeing and hearing Jonathan is an eye-opening experience. He is a real inspiration." Both authors of this book have had Jonathan as a student and can testify to his dynamic speaking style. One of Jonathan's speeches appears in Appendix A and is available on videotape.

Jonathan emphasizes the importance of "talking about what I know about, something I really care about." He feels that if speakers "feel passionately" about their topic, the other things, such as delivery, will fall into place. Jonathan often is called on to talk to children about living with a disability. He uses a question-and-answer technique to involve the youngsters in the speech. For example, he will ask, "Have any of you ever dropped a glass on the floor? What happened?" The answer is invariably, "It broke." So Jonathan tells his audiences: "Well, my bones kinda break like glass, which is why I tell people, when you carry me, treat me like your best crystal."

Jonathan adds an important thought for beginning speakers. A speech class is an opportunity. Three or four times during the semester you will have the chance to share something important with your classmates. Seize the opportunity to talk about something you really care about. Jonathan puts it this way: "Speaking isn't broccoli; it's fun!"

with a topic that interests you. Or a magazine or a newspaper may suggest a topic. For example, an article in *Consumer Reports* titled "Selling Green" was the source of an excellent speech for one of our students.[1] Moreover, because the article questioned advertisers' claims that their products were environmentally sound, the topic proved to be of interest to other students.

Television, newspapers, and magazines are but a few of the places where you might find a topic. Others include campus publications, instructors, and fellow students. Computer users who surf the Internet may find ideas there. The number of places to find a good topic, in fact, is limited only by how aware you are of what's going on around you. The following list summarizes a few good places to look for a topic.

Suggestions for Finding a Topic

Tips and Tactics

- *Make a personal inventory.* What hobbies, interests, jobs, or experiences have you had that would interest others?
- *Talk to friends.* Perhaps they have ideas to share with you, including topics they would like to know more about.
- *Read.* Newspapers, newsmagazines, and books are filled with ideas. You should commit to reading at least one newspaper a day and one newsmagazine a week while enrolled in this course.
- *Check the Internet.* So many subject areas are discussed on the Internet, and there is a wide range of interest-based chat groups. If you enjoy "surfing the Net," you may well find speech ideas there for the taking.
- *Brainstorm.* Brainstorming is a creative process used for generating a large number of ideas. A group of people get together and suggest a variety of ideas. One person writes them down. No one is allowed to evaluate the ideas until the group has listed every last one it can think of. Then one or more members go back and critically examine the ideas. When brainstorming, work down from the broad topic to narrower topics. "Wearing seat belts" might seem like an overdone topic. But a speech on how even drivers of cars with air bags aren't fully protected if they don't wear seat belts might be a new slant on an old topic. Use the situation, audience, and your own goals as criteria for judging the possible topics. (The activity on page 51 explains brainstorming in more detail.)

In addition to knowing *where* to look for a topic, it is important to know *what* to look for. To help you in this process, we offer the following criteria for what makes an appropriate speech topic.

Six Criteria for an Appropriate Speech Topic

Tips and Tactics

1. *The topic should be interesting to you.* If you don't care about the topic, how can you expect your audience to care?
2. *It should be interesting to your audience*—or at least be capable of being made interesting to them. This is why it is crucial to know as much as possible about your audience.
3. *It should be appropriate to the situation.* If your instructor has asked you to speak on your pet peeve, she or he probably is thinking of topics like "dorm food," "roommates," or "people who blow smoke in my face," not the destruction of the rain forests.

4. *It should be appropriate to the time available.* One limitation of a public speaking class is time. Know what your instructor expects and stick to it. Further, consider the time you have available to prepare. If the speech is due next week, you won't be able to send off for information from your state's senator. Pick a topic that you can research in the time available.

5. *It should be manageable.* Don't pick a topic that is beyond your abilities or resources. One of your greatest assets in speaking is your own credibility, which is the degree to which your audience trusts and believes in you. Nothing will undermine your credibility faster than speaking on a topic with which you are unfamiliar. Know more than your audience. Why else would you speak to them?

6. *It should be worthwhile.* We treat time in our society as a commodity. We bank time, spend time, and buy time. You are angered if someone wastes your time—so don't waste your audience's time. Pick a topic that will inform, persuade, or entertain the audience by presenting them with ideas or information they haven't already heard. Just as we hate to hear an old joke told over again, we don't like to hear for the umpteenth time that we ought to recycle our aluminum cans, unless the speaker tells us something new and insightful about why we should do just that. If you pick a well-worn topic, then you must give it a different "spin" or focus.

Choosing a General Speech Purpose

One of the first decisions a speaker faces is to decide on the **general purpose**— the primary function—of the speech. The three commonly agreed upon general purposes are to inform, to persuade, and to entertain. The most common types of speeches seek to *inform* others about things they do not already know or to *persuade* others to believe or behave in certain ways. Persuasive speeches not only seek change, they also may seek to reinforce social values, as when someone gives a Fourth of July speech or a sermon. Other speeches seek to *entertain* by sharing an enjoyable experience. Obviously, these general purposes are not mutually exclusive. A persuasive speech will also inform the audience, and an informative speech should be interesting enough that it persuades the audience to listen. Nevertheless, the general purpose you either have been assigned or have decided on yourself should tell you something about the topic you ultimately choose. Simply put, some topics may be inappropriate or only marginally appropriate to your purpose. Though controversial topics, for example, lend themselves to a persuasive speech, they are less well suited to an informative speech.

Writing Your Specific Purpose Statement

You may be assigned a general purpose—to inform, to persuade, or to entertain—for your early speeches. But you will not be assigned a specific purpose.

The **specific purpose** is the goal or objective you hope to achieve in speaking to a particular audience. What you want to accomplish specifically with your audience rests with you. For example, assume you are asked to introduce yourself to the rest of the class. What do you want your classmates to think and feel about you? Do you want them to like, respect, and admire you? Then your specific purpose might be "to have the class develop a favorable opinion of me." Clearly this is a persuasive effort. You are creating attitudes about yourself where none existed before. Thus, even in early speech assignments, you should try to articulate a specific purpose for your speech.

The specific purpose of a speech is typically expressed in terms of an infinitive phrase that begins with "to." Specific purposes usually fall under one of the general purposes: to inform, to persuade, or to entertain. If you were giving an informative speech on computer viruses, for example, you might express your specific purpose as "to inform my audience about the methods of transmission of computer viruses." This purpose, however, is somewhat vague. More specifically, you might express it as "to enable my audience to explain in their own words the ways a computer virus can be transmitted." Because this specific purpose includes a way of measuring your results—the audience should be able to describe how the virus is transmitted—it will point you toward a specified goal. The level of audience understanding should be realistic: One speech cannot make them computer experts, but they should know how to protect themselves against viruses.

On the same topic, you might have as a persuasive specific purpose "to convince my audience to purchase a virus-detection program for their personal computer." Thus, a successful speech given this goal would lead to a number of audience members eventually purchasing such a program. Of course, there is a difference in content as well as purpose between a speech to inform the audience on computer virus transmission and one designed to persuade them to purchase a particular virus-detection software product. The persuasive speech would probably require the speaker to compare products, prices, and ease of use. The informative speech would not. Both speeches, however, would need to explain the nature of the threat to computer data from viruses. The persuasive presentation might do more to raise the level of concern among audience members so as to motivate them to purchase software to combat the threat.

Some persuasive speeches are part of a longer process or campaign. For example, although State of the Union speeches delivered each January normally have as their primary purpose the definition of a presidential agenda for the coming year, at the end of the first term, a president who plans to run for reelection likely has a different ultimate purpose—to get votes in November. The State of the Union Address is just one step toward that goal. As a consequence, the president might express the specific purpose for such a speech as "to persuade voters that they are better off now than they were four years ago."

Speeches to entertain have the advantage of instantaneous feedback. Speakers know by the audience's laughter or applause whether they have succeeded. So, a speaker might express a specific entertainment purpose as "to entertain my audience with the story of my worst computer nightmares." It is not necessary to state how you will measure whether this goal has been met because success or failure is immediately evident.

As you continue to give speeches in your class, work on developing specific purposes that are realistic, that are worthwhile for the audience, and that fulfill your goals as a speaker. Realistic specific purposes are those that can be accomplished in the brief time you have to present your speech considering the views of the audience you are addressing. For example, you might well motivate your audience to drink alcohol responsibly—something that is noncontroversial for most people. But to convince an audience that disagrees with your point of view to change its opinion on a topic like gun control or abortion is unrealistic. On such topics your specific purpose should be more modest—perhaps to have the audience become more open to your point of view.

Thus, examples of realistic specific purposes for persuasive speeches would include

- To persuade audience members to avoid binge drinking.
- To persuade audience members to consider that gun control is not always a solution to violence.
- To persuade the audience that, at least in some circumstances, parents should be notified of a minor's desire to have an abortion.

For informative speeches, examples of specific purposes would include:

- To teach my audience the basic principles involved in the Heimlich maneuver.
- To have my audience understand the basic rules of soccer.
- To have my audience understand the basics of effective note-taking.

Again, your specific purpose must be realistic. It is one thing to explain the basics of the Heimlich maneuver, and quite another to successfully instruct people in using the maneuver in a brief time without any hands-on practice. You can explain the basic rules of soccer in a few minutes, but teaching someone to play the sport well takes years.

In addition to ensuring that your specific purposes are realistic, make sure they are worthwhile. For example, effective note-taking skills are important to every college student, and the Heimlich maneuver can save a life. But unless your audience has some interest in soccer or perhaps the World Cup is currently being played, why would audience members be motivated to listen to a speech on the rules of the game?

Finally, you need to assess your specific purpose carefully in terms of your own goals. What, exactly, do you want to achieve (other than a passing grade on your speech)? For example, what is your reason for teaching the rules of soccer? Are you a member of your college team who seeks to increase team support on campus? If so, it makes sense to develop an understanding and appreciation of the sport. On the other hand, if you just happen to like soccer and think it would be an easy topic on which to speak, then what will you have accomplished? So, understanding your own goals can help you write a clear and useful specific purpose.

As you develop your specific purpose, keep in mind these factors and the four guidelines listed below.

Guidelines for Refining the Specific Purpose of a Speech

- Describe the results you seek.
- Be as specific as possible.
- Express your goal in measurable terms.
- Set a realistic goal.

Whatever speech topic you select, therefore, you need to clarify in your own mind and for your instructor what specific purpose you intend to achieve through the speech. Make sure the specific purpose is realistic, worthwhile for your audience, and helps you achieve your own goals as a speaker.

Writing Your Thesis Statement

Every speech should have a central idea or point that it makes. If you want people to wear their seatbelts, your point might be that doing so can save their lives. You should be able to express this point in a single declarative sentence. We call this a **thesis statement,** a sentence that focuses your audience's attention on the central point of your speech. A thesis statement should make your central point clear; express your point of view on that point; and, if accepted, fulfill your specific purpose.

Your thesis statement should help the audience understand what response you seek from them. As a case in point, you might be opposed to a tuition increase at your university or college. Assuming you are speaking to a group of student colleagues, you may wish to focus your speech on what they can do to fight the tuition increase. Thus, your thesis statement might be, "We need to lobby the board of trustees of the university to stop this unjustified and harmful tuition increase." Notice that the thesis statement here is directly related to the specific purpose of your speech. In this instance, your specific purpose is "to convince other students to lobby the board of trustees to stop the proposed tuition increase." The thesis statement, if accepted and acted upon by the audience, will fulfill your specific purpose. While the specific purpose expresses your goal for the audience's response to the speech, the thesis statement expresses the essential message that is designed to fulfill that purpose.

Although the specific purpose is not normally stated explicitly to the audience, the thesis statement should be sufficiently related to that purpose to allow the audience to know what you want to accomplish. As an example, consider a speech on binge drinking. If your specific purpose was to persuade audience members to drink responsibly, your thesis statement might be, "Binge drinking can destroy lives." Or if you wanted to inform your audience of the basic principles of the Heimlich maneuver, your thesis statement might be, "The Heimlich maneuver involves applying pressure to the victim's diaphragm to expel air from the lungs and thus dislodge what is caught in the throat."

The thesis statement is usually stated in the introduction to the speech. There are some exceptions to this guideline, which will be discussed in later chapters. But as a general rule, letting your audience know your central point is important if you are to fulfill your goals as a speaker.

Even a speech to entertain should have a clear thesis. Obviously, there's no easier way to turn off an audience than to say, "Today I'm going to make you laugh." But it would be logical to say, "First dates are often a disaster, and mine was no different." Unlike a David Letterman monologue, which is often just a string of jokes, a speech to entertain should have a clear purpose, thesis, and structure.

INVENTING YOUR SPEECH

It may seem odd, at first, to think of a speech as an invention. However, just as it was not enough for Thomas Edison simply to have the idea for the lightbulb, it is not enough for you just to have an idea for a speech. You need to invest time and effort in inventing the substance of what you plan to say. **Invention** is the creative process by which the substance of a speech is generated. Where do you go for the substance of your speech? Here are some general suggestions, which we will develop in more detail in Chapter 7.

Developing Resources for Inventing Your Speech

Tips and Tactics

1. *Begin with your own experiences.* Each of us has had experiences that make us unique. Many early speech assignments require you to look no further than to the things that have happened in your own life. For example, you may be asked to introduce yourself or tell a story about a personally significant experience. You may be able to rely on hobbies or past job experiences for an early informative speech. Even if you cannot rely solely on personal experience, it is the logical place to begin searching for information.

Speaking about matters with which you have firsthand experience personally connects you to your message. What's more, this personal connection may also tell you how to connect your message to the personal and professional needs of your audience. For example, a successful actress, who was enrolled in one of the author's classes at the University of Southern California, gave a speech on how to break into "show biz." Unfortunately, she failed to mention her own experience, which included a role in a Clint Eastwood movie and a recurring role on the sitcom "The Odd Couple." Had she done so, her speech would have connected more effectively to the audience, in effect saying, "If I can do this, so can you!"

Even though your personal experience and knowledge is a good source with which to start, don't stop there. No matter how intense your experience or extensive your knowledge, there always is more to learn. In the effort to augment personal experience and knowledge, then, consult other sources as well.

2. *Look to general sources of information.* Books, reference books, general-circulation periodicals (*Time, Newsweek, U.S. News & World Report*, etc.), and even public affairs programs such as *60 Minutes, Dateline,* or *20/20* are good places to look for information on topics of general interest. Keep in mind that books may have a long lead time before they are published. Thus, on topics that require up-to-date information, you need to rely on more recent sources, such as periodicals, rather than books. A speech on why the United States got involved in the Vietnam War, for example, might well rely on books and encyclopedias, whereas a speech on the current situation in Iraq would require the most recent sources available.

3. *Interview experts.* Sometimes you can interview an expert on the topic of your speech. You may not have to look any further than the other classes you are taking. An interview with an environmental-science instructor, for example, could provide a wealth of information for a unique speech about recycling. Further, experts often provide leads to other sources of information the speaker can obtain. Be sure to prepare thoroughly for your interview so that you know what questions to ask. Chapter 7 contains specific guidelines for conducting interviews, which you should consult before interviewing sources for any speech.

4. *Conduct computerized searches, including the Internet.* At one time the beginning public speaker relied primarily on print indexes, such as the *Readers' Guide to Periodical Literature.* In some libraries, these may still be the best means of access. However, more and more libraries are providing computerized databases, such as the Academic Search. In addition, many students now have access to the Internet either through their universities or through private Internet service providers (ISP). Although one must be cautious about the reliability of many Web sites on the Internet, there is a wealth of information available to the average citizen. For example, according to one poll, some 20 million Americans read at least portions of the Starr report on the Internet.[3] Whatever you might think of the report's claims about President Clinton's conduct in office, never before in history have average citizens been able to read unedited government reports with such ease. However, the assumption that something must be true just because it is on the Internet is clearly false. As evidence, consider the bogus claim that TWA Flight 800 had been shot down by a missile, which was widely circulated on the Internet despite having been disproved by the FBI.

   Your school may also have access to Lexis-Nexis, a service that allows for searches of newspapers, magazines, wire service reports, court transcripts, law digests, and even television program transcripts. If you have access to such resources, they will provide a systematic way to find articles on your topic. Further, they will save you time and improve the quality of your research.

5. *Consider specialized sources of information.* Every discipline has specialized journals and books, as well as indexes to provide access to them. Chapter 7 discusses some of the more commonly used indexes. If you are dealing with a specialized topic early in the class, you probably should skip ahead to that chapter or meet with a reference librarian to help familiarize yourself with the resources available at your school. You might also consider other types of specialized sources, such as trade publications and government publications, if they are appropriate to your topic. For your early speeches, such specialization probably will not be necessary, but you should be aware that there is more to researching a speech than simply consulting the general books and periodicals found in most libraries.

As you gather information, whether from written sources or interviews, be sure to carefully record the facts and quotations you discover. Note not only what was said but also who said it, when, and where. As we discuss in Chapter 7, documenting your evidence for an audience will build your credibility, which will enhance the likelihood you will be effective in delivering your speech.

ORGANIZING YOUR SPEECH

Someone once said that every speech has three tell 'ems. First you tell 'em what you are going to tell 'em; then you tell 'em; and, finally, you tell 'em what you told 'em. That's a bit simplistic, but nevertheless, it captures the basic idea of the three parts of every speech: the introduction, the body, and the conclusion.

Though there are many ways to organize your speech, one of the most helpful patterns we have found for our own students is an adaptation of a system developed by Dr. Loretta Malandro for the business executives she coaches.[3] According to Dr. Malandro, the traditional introduction, body, and conclusion of a speech should include several important steps. Steps 1–4 are the introduction, step 5 is the body of the speech, and steps 6 and 7 are the conclusion. None of these steps should be skipped, and they should nearly always be presented in the order given here.

Seven Steps for Organizing Your Speech

1. *Open with impact.* In this step you capture your audience's attention.
2. *Focus on your thesis statement.* In this step you draw the audience's attention to the central point of your speech.
3. *Connect with your audience.* In this step you let the audience know "what's in it for them."
4. *Preview the body of your speech.* This is where you tell your audience what you are going to tell them in the body of the speech.

5. *Present your main points.* In this step you present the body of your speech. This step constitutes the bulk of your presentation.

6. *Summarize your main points.* In this step you tell the audience what you've told them.

7. *Close with impact.* In this step you leave your audience with a lasting impression.

Let's briefly examine each of these steps and how they relate to the traditional introduction–body–conclusion format of a speech. This relationship is illustrated in Figure 2.1.

Introduction

To present an effective introduction, you should follow four steps.

Open With Impact Introduce your presentation dramatically or humorously. There's no surer turnoff than beginning a speech, "Uh, um, well, I guess I'll talk about dorm food today." Begin the speech with something that captures your audience's attention, such as an appropriate joke, a startling statistic, an anecdote, or a reference to current affairs.

Focus on Your Thesis Statement As we noted earlier, the thesis statement captures the central point of your speech. For example, if you are opposed to a planned tuition hike on your campus, you should state clearly, "The students of this university should not be forced to pay more for less." On the other hand, you

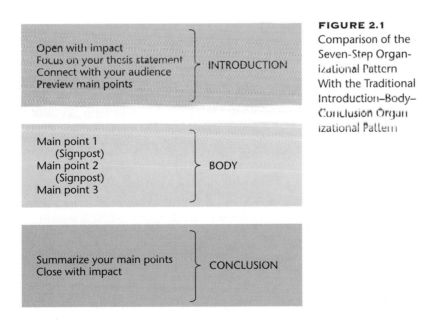

FIGURE 2.1
Comparison of the Seven-Step Organizational Pattern With the Traditional Introduction–Body–Conclusion Organizational Pattern

might want to inform your audience about the variety of financial assistance available to them: "With effort and persistence, you can obtain a student loan or scholarship to help meet your college expenses."

Connect With Your Audience   Answer the questions "What's in this for my audience? Why is it in their personal and/or professional interest to listen to me?" For example, will the proposed tuition hike keep some in your audience from completing their degrees? Make the connection to your specific audience clear in the introduction to the speech. This is also a good place to build your credibility as a speaker. Let the audience know you understand their concerns and have their best interests at heart. If you have expertise on the topic, let your audience know this now so that they can appreciate what is to come.

Preview   Most people like a map of the territory they're entering. The **preview** provides your audience with a map to where you are taking them. It forecasts the main points of a speech. You should mention all your main points briefly before treating each one in detail. This is the "tell 'em what you're going to tell 'em" part of the speech. It may be as simple as saying, "I'm going to present three ways to save money on your groceries: clipping coupons, watching for store ads, and buying generic brands." On the other hand, a preview may specifically enumerate the three main points of the speech: "You can save money on your groceries, first, by clipping coupons; second, by watching for store ads; and third, by buying generic brands." The preview helps reduce the audience's uncertainty about what is to follow, and it helps them see the relationship among your various points.

Body

The majority of your speech should develop the thesis you are trying to convey. Usually, the body of the speech is divided into three to five main points that in aggregate develop the thesis of your speech.

Organize Your Main Points   A speech that wanders off the topic or whose main points don't follow a logical pattern of development is likely to lose the audience. The same is true of an overly complex speech. Here are some basic patterns for organizing your main points:

- *Time pattern.* Most stories are arranged chronologically. One event follows another until the climax unfolds. Often speeches deal with topics in terms of past, present, and future.
- *Spatial pattern.* Some topics are best dealt with spatially. A speech on the solar system might begin with the sun and work out to the most distant planets.
- *Categorical pattern.* Many topics fall into obvious categories. A teacher explaining the federal government to a civics class, for example, is likely to talk about the legislative, judicial, and executive branches. This is sometimes called a topical pattern of organization. If a topic

Time Pattern

Specific purpose: to inform audience how to change a tire

I. Remove jack and spare from trunk
II. Use jack to raise car
III. Remove flat tire
IV. Replace with spare tire
V. Lower car

Categorical (Topical) Pattern

Specific purpose: to inform listeners about types of classes they may take at the university

I. General education courses
II. Courses in the major
III. Electives

Spatial Pattern

Specific purpose: to inform audience about regions of the U.S.

I   Eastern seaboard
II. Midwest
III. Rocky Mountains
IV. Pacific States

Problem-Solution Pattern

I. The problem is explained.
  A. The harm of the problem is shown.
  B. The qualitative or quantitative significance of the problem is shown.
  C. The cause or causes of the problem are identified.
II. The solution to the problem is proposed.
  A. The solution is described.
  B. The feasibility of the solution is explained.
  C. Advantages of the solution are explained.

FIGURE 2.2 Common Organizational Patterns for a Speech

lends itself to natural divisions, this is an excellent way to arrange your speech.

- *Problem–solution pattern.* Sometimes called the stock issues approach, the problem–solution pattern is a natural way to organize persuasive speeches. What's wrong and why are followed by how to solve the problem and how the solution will benefit the audience. Many sales pitches are built around a problem–solution pattern. For example, a salesperson selling water softeners would begin with the problems caused by "hard water," such as water spots on dishes and excessive use of expensive detergent. Then she would propose a solution: buying her company's product.

These four ways to organize a speech are summarized in Figure 2.2. Other ways to organize a speech are discussed at length in Chapter 8. For now, this will give you a start. The key thing to remember in this regard is to pick a simple pattern and stick with it for the entire speech.

Provide Signposts   We also want to emphasize the importance of using **signposts,** transitional statements that bridge your main points. For example, you might say something as simple as, "My second point is . . ." or "Now that you understand the problem, let's examine some possible solutions." The goal in using signposts is to provide your audience with guides along the path of your speech so that they will know where you have been, where you are, and where you are going next.

Conclusion

All too often, speakers invest so much energy in developing the introduction and body of their speeches that they run out of gas at the end. The impact with which you conclude a speech is just as important as the impact with which you began.

Summarize Your Main Points   Tell 'em what you've told 'em. That is the first and most important function of a conclusion. Remind the listeners of what they've heard.

Close With Impact   Just as a salesperson doesn't like the customer to walk out the door without buying something, you don't want your audience to leave without at least thinking about doing what you've asked them to do. So, find a way to reinforce your specific purpose. It's also your last chance to leave a favorable impression. Just as listeners are turned off by an introduction that begins "Today I want to tell you about . . . ," you can undermine the effectiveness of an excellent speech with a poor conclusion, such as "Well, I guess that's about it." Finish with a flourish that is as powerful as your opening.

Tips and Tactics

Ways to Close Your Speech Effectively

- Present a short, memorable *quotation.* This is often an effective way to reinforce your specific purpose and wrap up your presentation.

- Use an *anecdote* or a *story* that illustrates your point. However, it must leave a lasting impression on your audience. A long, drawn-out, pointless story will cause your audience to lose interest.

- Make a *direct appeal* or "call to action." Just as a successful evangelist asks the faithful to come forward at the end of a crusade, effective persuasive speakers seek a public commitment from their audience to act on their messages. If you are opposed to a tuition hike, appeal to the audience to contact the board of trustees or sign a petition supporting your position. Perhaps the most famous direct appeal to action was in President John F. Kennedy's inaugural, where he challenged his fellow Americans to "ask not what your country can do for you, but what you can do for your country."[4]

- *Return to your opening.* This is one of the best ways to end a speech because it brings the listeners full circle. Suppose you began your plea for people to sign organ donor cards with the story of a little girl who needed a liver transplant. At the end of the speech, you can describe how her life was saved because a donor was found. This gives the speech a sense of wholeness and completeness.

So, conclude your speech by *summarizing* your main points and *closing with impact*.

The speech outline in the box, "Accident or Suicide: Driving Without a Seatbelt" by Karen Shirk, follows the steps we have just discussed. Notice how Karen introduces her speech with examples of objects from her own automobile accidents. Her speech has four clear main points, which she previews for her audience. She cites a number of credible sources, which are also listed in her reference list. Finally, she summarizes and closes her speech with impact. We have noted a number of the features of the outline in the margin.

PRESENTING YOUR SPEECH

There's a story told about the great speaker of ancient Greece, Demosthenes, who said that the first, second, and third most important things in rhetoric were—delivery, delivery, and delivery.[5] Although the story is probably apocryphal, it does illustrate the importance of effective delivery. No matter how well-thought-out your speech, or how many hours you put in at the library, or how elegant your outline, unless the speech is effectively presented, your message will not have its desired impact. In Chapter 10 we deal at length with the nonverbal nature of delivery, including the important functions it serves for a speaker. In the meantime, however, the following guidelines will help you present your beginning speeches.

Keep in mind that you have three tools as a public speaker: your *voice*, your *face and eyes*, and your *body*. If you manage these effectively, you will be able to get your message across to your audience.

Use Your Voice Effectively

How you use your voice is critical to effective communication. Some basic guidelines will enable you to speak most effectively.

Breathe Properly Breathe deeply, from your diaphragm. Give your voice enough support to be heard, but avoid straining your voice or shouting.

Speak Conversationally Think of public speaking as heightened conversation. Don't attempt to emulate political orators: Most audiences are put off by their

VIDEO FILE

If you have access to the videotape that accompanies this book, view segment 2, which shows the speech by Karen Shirk outlined in the box "Accident or Suicide: Driving Without a Seatbelt."

Sample Speech Outline

Title of speech.

ACCIDENT OR SUICIDE: DRIVING WITHOUT A SEATBELT
by Karen Shirk

Specific purpose is to motivate audience to do what they know is right.

Specific Purpose: To persuade my audience to wear their seatbelts.

Introduction

Speaker begins with startling statements and visual aids of actual objects that survived a crash.

I. **Open With Impact:** This may be recognized as a piece of a brake light, but to me, it is a piece of brake light from my mother's car. This may be recognized as a CD-player face, but to me, it's the only thing left from an accident that happened earlier this year.

   A. Many times I have seen people getting in cars and driving away without a seatbelt on.

   B. This concerns me because I know how quickly a little drive can turn into a big accident.

   C. It doesn't matter if you are an expert driver, your safety is put into other people's hands, whether you're the passenger or the driver.

Thesis statement and connect with audience are clearly labeled.

II. **Focus on Thesis Statement:** It's important to take what little control you have on the road and utilize it.

III. **Connect With the Audience:** That's why it's so important to wear your seatbelt.

Preview of speech is provided.

IV. **Preview:** Today I will discuss the importance of seatbelts, the benefits of wearing a seatbelt, why some people still aren't wearing seatbelts, and some ways to remind you to strap on your seatbelt.

Body

Body of speech is labeled.

Main points begin with roman numeral I.

I. **Main Point:** Putting on your seatbelt may be the most important part of driving.

Direct quotations are indicated by quotation marks and source is cited in parentheses. Your instructor may prefer a different method of citing sources.

   A. After all, a seatbelt is defined as "an arrangement of straps designated to hold a person steady in a seat" (*Merriam-Webster's*, 1993, p. 1054).

   B. And, as Dr. Haddon says, "I would challenge those of you who do not use them to consider that . . . as persons sending something through the mail you would not ship things loose in an empty barrel to flop around with the barrel moving at high speed" (Haddon, 1968, p. 13).

   C. As an example, consider Barbie, who doesn't bother putting on her seatbelt (show overheads).

Speaker includes note to self to turn on overhead projector.

   D. Some important points to remember about seatbelts as listed online are:

      1. First, an adult can only hold back the weight of his body by the arms and legs at speeds of up to 7 kilometers per hour (*The seatbelt—a link with life*, 1998).

      2. Second, in a collision at 50 kilometers per hour, the force is the same as falling 10 meters.

Signposts are transitional statements between main points.

(**Signpost:** Now that you've been reminded of the importance of seatbelts, let's discuss how a seatbelt can benefit you.)

II. **Main Point:** A seatbelt can save you from serious or even fatal injury.

   A. First, if the vehicle you're in is rear-ended, a seatbelt will hold you from flying through the windshield.

   B. Second, if your vehicle rolls or flips, the seatbelt will keep you from banging into the sides and roof of the car.

C. And third, it can keep you from getting a hefty fine from the Highway Patrol.

(**Signpost:** Now that we've discussed the benefits, let's try to analyze why some people still aren't wearing seatbelts.)

III. **Main Point:** There could be several reasons why some people still aren't wearing seatbelts, although none of them serves as a valid excuse.
   A. One reason could be laziness.
   B. Another reason could be forgetfulness.
   C. One reason might be confidence.
   D. Some people are afraid that a seatbelt will trap them in the event of an accident.
   E. Finally, I've overheard someone say that wearing a seatbelt would wrinkle their clothes.

(**Signpost:** Basically, there's no excuse. But, instead of verbally abusing unsafe drivers, it's better to suggest a few solutions to remind yourself to strap on your seatbelt.)

IV. **Main Point:** These solutions are simple and don't require too much effort, considering the benefits involved.
   A. Make putting on your seatbelt the first thing you do upon entering a vehicle.
   B. Get into the habit of having it on.
   C. Wear it no matter how far you're driving—no exceptions.

Conclusion

I. **Summarize:** Today I've discussed seatbelts and the safety they offer.
   A. I've reinforced the importance of wearing a seatbelt.
   B. I've listed some of the immediate benefits of wearing a seatbelt.
   C. I've tried to explain some reasons why others may not wear a seatbelt.
   D. And I've tried to offer some useful suggestions on how to increase your control on the road by wearing a seatbelt.

Conclusion begins with a summary of main points.

II. **Close With Impact:** It shouldn't be necessary to have to persuade you to wear a seatbelt.
   A. But, as seen in the numerous fatalities each year in cases where someone wasn't wearing theirs, sometimes the message doesn't get through.
   B. I hope I've reinforced that message enough so that you might think twice before driving unbuckled.
   C. That way, if you're ever in an accident, your chances are much higher that you'll walk away unharmed.

Speech closes with impact. Ask yourself if it matches the impact with which the speech opened.

References

Haddon, W. (1968). The national highway safety program—18 months later. In J. O'Day (Ed.), *Driver behavior: Cause and effect.* Washington, DC: Insurance Institute for Highway Safety.

The seatbelt—a link with life. (1998). [Online]. Available: http://www.lycos.com/wguide/wire/wire_969214_2_0.html [1998, April 3].

Merriam-Webster's collegiate dictionary (10th ed.). (1993). Springfield, MA: Merriam-Webster.

Speaker lists references at end of speech with full bibliographic citation. We discuss American Psychological Association (APA) and Modern Language Association (MLA) methods of source citation in Chapter 7. Your instructor may prefer a different method of citing sources. Whatever method is used, accurate source citation is important.

Using your face, eyes, and hands can add to the effectiveness of your presentation.

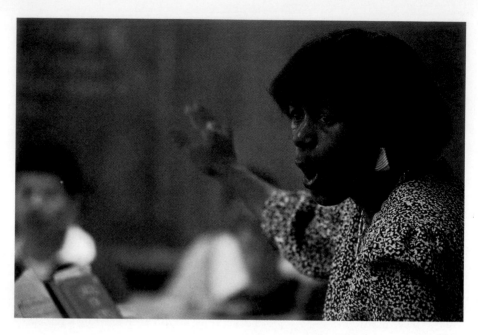

techniques. Speak as you do in conversation, but enlarge your voice sufficiently to be heard by all in the room. It is certainly appropriate and even advisable to ask those in the back of the room if they can hear you, should there be any doubt.

Vary Your Voice   Nothing is more deadly to a speech than a monotone voice. Vary the rate at which you speak, the pitch (high or low) at which you speak, and the volume (loudness). The goal is to present your speech enthusiastically, sincerely, and energetically. Let the audience know you care about your topic.

Use Your Face and Eyes Effectively

The face is one of the most complex and expressive parts of our anatomy, capable of communicating thousands of messages. Use your facial expression to reinforce your verbal message. The eyes, in particular, convey a great deal. Consider a person who gazes at you without pause. This will tend to make you uncomfortable. On the other hand, in our North American culture, a person who refuses to look at us communicates a negative message. (In some other cultures, such as certain Asian societies, no such negative message is communicated by avoiding eye contact.) As a speaker communicating to an American audience, therefore, maintain eye contact with your audience. This does not mean staring at just one portion of the room or shifting your eyes randomly. Rather, look at one member of your audience, then shift your gaze to another member, and so on. Be alert for audience responses to what you are saying. Are they restless, interested, puzzled? Such feedback can help you adapt to the audience as you speak.

Use Your Body Effectively

Your body is the third tool you use to communicate your message. Your body communicates to your audience through *posture, movement, gestures,* and *dress.*

Posture   How do you want to stand during your speech? Some speakers are comfortable behind a lectern, whereas others prefer to move away from it or dispense with it entirely. Choosing not to use a lectern can be an effective way of lessening the physical and psychological distance between yourself and the audience. If your preference is to use a lectern, do not use it as a crutch or bass drum. Avoid leaning on or clutching the stand, as well as beating on it with your open palm. Instead, find a comfortable, erect posture and stand slightly behind the lectern. Keep in mind that to breathe effectively, you need to have good body posture.

Movement   Movement should be spontaneous and meaningful. Though good speakers avoid pacing and random movements, it is perfectly appropriate—in fact, desirable—to move to emphasize an important idea or a transition between points. There is no reason a speaker's feet have to be nailed to the floor. Use your body to communicate your message whenever possible and practical.

Gestures   It is common in everyday conversation to gesture with your hands. In fact, try this experiment: Give someone directions from your school to your home *without* moving your hands. You will find it virtually impossible. The key to effective use of gestures in a public speech is that they should be appropriate to the point you are making and clearly visible to your audience. The larger the room, the larger the gesture needs to be for your audience to see it. On the other hand, too many gestures, especially if they appear to be the result of nervousness, such as fidgeting, can be distracting to an audience. Finally, your gestures should be natural extensions of what you do in everyday conversation.

Dress   Your dress as a speaker should be *appropriate* to the situation and the audience. A good rule of thumb is to dress as you might for a job interview. People make instant judgments about other people and, as one shampoo ad proclaims, "You never get a second chance to make a first impression." In no case should your dress detract from the message you want to convey.

Methods of Delivery

There are four common ways to deliver a speech:

- Write out a *manuscript* and read it to your audience.
- *Memorize* your speech and recite it from memory.
- Present a spontaneous, unrehearsed *impromptu* presentation.
- Combine preparation and spontaneity in an *extemporaneous* presentation.

We discuss each type of delivery in turn, along with its advantages and limitations.

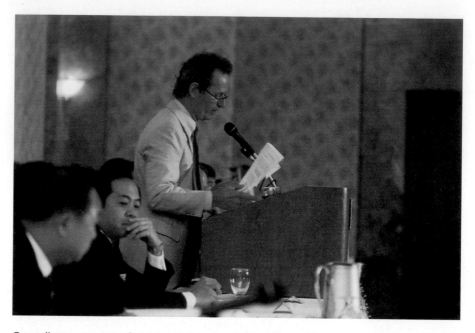

Overreliance on a speech manuscript can cause a speaker to lose contact with the audience.

Manuscript Delivery   When a speaker uses **manuscript delivery,** the speech is written out completely and read to the audience. Few speakers are very good at reading a speech. In fact, except for politicians and other officials who rely on ghostwriters to prepare their speeches, most of us will not have occasion to give a manuscript speech.

Though it might seem easy to write out your speech in advance and read it to the audience, this is easier said than done. One disadvantage of written speeches is that most people don't write as they speak. Speeches delivered from a manuscript have an artificial quality about them. Sentences are often too long and complex. The audience often loses track of the point being made. "Oral essays" are not an effective way to communicate with an audience.

If the manuscript pages get out of order or some are missing, you may be forced to improvise or stop your speech altogether. Most teachers have had the painful experience of watching a speaker fumble for words as he or she looks frantically for the next page of the speech. Overreliance on a manuscript can lead to such embarrassing moments.

Another disadvantage of manuscript delivery is that you lose eye contact with your audience. Not only does this inhibit feedback, it reduces your contact with the audience, which, as we will see later, is a major factor in establishing your credibility as a speaker.

The principal situation in which you will want to deliver a speech from a manuscript is if it is critical that you be quoted accurately. For example, public officials usually speak from a manuscript to ensure that they are accurately quoted in the media, to which copies are usually provided. For your first speeches, however, you should avoid the manuscript speech.

Memorized Delivery An alternative to reading a speech is to memorize it. **Memorized delivery** is a mode of presentation in which the speech is written out and committed to memory before being presented to the audience without the use of notes. This method of delivery does eliminate the problems associated with maintaining eye contact. And, presumably, an able speaker can quickly drop a section of a memorized speech should time run short. But, on the whole, memorized speeches today are confined to the theater and speech tournaments. The reason is simple: Memorization requires an enormous investment of time for even a brief speech. Further, if you forget the speech, you are faced with either a very noticeable silence or "winging it." Finally, memorized speeches usually sound memorized. They are simply oral essays without the physical manuscript.

Impromptu Delivery A spontaneous, unrehearsed mode of presenting a speech is termed **impromptu delivery.** We are frequently called on to give impromptu speeches, although we usually don't think of them as speeches. For example, when your instructor calls on you to explain the day's reading assignment—or when you explain to your bank why you really aren't overdrawn—you are making an impromptu speech. In fact, most of our everyday conversations are spontaneous.

Nevertheless, for most speaking situations, the impromptu method of speaking is of limited usefulness. Even experienced public speakers usually have "canned" or set pieces on which they rely when they are called on to make impromptu presentations. For example, candidates for public office prepare for their debates and press conferences for days beforehand. Every conceivable question is asked in rehearsal, and possible answers are practiced. The unprepared candidate is often caught off guard, and his or her attempt to ad lib can backfire, as when Bob Dole spoke about the "Brooklyn Dodgers" during the 1996 presidential campaign. Of course, the Dodgers haven't played in Brooklyn since the early 1950s, and Dole's flub was taken by many as a sign that he was out of touch.

For beginning speakers, impromptu speeches should be approached as a learning tool to enhance the principles that apply to other speeches. To rely on impromptu speeches for all of your assignments is not wise.

Impromptu speaking is discussed in more detail in Chapter 15, but here are a few pointers to keep in mind if you are called on to give an impromptu presentation early in the semester.

Making an Impromptu Presentation

Tips and Tactics

- Think about what basic point you want to make about the topic. If you are asked about lowering the drinking age to 18, are you for or against it? If you don't know what your stand is, you might list the pros and cons of the issue and suggest that the audience needs to reach its own conclusion. If you are not informed on the topic, try linking it to something on which you do have information. Note that most instructors give students a choice from among two or three topics for impromptu speaking exercises. It is not their purpose to embarrass or "stump" the speaker.

- Think of one or more points that support your position. If you want to lower the drinking age to 18, is it because that's the age at which people can vote, sign contracts, and enlist in the armed forces?

- If you have time, think of an attention-getter as an introduction. If you knew of a specific case of an 18- to 20-year-old who had served in the military and risked his or her life, you might use that example as a "hook" to begin your speech.

- State your topic in the introduction: It buys you time and then you are sure the audience knows what you are saying. "I'm in favor of lowering the drinking age to 18, and I have three basic reasons."

- As a conclusion, summarize what you've said. "So, because 18 is the age at which people can vote, sign contracts, and enlist in the armed forces, I believe it's only fair to extend all adult rights to 18-year-olds."

If you do not have time to organize your thoughts, at least take a moment to think of your thesis and two or three main points. Believe it or not, in a few seconds you can organize a fairly decent impromptu speech. We engage in spontaneous conversations all the time. Thinking and speaking are not mutually exclusive.

Extemporaneous Delivery   The best mode of presentation for most beginning speakers is **extemporaneous delivery,** which combines careful preparation with spontaneous speaking. The speaker generally uses brief notes rather than a manuscript or an outline. Some instructors require students to first outline their speech in a formal way, in which case the outline should serve as a preparatory tool, not an abbreviated speech manuscript. Other instructors require only that students prepare note cards to help them recall their main and supporting points. (For an example of a speaker's note cards, see Figure 2.3.) Practicing the speech in advance allows you to fix the ideas in your head without memorizing the exact wording.

The extemporaneous method allows you to be prepared yet flexible. If you see from the audience feedback that people are disagreeing with you, you can reexplain a point or add another example. If the audience seems bored, you might skip ahead to your most interesting example. Most teachers employ an extemporaneous method when lecturing to their classes. Students are invited to interact with their instructor, ask questions, and perhaps challenge a point. An extemporaneous speech should be a true transaction between speaker and listener.

SUMMARY

The essential steps in developing an effective speech are to (1) analyze the situation with which you are faced, (2) choose a topic that is suitable to both the situation and the audience, (3) decide on a general and specific purpose, (4) write a clear thesis statement, (5) invent the substance of your speech, (6) organize your speech, and (7) present your speech effectively.

In analyzing your situation, consider both the nature of your assignment and the *audience* you will face. Look for clues that will help you understand your au-

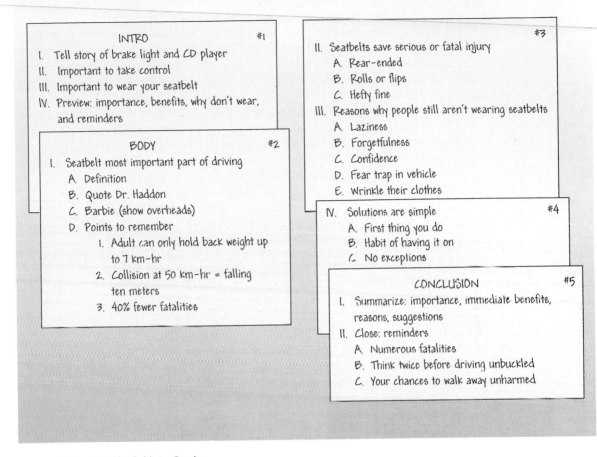

INTRO   #1
I.   Tell story of brake light and CD player
II. Important to take control
III. Important to wear your seatbelt
IV. Preview: importance, benefits, why don't wear,
     and reminders

BODY   #2
I.   Seatbelt most important part of driving
     A. Definition
     B. Quote Dr. Haddon
     C. Barbie (show overheads)
     D. Points to remember
        1. Adult can only hold back weight up
           to 7 km-hr
        2. Collision at 50 km-hr = falling
           ten meters
        3. 40% fewer fatalities

                                                       #3
II. Seatbelts save serious or fatal injury
     A. Rear-ended
     B. Rolls or flips
     C. Hefty fine
III. Reasons why people still aren't wearing seatbelts
     A. Laziness
     B. Forgetfulness
     C. Confidence
     D. Fear trap in vehicle
     E. Wrinkle their clothes

IV. Solutions are simple   #4
     A. First thing you do
     B. Habit of having it on
     C. No exceptions

CONCLUSION   #5
I.   Summarize: importance, immediate benefits,
     reasons, suggestions
II. Close: reminders
     A. Numerous fatalities
     B. Think twice before driving unbuckled
     C. Your chances to walk away unharmed

FIGURE 2.3 Speaker's Note Cards

dience, such as common experiences, age, sex, and social status. There are many ways to come up with an appropriate topic, including making a personal inventory, talking to friends, reading widely, checking the Internet, and *brainstorming*. Six criteria for an appropriate speech topic are that the topic should be (1) interesting to you, (2) interesting to your audience, (3) appropriate to the situation, (4) appropriate to the time available, (5) manageable, and (6) worthwhile.

The *general purpose* is the primary function of a speech. The three commonly agreed upon general purposes are to inform, to persuade, and to entertain. A *specific purpose* describes your goal or objective in speaking to a particular audience. The *thesis statement* focuses your audience's attention on the central point you wish to make in your speech.

The process of *inventing* your speech includes looking for sources of information for the substance of your speech. Such sources include: (1) your own experiences, (2) general sources of information, (3) interviews with experts, (4) computerized searches, and (5) specialized sources of information.

Then you need to develop a clearly organized speech that (1) opens with impact, (2) focuses on your thesis statement, (3) connects with your audience, (4) *previews* your main points, (5) organizes your ideas with three to five main points, (6) summarizes your main points, and (7) closes with impact. Common organizational patterns include time, spatial, categorical, and problem–solution. Transitional statements, called *signposts*, help the audience follow your organizational pattern.

In presenting your speech, you have three tools: your voice, face, and body. If you manage these effectively, you will most likely achieve your purpose in speaking. Although speeches may be delivered by *manuscript, memorization*, or in an *impromptu* fashion, for most speeches we recommend that you use an *extemporaneous* delivery. This involves fully preparing your speech, reducing it to note cards, and then presenting it in a spontaneous fashion.

Check Your Understanding: Exercises and Activities

1. Write a one- or two-page analysis of the audience for your first speech. What characteristics do your classmates seem to have in common? Are they similar to or dissimilar from you in age, social status, and background? What assumptions can you make about them based on their attendance at your university or college? How will what you know about your classmates affect your choice of speech topic and specific purpose?

2. Come up with three possible topics for your first speech. For each topic, consider whether it is (a) interesting to you, (b) interesting to your audience, (c) appropriate to the situation, (d) appropriate to the time available, (e) manageable, and (f) worthwhile. Based on this analysis, which topic do you believe is best for your first speech?

3. Once you have selected the best topic, determine what general purpose it would fulfill and phrase a specific purpose that you would hope to achieve in presenting the speech.

4. Make a list of appropriate sources for information about the topic you have chosen for your first speech.

5. Using the format discussed in this chapter, prepare an outline that organizes your speech so that it (a) opens with impact, (b) focuses on your thesis statement, (c) connects with your audience, (d) previews your main points, (e) organizes your ideas with three to five main points, (f) summarizes your main points, and (g) closes with impact.

6. View a speech on videotape and then read a manuscript of the speech. Appendix A contains manuscripts for several speeches that are available on the tape that accompanies this book. After both reading and viewing the speech, write a short paper that answers the following questions: (a) What seemed to be the greatest strength of this speech? (b) What seemed to be the greatest weakness of this speech? (c) What differences did you note between reading an outline or manuscript of the speech and actually seeing the speech delivered?

Alternatively, review the manuscript of a famous speech, such as Earl Spencer's eulogy of Princess Diana or Mary Fisher's speech on AIDS (in Appendix B). Then answer questions (a) and (b).

7. In a group of about five students, brainstorm different possible speech topics for about 15 to 20 minutes. During brainstorming the following rules apply:

   • The goal is quantity of ideas; even silly ideas should be listed.

   • No criticism or evaluation is allowed during the brainstorming process.

   • One person is designated to write down every idea. Ideally, write ideas on a chalkboard or an easel so that everyone can see them.

   • "Hitchhiking" ideas is encouraged. If you can add to or improve on someone else's idea, do it.

   • When you think everyone is out of ideas, try to get at least one more from each group member.

   • After all the ideas are listed, go through the list and select the best ideas. Look for ideas that fit the assignment, are feasible given the time limits, and would be appropriate for this class. Cross off ideas that don't seem to apply.

   • Now rank the remaining ideas in order of value. You may want to modify or combine ideas in this process.

   • When your instructor calls for your group to report, give the class your five best ideas. If there are five groups, that would mean 25 ideas listed for the class as a whole.

   As time permits, discuss the ideas in class. Which ones are most promising? How well do these possible topics fit the assignment? Will they be interesting and worthwhile for the members of the class? If you have an upcoming speech assignment, you might find one of these topics to be appropriate. You can also repeat the whole brainstorming process outside of class with some friends to see if you can come up with other topics as well.

Notes

1. "Selling Green," *Consumer Reports*, October 1991, 687–692.

2. "20 Million Americans See Starr's Report on Internet," CNN Interactive [Online]. Available: http://www.cnn.com/, 13 September 1998.

3. The formula was originally developed by Dr. Loretta Malandro and is taught in her program "Speak With Impact," offered by Malandro Communication Inc., Scottsdale, Arizona. We have modified it to add a preview to the introduction.

4. John F. Kennedy, "Inaugural Address," in *American Rhetoric from Roosevelt to Reagan*, 2nd ed., ed. Halford Ross Ryan. (Prospect Heights, Ill.: Waveland Press, 1987), 158.

5. George Kennedy, *The Art of Persuasion in Greece* (Princeton, N.J.: Princeton University Press, 1963), 283.

CHAPTER 3

Practice helps relieve anxiety about speaking.

Coping With Speech Anxiety

OBJECTIVES

After reading this chapter, you should be able to:

- Explain the relationship between arousal and anxiety.
- Define anxiety and distinguish it from speech anxiety.
- Identify common sources of speech anxiety.
- Understand and use skills that have proved effective in controlling arousal and speech anxiety.

KEY CONCEPTS

anxiety	physiological arousal
constructive self-talk	self-talk
coping skills	speech anxiety
negative self-talk	visual imagery

If your stomach disputes you—lie down and pacify it with cool thoughts.

— Satchel Paige

It often begins with butterflies in the pit of your stomach. Then your heart begins to noticeably palpitate. Your head starts to swim, making it difficult for you to concentrate, and a thin veil of perspiration begins to form on the palms of your hands. It may result from being asked to pinch-hit during a game of summer softball, from anticipating an important test you need to pass for your major, or from thinking about an interview for a needed internship.

What is this mysterious "it" about which we speak? **Anxiety** is the word we give to feelings of fear and uncertainty usually accompanied by physical symptoms such as butterflies in the stomach, perspiring, and unsteadiness. Not only is it a fact of life for college students, it frequently is a consequence of the subject of this book. In fact, as pointed out during a segment of ABC's program *20/20*, speech anxiety is regularly experienced by upward of 40 percent of all American adults. **Speech anxiety** refers to the feelings of discomfort that people experience before, during, or even after speaking in public.

Our concern in this chapter is the constructive control of speech anxiety before, during, and following your speeches. The information presented will help you to become a better, more confident public speaker. Further, we will present specific **coping skills,** which are mental and physical techniques used to control anxiety before, during, and following a speech. These techniques will help you to become a better speaker even if speech anxiety generally is not a problem for you. Of course, those with minimal speech anxiety will not need to employ all of these methods. We begin by discussing the relationship between physiological arousal and speech anxiety. We then describe the sources of speech anxiety. Finally, we present a number of well-researched techniques and coping skills you can use to become a less anxious and more confident public speaker.

PHYSIOLOGICAL AROUSAL AND SPEECH ANXIETY

The relationship between physiological arousal and speech anxiety is paradoxical. When we speak of **physiological arousal,** we mean the physical changes that occur when a person is aroused, such as increased pulse, greater alertness, and more energy. On the one hand, moderate arousal is necessary to effective speaking. Too little arousal, for example, decreases alertness, motivation, and overall performance.[1] On the other hand, too much arousal can cause constricted muscles and vocal cords, excessive sweating, and nausea. Too much arousal, in other words, can have a disastrous effect on public speaking transactions.[2] Everyone experiences some degree of physiological arousal when he or she speaks or, in some cases, anticipates speaking. This arousal is positive until it is interpreted by the person as uncomfortable.

The relationship between arousal and performance is illustrated in Figure 3.1. As you can see, as your level of arousal nears the top of the curve, motivation, alertness, and the potential for effective speaking are positively influenced. However, when your level of arousal begins to exceed this point, motivation, alertness, and the potential to speak effectively steadily decline. The optimal level of arousal is

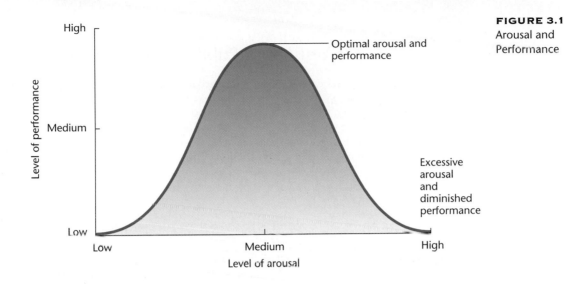

FIGURE 3.1
Arousal and
Performance

not the same for every person. However, the same factors influence the level of arousal each of us experiences.

The level of arousal you experience before, during, and following a speech will depend on the emotions you are experiencing. Of the many emotions that can influence your level of arousal in this respect, anxiety is the most common. Potentially, it also is the most troublesome.

As noted at the beginning of the chapter, anxiety is a type of fear and uncertainty usually accompanied by physical symptoms. Medical authorities note that such anxiety involves a sense of dread and distress over perceived threats, whether real or not, to either mental or physical well-being.[3] It is well documented that the more anxious we are about something, the greater are the chances that we will experience a performance-detracting level of arousal.[4]

The fear of speaking publicly is a specific type of anxiety. Generally, it is felt before, during, and following a public speech. Public speaking anxiety also shows itself in two major ways. The first is mental. Before a speech it is characterized by such things as excessive worrying, the inability to concentrate, and procrastinating about preparing the speech. During a speech it can take the form of feeling helpless, thinking highly negative thoughts, and erroneously believing that the audience wants the speaker to fail. Following a speech, it commonly expresses itself in terms of excessive self-criticism, unjustified feelings of embarrassment, and the inability to listen to feedback about the speech.

The second and most easily recognized way speech anxiety shows itself is physical.[5] Prior to speaking, for example, an anxious person stereotypically has butterflies in the stomach. While he or she is giving a speech, anxiety can involve excessive perspiration, blushing, forgetfulness, trembling hands, and poor eye contact, among other symptoms. After sitting down, moreover, the anxious speaker may feel physically exhausted, mentally drained, and unable to focus on constructive feedback.

How Anxious Are You About Public Speaking?

The following scale measures communication anxiety in general, as well as anxiety resulting from communication in four specific contexts: (1) dyads, (2) small groups, (3) meetings, and (4) public settings. You may find upon completion of the measure that although your overall score is indicative of mild levels of communication anxiety, you are moderately to highly anxious about communicating in one or more specific contexts. Some research, for example, indicates that communicating in groups, meetings, and public settings is most anxiety arousing for students much like you. In any case, the techniques introduced in this chapter will help you cope with your communication anxieties, regardless of their contextual source.

PERSONAL REPORT OF COMMUNICATION APPREHENSION (PRCA-24)

Directions: This instrument is composed of 24 statements concerning your feelings about communication with other people. Please indicate in the space provided the degree to which each statement applies to you by marking whether you (1) Strongly Agree, (2) Agree, (3) Are Undecided, (4) Disagree, or (5) Strongly Disagree with each statement. There are no right or wrong answers. Many of the statements are similar to other statements. Do not be concerned about this. Work quickly; just record your first impression.

_____ 1. I dislike participating in group discussions.

_____ 2. Generally, I am comfortable while participating in a group discussion.

_____ 3. I am tense and nervous while participating in group discussions.

_____ 4. I like to get involved in group discussions.

_____ 5. Engaging in a group discussion with new people makes me tense and nervous.

_____ 6. I am calm and relaxed while participating in group discussions.

_____ 7. Generally, I am nervous when I have to participate in a meeting.

_____ 8. Usually I am calm and relaxed while participating in meetings.

_____ 9. I am very calm and relaxed when I am called upon to express an opinion at a meeting.

In the context of public speaking, mental and physical anxiety interact with one another. If you are so anxious prior to giving a speech that you procrastinate and do not adequately prepare, you likely will experience symptoms of physical anxiety as you begin to deliver your speech. In turn, as you begin to sense the telltale symptoms of physical anxiety, the more likely you will be to begin to mentally interpret your presentation in a negative light.

Therefore, optimizing your success as a public speaker depends on your ability to achieve and maintain an optimal level of arousal during all phases of the preparation and delivery of your speech. Before examining the sources and remedies for public speaking anxiety, you may want to evaluate your speech anxiety

_____ 10. I am afraid to express myself at meetings.

_____ 11. Communicating at meetings usually makes me uncomfortable.

_____ 12. I am very relaxed when answering questions at a meeting.

_____ 13. While participating in a conversation with a new acquaintance, I feel very nervous.

_____ 14. I have no fear of speaking up in conversations.

_____ 15. Ordinarily I am very tense and nervous in conversations.

_____ 16. Ordinarily I am very calm and relaxed in conversations.

_____ 17. While conversing with a new acquaintance, I feel very relaxed.

_____ 18. I'm afraid to speak up in conversations.

_____ 19. I have no fear of giving a speech.

_____ 20. Certain parts of my body feel very tense and rigid while giving a speech.

_____ 21. I feel relaxed while giving a speech.

_____ 22. My thoughts become confused and jumbled when I am giving a speech.

_____ 23. I face the prospect of giving a speech with confidence.

_____ 24. While giving a speech I get so nervous, I forget facts I really know.

SCORING

To determine your anxiety level, compute the following formulas. The higher your score, the more significant your level of anxiety. (The numbers in parentheses in the formulas refer to the numbered questions above.)

Group = 18 − (1) + (2) − (3) + (4) − (5) + (6)

Meeting = 18 − (7) + (8) + (9) − (10) − (11) + (12)

Dyadic = 18 − (13) + (14) − (15) + (16) + (17) − (18)

Public = 18 + (19) − (20) + (21) − (22) + (23) − (24)

Overall CA = Group + Meeting + Dyadic + Public

Source: James C. McCroskey, _An Introduction to Rhetorical Communication_, 7th ed. (Needham Heights, Mass.: Allyn & Bacon, 1997).

by filling out the self-assessment exercise in the box "How Anxious Are You About Public Speaking?"

RECOGNIZING THE SOURCE OF YOUR ANXIETIES

Not all people have the same reason for being anxious about speaking in public. The underlying sources of mental and physical anxiety are varied. Still, research over the past three decades has given us a good picture of the most common sources of our anxieties about speaking in public.[6] This picture includes a pessimistic attitude toward speaking, inadequate preparation and practice, negative or insufficient experience, unrealistic goals, inaccurate perception of the audience, negative self-talk, and misdirected concerns. Let's discuss each of these sources of anxiety in turn.

Pessimistic Attitude Toward Speaking

The first and most immediate source of anxiety is your perception of and reaction to the situation you face. Though actual physiological arousal is neither positive nor negative in itself, your perception of it can be either positive or negative. If you perceive and react to a situation positively, the arousal you feel will be perceived as a pleasant rather than an aversive sensation. What's more, it is not likely to exceed its optimal level. Conversely, if you perceive a situation negatively, you will perceive the arousal you feel as an unpleasant, even worrisome sensation. This increases the probability of arousal exceeding the optimal level as you become more and more anxious, further pushing your physiological arousal level.

Research shows that the difference between being positively excited or negatively threatened by a situation such as public speaking is not a matter of arousal per se. It is a matter of how the arousal is initially interpreted. Consider riding a roller coaster. Some people love it; others hate it. If you were to measure arousal while people actually rode a roller coaster, however, you would find, in the beginning, very little difference in their level of physiological arousal. But as the ride progressed and their positive or negative interpretation of the experience began to kick in, differences in arousal would begin to appear.

So it is with public speaking. If you perceive it as an opportunity to become a more skilled communicator, chances are you will be able to maintain an optimal level of arousal before, during, and following your speeches. Of course, the reverse also is true. If you perceive public speaking as an anxiety-producing task you prefer to avoid, you probably will become so aroused that you will experience the mental and physical signs of anxiety we discussed earlier. The question we now need to address, then, is why some people perceive and react to public speaking so negatively.

Inadequate Preparation and Practice

An obvious reason for viewing the speech transaction as aversive is inadequate preparation and practice. Whereas most students would never dream of entering an athletic competition or taking a test crucial to their success in their major without preparation and practice, many seem to think that public speaking is different in this regard. So they put off preparing and practicing their speech until the last moment. Then they wonder why the act of speaking itself is so traumatic.

Minimizing the importance of preparation and practice to the speaking experience only increases the amount of uncertainty surrounding the speaking assignment. Further, this uncertainty is one of the chief causes of the excessive arousal and anxiety that students feel in the course of speaking in public. Frequently, then, the real source of their discomfort is a result of their own shortsightedness.

Sometimes students recognize the importance of preparation and practice but simply cannot confront the public speaking assignment. Much like "writer's block," such aversion to preparing and practicing a speech occurs because students are afraid to get started. Perhaps they fear failure or they just don't know where to begin. Whatever the reason, procrastination is a sure source of speech anxiety.

Negative or Insufficient Experience

Your prior experiences with any task influence how you approach and complete your present task. If your past experiences with public speaking proved both successful and personally rewarding, chances are you look forward to your speaking assignments in this class. But if your prior experiences with public speaking were unpleasant, chances are you harbor some doubt about your abilities to succeed in this class. Finally, if you have had little or no opportunity to speak in public, you too may be mildly or even considerably anxious about speaking before your teacher and peers.

If you are in one of these latter two groups, your anxieties are understandable. It is natural to initially perceive a task such as speaking as a threat if your past experience with the task seemed more punishing than rewarding. It also is natural to feel anxious about a task with which you have little or no familiarity. But the fact that your past efforts as a speaker were unrewarding, or even traumatizing, need not mean that your efforts in this class will prove likewise. As we discuss in the next section, dwelling on unpleasant experiences in your past can be a major obstacle to self-improvement.

By the same token, the fact that you think you have had little experience with the skills necessary to effective public speaking shouldn't make you overly anxious. As pointed out earlier, public speaking is an extension and refinement of the communication skills you put to use daily. Through your class and this book you can learn to successfully extend your everyday communication skills to the task of speaking in public.

Unrealistic Goals

A common source of anxiety for student speakers, especially inexperienced ones, involves the goals they set for themselves. Though it is important to set high goals for yourself, they also should be realistic. Unrealistic goals can lead to irrational fears about the speaking situation. Research shows that people who set realistic goals for themselves are less anxious and more successful than their counterparts with unrealistic goals.[7] This finding also has been reported in studies of elite athletes, businesspeople, and students enrolled in public speaking courses.

Speech-anxious students often hurt themselves by establishing goals that are not only unrealistic but also well beyond their reach. They tell themselves that despite their inexperience and unwillingness to make their speech class a priority, they must be the best in their class or they have to get an A. Such

Despite previous bouts with anxiety, Barbra Streisand is back speaking and performing in public.

illogical and unrealistic goals, the research shows, harm much more than help students in coping with their speech anxiety.

Inaccurate Perception of the Audience

Another source of speech anxiety involves your perception of the audience. Many beginning speakers view the public speaking situation in general, and their audience specifically, as a threat to their mental well-being. They convince themselves that the members of their audience are just waiting for them to commit some faux pas (social blunder), lose their train of thought, blow a quotation, or mumble through a sentence. Along the same lines, it is not uncommon for beginning speakers to read into the nonverbal feedback they receive from their audience such false conclusions as "they're bored to tears" or "they think I'm terrible." This is anything but the case, of course. Audiences, with rare exception, want speakers to succeed and are silently rooting for them to do so.

In recognition of this fact, consider the case of the late Mary Martin, a well-known and highly praised stage actress. She used to do something before a performance that you may wish to try. Just before going on stage, she would close her eyes, take a deep breath, and say 100 times to herself, "I love my audience." Next she would repeat the process, but this time tell herself, "My audience loves me."

In addition to misperceiving their audience as a threat, beginning speakers may convince themselves that their audience expects more from them than they can deliver. Such expectations about an audience can easily become a self-fulfilling prophecy. These unwarranted expectations also can make you anxious and overly aroused. The students you face share the same boat with you and want you to succeed as much as you do. If you still need convincing, consider how you feel when you are a member of an audience gathered to watch a public performance. Do you silently root for the performer to fail miserably? Do you take perverse joy in seeing the performer make an obvious mistake? We didn't think so!

Negative Self-Talk

Closely aligned with the problem of unrealistic personal goals is the more widespread problem of self-defeating patterns of self-talk. **Self-talk** describes communicating silently with oneself, sometimes referred to as intrapersonal communication. **Negative self-talk,** a self-defeating pattern of intrapersonal communication, can result from several causes, including the following:

- undue worrying about your speech, including unnecessary comparisons of your speeches with those of other students before the fact
- dwelling excessively on negative past experiences with public speaking
- spending too much time thinking about the alternative approaches you might take in preparing your speech
- preoccupation with feelings of mental and physical anxiety, such as trembling hands and a racing heart
- thinking about the worst and usually most unlikely consequences of your speech—people laughing at you or ridiculing your performance
- thoughts about or feelings of inadequacy as a public speaker

Such negative thinking usually leads to three specific types of negative self-talk: self-criticizing, self-pressuring, and catastrophizing. Let's look at each.

Self-Criticizing   Though realistic self-evaluation is important to self-improvement, it is well documented that many of us berate and derogate ourselves without sufficient cause. Without much evidence at all, we say all sorts of negative things about ourselves.

Not just students but people in all walks of life tell themselves they are poor speakers. Many of them do so, moreover, despite the fact that they have never received any training in public speaking and have had few if any opportunities to speak in public. Their lack of skill doesn't justify their self-criticism.

Self-Pressuring   We also bring undue and added pressure on ourselves through our self-talk, never once thinking about whether such pressure will help us to perform better. We tell ourselves, for example, that we must be "the best speaker in the class" without first considering why. As it is, you invariably will experience some degree of pressure and arousal when speaking publicly. A small amount of pressure can help you reach the optimal level of arousal that will help you deliver your speeches effectively. If you feel no pressure at all, you will lack the motivation to properly prepare and practice. But telling yourself that anything but being the best isn't good enough frequently will hurt rather than help your speaking.

Catastrophizing   We may blow things out of proportion when talking to ourselves. For example, a speech becomes the worst thing that has ever happened to you, something that you will never be able to live down for the rest of your life, or important enough to hate yourself should you receive a low grade.

As was the case with unrealistic goals, this kind of self-talk increases arousal and speech anxiety. The more negative your self-talk is, the more probable it is that you will exceed your optimal level of arousal. Fortunately, substituting constructive self-talk for negative self-talk is one of the easiest and best ways you can control your level of arousal while preparing and delivering your speeches. We discuss the specifics of this process later in the chapter.

Misdirected Concerns

Finally, some research suggests that students who are highly anxious about speaking express very different concerns about an upcoming speech than do those who are only moderately anxious.[8] For example, researchers found that highly anxious students were most concerned with how they would be evaluated, how long they should speak, what specific topic they should choose, whether they could use notes, and how long they had to prepare. In short, these students were concerned primarily with immediate factors that affect how they would be evaluated in the classroom situation. These concerns are classic signs of mental anxiety. Moreover, they suggest that truly anxious students may be so preoccupied with themselves, they will neglect the public speaking situation itself.

These researchers also found that students who reported little anxiety about speaking were most concerned with factors that would enable them to successfully attain their goals as speakers. In fact, these are the kinds of issues that even professional and highly paid speakers want to know about—for instance, the arrangement of the room, the availability of a microphone, and whether the audience would ask questions. To get a clearer idea of what lies behind your anxiety, see the box "What Are the Sources of Your Speech Anxiety?"

CONTROLLING THE SOURCES OF YOUR SPEECH ANXIETY

In the past 25 years, researchers have learned much about the control of arousal and anxiety. In the process, they have also learned that anyone can benefit from following certain arousal- and anxiety-controlling steps regardless

What Are the Sources of Your Speech Anxiety?

Listed below are common sources of speech anxiety. As you read each item, consider how much it contributes to the anxiety you experience about public speaking. Rate each item on a scale of 1 to 10, from least important to most important.

Sources of Speech Anxiety	Least Important/Most Important									
	1	2	3	4	5	6	7	8	9	10
Your attitude toward speaking	—	—	—	—	—	—	—	—	—	—
Lack of preparation and practice	—	—	—	—	—	—	—	—	—	—
Previous experiences with speaking —lack of or bad experiences	—	—	—	—	—	—	—	—	—	—
Unrealistic goals	—	—		—	—	—	—	—	—	—
Perception of your audience as hostile or unsympathetic	—	—	—	—	—	—	—	—	—	—
Negative self-talk	—	—	—	—	—	—	—	—	—	—
Misdirected concerns with how you will be evaluated	—	—	—	—	—	—	—	—	—	—

Rearrange the items in order of importance. Use this hierarchy to better understand the sources of your speech anxiety. What steps can you take to address and change your patterns of thought and behavior?

1. _____
2. _____
3. _____
4. _____
5. _____
6. _____
7. _____

of their individual level of anxiety about speaking in public. Let's now look at each of these steps.

Develop an Optimistic Attitude Toward Speaking

To begin with, the slightest shift in our point of view can drastically change the way we see things. For example, shifting your point of view about public speaking from one of performance to one of communicating can make a tremendous difference in the way you look at and respond to the speech transaction.

The first step in controlling speech anxiety for many people, then, requires that they start thinking about public speaking differently. Instead of thinking of it as a public performance during which they will be "on stage," for instance, they might be better off viewing it as a slightly different and more formal way of carrying on a conversation with a group of interested friends or perhaps telling them a story. Certainly the latter is a more inviting view of the speech transaction.

Research shows that this kind of thinking works because it forces people "outside the box" they customarily stay within. Once outside the box, moreover, people begin to understand not only that there are multiple ways to view a task but that these alternative ways of viewing a task actually influence the way they complete it.

Don't Procrastinate Preparing Your Speech

The second step in controlling arousal and anxiety is to commit to preparation well in advance of the actual speech. Although only you know how much time you need to prepare, our experience as instructors is that students usually need more time than they think they do. As we have said, most students do not have a great deal of experience in public speaking, nor are most students exceptionally skilled in public speaking at the outset.

Preparation begins with making sure that you clearly understand the nature of the speech you are asked to share, the conditions under which it will be shared, and the expectancies that will guide your instructor's evaluation. If you have a *clear* understanding of what is being asked of you, you will be less likely to procrastinate. Make sure you have all the information you need about the assignment to get off to a good start.

Preparation also involves making sure that you waste neither your nor your audience's valuable time. This means such things as topic selection, deciding on a general purpose, organizing your message, and gathering evidence should be undertaken with considerable care. Nowhere is such care more apparent than in the time you spend in selecting a topic and researching it. Hastily selected and poorly investigated topics not only are easily discerned, they also tell your audience that you didn't consider them worth the time it would have taken you to genuinely prepare. The response you receive from the audience, moreover, likely will make you more aroused and anxious.

Look for Opportunities to Gain Speaking Experience

Of course you have made the first step to gaining public speaking experience by enrolling in this class. Realistically, however, you probably will be able to give only four to six speeches during the course of an academic term. To build up your repertoire of public speaking experience, you should seek out other opportunities to speak. Many colleges and universities offer a competitive speech team. Though this might seem intimidating at first, competition is geared to levels of experience, with beginning speakers normally placed at the "novice" level. There may also be other opportunities to speak on your campus or in your community. Some communities have a Toastmasters International club, which provides an opportunity to gain a great amount of experience in a group devoted to building public speaking confidence.

You also can use assignments in other classes to gain experience. Cara Cupp, who was introduced in Chapter 1, used her oral assignments in many different courses to refine her speaking skills. She recognized and took advantage of a fact overlooked by many: A book report or an oral presentation covering a term project is a form of public speaking.

You can expect to speak more rather than less once you get started in your career. Your public speaking course, therefore, should be viewed as the beginning—not the end—of your education in public speaking.

Set Realistic Goals

Usually realistic goal-setting begins with an assessment of the unrealistic goals that lead to irrational fears that misguide anxious speakers in the preparation, presentation, and evaluation of their speeches. For example, research shows that anxious speakers often report that they are afraid because they believe that they must be perfect and they must be the best. No one is perfect. To think that *you* always must be perfect simply isn't realistic. By the same token, it is impossible for anyone to be the best at everything. Unnecessary and anxiety-arousing comparisons arise among people when they tell themselves they must always be the best.

In a public speaking class, you have the opportunity to work on improving your public speaking incrementally. You do not need to be a perfect or ideal speaker with each speech. Rather, as you approach each assignment, focus on one or two areas that you think are most in need of improvement. Perhaps in a particular speech you'll want to focus on organization, in another on delivery skills, and in another on your use of visual aids.

Realize the Audience Wants You to Succeed

Just as anxious speakers set unrealistic goals for themselves, research shows that they often report that they are afraid because they believe that their audience will ridicule them and they will look ridiculous. These fears are as irrational as expecting perfection in yourself as a speaker. For example, as an audience member, do you routinely ridicule the speaker or performer? Of course not. And audiences don't want to be made uncomfortable. As a result, when a single audience member tries to ridicule a speaker or performer with heckling, it usually is the heckler who becomes the object of audience scorn.

Probably no situation will provide you with as supportive an audience as your public speaking class. Remember, every member of the class faces exactly the same challenges you do. If you do make a mistake when giving a speech, their reaction is far more likely to be empathy and support than ridicule. In fact, in many public speaking classes, it is customary for every speaker to receive a round of applause on the completion of each speech.

Practice Constructive Self-Talk

Another step to take in your efforts to control arousal and anxiety involves **constructive self-talk:** the use of positive coping statements instead of negative self-talk. Just as researchers have found that anxious speakers set unrealistic goals and

TABLE 3.1 Positive Coping Statements for Speeches

BEFORE SPEECH	DURING SPEECH	AFTER SPEECH
Task Statements	*Task Statements*	*Context Statements*
What do I have to do?	Keep using coping statements.	It wasn't as bad as I feared.
Remember to use coping statements.	Speak slowly, it helps.	It was not a big deal.
Speak slowly and I'll be fine.	*Self-Evaluation*	Each time will get easier.
Context Statements	How am I doing?	*Self-Evaluation*
It's only my class.	So far so good.	What did I do well?
It's only one speech.	I've started and it was okay.	I used coping statements.
We're all in the same boat.	I was anxious, but now I've calmed down.	I spoke.
I know as much as anyone.	This is a little easier than I thought.	I spoke slowly.
I can't be any worse than previously, only better.		What do I want to improve next time?
		Remember to speak slowly and rehearse my statements.

inaccurately perceive their audiences, they have also found that speakers fear they will make extreme and obvious mistakes. This, too, is an irrational fear. Why should you appear any more ridiculous or make more mistakes than your classmates? If you've followed our advice for preparing and practicing your speech, you should neither appear ridiculous nor make more mistakes than other speakers. All speakers, including the most polished and practiced, make mistakes. The difference is that this latter group doesn't dwell on them, preferring to treat mistakes as an inevitable part of the process of public speaking. Polished and practiced speakers, in other words, know that no one is perfect—including themselves.

Once unrealistic goals and irrational fears about speaking have been confronted and exposed as such, constructive self-talk becomes a genuine possibility. Table 3.1 shows examples of positive coping statements. Note that positive coping statements (1) accentuate your assets—not your liabilities; (2) encourage you to relax; and (3) emphasize a realistic rather than catastrophic assessment of your situation before, during, and after your speech.

Instead of telling yourself you'll look ridiculous or sound funny, positive coping statements suggest you're attractive and sound sensible. Instead of telling yourself you must present the best speech in your class, positive coping statements suggest you should give the best speech of which you are capable. And instead of telling yourself you were terrible, positive coping statements suggest you'll get better with preparation, practice, and coaching.

Overcoming negative self-talk requires commitment and routine practice. Learning to substitute positive coping statements for negative self-talk also requires dedication and stick-to-itiveness. Thus, what you get out of this particular technique will very much depend on what you put into it.

Direct Your Concerns at Important Issues

As noted earlier, overanxious speakers tend to focus on concerns related to the evaluation of their presentation rather than the overall speech situation. Though it is certainly important that students know how they will be evaluated and what the instructor expects of them, an exclusive focus on such concerns is a case of the proverbial "missing the forest for the trees." Focus on your goal as a speaker and what you want to accomplish in a given situation. Ask yourself what your audience is like, what they expect, and how you can best meet their needs. Find out about the arrangement of the room, whether the audience will have an opportunity to ask questions, and the like. These factors are directly related to accomplishing your specific purpose, rather than getting a good grade. Our experience as instructors suggests that it is not the student who is overly concerned with the mechanics of evaluation who does best in our classes. Rather, students who do their best to manage the larger speech situation are most likely to give a successful speech.

In sum, then, there are numerous approaches to controlling the most common sources of speech anxiety. Experiment with them to see which ones help you the most. As a reminder, we list them below.

Controlling the Sources of Speech Anxiety

Tips and Tactics

- Develop an optimistic attitude toward speaking.
- Don't procrastinate preparing your speech.
- Look for opportunities to gain speaking experience.
- Set realistic goals.
- Realize the audience wants you to succeed.
- Practice constructive self-talk.
- Direct your concerns at important issues.

TECHNIQUES FOR CONTROLLING ANXIETY AND AROUSAL

The preceding section focused on directly attacking each source of public speaking anxiety. Nevertheless, regardless of how irrational some of the fear may be or how often you are reassured that your audience will be supportive, you may still experience symptoms of speech anxiety and heightened arousal. The techniques we now discuss do not depend on identifying particular sources of anxiety. Rather, you should think of these as general techniques for coping with speech anxiety. In addition, because they treat the symptoms directly, these techniques are applicable to other anxiety-producing situations, such as athletic competition and public performances.

An Athlete's Approach to Anxiety: Kristi Yamaguchi

Champion figure skater Kristi Yamaguchi not only practices physically for a performance, she practices mentally in order to cope with anxiety. Here, she describes her techniques:

> I usually get by myself before I go out for a routine. I walk through the program, visualizing myself completing all the moves. Right before a performance, I start talking to myself: "Okay, get out there, skate like it's an everyday practice."

The techniques Kristi Yamaguchi uses illustrate the importance of practice and mental imaging in dealing with anxiety. Notice that she mentally rehearses her moves right before a performance. She also engages in constructive self-talk when she tells herself that a competition is like an everyday practice. How do you think Yamaguchi's techniques could be successfully used by a public speaker? What can we learn as public speakers from the ways that elite athletes deal with the enormous pressure under which they must perform?

Source: American Health © 1992 by Steve McKee.

Using Visual Imagery and Practice to Enhance Performance

Using **visual imagery** is the opposite of rehearsing your speech. It is the process of mentally seeing (imagining) yourself performing an action or a series of actions. Instead of practicing your speech out loud, visually imagine yourself confidently and successfully giving the speech. At the 1998 Winter Olympiad, TV viewers were treated to pictures of gold and silver figure skating medalists Tara Lapinski and Michele Kwan both rehearsing through visual imagery before their performances. You may have caught a glimpse of them as they moved their heads side to side and up and down with eyes closed, while seated backstage. These two top performers are the tip of the iceberg of elite athletes who include visual rehearsal as a part of their everyday routines. See the box "An Athlete's Approach to Anxiety: Kristi Yamaguchi" for more information on visual rehearsal.

More to the point of this book is the case of Dr. Loretta Malandro. The founder of a successful communication consulting firm, Dr. Malandro travels worldwide as a professional speaker. One of the things she tries to do before each speaking engagement is to visually imagine herself giving the speech. Even if it means getting up before dawn, for example, she tries to run 5 miles and visualize her upcoming presentation as she runs. Because Dr. Malandro does this routinely, she sees not only herself as she shares her message, but also the positive feedback she is receiving from her audience.

Visual imagery is a highly effective complement to actual practice. Study after study has demonstrated that when used in combination with practice, visual imagery significantly enhances performance. That's why it is part of the routine practice of Olympic athletes in events ranging from archery to weight lifting.

Because it is yet another way that you can reduce your uncertainty about an upcoming speech, visual imagery also can assist you in controlling your level of anxiety and arousal. This technique works best when you are in a relaxed state and familiar with the content of your speech. It involves controlled visualization of your actual speaking situation, which will require practice on your part. The idea is to see yourself during all phases of your speech. For example, you might first visualize yourself seated at your desk, relaxed but appropriately aroused as you wait your turn to speak. Next, you might visualize yourself leaving your desk, moving to the front of the room, confidently facing your audience and introducing your speech. From here on, you would visualize yourself speaking—moving, gesturing, and making eye contact with individual members of your audience right up to your conclusion. Finally, you would see your audience and teacher enthusiastically responding to your presentation. Once you become adept at visualizing, you can even add sound to the picture in your mind's eye. Hearing yourself take command of an audience as you turn a phrase or smoothly make a transition from one point to another will enhance the impact of visual imagining.

To be most effective, this skill works best as a complement to actual practice. To maximize the enhancement of public speaking skills, therefore, you will also need to rehearse your speech. You can practice in front of friends, record your speech on videotape so that you can see the dynamics you may wish to modify, or practice in other ways. Regardless of how you practice, here are eight steps that will help you make the most of your practice time.

Steps for Practicing Your Speech

Tips and Tactics

1. Find a place where you will not be disturbed.
2. Set up the area as similar to the actual speech situation as possible. If you will be using a lectern, for example, use some object (like a chair or stool) to represent the lectern.
3. Practice alone first, only later in front of friends. Or tape-record your practice for later review.
4. Run through the whole speech at least once to see what areas need work.
5. Practice particular sections of the speech that are giving you trouble. Get these down "pat."
6. Go back and run through the entire speech again.
7. To work on nonverbal aspects of delivery, use a mirror or videotape yourself, if possible. At a minimum, try to tape-record your speech.
8. Finally, be sure to try a run-through with an "audience" of friends, roommates, or classmates.

Practicing your speech is essential to building confidence.

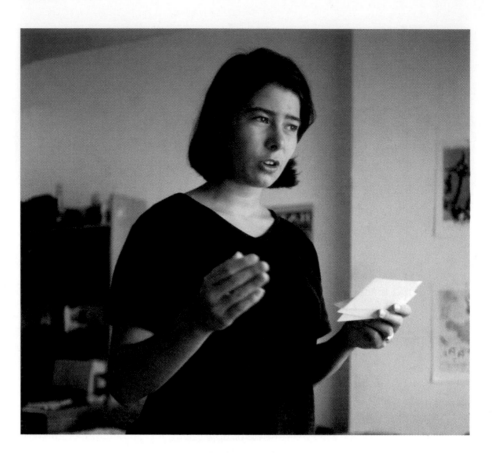

VIDEO FILE

If you have access to the videotape accompanying this book, view segment 3. Compare the relaxation techniques discussed in this chapter with those illustrated on the tape. After reading this chapter and before your next speech, review this segment and apply at least one relaxation technique to your own presentation.

Allow yourself plenty of time for practicing your speech. Make sure you have the speech ready a couple of days before it is due so that you can practice and, if necessary, revise it. Be sure to time the speech to make sure it fits the time limits of your assignment. And remember, practice doesn't make perfect, it makes permanent. So it is not just how much you practice, but how well you practice, that will make a difference in your success.

Making Effective Use of Relaxation Techniques

Butterflies, a racing heart, trembling hands, and weak knees are the result of the excessive adrenaline that is pumped into your system when you are overly aroused. The best way to prevent these symptoms is to condition your body to relax in situations that are, characteristically, overly arousing. You can accomplish this in one of several ways.

Exercise   The first way to help your body relax is to engage in some form of intense exercise 1 to 2 hours before you speak. The effects of physical exercise on physical and mental well-being are well known. Intense exercise assists us in decreasing signs of stress and has been linked to improved thinking and performance, regardless of the task.

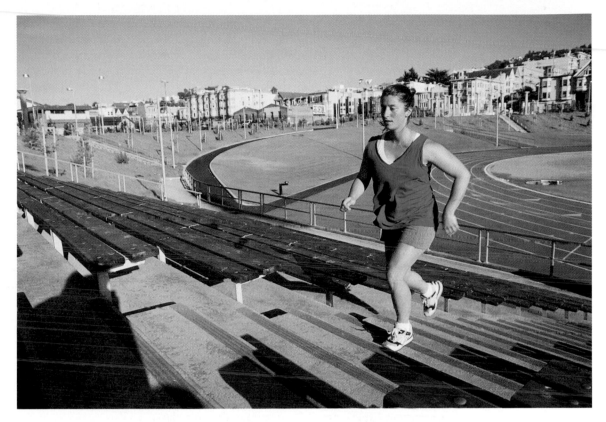

Exercise is a great way to manage the stress and anxiety you feel in anticipation of speaking.

Relaxation Imagery   If exercise is either inconvenient or impractical, another way to induce relaxation before you speak is to use relaxation imagery. Imagery is not the same as merely thinking. Imagery involves pictures, whereas thinking is a verbal process. Relaxation imagery involves visualizing pleasant and calming situations. Lying in a hammock or on the beach during a warm summer day are but two examples of such pleasant and calming situations. If you were to visually linger on such situations, you would find your body becoming increasingly relaxed. As a result, you would significantly lower the level of arousal customarily felt as a result of the day's activities.

This latter point is important. As a busy college student, you may find your up-coming speech to be the most significant but not the sole source of arousal you experience during the day. By practicing relaxation imagery before you speak, therefore, you can reduce the arousal that began to climb with the start of your day.

Muscular Relaxation   This technique involves systematically tensing and relaxing the various muscle groups. It usually begins with the muscles in your face and neck, then gradually moves to your middle and lower torso. The idea behind this technique is to teach your body the difference between tension and relaxation.

By first tensing and then relaxing your muscles systematically, you can also condition your muscles to relax even under the most stressful circumstances.

There's a good reason for practicing muscular relaxation. When we tense up, the range of movement in our muscles is restricted. They don't work as they are intended. In a game of basketball, we sometimes see this when a free-throw shooter hits the front of the rim, loses "touch," or puts up an air ball. With a speaker, we sometimes see this either in the absence of movement or gesturing or in movement and gesturing that are awkward and unnatural.

Combining Techniques

Visual imagery and relaxation techniques work best when used in combination. By combining relaxation with visual imagery, you can enhance the effectiveness of both techniques. You will come to associate the speaking situation with relaxing images rather than anxiety-producing ones.

These techniques also work best when they become a habitual routine that you practice as you prepare to speak. Elite athletes don't use them only before they are about to compete. Speakers shouldn't put off using them, moreover, until the night before they speak. The research is clear. These techniques will serve you well only if you commit to their systematic use. We suggest that you develop a routine like the one that follows.

Tips and Tactics

Five Steps to Reducing Speech Anxiety

1. Immediately begin to analyze your goals. Ask yourself if they are realistic given your experience and commitment to this class.

2. Begin today to assess the degree to which you routinely engage in negative self-talk. Write down the self-criticizing, self-pressuring, and catastrophizing statements you routinely make to yourself. Describe in writing how these statements affect your level of arousal and anxiety before, during, and following your speeches.

3. Make a list of the positive coping statements you could substitute for the negative ones you now make. Begin to use these statements as you prepare and practice your speech.

4. Once you're confident that you have thoroughly prepared your speech, find a quiet time in which you can both practice relaxation imagery and visually rehearse your speech. Do this for 15 minutes every other day, actually practicing your speech in between.

5. Use your positive coping statements as you are about to speak, while speaking, and after speaking.

Postpresentation Techniques

As important as it is to use anxiety-reducing techniques prior to and during your presentation, it is equally important to use these techniques after your presentation. We offer several techniques to reduce anxiety after a presentation.

Techniques for Reducing Postpresentation Anxiety

- Describe to yourself what you did well.
- List areas in which you still hope to improve. Write down at least three realistic goals for your next presentation.
- Engage in positive self-talk, such as "It wasn't as bad as I thought," "I did okay," "People smiled at me and gave me positive feedback."
- Breathe deeply; practice muscular relaxation.

SUMMARY

Speech anxiety is a result of our subjective interpretation of the *arousal* we experience when called on to speak publicly. Although some degree of arousal is necessary to prepare and deliver an effective speech, too much of it can lead to psychological side effects, such as excessive worry, and physical side effects, such as trembling hands. Too much arousal can lead to a debilitating level of speech anxiety.

To control speech anxiety, you must learn to control the arousal you feel before, during, and after a speech. This learning process begins with a search for the source of your speech anxiety. The most common sources are a pessimistic attitude toward speaking, inadequate preparation and practice, negative or insufficient experience, unrealistic goals, inaccurate perception of the audience, *negative self-talk*, and misdirected concerns.

Once the source or sources of speech anxiety have been discovered, there are several ways in which its negative side effects can be overcome. Research demonstrates that the most effective ways to manage such anxiety include attacking the source of the anxiety directly. This involves developing an optimistic attitude toward speaking, not procrastinating the preparation of your speech, looking for opportunities to gain speaking experience, setting realistic goals, realizing the audience wants you to succeed, practicing *constructive self-talk*, and directing your concerns at important issues. More general ways to control speech anxiety and the accompanying arousal include using *visual imagery* and practice and teaching your body to relax under stressful conditions. Finally, research suggests that these techniques work best in combination.

Remember, some level of arousal when you speak is natural. Moderate levels of arousal, moreover, are necessary for effective speaking. Too much arousal, though, is the difference between being "psyched up" and "psyched out" by the speeches you have yet to share.

Check Your Understanding: Exercises and Activities

1. In a short paper, describe the relationship between physiological arousal and speech anxiety and give examples of both physical and mental symptoms of anxiety. Be sure to define anxiety and distinguish it from speech anxiety.

2. The chapter lists seven common sources of speech anxiety and steps for controlling them. For your next speaking assignment, identify at least one such source of anxiety that concerns you and make an effort to remedy it. For example, if you have a tendency to procrastinate, make sure you start your speech sooner than usual. After the speech, assess how the remedy worked in alleviating at least one source of public speaking anxiety.

3. Before your next speech, make a list of the negative self-talk you have engaged in regarding speech assignments. Then come up with a series of constructive self-talk statements you will use in preparing for and while giving your next speech. Your instructor may ask you to turn in your list before you speak.

4. Two of the most convenient relaxation techniques you can use are relaxation imagery and muscular relaxation. Both initially require a quiet place and time where you will not be interrupted. This exercise allows you to practice relaxation on your own or with a friend. It is sometimes useful to have someone read the steps to you so that you can completely relax.

   a. Find a reclining chair or couch where you can make yourself comfortable.

   b. Lower or turn off bright lights.

   c. With your eyes closed, tense and then relax your muscles in this order: face, neck and shoulders, biceps and triceps, forearms, wrists and hands, chest, solar plexus, buttocks/hamstrings, quadriceps, calves, ankles and feet.

   d. Once you are completely relaxed, imagine a peaceful setting in which you feel calm. Learn to hold this image for as long as you can. After a minute or two move on to step 5.

   e. Imagine your speech class. If you feel any sign of anxiety, return to the preceding image.

   f. Continue to imagine your speech class and add yourself to the picture. See yourself calmly seated, enjoying others as they speak.

   g. See yourself writing down the requirements of an assigned speech. See yourself involved with the various stages of preparation, including seeing yourself practice.

   h. See yourself waiting to be called on, aroused but not anxious.

i. See yourself walking to the front of the room, turning to face your audience, smiling, and opening your presentation with impact.

j. See yourself speaking energetically, gesturing, and using your eyes, face, and voice.

k. See students and your instructor listening attentively.

l. See yourself concluding and your audience responding with genuine applause.

Practice this series of steps at least twice a week for 15–25 minutes each time. Remember, any time you begin to feel anxious during this exercise, replace whatever image you're holding with a pleasant and relaxing one.

Notes

1. R. M. Yerkes and J. D. Dodson, "The Relation of Strength Stimulus to Rapidity of Habit Formation," *Journal of Comparative Neurology and Psychology* 18 (1908): 459–482.

2. William J. Fremouw and Michael D. Scott, "Cognitive Restructuring: An Alternative Method for the Treatment of Communication Apprehension," *Communication Education* 28 (1979): 129–133.

3. C. L. Thomas, *Taber's Cyclopedic Medical Dictionary*, 12th ed. (Philadelphia: F. A. Davis, 1973), A-101.

4. Michael D. Scott and Louis Pelliccioni, Jr., *Don't Choke: How Athletes Can Become Winners* (Englewood Cliffs, N.J.: Spectrum Books, 1982).

5. William J. Fremouw and M. G. Harmatz, "A Helper Model for Behavioral Treatment of Speech Anxiety," *Journal of Consulting and Clinical Psychology* 43 (1975): 652–660.

6. J. A. Daly and J. C. McCroskey, eds., *Avoiding Communication: Shyness, Reticence and Communication Apprehension* (Beverly Hills, Calif.: Sage, 1984).

7. Albert Ellis and Robert A. Harper, *A New Guide to Rational Living* (Hollywood, Calif.: Wilshire Book Company, 1975).

8. Joe Ayres, "Perceptions of Speaking Ability: An Explanation for Stage Fright," *Communication Education* 35 (1986): 275–287; Michael Beatty, "Situational and Predispositional Correlates of Public Speaking Anxiety," *Communication Education* 37 (1988): 28–39; Bruskin Associates, "What Are Americans Afraid Of?" *The Bruskin Report* 53 (July 1973); J. A. Daly, A. L. Vangelisti, H. L. Neel, and P. D. Cavanaugh, "Pre-Performance Concerns Associated With Public Speaking Anxiety," *Communication Quarterly* 37 (1989): 39–53.

9. J. A. Daly, A. L. Vangelisti, and D. J. Weber, "Speech Anxiety Affects How People Prepare Speeches: A Protocol Analysis of the Preparation Process of Speakers," *Communication Monographs* 62 (1995): 383–397; T. Freeman, C. R. Sawyer, and R. R. Behnke, "Behavioral Inhibition and Attribution of Public Speaking State Anxiety," *Communication Education* 46 (1997): 175–187.

CHAPTER 4

Listening is an important part of the speech transaction.

Listening

OBJECTIVES

After reading this chapter, you should be able to:

- Explain what listening involves.
- Describe the significant role that listening plays for both speakers and audience members.
- Recognize and demonstrate the difference between hearing and listening.
- Identify common misconceptions about listening.
- Exhibit behaviors consistent with those of an active listener.
- Demonstrate understanding, appreciative, and critical listening skills.
- Identify and overcome obstacles to listening.

KEY CONCEPTS

active listening	denotative meanings
active mindfulness	listening
appreciative listening	metacommunication
comprehension	pinpoint concentration
connotation meanings	retention
context	selective attention
critical listening	sensorial involvement
cross cue–checking	wide-band concentration
culture	

To listen is an effort, and just to hear has no merit. A duck hears also.

— Igor Stravinsky

Nationally syndicated humorist Dave Barry wrote about traveling in Japan. To illustrate how "the Japanese tend to communicate via nuance and euphemism," he described an encounter between his wife, Beth, and a Japanese travel agent just prior to their trip:

Beth: . . . and then we want to take a plane from Point A to Point B.

Travel Agent: I see. You want to take a plane.

Beth: Yes.

Travel Agent: From Point A?

Beth: Yes.

Travel Agent: To Point B?

Beth: Yes.

Travel Agent: Ah.

Beth: Can we do that?

Travel Agent: Perhaps you would prefer to take a train.

Beth: No, we would prefer to take a plane.

Travel Agent: Ah-hah. You would prefer to take a plane?

Beth: Yes. A plane.

Travel Agent: I see. From Point A.

This exchange continued along these lines with Beth still seeking an answer to what she perceived to be a straightforward and simple question. Hearing no answer, she broke off the exchange, perplexed by what she perceived to be the agent's evasive and unresponsive behavior.[1]

Scenarios such as this one can be common between communicators from different societies that have different norms for appropriate communication behavior. In this case, it wasn't that the Japanese agent was purposely trying to evade Beth Barry's question. To the contrary, coming from a society where it is impolite to tell others "no" explicitly, the agent was trying to assist Beth in coming to the realization that her request was impossible because there was no plane between Points A and B. To come to such a realization, though, Beth would have had to realize that to understand the Japanese it is not enough to *hear* the content of the message. In a collectivist culture like Japan, where the context often contains more information than the words, you must *listen* for the nuance of the message as well.

Of course, we don't need a cross-cultural example to know that simply hearing what people say isn't the same as listening to them. Most of us have had plenty of experiences where our understanding of what we heard didn't correspond to the message the speaker intended. This is because although we may have heard what was said, we weren't listening for the underlying message that was being sent. *Hearing* is a physical process that in no way guarantees understanding. *Listening,* which is paramount to understanding, is both physical and psychological.

Listening is one of those concepts to which we all pay lip service. Yet how many of us truly understand what it means to listen, what listening involves, and what a significant role it can play in making us more competent communicators, both as speakers and interested audience members? Research suggests that fewer of us understand than we might think.

There are tremendous benefits to learning to be a good listener. On a daily basis, we are given directions, instructions, and advice that can be very important to our personal well-being. Anyone who's ever been lost and had to follow directions from a stranger knows how important it is to fully understand what is said. Few bosses are tolerant of employees who say, "Sorry, I didn't hear you tell me to do that." Whether seeking financial, career, or even personal advice, it is important to understand fully what is being said. Listening is one of those skills people take for granted, yet their very lives can depend on it.

Listening to other people is essential not only to our daily lives but also to our development as speakers and responsible audience members. Further, the information we receive in our daily lives is often rich in cues about the nature of our potential audiences. Thus we are more likely to achieve our speaking goals if we have listened carefully to the people around us.

This chapter is designed to assist you in becoming a better public speaker and audience member by first becoming a better listener. We discuss (1) the nature of listening, including its importance to our overall communication competence; (2) misconceptions about listening; (3) obstacles to effective listening; (4) types of listening especially relevant to the speech transaction; and (5) a series of interdependent techniques you can begin to use immediately in the effort to improve your listening behavior.

EVERYDAY IMPORTANCE OF LISTENING

The ability to listen effectively is important to succeeding (1) in school, (2) at work, (3) in relationships with friends and family, and (4) in situations where we need to share information with others. First, consider the fact that as a college student you are exposed to hundreds of hours of lectures, group discussions, and mediated communication. The ability to process and absorb information is the essence of learning. Not every professor is a brilliant speaker, holding your attention with ease. You need to listen especially well if you are to obtain the maximum benefit from your college career.

Second, effective listening is essential to success in the workforce. One of the key complaints of many employers is that employees do not listen effectively, costing millions of dollars each year in mistakes and inefficiencies. Among the skills employers value in listeners are "listening for content; listening to conversations; listening for long-term contexts; listening for emotional meaning; and listening to follow directions."[2]

Third, listening is essential to interpersonal communication, especially in families. How many times have you heard children or parents complain that no one listens to what they say? In interpersonal contexts, listening must go well beyond content, focusing on the emotional and relational components of the communication transaction.

FIGURE 4.1
Listening Relative to
Other Types of
Communication

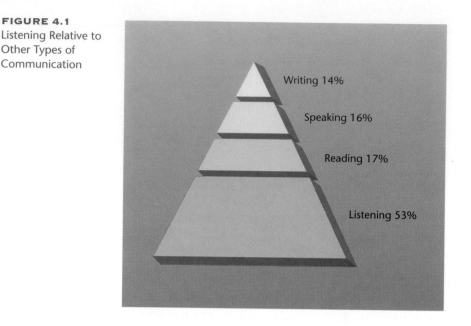

Writing 14%

Speaking 16%

Reading 17%

Listening 53%

Fourth, listening is essential to effectively communicate information to others. You need to adapt your own messages to the feedback you receive from others. Understanding what others need is essential to successfully influencing their beliefs, attitudes, and actions through the speeches you share.

As you can see in Figure 4.1, which shows the types of communication activities in which people engage daily, listening is by far the most dominant. But it also may be the activity at which people are the least skilled. The average listener remembers only about half of what was said immediately after it was said. And, as if that weren't bad enough, after 48 hours the average listener remembers only about one quarter of what was said.[3]

THE NATURE OF LISTENING

There is no universally accepted definition of listening. For our purposes, though, **listening** is the process of receiving, attending to, and assigning meaning to aural as well as visual and tactile stimuli.[4] Important to this comprehensive definition is the idea of **active listening,** which involves conscious and responsive participation in the communication transaction.[5] Such active and complete participation encompasses the following:

- active mindfulness
- selective attention
- sensorial involvement
- comprehension
- retention

Active Mindfulness

Active mindfulness involves the degree to which speakers and audiences are consciously aware of the transactions between them. For example, the fact that someone responds to your message with a look of puzzlement doesn't automatically mean the person is hard of hearing. Yet, many people automatically speak louder when their message is greeted with such a look, rather than considering the alternatives. Before raising their voice, such people should at least consider the possibility that they were unclear or that the other person speaks another language. This kind of consideration, though, demands complex instead of simplistic thinking.

Active mindfulness also requires open-mindedness to ideas contrary or unfamiliar to the way we customarily think. This doesn't mean that you have to accept such ideas uncritically. Instead, it means that you do not automatically reject these ideas.

Selective Attention

As our discussion of mindfulness suggests, we are most likely to seek out and pay attention to speakers and messages that we perceive to be reinforcing. A person whose speech reflects our viewpoint, therefore, is more likely to get our undivided attention than one whose speech presents a diametrically opposed viewpoint. Similarly, professors whose lectures involve your major are more likely to "have your ear" than those who lecture on topics you perceive to be less important to your future.

Understanding **selective attention** is important to your development as an audience-focused speaker and as an attentive and responsive audience member. You cannot learn to effectively communicate to your audience, for example, unless you first selectively choose to pay attention to the thoughts and concerns of the people in it. You can't be a responsive audience member unless you make the conscious choice to pay attention to what a speaker shares.

Listening to others speak, moreover, is one of the best ways to improve your own speaking ability. For instance, listening for such things as the developmental pattern a speaker follows, changes in pitch and rate, and the sources a speaker cites can assist you tremendously in preparing and delivering your own speeches. In a sense, listening facilitates the "modeling" of effective speakers and their speeches. However, you first must decide to consciously pay attention—selectively attend—to these models of effective public speaking.

Sensorial Involvement

Once you've chosen to pay close attention to the speech transaction, you then need to practice **sensorial involvement,** that is, to involve all of your senses in the transaction. As noted in Chapter 1, every message has two dimensions: a content and a relationship dimension. Reading the text of a speech is not the same as physically participating in the transaction. Reading just text limits us to the *content* of the message and its compositional elements. While *what* a speaker says is important, *how* a speaker says it is equally important. Gestures, movements, facial expressions, and eye contact serve to visually punctuate the content of a speech and suggest nuances of meaning, including what a speaker is saying "between the lines." The reaction of people to a speaker's message and the physical setting in which it's shared also affect the meaning of the message.

To truly appreciate the speech transaction, therefore, you need to involve as many of your senses as you can. Not only must you try to hear what is being said, but you also must try to see and feel what is being said. Only then will you be in a position to measure the totality of the message that has been communicated.

Comprehension

Comprehension is the act of understanding what has been communicated. Careful listeners make sure that they truly understand what a speaker means and do not hesitate to ask for clarification if the speaker's message is unclear. It is also important to make sure that understanding includes not just the explicit content of a message, but the relational component as well. And speakers need to make sure that their choice of words is appropriate for their audience. Speaking in technical language to a nontechnical audience, for example, is a sure way to guarantee noncomprehension of your message.

Retention

Retention is the act of storing what has been communicated in either short- or long-term memory. Often what is viewed as a failure to remember is actually a failure to comprehend or attend to the original message. But assuming a listener fully attends to and comprehends a speaker's message, there is still the important issue of retaining that message. The use of careful note-taking can help a listener to retain messages that would otherwise be forgotten. And a good speaker will repeat and reinforce the key concepts of a message to help the audience remember it.

MISCONCEPTIONS ABOUT LISTENING

There are a number of common misconceptions about effective listening. These include but are not limited to the idea that listening (1) is easy, (2) is correlated with intelligence, (3) does not need to be planned, and (4) is related to skill in reading.[6]

"It's Easy to Listen"

Some people think that listening is like breathing, that we are born competent listeners. Of course, that is just as fallacious as assuming that because we breathe, we all breathe well enough to become professional singers. Just because someone can carry a tune and sing in the shower doesn't mean the person is ready for the New York Metropolitan Opera. Similarly, just because we've heard others talk to us all of our lives does not mean we are effective listeners. Quite the contrary, our complacency about listening is one of the very things that makes us susceptible to poor listening habits. As illustrated in the box "Misheard Lyrics," our poor listening habits even carry over to the messages communicated by popular musicians.

"I'm Smart, So I'm a Good Listener"

Even highly intelligent people can fail to listen. For example, submarine crew members are among the most intelligent, tested, and trained members of the Navy. But failure to listen caused the submarine U.S.S. *Stickleback* to collide with a destroyer escort and sink off Hawaii in May 1958. Although no personnel were lost, tragedy was narrowly avoided. And it all happened because an electrician's mate thought he heard the order "Come on" when the actual order was "Come off." Instead of turning his rheostat *down*, as he was ordered, therefore, he turned it *up*, tripping the circuit breakers, cutting off power, and causing the sub to lose control, plunging it directly into the path of the destroyer escort.[7]

Despite what we may think, intelligence far from guarantees effective listening. Although some highly intelligent people have been trained to use effective listening skills, equal numbers have not. As the U.S.S. *Stickleback* incident illustrates so well, some people may fail to listen carefully in spite of their intelligence.

Misheard Lyrics

This list of "misheard" lyrics is reprinted with permission of Simon and Schuster from *'Scuse Me While I Kiss This Guy and Other Misheard Lyrics* by Gavin Edwards, copyright © 1995 by Gavin Edwards, in which Edwards reveals what people thought they heard in popular song lyrics. The title, by the way, comes from a mishearing of a Jimi Hendrix lyric, " 'Scuse me while I kiss the sky."

Misheard lyric:
"The girl with colitis goes by."

Correct lyric:
"The girl with kaleidoscope eyes."
—The Beatles

Misheard lyric:
"And doughnuts make my brown eyes blue."

Correct lyric:
"And don't it make my brown eyes blue."
—Crystal Gayle

Misheard lyric:
"They sent you a tie clasp."

Correct lyric:
"They said you was high class."
—Elvis Presley

Misheard lyric:
"I'll never leave your pizza burnin'."

Correct lyric:
"I'll never be your beast of burden."
—The Rolling Stones

Misheard lyric:
"Mice aroma."

Correct lyric:
"My Sharona."
—The Knack

Misheard lyric:
"Baking carrot biscuits."

Correct lyric:
"Takin' care of business."
—Bachman-Turner Overdrive

"There's No Need to Plan Ahead"

A third common misconception is that listening just happens—that there's no need to plan for it. Of course, sometimes you will end up listening to an unexpected conversation. But if you know in advance that you will be in a listening situation such as the one you face in your speech class, you should plan ahead. For example, in most introductory speech courses, students provide each other with both oral and written feedback. Who do you think will do a better job: the student who prepares in advance, including a review of criteria for the speech, checklists for speech evaluation, and a clear understanding of the speech assignment, or the one who shows up to class only to be surprised by the fact that he or she will be responsible for providing classmates with feedback about their speeches? Finally, when the tables are turned, whose speeches do you think most likely will benefit from critical evaluation by classmates?

"I Can Read, So I Can Listen"

Although one might assume that reading and listening skills are correlated, that is not the case. In fact, the skills required are quite different. The reader controls the pace of communication, whereas a listener is at the mercy of the person

In a bar, listening is extremely difficult because of physical conditions.

speaking. A reader can reread a confusing passage, whereas a listener may have only one chance to get the point. Reading is typically a solitary activity; listening most often takes place in groups where it might be hard to hear the speaker or there might be distractions. Listening skills, as you can begin to see, require development in their own right.

OBSTACLES TO LISTENING

Several factors can intervene to prevent effective listening. Six of the most important obstacles to listening are physical conditions, cultural differences, personal problems, bias, connotative meanings, and anxiety.[8] Most of these obstacles are directly influenced by our perceptions. Thus the discussion of perception and communication in Chapter 1 directly relates to problems in listening.

Physical Conditions

The physical environment clearly affects our ability to listen. Among the factors that can inhibit listening are noise, an unpleasant room temperature, poor lighting, physical obstacles, and uncomfortable chairs. A noisy, hot, poorly lit

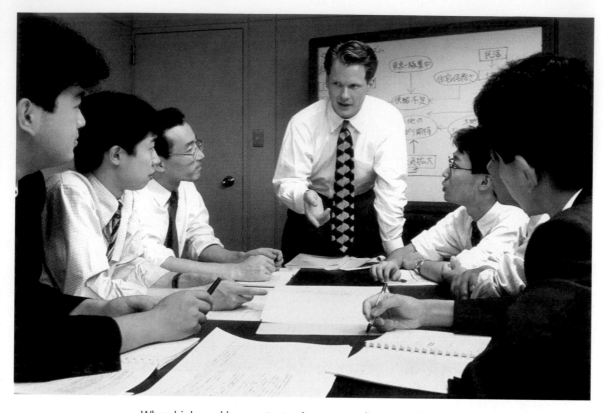

When high- and low-context cultures meet, listening often becomes more difficult.

room, with a post blocking your view and hard chairs, is hardly an ideal listening environment. On the other hand, a quiet, well-lit room with a clear line of sight, comfortable (but not too comfortable) chairs, and a pleasant temperature allows you to concentrate on the speaker. Although there is usually not much the listener can do about the physical environment, being aware of its impact on listening helps you know how much you need to focus. In addition, you can often choose your location to listen. Students who sit in the back of the classroom, where their view is limited, often are tempted to let their attention drift. Those who move front and center clearly are interested in listening to what is said.

The best speakers try to minimize the effects of a troublesome physical environment on audience listening. If the acoustics are bad, they may raise or amplify their voice so that it is more audible. If their line of sight is blocked from some audience members, they may move toward audience members in the back of a room. If some loud activity is occurring within earshot of the audience, they may make light of the situation rather than show that the noise bothers them. No matter what a speaker does to overcome a problem environment, however, audience members also bear some responsibility in this regard.

Cultural Differences

Communication patterns vary from culture to culture. **Culture** is a learned system of language, beliefs, customs, and values with which specific people identify. The relative importance of the context in which listening takes place differs from one culture to another. Anthropologists Edward T. Hall and Mildred Reed Hall define **context** as the information that surrounds an event and contributes to the meaning of that event.[9] For example, suppose you receive a message on your answering machine from a relative you almost never hear from except in an emergency. The message simply says, "Call me right away." Needless to say, you would be alarmed, because you know this person never calls you unless there is a serious problem. On the other hand, if you received the same message from a friend with whom you often get together, you might assume he or she just wants to set up a meeting. The same message has a very different meaning because of the context in which it occurs.

As our opening story illustrated, some cultures rely more than others on unspoken information contained in the context to determine the meaning of a message. In high-context (HC) cultures, such as Japan, the Arab states, and the Mediterranean countries, the context of statements can be extremely important. Much of the meaning in such cultures is carried not only by the words that are spoken but also by the situation in which they are uttered. On the other hand, in low-context (LC) cultures, such as the United States, Germany, and most northern European countries, people rely less on the overall communication situation and more on the words spoken to convey meaning.

When low- and high-context people communicate with each other, the results can be frustrating. Hall and Hall note that HC people are apt to become impatient and irritated when LC people insist on giving them information they don't need. Conversely, low-context people are at a loss when high-context people do not provide *enough* information. Too much information frequently leads people to feel they are being talked down to; too little information can mystify them or make them feel left out.[10]

Although we cannot give you any simple rule of thumb for dealing with cultural differences in listening, our best advice is to be aware of the culture of the person(s) to whom you are listening or with whom you are speaking. Then, take differences from your own culture into account and try to adjust your behavior accordingly. Finally, if you expect to be listening or speaking to someone from a different culture, which is increasingly likely on a college campus, learn as much as you can in advance about the person's culture.

Personal Problems

Most people have had the experience of being so preoccupied with a personal problem they couldn't pay attention to what someone was saying. Personal problems can easily detract us from listening to what is being said. The best advice for overcoming this obstacle is to recognize the situation and to focus on what is being said, as difficult as that may be. For example, if you were plagued by a

Listening in High- and Low-Context Cultures

As discussed in this chapter, some cultures place greater emphasis on the context in which communication occurs than on what is actually said. In such high-context cultures, as they are called, people realize that what one hears while listening must be deciphered only after thoroughly considering the context in which it is heard. Yes may mean no and vice versa, for example, depending on where and under what circumstances they are uttered. The opposite is true in low-context cultures, where the greatest emphasis is given to the spoken word. People trust what they think they hear without giving undue attention to the context in which it is heard.

What kinds of problems do you see occurring when people from high- and low-context cultures listen to each other's speeches? Which of the listening skills discussed in this chapter do you think would most help in overcoming these problems. Be specific!

Source: Edward T. Hall and Mildred R. Hall, *Hidden Differences: Doing Business With the Japanese* (Garden City, N.Y.: Anchor/Doubleday, 1987).

personal problem prior to an important job interview, chances are you would tell yourself to "get your act together." You need to do exactly the same thing before listening to (or giving) a speech.

Bias

As you might suspect, bias gets in the way of active mindfulness. All people are biased, though not to an equal degree. Bias reflects an opinion formed without evidence, usually about a person or group of people. Racial, religious, sexual, and other such biases, although forbidden by law, often exist in the reality of people's opinions. Recognizing bias is an important step to overcoming it.

Bias isn't always based exclusively on false generalizations about groups of people. Prior, but incomplete, knowledge can cause us to form hasty judgments. Consider the case of the bombing of the federal building in Oklahoma City in 1995. Such terrorist acts previously were associated with Arab or Muslim terrorist groups almost exclusively. Despite only partial information, many people chose to jump to unsupported conclusions about who was responsible for the bombing, even calling for military retaliation against Islamic countries like Iran. They quickly quieted down when a young American with no ties to Islam was arrested for the crime.

Regardless of its source, bias is a serious impediment to listening. To overcome bias, listeners need to first recognize its existence, mentally set it aside, and recognize its irrationality. Although this may seem easier said than done, the ability to put bias in its rightful place is one of the keys to critical thinking and decision making.

Connotative Meanings

Important to this discussion are the related concepts of denotation and connotation. **Denotation** involves the objective, conventional meanings you find

TABLE 4.1   Goals of Listening

TYPE	GOAL	EXAMPLE
Listening to understand	To recognize meaning based on auditory and visual cues and to comprehend meaning	Listening to a lecture on Einstein's theory of relativity
Appreciative listening	To experience stimulation and enjoyment	Listening to a speech to entertain
Critical listening	To arrive at an informed judgment	Listening to candidates to determine how to vote

in a dictionary for a word. **Connotation** involves meanings you won't always find in a dictionary for a word, or the ideas, images, and emotions people associate with a word. Although denotative meanings can be learned by reading a dictionary, connotations, which are largely determined by cultural usage, are learned over time from seeing and listening to examples. As an illustration of connotation, consider some of the various words used to describe a person who weighs more than average. The word *chubby* is appropriate when describing a baby or toddler, but would prove hurtful when used to describe a teenager. The word *stocky* doesn't mean the same when used to describe a man as when it is used to describe a woman. And, although it would be okay for a physician to write on a chart that a patient was overweight, it wouldn't be appropriate to write "tubby."

Anxiety

As discussed in Chapter 3, anxiety significantly detracts from our ability to process the information to which we are exposed. Anxious speakers often are unable to focus on audience feedback as they speak or actively listen to an instructor's feedback when they finish speaking. Likewise, anxious audience members have difficulty listening actively. To evaluate yourself in this area, see the box "What Is Your Level of Receiver Apprehension?"

GOALS OF LISTENING

The purpose or goal of a listener shapes the context in which listening occurs. It is one thing to listen to a stand-up comic and another to sit through a lecture on the theory of relativity. Just as speakers can have different general purposes, such as speaking to entertain, inform, or persuade, listeners can approach the public speaking transaction with different goals. The three listening goals most relevant to our purposes are (1) listening to understand, (2) listening to appreciate, and (3) critical listening (Table 4.1).

What Is Your Level of Receiver Apprehension?

The following statements apply to how various people feel about receiving communication. Although this measure was developed specifically for persons without hearing disabilities, people who are hard of hearing may think about analogous situations in which they become anxious while receiving messages through nonaural means, such as sign language, closed captions, reading lips, or via a TDD. Indicate if these statements apply to how you feel by noting whether you (5) strongly agree, (4) agree, (3) are undecided, (2) disagree, or (1) strongly disagree.

_____ 1. I feel comfortable when listening to others on the phone.

_____ 2. It is often difficult for me to concentrate on what others are saying.

_____ 3. When listening to members of the opposite sex, I find it easy to concentrate on what is being said.

_____ 4. I have no fear of being a listener as a member of an audience.

_____ 5. I feel relaxed when listening to new ideas.

_____ 6. I would rather not have to listen to other people at all.

_____ 7. I am generally overexcited and rattled when others are speaking to me.

_____ 8. I often feel uncomfortable when listening to others.

_____ 9. My thoughts become confused and jumbled when reading important information.

_____ 10. I often have difficulty concentrating on what others are saying.

_____ 11. Receiving new information makes me feel restless.

_____ 12. Watching television makes me nervous.

Listening to Understand

Understanding, in the truest sense of the word, is a multistep process. Further, there are different levels of understanding, depending on the goal of the listener. The first step in the process of understanding is to discriminate between differing auditory and/or visual stimuli.[11] As infants we first recognize parental voices, then sounds, words, and eventually the complex structures of language. Visual stimuli, such as facial expression, gesture, and movement, become part of meaning for us, as does touch. The careful listener is sensitive to both the verbal and the nonverbal nuances of messages. This is especially true for public speaking. Listeners in the audience need to look beyond just the words of a speaker's message. By the same token, speakers need to listen to the entire message received from the audience. This means they should listen not only for aural feedback but for feedback from other sources as well. These sources include the expressions on audience members' faces, their body orientation, and head movements such as nodding in agreement.

_____ 13. When on a date, I find myself tense and self-conscious when listening to my date.

_____ 14. I enjoy being a good listener.

_____ 15. I generally find it easy to concentrate on what is being said.

_____ 16. I seek out the opportunity to listen to new ideas.

_____ 17. I have difficulty concentrating on instructions others give to me.

_____ 18. It is hard to listen or concentrate on what other people are saying unless I know them well.

_____ 19. I feel tense when listening as a member of a social gathering.

_____ 20. Television programs that attempt to change my mind about something make me nervous.

To determine your score, first total the scores you gave yourself for statements 2, 6–13, and 17–20, and *add* 42 to that total (maximum 107, minimum 55). From this result, *subtract* the total of the scores you gave yourself for statements 1, 3–5, and 14–16. Your score should be in the range of 20 to 100. The higher your score, the more apprehensive you are about listening. Scores above 80 indicate a relatively high level of receiver apprehension. A mid-range score would be about 60. Scores below 40 indicate a relatively low level of receiver apprehension.

Based on your score, what sorts of listening behaviors do you think you could improve? For example, do your answers suggest a need to work harder at concentration? Should you seek greater opportunities to practice listening skills and learn new information? Could the same type of relaxation exercises suggested in Chapter 3 be useful in listening situations, as well as when you are a public speaker?

Source: Copyright by the Speech Communication Association, 1975, from Lawrence R. Wheeless, "An Investigation of Receiver Apprehension and Social Context Dimensions of Communication Apprehension," *The Speech Teacher* 24 (1975): 261–268, by permission.

Once you have discriminated among various sounds and sights, the next step to understanding is making sense of the aural and visual stimuli received.[12] Successful listening to understand demands that the meaning you assign to a message closely approximates that of the source of the message. How well you understand depends on several factors. Chief among them are vocabulary, concentration, and memory.[13]

Vocabulary Obviously, you cannot comprehend something for which you don't have meaning. Thus a limited vocabulary has the undesirable effect of limiting your ability to understand messages. In fact, failure to master the necessary vocabulary can lead to disaster. For example, both of the authors of this text were high school debaters. One of us recalls a particularly embarrassing incident that resulted from not knowing the meaning of the word *superfluous*. Unaware that the other team's plan to remove all "superfluous United States tariffs" meant that they would remove only the unnecessary ones, the author's team produced several examples of

FIGURE 4.2
Wide-Band Versus Pinpoint
Concentration. If you were
listening to a symphony
orchestra, you would use
wide-band concentration to
focus on the total sound of
the orchestra. Pinpoint
concentration would involve
focusing on a single section
of the orchestra.

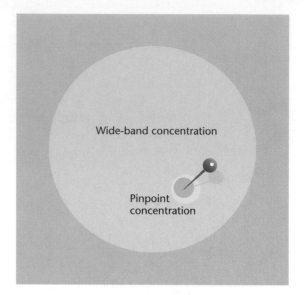

tariffs that were essential to American industries. During cross-examination, an opposing team member asked the author, "Do you know what *superfluous* means?" Of course, the author did not know. When the opposition pointed out that every tariff the author's team had cited was, by definition, *not* superfluous, and that only superfluous tariffs would be removed, the debate was, for all practical purposes, lost. Needless to say, a dictionary became standard material for all future debates.

Concentration   A second important factor for listening to understand is concentration. As we know all too well, our minds are easily distracted from the task at hand. If you doubt that, think back to the last time you immediately forgot the name of someone to whom you had just been introduced.

There are two types of concentration: wide-band and pinpoint (Figure 4.2). Whereas pinpoint concentration is most relevant to critical listening, wide-band concentration is most central to listening to understand. **Pinpoint concentration** focuses on specific details. **Wide-band concentration** focuses on patterns rather than details. As a result, wide-band concentration assists you in listening for the tone of the speech, or its larger meaning in a particular context.

Both types of concentration, however, demand that you try to block out stimuli that compete with the message on which you are trying to focus. These competing stimuli range from the obvious, such as a heavy-metal band playing in the free-speech area outside your classroom, to the subtle, for example, the gastrointestinal growls your stomach makes when you are hungry.

Memory   Closely related to concentration is the third factor that influences listening to understand: memory. Often failure to remember reflects the fact that you also failed to concentrate. Consider the example of forgetting the name of someone to whom you have just been introduced. Although this very common experience simply may be the result of "mental laziness," most often it is the product of the anxiety accompanying the situation. Both anxiety and preoccupation with feelings of anxiety have a devastating effect on our powers of concentration and memory. As you are being introduced to someone, you may be too busy thinking about how you are being perceived to concentrate on the person's name. It isn't that you forgot the name—it's that you didn't listen for and process the name in the first place.

Much of your day is spent in situations that require comprehensive listening. And nowhere is this more likely to be true than in your speech class. Here are some skills that will help you improve your listening to understand.[14]

Improving Listening to Understand

- *Utilize the time difference between speech and thought effectively.* Most people speak at a rate of about 125 to 150 words per minute, but the human brain can process 400 to 500 spoken words per minute, although that is possible only with a special process known as "compressed speech." By using the time differential to think about what you are hearing, you can better interpret and understand the significance of what is said.

- *Listen for main ideas.* Don't get bogged down in insignificant detail. Rather, focus on understanding the main ideas and principles a speaker is discussing.

- *Listen for significant details.* Though not as important as main ideas, some details are fairly significant. Try to determine which details are illustrative of the main ideas and have significance in understanding what is being said.

- *Learn to draw valid inferences.* What does it all mean? Try to determine what conclusions you can draw from the speech.

Listening to Appreciate

Appreciative listening involves obtaining sensory stimulation or enjoyment from others.[15] This could include listening to music, drama, poetry, or a speech to entertain. Though it might appear that such listening "just comes naturally," the fact is that you can enhance your pleasure by expanding your listening experiences, improving your understanding of what you are listening to, and developing your powers of concentration. Music appreciation classes, for example, help students learn what to listen for in different kinds of music.

This is also true of your speech class. Learning about the various types, styles, and structures of speeches should help you appreciate what a rarity a good speech is. Learning how important it is to construct and share a good speech, moreover, should reinforce your appreciation and give you a more finely tuned ear. Here are some skills that will help you improve your appreciative listening.[16]

Improving Appreciative Listening

- *Use opportunities to gain experience with appreciative listening.* Listening appreciatively, as with all forms of listening, requires experience with different situations.

- *Be willing to listen appreciatively to a variety of writers, speakers, composers, and so on.* Even if you've developed preconceptions about a particular composer or type of music, for example, be willing to listen with an open mind. You may not appreciate Beethoven, and someone else may not appreciate The Wallflowers. Chances are that with a proper frame of mind you can learn what it is that makes them both appealing to large numbers of people.

- *Develop the ability to concentrate while listening appreciatively.* Many forms of appreciative listening depend on not letting your mind wander. Of course, the greater your experience with a variety of situations that involve listening, the more ability you will have to concentrate on the important aspects of the experience.

Critical Listening

Critical listening, which is an extension and refinement of the two types of listening just discussed, often requires skills similar to those required by listening to understand as well as to appreciate. There is a crucial difference, however: **Critical listening** is listening for the purpose of making reasoned judgments about speakers and the credibility of their messages.

Much of the daily information we receive is targeted at influencing us, as well as making us compliant to the wishes of others. If information directed at influencing us or making us comply was always in our own self-interest, this wouldn't be a problem. Of course, this is anything but the case. Cigarette advertising, for example, is notorious for encouraging people to pursue a habit that can cost them their health or even their life. Beer companies, moreover, glamorize drinking to excess, even though alcohol is the single most abused substance in the United States.

Thus learning to listen critically is a form of self-protection. It guards us against being taken advantage of by unscrupulous salespeople, politicians, and plain old con artists. But learning to listen critically also enhances our ability to communicate while delivering a speech.

At a minimum, critical listening involves focusing on both the speaker and the message in the attempt to verify the validity of what is being said. Is the speaker competent and trustworthy? If you think so, what evidence have you been given that makes this the case? Is the message directed at getting you to change, stay the same, or buy something? Is it merely informative, or is it argumentative? In either case, how do you know the information is representative of the facts? Is it logical? Is it supported with evidence, and are the sources clearly cited?

Here are some skills that will help you improve your critical listening.[17]

Improving Critical Listening

- *Consider the credibility of the source.* How much confidence do you have in the goodwill, trustworthiness, and competence of the person to whom you are listening?

- *Recognize that the credibility of the source can influence you.* Although credibility is important and can be influential in and of itself, do not let another person's judgment automatically replace your own thinking. Even the most credible sources can be wrong.

- *Evaluate the validity of arguments.* Are the arguments presented reasonable? Don't be afraid to question the logic of a speaker if it seems fallacious.

- *Evaluate the evidence presented in support of arguments.* Is the evidence presented believable, from reliable sources, and documented for you?

- *Recognize fallacies of reasoning.* In Chapter 14 we discuss a number of ways arguments that appear to be valid can be deceptive or fallacious.

- *Identify emotional appeals.* Determine the type of emotions the speaker appeals to. Are these appeals ones with which you are proud to identify? Whereas appealing to legitimate human emotions is a necessary aspect of persuasion (as we see in Chapter 13), misguided appeals can be destructive. Use of appeals to hate, irrational fears, and prejudice should be rejected.

The critical perspective you bring to bear when listening to speakers and their messages is just as relevant to you and the message you ultimately share with others. Thus, learning to listen critically to others will help you become more objectively critical of yourself. This will assist you in both the preparation and the delivery of your own speeches because it will force you to apply a similar set of critical questions to yourself.

TECHNIQUES TO IMPROVE YOUR LISTENING SKILLS

Actually, listening begins within our own minds. We all carry on an internal dialogue. Sometimes this is limited to our own thoughts, whereas at other times, it is in response to what someone else has said. For example, imagine you are about to ask a friend for money. You might hear yourself saying silently, "Oh no, he'll never loan me the money. All I will do is tick him off." On the other hand, you might think, "I've helped her out before. She knows I'm good for it. What have I got to lose?"

Sometimes we listen to our thoughts in response to another's words, although we don't verbalize them. For example, suppose you listen to someone speaking about a controversial topic. If you agree with the speaker, you may find yourself thinking, "Yeah . . . yes!" On the other hand, if you disagree with the speaker, you may mentally hear yourself saying things like, "You've got to be kidding." Listening to your own thoughts affects how you listen to others and can

Advertisers (such as the tobacco and alcoholic beverage industries) would go broke if people listened critically to their messages.

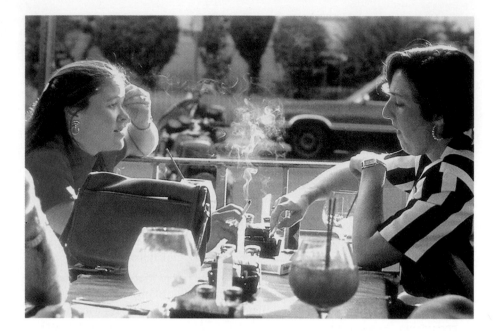

interfere with your processing of the message you are receiving. For example, if you think you already know what a speaker is going to say, you might say to yourself, "Heard that before" and tune out, missing an important message you did not anticipate. Or thinking about what you are going to say to another person can cause you to miss what he or she is saying to you.

To begin with, no one can make you listen. The decision to actively attend to speakers and their messages is yours and yours alone. The same is true for speakers listening to their audiences. All the techniques in the world, therefore, won't help you become a better listener unless you consciously choose to attend to a specific speaking transaction.

The techniques that follow are best viewed as a collection or system of techniques that are interdependent. Your skill in using one of these techniques, consequently, will have a direct bearing on your skill in using them all. The techniques we discuss are setting goals, blocking out distracting stimuli, suspending judgment, focusing on main points, recognizing highlights and signposts, taking effective notes, being sensitive to metacommunication, paraphrasing, and questioning.

Setting Goals

The first technique is straightforward: Establish a goal you hope to achieve as a consequence of listening. This goes back to the goals of listening described earlier. The goal of appreciative listening is not the same as the goal of critical listening.

Your goal guides your behavior as you listen. When listening critically, for example, much of your attention will be focused on distinguishing what part of a speaker's message is fact from what part of it is opinion. In contrast, when you are listening appreciatively, your attention will be more general, focused on the gist of the message's meaning, not on each and every fact offered by a speaker or interviewee. The listening goal established tends to dictate the listening behaviors in which people engage. Thus, when people fail to establish a goal at the outset of the listening process, they run the risk of focusing on what is peripheral rather than central to their needs.

Blocking Out Distracting Stimuli

The second technique is even more straightforward: To listen actively, you must clear your mind of distracting stimuli. Trying to force yourself to rid your mind of distracting thoughts, however, is not the answer. Relaxation may be.

Research suggests that a relaxed mind is a receptive mind. Moreover, we know that there is a mind-body relationship in this regard. When the body feels relaxed, so does the mind. As a result, anything you do to promote self-relaxation prior to listening should help you diminish the potential impact of distracting stimuli. In Chapter 3 we provided a number of ways to help you relax before speaking. The same techniques can also help you relax so that you can become a more receptive listener.

Suspending Judgment

As the Oklahoma City bombing example illustrated, people can be excessively judgmental, even when they have been provided with little concrete evidence on which to base their judgments. People cannot listen when they prematurely judge others and their messages. They may hear what they want to hear, but they cannot listen. Critical listening especially demands an open mind.

In the attempt to suspend judgment when you are listening to a speaker, you can do three things. First, recognize and accept the fact that you—and everyone else—bring subjective experience and bias to the speech transaction. This subjective experience colors and filters your perceptions of the speaker and the message. Second, try not to judge a book by its cover. Stereotypes on the basis of physical appearance are notoriously unreliable. Finally, try to process the message rather than immediately reacting to the speaker and the message.

Focusing on Main Points

You may also find it helpful to prioritize what you listen for in a communication transaction. The content of all messages varies in importance. Some ideas expressed are central, whereas others are more peripheral. As mentioned earlier, listening to the main ideas in a message is most important.

Some students make the mistake of trying to write down verbatim everything a professor says in class. They risk missing the main points of the lecture. For example, one of the authors had a classmate in college who tape-recorded and then transcribed every class lecture. Despite an extraordinary effort on her part, she rarely earned better than a C. Why? Because she focused so much on trying to record and memorize every word her professors said, she never learned to separate the important points from the insignificant ones.

Recognizing Highlights and Signposts

Two things you can look for in the attempt to make sure you are listening for main ideas are highlights and signposts. Highlights and signposts also are something you'll want to include in your own speeches to assist the listeners in your audience. The best speakers go out of their way to highlight what is most important in their message. They might say:

> "Of the three ideas I've shared, this one is far and away the most important."

> "In my mind, the most precious freedom we enjoy is the freedom of speech."

> "How can anyone ignore the magnitude of environmental problems caused by automobiles?"

Signposts are transitional statements that tell people when one main idea is ending and another is beginning. Examples of such signposts might be:

> "Having established the importance of a speaker's credibility, let's now look at . . ."

> "This key to understanding the poetry of Edgar Allan Poe leads me to my second point about the interpretation of *The Raven*."

> "Equally important to this idea is the notion that an open society demands a free press."

Taking Effective Notes

Much as professors might like to think otherwise, not every word they utter in their lectures deserves to be recorded. Yet they routinely have to ask students to quit writing, sit back in their seats, and listen to an idea before writing it down. Effective note-taking is a science. Like any other science, it demands an appropriate methodology. Ralph G. Nichols and Thomas R. Lewis, two of the earliest researchers on the process of listening, describe four basic note-taking methods for listening to speeches and lectures.[18] They point out that no one method will work with every situation. The four methods are outlining, annotating of a book or manuscript, précis writing, and recording fact versus principle.

Outlining   We will discuss outlining from the point of view of the speaker at greater length in Chapter 8, so we won't go over the details of the process here. The listener using outlining basically tries to capture the main points of the speech as they are presented, as well as the subordinate or supporting ideas under each point. A well-done outline is a good guide to what has been said. But outlining requires considerable effort on the part of the listener and can distract attention from what is being said. It also depends on the speaker using clear sign-posts and a consistent organizational pattern. Trying to outline a disorganized speech is the height of frustration.

Annotation   This technique works well only when a speaker or lecturer is going over material you have already read. For example, if a literature professor is discussing a short story you have been assigned to read, you would write marginal comments called annotations at each place in the book the professor discusses. Although the technique does not require great effort on the part of the listener, it can be messy and there is no way to organize your notes for later review.

Précis Writing   With this technique, you listen for a few minutes, get the gist of what the speaker is saying, and then write a brief paragraph to yourself summarizing what has been said. This technique involves alternating between intense listening for 3- or 4-minute intervals and brief periods of note-taking. While listening to the speaker, you should be focusing on what is being said and how to summarize it for your notes. Though the notes produced are brief, clear, and easy to review, the downside is that you must divert your attention from the speaker to write your précis.

Recording Fact Versus Principle   First, you divide your page vertically down the middle. On the left write "facts"; on the right, "principles." As you listen to the speaker, list each important fact presented on the left, numbering them 1, 2, 3, and so on. On the right, list only broad general principles, using roman numerals (I, II, III, etc.) to distinguish them from facts. Under each principle, list the numbers of the facts that correspond to the principles. This method of note-taking is illustrated in Figure 4.3. The system avoids excessive writing and requires the listener to think about what the speaker has said. In addition, you can leave space at the bottom for ideas and questions that occur to you as you listen. Although this is a very useful technique, it works better for the social sciences and humanities than for the natural sciences.

Whatever note-taking system you employ, the important thing is to focus attention on the speaker's ideas and try to think about what is being said, not simply try to produce a transcript. Writing down too much can cause you to miss the most important ideas and get bogged down in minute details.

Being Sensitive to Metacommunication

Another important technique involves listening for metacommunication. **Metacommunication** is the message about the message. It is generally conveyed nonverbally. You can listen for metacommunication in a speaker's eyes, voice, gestures, movements, posture, and use of time. You can also listen for metacommunication in other people's reaction to your message.

Chief among the reasons for listening carefully to metacommunication is cross cue–checking. **Cross cue–checking** involves gauging what a person says

FACTS	PRINCIPLES
1. 1455, Gutenberg invented moveable-type printing	I. Technological developments in communication have accelerated at an ever more rapid pace.
2. 1920s, first radio broadcasts	(1, 2, 3, 4, 5, 6)
3. 1952, 9% of households had TV	
4. 1960, 85% of households had TV	
5. 1980s, 1.1% of households had VCRs	
6. 1995, 67% had VCRs	II. TV & radio are becoming more important to average Americans than print.
7. Average American watches TV 7 hours a day	(7, 8, 9)
8. 96% of population listens to radio	
9. Newspaper subscriptions per household are about half of what they were in 1960	IDEAS & QUESTIONS
	Has the increase in VCRs cut into broadcast TV?

FIGURE 4.3 Recording Fact Versus Principle While Listening

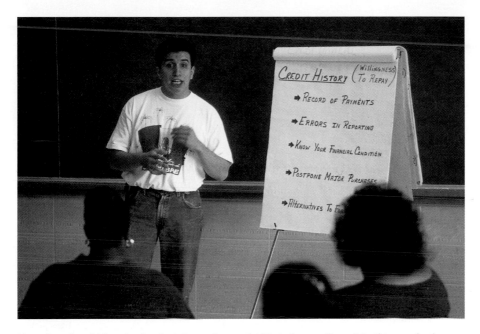

Listening should involve both sight and sound. What do you "hear" in this speaker's metacommunication?

verbally against the nonverbal behaviors that make up metacommunication. Cross cue–checking enables people to ferret out the subtleties in a speaker's message—for example, irony, sarcasm, and sometimes deception. Metacommunication is a potentially rich source of meaning. Because shared meaning is the bottom-line goal of listening, it would make no sense to ignore this source.

A word of caution is in order. At the outset of this discussion, we stated that techniques for listening are interdependent. This is especially true of the last technique. Never infer the meaning of a speaker's or an audience member's message on the basis of metacommunication alone. It is not a substitute for the spoken word. It also can be tremendously misleading when isolated from its spoken counterpart.

Paraphrasing

One of the techniques you may use when researching your speeches is the interview. Successful interviewing depends on active listening. A key element of active listening is seeking confirmation from people that you have understood their message. The techniques of paraphrasing and questioning (discussed next) are valuable tools for ensuring accurate communication. Moreover, paraphrasing encourages the interviewee to talk because it reinforces the fact that you are actively engaged with what the interviewee is saying.

To paraphrase a message, you briefly repeat in your own words the essence of what has been said. Paraphrasing should be nonevaluative. Your goal is not to convey your opinion of what was said, but merely to confirm that you understand it. Often you will paraphrase not only the denotative content of the message but the emotional aspects as well. For example: "What I'm hearing you say is . . . ," "Let me make sure I understand what you are saying . . . ," or "You seem to be feeling. . . ."

Questioning

Similar to paraphrasing, questioning is another way of determining if you correctly understand the message. But rather than simply repeating back what you think you have heard, you ask the other person for information as well as confirmation. Avoid hostile and loaded questions. A *hostile question* signals your strong disagreement with the other person: for example, "How can you possibly say such a stupid thing?" *Loaded questions* assume something that is not necessarily the case. The classic loaded question is "Have you stopped beating your wife (or husband)?" Your goal is not to embarrass or trap people, but to give them an opportunity to clarify and elaborate on what they have said.

When listening to a speech, you should not interrupt to ask a question unless the speaker has clearly indicated a willingness to take questions during the presentation. Even then, the common courtesy of raising a hand to indicate you wish to ask a question is recommended. Some public speakers ask people to hold their questions until the end of a speech. When interviewing people, of course, the flow of questions is much freer. But you should still wait until the opportunity arises to ask your question without interrupting the other person mid-sentence. Often, paying close attention to nonverbal behaviors will help you know when it is appropriate to interrupt with a question. A pause, a glance, or a facial expression that indicates finality are all ways of signaling that a person is waiting for a response.

SUMMARY

Listening is but one more skill necessary to becoming a competent speaker and audience member. Hearing and listening are not the same thing. *Listening* is the process of receiving, attending to, and assigning meaning to aural as well as visual and tactile stimuli. *Active listening* involves conscious and responsive participation in the communication transaction. *Active mindfulness* has to do with the degree to which speakers and audiences are consciously aware of the transactions between them. *Selective attention* involves making a conscious choice to focus on some people and some messages, rather than others. *Sensorial involvement* means listening with all the senses, not simply the sense of hearing. *Comprehension* is the act of understanding what was said. *Retention* is the act of storing what was said in either short- or long-term memory. Listening begins in your mind with an internal dialogue.

There are quite a few misconceptions about listening. Many people think listening is easy, whereas it requires effort. Intelligence is no sure guarantee of effective listening. Those who believe there is no need to plan ahead are misguided. And though it might seem that reading skills correlate with listening skills, such is not the case.

Obstacles to effective listening include physical conditions, cultural differences, personal problems, bias, connotative meanings, and anxiety.

There is more than one goal of listening. Much listening is targeted at understanding. *Appreciative listening* involves obtaining sensory stimulation or enjoyment through the words and experiences of others. *Critical listening* has the purpose of making reasoned judgments about speakers and the credibility of their messages.

Once you have made the conscious choice to actively listen, there are several techniques you can use to increase your overall listening skill. These include setting goals, blocking out distracting stimuli, suspending judgment, focusing on main points, recognizing highlights and signposts, taking effective notes, being sensitive to *metacommunication*, paraphrasing, and questioning.

Remembering that we will spend far more of our communication lifetime as listeners than as speakers, it is important that we work on mastering listening skills. Communication is a two-way street, and the person who ignores the importance of listening is in danger of a head-on collision.

Check Your Understanding: Exercises and Activities

1. In a short paper or speech, describe an incident where your message was misunderstood or where you misunderstood another person's intended message. Were there any tip-offs that the speech transaction was not effective? How could the misunderstanding have been avoided?

2. Planning for upcoming listening situations is important. Consider one of your classes in which the instructor regularly lectures. In what ways can you prepare for listening to the next lecture? Are there any specific listening obstacles you need to overcome? After attending the lecture, see if your understanding was enhanced by your preparation for the class.

3. In a short paper, describe a situation you have experienced in which bias affected the listening process. Choose a situation in which you feel your meaning was distorted due to bias or a situation in which you feel your own biases handicapped you in the listening process.

4. Make a list of 10 words that have varying connotations to different people or in different situations. Be prepared to share your list with classmates in small groups or before the full class, depending on your instructor's directions.

5. Describe three times in a given day during which you engaged in critical listening. Be prepared to share your list with classmates in small groups or before the full class.

Notes

1. Dave Barry, *Dave Barry Does Japan* (New York: Random House, 1992), 35–36.

2. Anthony P. Carnevale, Leila J. Gainer, and Ann S. Meltzer, *Workplace Basics: The Skills Employers Want* (Washington, D.C.: American Society for Training and Development and U.S. Department of Labor, 1988), 12.

3. Lyman K. Steil, L. Barker, and Kittie W. Watson, *Effective Listening* (New York: Random House, 1993), 12–13.

4. Andrew D. Wolvin and Carolyn Gwynn Coakley, *Listening*, 3rd ed. (Dubuque, Iowa: W. C. Brown, 1988), 93.

5. Wolvin and Coakley, *Listening*, 115.

6. Melvin L. DeFleur, Patricia Kearney, and Timothy G. Plax, *Fundamentals of Human Communication* (Mountain View, Calif.: Mayfield, 1993), 112–113.

7. Robert Haakenson, *The Art of Listening* (Philadelphia: Smith Kline & French Laboratories, n.d.), 3.

8. DeFleur, Kearney, and Plax, *Fundamentals of Human Communication*, 113–117.

9. Edward T. Hall and Mildred Reed Hall, *Hidden Differences: Doing Business With the Japanese* (Garden City, N.Y.: Anchor Press/Doubleday, 1987), 7.

10. Hall and Hall, *Hidden Differences*, 10–11.

11. Wolvin and Coakley, *Listening*, 140.

12. Wolvin and Coakley, *Listening*, 188.

13. Wolvin and Coakley, *Listening*, 189–206.

14. Wolvin and Coakley, *Listening*, 207–225.

15. Wolvin and Coakley, *Listening*, 320.

16. Wolvin and Coakley, *Listening*, 330–333.

17. Wolvin and Coakley, *Listening*, 287–313.

18. Ralph G. Nichols and Thomas R. Lewis, *Listening and Speaking: A Guide to Effective Oral Communication* (Dubuque, Iowa: W. C. Brown, 1954), 41–53.

Adapting to the Audience

Effective public speakers focus their analysis on the audience they will be addressing.

Audience-Focused Speaking: Mastering the Rhetorical Situation

OBJECTIVES

After reading this chapter, you should be able to:

- Discuss the historical development of the study of the rhetorical situation.
- Define the nature of the rhetorical situation.
- Identify the goals, audience, and constraints you face as a speaker.
- Describe how you can analyze the cultural, demographic, and individual diversity that characterizes today's audiences.
- Explain the relationship between general speech purposes and various rhetorical situational factors.
- Be able to evaluate the effectiveness of your speeches in terms of how they help you achieve your goals.

KEY CONCEPTS

attitude	demographics
audience diversity	incremental goals
belief	long-term goals
canons of rhetoric	rhetorical situation
constraint	short-term goals
cultural diversity	values
demographic diversity	

"I was not planning on speaking here tonight, but this is where my journey has taken me. . . ."

— Carolyn McCarthy, wife and mother of victims of the Long Island Railroad massacre.[1]

December 7, 1993, should have been a day of fond remembrance for Carolyn McCarthy, her husband, Kevin, and her 26-year-old son, Dennis. December 7 marked Carolyn's 50th birthday, a milestone in anyone's life. What should have been a day for celebrating turned to tragedy, however, when Carolyn learned that a crazed gunman aboard a Long Island railroad commuter train had murdered her husband along with five other passengers and had seriously wounded twenty-five others, including her son, who had been partially paralyzed from a gunshot wound to the head.[2]

Devastated, but not defeated, Carolyn McCarthy shortly thereafter dedicated her life to a dual purpose. First, she pledged to help her son Dennis relearn how to walk. Second, she made a commitment to curb the kind of senseless gun violence that had so radically changed the life of her family.

A former intensive care nurse, McCarthy was well suited to the first purpose. Against the odds given by his doctors, she succeeded in helping her son regain the use of his legs and walk again. A lifelong Republican, however, McCarthy was less prepared to meet her second purpose. She was shocked, in fact, to learn that her Republican congressman had actually voted to repeal the ban on semiautomatic weapons exactly like the Ruger P-89 semiautomatic pistol that had been used against her husband, her son, and their fellow passengers.

In response to this bitter lesson, Carolyn McCarthy did the unexpected. She changed her political affiliation, becoming a Democrat, and declared herself a candidate for the congressional seat occupied by the man she once supported. She not only won her party's nomination in the primary, but also was cast into the national spotlight when she addressed the National Convention of the Democratic Party. (See the box "Remarks. . . .") That didn't change, moreover, when she proved the experts wrong and defeated the Republican incumbent in the general election.

Although Carolyn McCarthy's example may seem distant from you, none of us knows what tomorrow may bring. Further, none of us knows whether one day the circumstances in which we find ourselves will make extraordinary and unexpected demands on our public speaking skills.

So it was with Carolyn McCarthy. One day she was a nurse, spouse, and mother, content to let others practice politics. The next day, however, events set her on a path of public life and rhetorical demands she never could have anticipated.

This chapter focuses on situations you can expect to confront in your public speaking life—and on others you may not expect. Our immediate goal is twofold. First, we want to introduce you to situations that demand a rhetorical response. Second, we want to show you that only through a process in which you carefully analyze your audience can you make the most of those rhetorical responses.

SITUATIONS THAT DEMAND PUBLIC SPEAKING

Rhetorical scholar Lloyd Bitzer is interested in determining what it is that calls forth the need for public speaking. He believes that public speaking occurs in response to what he defines as a **rhetorical situation,** or "a natural context of persons, events,

Remarks Before the Democratic National Convention: Carolyn McCarthy

December 7th, 1993—that was the day of the Long Island Railroad massacre. My life and the lives of many others changed forever. A man with a semiautomatic weapon boarded the train that my husband and my son took to work every day. He killed 6 people and wounded 19. My husband, Dennis, was one of those killed. My son, Kevin, was left partially paralyzed. Kevin has had a courageous recovery. He's back at work. But he still spends many hours a day with rehabilitation. It's every mother's dream to be able to stand up on national TV and say she's proud of her son. Kevin, I'm very proud of you.

On that day I started on a journey, a journey against gun violence in this nation. Today I am here as a nurse, as a mother, as a person who isn't afraid to speak up on what is going on in this country.

Gun violence adds millions of dollars in hospital costs every year, and threatens families with a mountain of bills, and so much pain. Until our government listens to ordinary people speaking out against gun violence, of listening—instead of listening to special interest groups like the NRA leadership, we are not going to have safety in our streets!

I was not planning on speaking here tonight, but this is where my journey has taken me—to the Democratic Party, the party that believes in including ordinary citizens. That's why I'm here. I am here as a woman with common sense and determination, and I am going to make a difference.

I will fight to keep the assault weapons ban the law of the land. I—Yeah, I will. I will work for the day when President Clinton's Victims Rights Amendment is in the Constitution. And those of us who are concerned about gun violence will not tolerate being ignored, as I was by my congressman, who voted to repeal the assault weapons bill.

We have all been ignored by the Gingrich congress. They have not listened to us on education, on the environment, or on making our streets safe. We will not be ignored. We will make them listen.

The journey I began in 1993 wasn't one that I had planned. Getting involved in politics wasn't anything I ever wanted to do. But this journey will make a difference when our neighborhoods pull together, when government listens to us again. When all of us, Democrats and Republicans, come together to solve our problems, not just fight about them. We have a responsibility to our children to speak up about what we know is right and to do what is right. I ask you to join me and my son, Kevin, on that journey. Thank you so very much.

Source: Reprinted by permission of the author.

objects, relations, and an exigence [goal] which strongly invites utterance."[3] Although the specific term *rhetorical situation* wasn't coined until the late 1960s, its roots can be traced to ancient Greece and the 5th century B.C. Then as now there was a need for public speaking skills because democracy required people to deliberate about public policy. Further, there were no lawyers, and people had to plead their own case in court. A group of teachers of rhetoric, known as *Sophists*, taught the skills of speaking for a fee. Plato opposed their approach to rhetoric as lacking in regard for the truth and proposed his own philosophy of rhetoric in two dialogues, the *Gorgias* and the *Phaedrus*. Plato believed that one should first discover the truth philosophically and then use rhetoric only in service to truth. In Chapter 6 we discuss the controversy between these schools of rhetoric in more detail.

Plato's famous student Aristotle brought order and systematic focus to the study of the rhetorical situation. Aristotle wrote the *Rhetoric*, probably the most influential book on the subject to this day. Aristotle defined rhetoric as the "faculty of observing in any given case the available means of persuasion."[4] He specified that rhetoric consisted of three modes of proof: *ethos*, the personal credibility of the speaker; *pathos*, the putting of the audience into a certain frame of mind; and *logos*, the proof or apparent proof provided by the actual words of the speech (*logos* being the Greek word for "word"). In many ways this classification foreshadows much of contemporary communication research, with its emphasis on source credibility (*ethos*), audience analysis and reaction (*pathos*), and message construction (*logos*).

The study and practice of rhetoric was further refined by Roman rhetoricians such as Cicero and Quintilian, who developed the **canons of rhetoric,** classic laws of invention, arrangement, style, delivery, and memory. Recall from Chapter 2 that *invention* concerns the creative enterprise of discovering the materials to be used in a speech. *Arrangement* refers to how the speech is organized. *Style* deals with the way language is used in the speech. *Delivery* concerns the actual presentation of the speech. Finally, *memory* is concerned with ways to learn to recite a speech by heart. With the exception of memory, public speaking instruction to this day is largely concerned with these canons. A glance at the table of contents of this or any other public speaking book will find chapters concerned with gathering the materials for your speech (invention), organizational patterns (arrangement), language use (style), and nonverbal communication (delivery). Memory is largely confined to forensic competition, although making your speech memorable to your audience is also a focus of most public speaking books.

Given this rich history, rhetorical scholar Bitzer was following well-established tradition when he sought in 1968 to ground rhetoric in situational factors. Recall that Bitzer saw rhetoric as a response to a situation that strongly invites utterance. The elements of that situation include an exigence (goal), an audience, and a set of constraints that set the parameters for the rhetorical response.

GOALS AND THE MOTIVATION TO SPEAK OUT

Let's begin with what motivates you to speak out. Motives are the things that drive us to confront and hopefully master the rhetorical situation. Motives can be as selfish as convincing people to help you complete a task that will benefit only you. But motives also can be as altruistic as convincing the fortunate to share what they have with those less blessed. So what specifically motivates you? A good grade? Meeting still another requirement for graduation? How about self-improvement? In the effort to truly understand what motivates you, you need to thoroughly analyze the goal or goals you hope to achieve as a result of speaking.

A goal is an end. When we fully understand our speaking goals, they tell us about the destination we hope to reach as a result of speaking publicly. But we need to be careful in this regard. People commonly make mistakes in analyzing and identifying their speaking goals. Carolyn McCarthy did not simply decide one day to run for Congress. Rather, that goal developed as she learned about the causes and prevention of gun violence and about the limitations of the justice system. Colin Ferguson, who was the perpetrator of the Long Island Rail Road massacre, engaged in a long and somewhat bizarre trial, in which he not only defended himself, but directly interrogated many of the survivors of the attack. As a regular observer at the trial, McCarthy soon emerged as the spokesperson for the families of the victims. At the same time, she learned as much as she could about guns and about the issue of gun control. As she weighed the decision to run, even President Clinton tried to influence her decision. But she ultimately relied on her own judgment as well as the advice of her son and close friends. Her ultimate goal of being elected to Congress emerged over time, as she learned more about the issue of gun violence and how laws could be changed to help curb it.

Short-Term and Long-Term Goals

Some goals are short term and others are long term. Recognizing the difference is central not only to goal analysis but to your mastery of the rhetorical situation as well. **Short-term goals** are those ends you can accomplish in the near future. **Long-term goals** are ends that you can hope to achieve only over an extended period of time. Generally speaking, the realization of your short-term speaking goals should increase the chances of your realizing your long-term goals. Simply identifying what you need to accomplish in the short term, moreover, forces you to stay in the moment. Although it's good to think about an imagined future, it's what you do in the here and now that will first determine whether your imagined future becomes a reality.

Incremental Goals

Your analysis also requires thinking about goals in order of difficulty of achievement. The shopworn but accurate saying that "a journey of a thousand miles begins with a single step" is apropos here. Just as it makes good sense to go after short-term goals before long-term ones, it also makes good sense to first go after those goals you have the greatest chance of achieving. Typically this means organizing your speaking goals incrementally, from least to most important. **Incremental goals** are those steps you must complete to accomplish your long-term goal.

Consider again the case of Carolyn McCarthy. Once she decided to seek a seat in Congress, there were literally hundreds of steps that she had to take—

from making a formal announcement to raising money to speaking in front of a national audience at the Democratic National Convention. As a person who suffered from dyslexia, she feared that reading her speech from the TelePrompTer would be difficult because she often would misread what was on the screen. Instead, she spoke extemporaneously—from her heart.

ANALYZING YOUR AUDIENCE

VIDEO FILE

If you have access to the videotape that accompanies this book, view segment 4, which covers audience analysis.

So far we have said that rhetorical situations first must be analyzed in terms of the goals you hope to achieve. Any hope you have of achieving your speaking goals, however, depends on whether there is an audience "capable of being influenced by discourse and of being mediators of change."[5]

Audience analysis begins by knowing who your audience is. Then you need to know what power they have to help you achieve your goals. You also need to know whether they favor, oppose, or are indifferent to those goals. Finally, you need to analyze **audience diversity**—the cultural, demographic, and individual characteristics that differ among audience members. Once you know what audience you will be addressing, your task becomes more complex. Today's audience, whether selected or assigned, is a diverse one. This will increasingly become the case as you complete your education and pursue your career. There are many ways to break down audience diversity for the purpose of analysis.

In Figure 5.1, we have divided audience diversity into three types—cultural, demographic, and individual. Recognize that these types overlap each other and are interdependent rather than independent. For example, the demographic characteristics "religion" and "language" are also cultural characteristics, just as the demographic characteristics "gender" and "age" are also individual characteristics. Still, this division is a useful way to start. Don't let yourself get trapped, however, into thinking that knowing one or two things about the makeup of your audience is sufficient to succeed.

Cultural Diversity

Culture, as you may recall from Chapter 4, is a learned system of language, beliefs, and customs with which specific people identify. **Cultural diversity,** therefore, refers mainly to differences among people in terms of language, beliefs, and customs. At the most basic level, you need to familiarize yourself with the cultural diversity inherent in your audience.

Because culture is learned, what is appropriate in one culture may not be appropriate in another. The list of specific things that make one culture unique from another is inexhaustible. However, recognizing and responding to cultural diversity does not demand that you try to learn everything that is most peculiar about a specific culture. To the contrary, discovering what is *common but variable* among cultures is the key to culturally responsive speaking.

Dutch communication scholar Geert Hofstede says that all national cultures vary in terms of four dimensions: "*power distance* (from small to large), *collectivism*

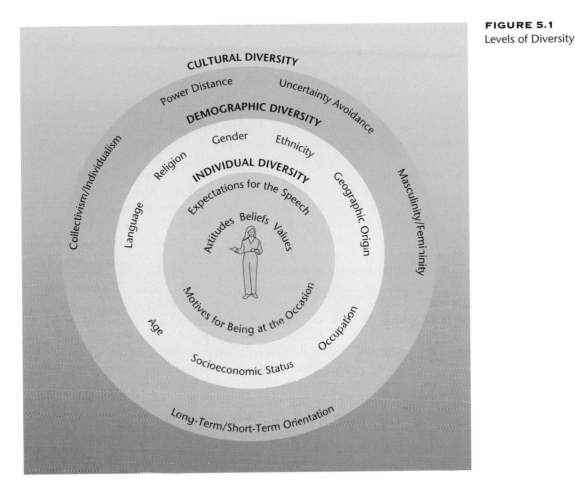

FIGURE 5.1
Levels of Diversity

versus *individualism, femininity* versus *masculinity,* and *uncertainty avoidance* (from weak to strong)."[6] In addition, Hofstede notes that a fifth dimension has been recently discovered, *long-term orientation* versus *short-term orientation* to life.[7] Cultures vary in their positions on these dimensions—for example, the extent to which they accept a large degree of power inequality or the degree to which they favor rugged individualism over collectivism. Your competence in identifying and adapting to cultures that differ on these dimensions will have an important effect on how well you adapt to the cultural diversity of your audience.

Power Distance   Hofstede defines power distance as "the extent to which the less powerful members of institutions and organizations within a country expect and accept that power is distributed unequally."[8] All societies are unequal, some more than others. However, different societies handle inequality in different ways. For example, there are large power distances in countries in Latin America, Asia, and Africa and in some European countries such as Spain. On the other hand, countries such as the United States and Great Britain and some parts of Europe have smaller power distances. Sweden, for example, is an egalitarian country with a small power distance, whereas France has a large power distance.

The importance of small power distance to American audiences is illustrated by the case of Carolyn McCarthy, an average mother and nurse, who ended up speaking to a national audience and subsequently defeated a powerful member of Congress. In her speech, she capitalized on Americans' willingness to back the average citizen against the powers in Washington, by pointing out how the party in control of Congress had, in her view, ignored the will of the average person on gun control.

Power-distance differences have important implications for you as a public speaker. For example, suppose you are a manager in an international organization announcing company downsizing. You could not assume that an audience from a small-power-distance culture, such as Sweden, would react in the same way to your speech as would one from a large-power-distance culture, such as Japan. Similarly, teachers are treated with deference in large-power-distance cultures, whereas they are treated as equals in small-power-distance cultures. For example, a professor from a Japanese university teaching in the United States might be surprised to be called by his or her first name, though such a practice is not uncommon at American universities. Conversely, a Japanese student studying in the United States might find it odd that professors expect students to treat them less formally than professors are treated in Japan. For an example of how one Japanese student reacts to the culture of an American university, see the profile, "Between Two Cultures: Tomoko Mukawa."

Further, power distance can vary within the larger culture, for example, by social class, educational level, and occupation. Of course, in most societies these factors are closely linked. People with higher levels of education tend to belong to the middle or upper social class and hold the most powerful positions. Generally, those occupations with the lowest status tend to have the largest power distance, and those with the highest status tend to have the smallest power distance. Thus, whereas a factory manager might expect workers with little education who occupy the lowest ranks to accept her authority with little questioning, the president of a university might expect her highly educated faculty members to demand a share in the governance of the institution.

Collectivism Versus Individualism   The second dimension common to all cultures is collectivism versus individualism. Hofstede explains: "Collectivism stands for a society in which people from birth onwards are integrated into strong, cohesive ingroups, which throughout people's lifetime continue to protect them in exchange for unquestioning loyalty."[9] In an individualistic society, on the other hand, "Everyone is expected to look after himself or herself and his or her immediate family only."[10] Some cultures, notably Asian and Native American, believe the good of the many far outweighs the good of the few. In these collectivist cultures, people shun the individual spotlight. Singling out a member of a collectivist culture while you're giving a speech is likely to embarrass the person.

Between Two Cultures: Tomoko Mukawa

Tomoko Mukawa was born in Japan and lived there until she was 15, when she came to the United States as a high school exchange student for a year. After completing her high school education in Japan, Tomoko decided to return to the United States to attend college. First as a community college student, and then as a student at a four-year university, Tomoko was struck by the differences in the way students and professors communicate in the two different cultures. Now a graduate student at California State University, Chico, majoring in communication, Tomoko related an experience that illustrates the differences between the two cultures.

"I wanted to keep my fluency in Japanese, so I took a class from a Japanese professor. Although the American students were allowed to call the professor by his American nickname, I was required to follow the Japanese tradition of always using his title and surname. He stressed that, as a Japanese student, I needed to preserve my cultural heritage."

Not only did Tomoko notice the difference between how students and professors related to each other in Japan and the United States, she also noticed that the language in which she spoke made a difference in how she was treated. As an English tutor for Japanese students coming to America, Tomoko discovered that when she spoke English she was perceived as more assertive than when she spoke Japanese. "You are like a different person when you speak Japanese," she was told by one of her students.

These experiences illustrate the differences between a large-power-distance culture like Japan and a small-power-distance culture like the United States. In Japan, students would never be familiar with professors, and women are generally not assertive. Simply speaking in her native language changed the way Tomoko was perceived. Language and culture are closely intertwined, as her experience has shown.

In cultures where so-called rugged individualism is admired and encouraged, the opposite is true. In the United States, for example, the dominant culture is very individualistic. We champion lone-wolf entrepreneurs who strike it rich, quarterbacks who stand alone in the pocket, and politicians who march to the beat of a different drummer. There is evidence to believe, in fact, that the United States is the most individualistic nation on Earth.[11]

This may be changing given immigration patterns and birth rates. Census data show that more people from collectivist cultures reside in the United States today than at any other time in history. American college students today find that people from collectivist cultures are an increasing part of their audience, a fact that must be included in the analysis of the rhetorical situation. To find out

How Collectivistic or Individualistic Are You?

The purpose of this questionnaire is to help you assess your individualistic and collectivistic tendencies. Respond by indicating the degree to which the values reflected in each phrase are important to you: Opposed to My Values (answer 1), Not Important to Me (answer 2), Somewhat Important to Me (answer 3), Important to Me (answer 4), or Very Important to Me (answer 5).

_____ 1. Obtaining pleasure or sensuous gratification

_____ 2. Preserving the welfare of others

_____ 3. Being successful by demonstrating my individual competency

_____ 4. Restraining my behavior if it is going to harm others

_____ 5. Being independent in thought and action

_____ 6. Having safety and stability of people with whom I identify

_____ 7. Obtaining status and prestige

_____ 8. Having harmony in my relations with others

_____ 9. Having an exciting and challenging life

_____ 10. Accepting cultural and religious traditions

_____ 11. Being recognized for my individual work

_____ 12. Avoiding the violation of social norms

_____ 13. Leading a comfortable life

_____ 14. Living in a stable society

_____ 15. Being logical in my approach to work

_____ 16. Being polite to others

_____ 17. Being ambitious

_____ 18. Being self-controlled

_____ 19. Being able to choose what I do

_____ 20. Enhancing the welfare of others

To find your individualism score, add your responses to the *odd-numbered* items. To find your collectivism score, add your responses to the *even-numbered* items. Both scores will range from 10 to 50. The higher your scores, the more individualistic and/or collectivistic you are.

Source: William Gudykunst, *Bridging Differences*, 2nd ed. Copyright © 1994 by Sage Publications. Reprinted by permission of Sage Publications, Inc.

where you stand as an individual on this dimension, see the self-assessment "How Collectivistic or Individualistic Are You?"

Femininity Versus Masculinity The third dimension of culture in Hofstede's scheme is femininity versus masculinity. Hofstede explains: "Femininity stands for a society in which social gender roles overlap: both men and women are supposed to be modest, tender, and concerned with the quality of life."[12] Masculinity, on the other hand, "stands for a society in which social gender roles are clearly distinct: men are supposed to be assertive, tough, and focused on material success."[13] The United States ranks relatively high on measures of masculinity. Comparing the scores on an index of masculinity, the United States is ranked 15 out of 53 countries—with Japan the most masculine and Sweden the most feminine. The most feminine cultures are found in Scandinavia and tend not to assign one set of roles to men and another set of roles to women. In these cultures, the professional role a person assumes is a product of ability rather than biological sex. Thus, when imagining a physician or chief executive officer of a company, people don't automatically see a man. In imagining a nurse or secretary, they don't automatically see a woman.

The opposite is true for many other cultures. Some go to extremes in the degree to which one's sex decides one's role. In contrast to Scandinavia, countries such as Japan, Austria, and Venezuela have few women in positions of corporate or public authority. Women are assigned roles out of view and out of power.

This dimension is important to analyzing your audience and constructing your speech. An audience of Japanese men, as a case in point, would be polite but predictably unreceptive to a woman speaking on a topic such as reengineering the Japanese corporation. By the same token, a Scandinavian audience would derogate the credibility of a male speaker suggesting women belong in the home.

This dimension can be important in a number of settings. For example, in masculine cultures, children in school tend to speak out and compete openly. Failure is viewed as a disaster and can even lead to suicide. Boys and girls tend to study different subjects. On the other hand, in feminine cultures, students tend to behave less competitively, failure is not viewed as a catastrophe, and boys and girls tend to study the same subjects. Obviously, teachers need to know which type of culture they are dealing with if they are to be effective.

Even with an American audience, there are likely to be differences in masculinity and femininity based on cultural heritage. Carolyn McCarthy knew that in addressing the Democratic National Convention she was addressing not only her immediate audience, but millions of Americans of differing cultural backgrounds. Her speech includes appeals based on her roles as mother, nurse, and citizen—roles that appeal to both feminine and masculine cultural values.

Uncertainty Avoidance   The fourth dimension Hofstede discusses is uncertainty avoidance, which is "the extent to which the members of a culture feel threatened by uncertain or unknown situations."[14] As a student you know all about uncertainty and the feelings of discomfort that can accompany it. Instructors who are vague about assignments, tests, due dates, and evaluation not only create uncertainty but also are the ones you try to avoid. Just as people vary in terms of the amount of uncertainty they can tolerate, so it is with whole cultures. People who live in "low-uncertainty-avoidance cultures" have considerable tolerance for the kind of ambiguity that can drive some people nuts.

The greatest difference among cultures on this dimension exists between Asian (except Japan and Korea) and European ones. Hofstede says this is likely the result of the different directions the ancient Chinese and Roman empires took in making laws. In the Chinese Empire, laws were loosely defined and seldom codified. Thus, lawbreakers could not reliably predict their punishment. Conversely, the Roman Empire codified its laws and enforced them rigidly. Thus, lawbreakers knew exactly what they could expect for committing a specific offense.

Cultures whose roots can be traced to the Chinese Empire have a predictably higher tolerance for living with uncertainty than cultures whose roots can be traced to the Roman Empire. Further, tolerating uncertainty with respect to the law appears to have generalized to tolerating uncertainty in general in these cultures. This is important for speakers to know. People from cultures high in tolerance for uncertainty are less likely to be bothered by ambiguities or loose ends following a speech. People from cultures low in tolerance for ambiguity, however, want a speech to close with concrete recommendations, or better yet, a solid solution to the problem presented in the speech.

Long-Term Versus Short-Term Orientation   The fifth and final dimension Hofstede discusses is long-term versus short-term orientation to life. "Long-term orientation stands for the fostering of virtues oriented toward future rewards, in particular perseverance and thrift."[15] "Short-term orientation stands for the fostering of virtues related to the past and the present, in particular respect for tradition, preservation of 'face,' and fulfilling social obligations."[16]

Asian countries, such as China, Hong Kong, Taiwan, and Japan, tend to rank very high on the long-term dimension. In fact, this dimension is sometimes called Confucian because many of the values, on both sides of the dimension, are the same as the teachings of Confucius. The United States is in the lower third of countries and Pakistan is at the bottom of the list, meaning both have a more short-term orientation.

Those cultures with a long-term orientation to life tend to adapt long-standing traditions to modern situations, are willing to save and persevere to achieve long-term goals, are willing to subordinate themselves for a purpose, and are thrifty in their use of resources. Short-term-oriented societies respect traditions, are willing to overspend to maintain their lifestyle, and expect quick results.

For speakers, therefore, it is very important to know whether their audience members share a short- or a long-term culture. Appeals to thrift and patience are likely to be effective in those societies with a long-term orientation, whereas appeals to instant gratification are more effective in societies that have a short-term view of the world. The current debate in the United States over the need to change the Social Security system to protect future generations reflects the results of years of a short-term orientation on the part of American society. That this issue is now being seriously debated suggests that both short- and long-term orientations are competing within the American culture.

All five dimensions are important to analyzing cultural diversity. You shouldn't give one greater credence than another. Further, the days of the homogeneous audience are numbered. No longer can one assume a uniform cultural background on the part of audience members. Both now and in your future you can count on audience membership that is not only culturally diverse but also variable with regard to such dimensions as femininity versus masculinity.

Cultural Variations in Audience Response

Both your method and style of delivery should reflect the cultural and group diversity of your audience. For example, consider how three different audiences might respond to the same speech. A North American audience returns your eye contact and nods in agreement as you speak. A British audience also returns eye contact, but their heads remain motionless. And a West African audience avoids making direct eye contact with you altogether. What should a speaker make of the differences in feedback?

Before you decide, perhaps it would help to know more: When the British agree with a speaker, they sometimes blink rather than nod their heads. Further, the more direct the eye contact of West Africans, the less they respect the person to whom they direct the eye contact. Knowing the typical patterns of nonverbal behavior in a given culture is essential if you are to accurately interpret its members' nonverbal behaviors.

Another example of differences among diverse audiences concerns the voice. Almost from birth, the norm for the North American culture is "to speak up and let yourself be heard." What is normative here, however, may be loud in Japan or among the upper class in Great Britain. And much as we may want to be heard, we don't want to be perceived as loudmouths.

Thus, developing and delivering a speech that appeals to a majority of the cultures represented in your audience is tougher than ever. The importance of understanding the effects of cultural diversity on audience response to the delivery—in addition to the content—of your message is discussed in the box, "Cultural Variations in Audience Response."

Important as it is to recognize how cultural dimensions like uncertainty avoidance are significant to your audience analysis, you need more specific advice about audience diversity as well. Just because a culture at large is high in uncertainty avoidance, we shouldn't be trapped into thinking that everyone we identify as a member of that culture is so inclined. The formerly collectivist cultures of Eastern Europe, for example, are full of people who are working to make them more individualistic.

It is also important to recognize that the next audience variable we discuss, demographic diversity, is closely related to cultural diversity. As Hofstede notes, culture operates in a number of layers: national, regional, ethnic, religious, linguistic, gender, generational, social class, and occupational. He points out, "Regional, ethnic, and religious cultures account for differences within countries; ethnic and religious groups often transcend political country borders."[17] Thus, in analyzing the demographic diversity of the audience members, you will also be refining your understanding of their cultural diversity on a number of levels.

Demographic Diversity

Demographic diversity is the second factor you'll want to examine to better understand your audience and the overall rhetorical situation. **Demographic diversity** refers to the differences among people in terms of demographics. **Demographics** are the basic and vital data regarding any population. Demographic factors include age, socioeconomic status, occupational role, geographic origin, ethnicity, gender, religion, and language.

Students in today's classrooms represent a wide diversity of ages.

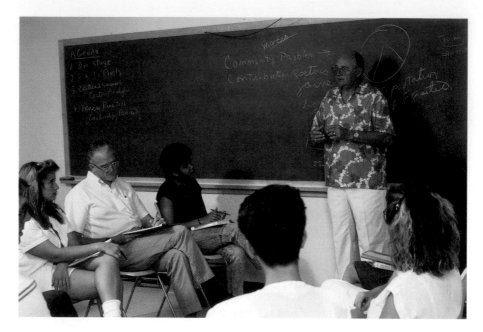

Age   The age demography of the United States is changing at an accelerated rate. So is the demography of the classroom. It used to be, for example, that traditional college classrooms consisted of a relatively homogeneous group of 18- to 22-year-olds. Today's classroom comprises a much more diverse mix of students. For example, college classes in a state university in the 1990s are likely to be of mixed gender and age. It's common for students to be as young as 17 or as old as 75. As a speaker, you need to take into account this demographic diversity in both the preparation and delivery of your speech. You have to consider not only how 18- to 22-year-olds are likely to respond to your presentation but also how continuing and reentry students are likely to respond. Likewise, you also will have to think through the response of students who may or may not be similar to you or other members of your audience.

This makes it especially important that you compare your audience with yourself. Some of the most effective speakers are similar but not too similar to their audience. Reentry students in their 40s can be somewhat intimidated by speaking to classes of 18- to 22-year-old classmates. Similarly, a 20-year-old asked to speak to a group of middle-aged businesspeople may feel uneasy. In situations where there is a big difference in age between speaker and audience, points of similarity can be stressed. For example, older students speaking to a younger audience can discuss their children, who might be the same age as the rest of the class. Similarly, younger persons facing an older audience can make reference to parents or grandparents in an effort to find a common thread linking them with the audience.

Socioeconomic Status   Social grouping or socioeconomic status, which is another type of demographic diversity, is not always directly observable. Most universities are working to increase the diversity of their student populations. Thus, in your class there may be students who come from impoverished backgrounds as well as students from affluent families. Although you can sometimes make inferences regarding the social status of your audience, these are not always reliable.

Occupation   Demographic diversity also is reflected in one's occupational role. On a residential campus, occupational roles generally are expressed in terms of major. At many schools, however, students already are involved in an occupation and pursuing a degree for purposes of advancement or career change. This is especially true of urban and metropolitan schools in or near major cities.

Our occupation and the people we routinely come into contact with at work influence how we look at things. People who are self-employed, for example, probably see things differently than do people working in the public sector, at a large corporation, or in the home. Because Carolyn McCarthy was both a mother and a nurse, for example, she appealed to both homemakers and women who have chosen careers outside the home. Just as it is important for speakers to analyze age and social diversity, so it is with occupational diversity.

Geographic Origin   The heterogeneous makeup of today's audience also is reflected in the geographic origins of the audience members. To understand how important this is to your analysis of the rhetorical situation, look around your campus. The chances are good that your campus reflects national and regional demographic diversity. International student attendance at U.S. colleges and universities is at an all time high. Faculties are becoming more international as well. Many campuses, especially large urban ones, look like mini-assemblies of the United Nations. To deny or ignore how this national diversity influences people's perceptions of each other, including how you are perceived as a public speaker, is foolish. The same can be said for the regional diversity reflected in your student body. Some campuses are near-mirror images of the region in which they exist. Still others look more like international cities than like their regional environment.

Ethnicity   Just as national and regional diversity are features of your campus, so too is ethnic diversity. With the exception of Native Americans, the ancestry of the people on your campus usually can be traced to other continents and countries. The ethnic origins of many of your classmates may be significant to their self-concept. These same classmates may be actively involved in maintaining and passing on the traditions that define their ethnicity. Thus, if you are ignorant of the ethnic diversity present on your campus, you may inadvertently violate or be insensitive to one or more of these traditions. (See the box "Rhetorical Sensitivity" on the next page.)

Gender   Gender's influence on how people perceive themselves and others is a subject receiving considerable scholarly attention. As scholars such as Julia Wood point out, gender is much more than your biological sex.[18] Gender is the blend of social and cultural characteristics that are associated with maleness or femaleness in a particular culture. Individuals learn gender roles—the expectations their cultures have of them as males or females—in the course of growing up.

Rhetorical Sensitivity

Anyone who listened to sports talk radio during the 1995 World Series knows about the controversy surrounding the Atlanta Braves' "Tomahawk Chop" and the Cleveland Indians' "Chief Wahoo." Both teams were accused of disparaging Native American traditions and tribes. Native Americans and their supporters pointed out that the public would be incensed at a team named after Jews or Blacks or Asians. Others thought Native Americans were being overly sensitive. They pointed out that no one complains about Notre Dame's "Fighting Irish."

Rhetorical scholar Roderick Hart suggests that this kind of scenario begs for what he calls *rhetorical sensitivity*. People who are rhetorically sensitive routinely take other people's point of view into consideration before speaking or acting. Do you think the baseball teams and their fans were rhetorically insensitive? Were you offended by their behavior? If so, what would you suggest they change?

Source: Roderick P. Hart and Don M. Burks, "Rhetorical Sensitivity and Social Interaction," *Speech Monographs* 39 (1972): 75–91.

As you look out at an audience, you can usually tell who is male and who is female by such outward signs as dress and hairstyle. But this distinction gives you little information about gender-based diversity. You can't tell what part of the United States or what country audience members come from, what their community and family values are, or what their personal preferences and opinions are. Even in an all-female or all-male group, such as a sports team or a men's or women's chorus, there may be great diversity among members. Thus, basing an audience analysis on how many women and men are in it is ineffective. In no way would it approximate the gender-based diversity of today's audience.

Religion   Religious diversity is still another form of demographic diversity for you to consider. Even at well-known sectarian universities like Notre Dame, you will find diversity in the religious beliefs of groups of students. Of course at public colleges and universities this is even more so. In some cases, a person's religion can be identified on the basis of apparel and appearance. Such cases include the Amish, Hasidic Jews, some Muslims, and Hindu Sikhs. Usually, however, the religious diversity on your campus or at work will not be outwardly visible. You cannot tell a devout Catholic from an atheist by outward appearances. We cannot emphasize enough, therefore, how important it is for you to consider religious diversity as an inherent feature of your rhetorical situation.

Language   Finally, there is language diversity. As illustrated in Chapter 1, people often use their language group to distinguish themselves from other groups. Such is the case with the residents of Boonville, California. If you ask for directions in this small Mendocino County town, a native in his mid-70s might reply: "Take your wee moshe, pike toward the Deep End, and you'll deek on the Big Crik chiggrul and sluggin' region. And jape easy!"[19] You would have encountered one of the few living speakers of a home-grown American language known as Boontling, which evolved in the isolated community of Boonville in the late 19th century. By speaking the lingo, residents could "shark" (play games) with "bright-lighters" (city slickers) passing through town.[20] The culture of the town was bound up with its own unique language. Today, however, only a few older native speakers still know how to speak Boontling. With the coming of modern transportation and communication, the language is dying out.

Language groups are not necessarily based on geographic location or boundaries. Some languages and vocabularies develop around an activity or interest. Surfers and sailboarders, snowboarders and skiers all have a vocabulary peculiar to their sport. The same can be said about computer hackers, photographers, and serious backpackers. What's more, these groups use their vocabulary not only to identify their own kind but also to differentiate themselves from others.

Individual Diversity

Up to this point, we have talked about diversity in collective terms such as cultures and demographic groups. But as you well know, what makes humans interesting is the fact that despite their cultural and demographic characteristics, they still can be individuals. It is at this level that diversity is both most meaningful and most difficult to assess. Individual diversity is deeply embedded in our beliefs, attitudes, values, motives for being at the occasion, and expectations for the speech.

Beliefs   We all hold certain beliefs about a variety of topics. A **belief** is "an assertion about the properties or characteristics of an object."[21] Some beliefs are relatively obvious and incontrovertible. For example, we all (presumably) share a belief that the Earth is round. On the other hand, some beliefs are very controversial—for instance, those concerning life after death, abortion, and evolution. When you are dealing with matters on which people hold different beliefs from your own, you face a serious obstacle. You must either change their relevant beliefs or convince them that such beliefs are not relevant and not necessarily in opposition to your own point of view.

Social psychologist Milton Rokeach pointed out that some beliefs are more resistant to change than others.[22] *Primitive beliefs*, also known as type A beliefs, are learned by direct contact with the object of belief and reinforced by unanimous social consensus. An example would be the belief that "death is inevitable." Primitive beliefs based on direct experience, but not subject to social support, are called *zero consensus*, or type B, *beliefs*. These beliefs are also very resistant to change. For example, "I like myself" is a type B belief; it is not reinforceable by social consensus. Together, type A and B beliefs are *core beliefs*, which are very resistant to change. The next two types of beliefs are known as *central beliefs* and are still very resistant to change. Type Cs are *authority beliefs*. For example, one's belief in the truth of the Bible or the Koran would be a type C belief. Type Ds are *derived beliefs*, based on authorities' beliefs. For example, a conservative Catholic's belief in the infallibility of the pope is a derived belief.

Together, type C and D beliefs are more central to a belief system than the final type of beliefs, type E, or *peripheral beliefs*. For example, someone might like rap music, whereas another detests it. These are the most inconsequential of

FIGURE 5.2
A Belief System

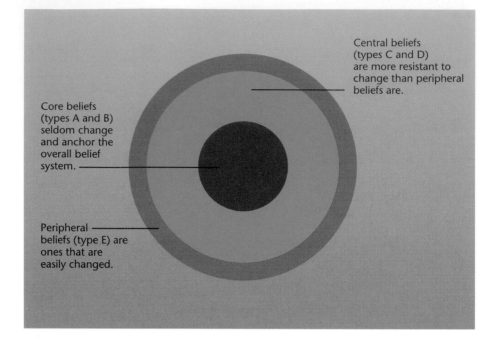

Central beliefs (types C and D) are more resistant to change than peripheral beliefs are.

Core beliefs (types A and B) seldom change and anchor the overall belief system.

Peripheral beliefs (type E) are ones that are easily changed.

beliefs. Figure 5.2 illustrates the relationship among these levels of belief. Clearly your chances of changing an audience member's core beliefs are far less than changing central or peripheral beliefs. Changing a type D belief requires an understanding of the type C belief from which it is derived. Thus, one might point to scripture to try to change a believer's views on a religious matter, but such an argument would have no impact on an atheist or a practitioner of a different religion.

Attitudes   An **attitude** is "a learned predisposition to respond in a consistently favorable or unfavorable manner with respect to a given object."[23] Attitudes are not simply beliefs but rather ways of potentially responding to various objects, based in part on one's beliefs about those objects. Over the course of our lives, we develop innumerable attitudes on everything from our favorite brand of soft drink to the burning political issues of the day. These attitudes mediate how we respond to the messages we hear. Thus, knowing your audience's attitudes toward your topic is crucial to your success as a speaker.

Of course, it is entirely possible in a diverse audience to have different and even conflicting attitudes among members of the same group. The more you know about the predominant or prevailing attitudes of the group, the better are your chances of convincing at least a majority of the audience of your position. When an audience is fairly evenly divided, you need to attempt to find some middle ground. Finding areas of common agreement while recognizing and respecting differences of opinion is essential to dealing with an audience of mixed attitudes.

Values   **Values** are "more general than attitudes." They are "enduring beliefs that hold that some ways of behaving and some goals are preferable to others."[24]

Underlying opposition to capital punishment, for example, is not only a belief regarding the improbability that it functions as a deterrent but also a value system about the preservation of human life.

According to Rokeach, some values are terminal, whereas others are instrumental.[25] *Terminal values* are those that concern "end states of existence." Examples of terminal values include a comfortable life, an exciting life, a sense of accomplishment, a world at peace, a world of beauty, equality, family security, freedom, and happiness. *Instrumental values* concern "modes of conduct." These are guides to behavior, the means to achieve the ends specified in the terminal values. Examples of instrumental values include ambitiousness, broad-mindedness, capableness, cheerfulness, cleanliness, courage, forgiveness, helpfulness, and honesty.

Although one might not always agree with Rokeach's classification—for example, honesty can certainly be viewed as an end in itself—the basic notion is useful. Some values are desirable in and of themselves, whereas others are instruments for achieving higher, terminal values. For example, forgiveness and courage may be seen as means to achieving a world at peace.

Values, particularly terminal values, are very difficult to change because they are learned at an early age and widely shared among people. Such values as fairness, justice, life, our nation, and so on not only are fundamental but also are taught to us in our most formative years. In fact, our basic value system probably is pretty well determined by the time we finish kindergarten, as Robert Fulghum pointed out in his best-selling book, *All I Really Need to Know I Learned in Kindergarten*.[26]

Speakers are best advised to appeal to known values shared by their audience rather than to try to convince their audience to adopt new values. Carolyn McCarthy illustrated this principle in her speech to the Democratic National Convention, which appealed to such key American values as the sanctity of human life; her son's courage; her pride in her son; the importance of common sense; and most of all, safety—freedom from gun violence in the streets. There are occasions, however, when speakers are called on to strengthen and reinforce values. A Fourth of July speech, a eulogy, or an inspirational speech can be thought of as fulfilling a value-strengthening function. For the most part, however, speakers need to treat values as a given and build on them. For example, Martin Luther King, Jr.'s "I Have a Dream" speech was not so much a call for new values as for Americans to live up to the values stated in the Declaration of Independence and the Bill of Rights. The same was true of Louis Farrakhan's speech at the 1995 Million Man March, which called for a return to core values among African Americans.

Motives for Being at the Occasion   Why are audience members attending your speech? In most classroom situations, the answer is simple: because they have to. In those situations, you have to work harder at holding the audience's interest and connecting to their needs than if they had come especially to hear you speak. In Chapter 8 we offer some suggestions that will help you connect with an audience and gain their attention. Even an audience who has come to hear you needs to be held. It is easy to lose an audience and very difficult to recapture their attention, as any experienced speaker can testify.

Expectations for the Speech   If audience members expect to be entertained, and you deliver a serious speech on the dangers of ozone depletion, you are unlikely to receive a favorable reception. Similarly, if most audience members expect a serious lesson on a topic not to be taken lightly, you owe it to them to meet this expectation. Always strive to match your speech as much to the audience members' expectations as is possible while still achieving your goals.

Generally, speeches contrary to a majority of audience members' expectations may backfire or, at the very least, be apathetically received. For example, the authors attended a graduation ceremony where the speaker used the opportunity to preach his view on "political correctness." While family and friends were there to honor and celebrate the graduates' accomplishments, they were instead treated to a political statement. Whereas such an address might have been appropriate at a meeting of the faculty senate, it missed the mark for the assembled graduates and their guests. The fact that the audience prematurely applauded and shouted loudly at what they thought was the conclusion of the speech reinforced how inappropriate the address was.

CONFRONTING CONSTRAINTS

Obviously, there is more to the rhetorical situation than the cultural, demographic, and individual characteristics of your audience. There are certain constraints on action that we all face. A **constraint** is a limitation on one's choices. Among the common constraints you may face in a rhetorical situation are the facts pertaining to the situation, legal constraints, ethical constraints, nature of the occasion and circumstances, traditions, time factors, and resource factors. Let's examine each of these.

Facts Pertaining to the Situation

Former President Reagan once observed that "facts are stubborn things." Although some people seem oblivious to the facts governing their situation, sooner or later they must face reality. As a private citizen, for example, Carolyn McCarthy learned there was very little she could do to influence her congressman to support the ban on assault weapons. Only as a candidate and effective public speaker was she able to change the stubborn facts of the situation in her congressional district. As a speaker, you should always try to fully understand the facts of your situation before speaking.

Legal Constraints

We all must abide by certain legal constraints in our speaking. Libel and slander laws, for example, proscribe certain types of speech. There are also laws that cover when and where one may peaceably assemble. Some pro-life activists have been successfully prosecuted, for example, for blocking the entrances to abortion clinics. Although the First Amendment guarantees freedom of speech and assembly, these rights are not an absolute license to do what you please.

Some speakers, however, have effectively challenged and even broken the law for a purpose. Following the principles of Mahatma Gandhi, Martin Luther King, Jr., practiced peaceful civil disobedience in the civil rights movement of the 1960s. So strong was his conviction, King was willing to risk great bodily harm as well as jail for his actions. Ultimately, this self-sacrifice served to sway public opinion to his side.

In your case, it is highly unlikely that you will choose to purposefully break the law to further the cause advanced in one of your speeches. Yet, unless you check on the legal constraints relevant to your situation, you may accidentally break a law of which you are unaware. In our own experience, we've had students show up to class with everything from exotic beers to poisonous pets, both of which are illegal on our campus. We've learned, consequently, that it is necessary for us to check on the topics and plans of our students well before their time to actually speak. So, check with your instructor before you unintentionally pit yourself against the law.

Ethical Constraints

We discuss ethical considerations for public speaking in detail in Chapter 6. At this point, we simply want to alert you to the fact that as a speaker and as a listener, you will face ethical constraints. Although something may be technically legal, that doesn't make it ethical.

One common example of the ethical constraints faced by speakers is the distinction between worthy goals and unethical means for achieving those goals. It is not unusual for people to attempt to justify ethically suspect rhetoric because it serves a noble end. For example, consider Louis Farrakhan and the Million Man March in 1995. To achieve a worthy end, somewhere between 400,000 and 2 million men marched on Washington, D.C., to hear what Farrakhan had to say. But Farrakhan himself has been widely denounced for views that promote Black separatism and smack of anti-Semitism. *Newsweek*, for example, reports that Farrakhan has a "long history of verbal assaults on Jews, Koreans, Palestinian Arabs, homosexuals—and whites in general."[27] If his rhetoric ends up promoting greater self-reliance and responsibility among African American men, is it ethical by virtue of his goal? Or is no end, no matter how noble, sufficient to justify such rhetoric?

Nature of the Occasion and Circumstances

What is the nature of the occasion prompting you to speak? You probably remember the day the world learned that Princess Diana had been killed in a traffic accident in France. When her brother, Earl Spencer, delivered her eulogy on September 6, 1997, he sought to both honor her and make the point that the *paparazzi* bore a share of the responsibility for her death. Was Diana's state funeral an appropriate forum for making this point? While some Britons applauded his efforts, others were shocked at his breach of etiquette.

Your speeches most likely will be given to classes during normal class times. Your audience is a captive one. Given that unavoidable fact, you must always decide whether your topic and presentation are appropriate to this context and occasion.

Traditions

Many speeches are governed by tradition. Whereas this is not a major factor in most classroom speeches, it could be when you are called on to speak in situations outside the classroom. For example, many service clubs, such as Rotary or Lions, have a whole set of traditions that may seem puzzling to the outsider. For instance, there is a good deal of good-natured poking fun at certain members, "fines" are levied for infractions such as getting your name in the paper, and so forth. Major corporations, such as IBM and Apple, each have their own set of traditions. IBM is formal; Apple is much less so. In speaking to either group, therefore, you would want to reflect the degree of formality each expected in terms of dress, demeanor, and style of presentation.

Time Factors

How much time do you have to give your speech? If you have been asked to speak for 5 minutes and you ramble on for an hour, the response will be predictably negative. On the other hand, imagine paying to hear an hour lecture by a major public figure and having the speech end in 10 minutes. You need to know and respect time limits, as well as match how much information you cover in your speech to your allotted time. For instance, it is generally better to cover a narrow topic thoroughly than to try to cover a wide range of points superficially. Carolyn McCarthy had only about 3 minutes to present her case to the American people when she spoke at the Democratic National Convention. Given that time constraint, she was forced to speak in generalities rather than specifics.

Time also is a factor you need to consider in your preparation. If you have a week to prepare a speech, you probably don't have time to write for information from outside sources. If you have a month, you probably do. You also will need time for practice. Because speaking is in part a behavioral skill, it deserves the same degree of practice as shooting free throws, swinging a golf club, or learning a new exercise in gymnastics. Simply put, it cannot possibly be mastered without some degree of repetition. And this means committing time to practice as far in advance of the speech as possible. Relaxation techniques and other approaches to managing anxiety also require time to master.

Resource Factors

Two questions are involved here. First, what resources do you have available to you? Resources include money, information sources, other people who might assist you, and the like. Second, what resources do you need to accomplish your speaking goal? If your resources match or exceed what you need, you are fine. If you lack the necessary resources, however, you must either redefine your goal or obtain more resources. Carolyn McCarthy faced an opponent who not only held a seat in Congress, but who had three times her financial resources to campaign. Thus she was forced to run a grass-roots campaign and to rely on free media coverage, which she often was able to command because of her public recognition as a spokesperson for victims of the Long Island shooting incident.

The same principles apply to a classroom speech. Suppose you are assigned to give a speech with at least three visual aids. How do you go about getting these? If you have enough money, you may be able to pay to have pictures enlarged to poster size or overhead transparencies prepared. If not, what alternative resources do you have? If you have a friend who is an art major, perhaps he or she can help you make posters. Whatever your rhetorical situation, you need to give careful consideration to the resources you have or will need to obtain to achieve your goal.

SPEECH PURPOSES

Given the preceding constraints with which you must deal, we can now look at your purpose. All speeches are motivational. Although the three common general speech purposes are to inform, to persuade, and to entertain, each of these purposes still involves motivating your audience. Information without direction is useless to an audience. You may be asking yourself how the rhetorical situation fits into these purposes. Although general speech purposes can be identified for frequently recurring rhetorical situations, each rhetorical situation involves a unique complex of persons, events, objects, relations, and goals. Whether a speech is predominantly informative or persuasive, for example, is not simply a matter of a speaker's choosing what he or she wants to accomplish. Rather, it depends on all three elements of the rhetorical situation: goals, audience, and constraints. Table 5.1 lists some of the complexities involved in understanding the dynamics of the rhetorical situation.

To illustrate this point, suppose you are giving a speech about crack cocaine. Speaking to an audience of parents, you might inform them about symptoms of crack use among their own children. Addressing an audience of teenagers, you

TABLE 5.1 Factors in Determining Speech Purpose

	PURPOSE		
	To Inform	*To Persuade*	*To Entertain*
Goal	Knowledge	Influence on attitude, value, or behavior	Enjoyment
Audience	Uninformed	May be informed, may be hostile	Seeks pleasure, diversion
Message	Noncontroversial	Controversial or reinforcing	Humorous, dramatic
Contexts	Classroom, training session	Political rally, business meeting	After-dinner speech

In the 1960s and '70s drug use was frequently treated as an object of humor.

might seek to persuade them to avoid the drug. For an audience of elementary children, you might seek to persuade them to "just say no" to drugs. The fact that it is difficult to imagine an entertaining speech today on drugs is a sign of how much attitudes have changed regarding drugs as a serious problem. During the '60s and '70s, drugs were frequently the topic of jokes. Two comics of the time, Cheech and Chong, made their reputations with drug-related humor in both their stand-up routines and a series of cheap, still popular, and extremely profitable movies.

The point of this example is that, depending on goals, the audience, and certain constraints, one may take essentially the same topic and shape it to any of the possible general purposes described. Further, it should be clear that these purposes are not mutually exclusive. It is difficult to imagine a successful persuasive speech that does not also inform. Clearly an informative speech may also persuade someone to act differently. If we were to inform you about methods for preventing AIDS, you might change your behavior, even without our urging. Speeches to inform or persuade also sometimes contain entertaining moments. In fact, humor, particularly irony, is sometimes very persuasive. Comics such as Bill Maher and Jay Leno typically have a strong political message embedded in their humor. Finally, the building of new attitudes and values is usually a long process. The persuasive efforts of Carolyn McCarthy, Sarah Brady, and other individuals and groups in favor of gun control have faced considerable opposition from those, such as the National Rifle Association (NRA), who interpret the Second Amendment to the Constitution literally. We are far from achieving a consensus in this country on the issue. For example, actor Charlton Heston, president of the NRA, has forcefully argued against those who would limit the

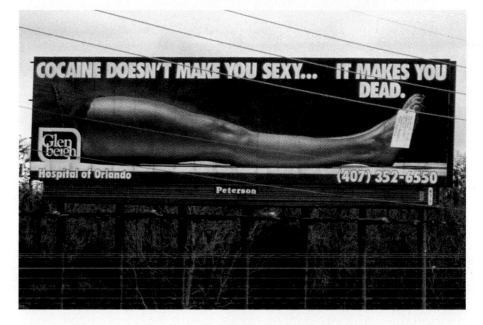

Today drug use is the target of government programs to persuade youth to say no to drugs.

Second Amendment right to bear arms. According to Heston, "There's no such thing as a good gun. There's no such thing as a bad gun. A gun in the hands of a bad man is a very dangerous thing. A gun in the hands of a good person is no danger to anyone except the bad guys."[28]

When you are assigned a speech, therefore, you must take into account the whole rhetorical situation, whether the speech is labeled informative, persuasive, or entertaining. Be particularly careful to consider your audience in this regard. You could deliver the same speech on evolution to a group of biology teachers and to a group who believes the Bible is literally true, including that God created the world in six days. Whereas the biologists might see your speech as informative, the other group undoubtedly would see it as an attempt to persuade them to change their beliefs. Same speech, different audiences, different perceived purposes. You cannot merely assume that your audience shares your perception of the purpose of the speech. Only by fully analyzing the rhetorical situation can you be reasonably confident that your intentions will be accurately perceived.

Because an audience is made up of many different individuals, a diverse audience may include those who see your purpose as informative and others who see it as persuasive. There is nothing wrong with this; in fact, it is inevitable. It is best to know this in advance, however, and to adapt to that segment of the audience most relevant to reaching your goal. Thus, though you may want only to inform your classmates who believe in evolution of the latest advances in the theory, some of your class may disbelieve the theory. For them, you will need to preface your speech by making it clear that you do not intend to challenge their beliefs. On the other hand, if you are seeking to persuade this latter group, then you will need to deal specifically with some of their objections to the theory of

Attitudes on gun control remain controversial in the United States, as illustrated by Charlton Heston's strong opposition to it.

evolution. The more heterogeneous an audience, the more difficult it becomes for the speaker to adapt to the rhetorical situation.

Once you have presented your speech, it is important to evaluate what you have accomplished. Talk to members of the audience. Observe the outcome of your speech. If you are seeking to persuade an audience in the short term, you may want to survey your audience before and after your speech to see if their attitudes have changed. Measuring the extent of long-term persuasion is more difficult because the results may not show up for years. You can usually tell if an audience is entertained: immediate laughter and applause are often their own rewards.

If time permits, don't be afraid to take audience questions. This sort of interaction gives you another chance to make your point. It also helps you know how well you have succeeded. Taking questions in a nonhostile, positive way is to your advantage.

In the classroom environment, there are frequently opportunities for classmates and your instructor to critique your speeches orally or in writing. These are valuable sources of feedback. Your goal in this class, presumably, is to become a better speaker. More often than not, one speech is not enough to achieve this goal. Thus, you should view each speech as a step in a process. After each speech, we recommend that you take stock and assess where you are. As you learn from the inevitable mistakes as well as the things you do correctly, your goal should become more attainable. Learning to be an effective public speaker is a dynamic process, and the more open you are to change, the more successful you are likely to become.

SUMMARY

The *rhetorical situation* is "a natural context of persons, events, objects, relations, and an exigence [goal] which strongly invites utterance." Our rhetorical heritage extends back to 5th-century-B.C. Greece. Sophists believed that truth is relative, and they taught public speaking skills for a fee. Plato believed that rhetoric should be in the service only of truth. Aristotle defined *rhetoric* as "the faculty of discovering in any given case the available means of persuasion." The Romans codified the principles of rhetoric into *canons* governing invention, arrangement, style, delivery, and memory.

Among contemporary theorists, Lloyd Bitzer has grounded rhetoric in the situation. The rhetorical situation contains an exigence (goal), an audience, and a set of constraints. Carefully analyzing each of these elements is essential to successful public speaking.

A goal is an end that a speaker seeks. *Short-term goals* are those ends you seek to accomplish in the near future; *long-term goals* require an extended period of time; *incremental goals* are steps along the way to a long-term goal.

Audience diversity refers to the cultural, demographic, and individual characteristics that differ among audience members. *Cultural diversity* refers to the differences among people in language, beliefs, and customs. Cultures vary in terms of five dimensions: power distance, collectivism versus individualism, femininity versus masculinity, uncertainty avoidance, and long-term orientation versus short-term orientation to life. *Demographic diversity* involves differences related to basic and vital data regarding any population, including age, socioeconomic status, occupational roles, geographic origin, ethnicity, gender, religion, and language. Individual diversity is deeply embedded in our beliefs, attitudes, values, motives for being at the occasion, and expectations for the speech.

Beliefs are assertions about the properties or characteristics of an object. *Attitudes* are predispositions to respond in a consistently favorable or unfavorable manner with respect to an object. *Values* are more general and enduring than attitudes and hold that some ways of behaving and some goals are preferable to others. An individual's motives for being at a speech are important to audience analysis, as are individual expectations of a speech.

The rhetorical situation also includes various *constraints* on the speech, such as factual, legal, ethical, nature of the occasion, traditions, time, and resources. Each of these factors can limit the speaker's choices as well as the likelihood that the speaker will achieve his or her goal.

Although general purposes, such as to inform, persuade, or entertain, can be identified, each rhetorical situation includes goals, an audience, and constraints that define the actual purposes of the speech. Only through careful audience analysis and adaptation can speakers match their speeches to the rhetorical situations they face. Finally, evaluation by self and others is an important part of becoming a better speaker.

Check Your Understanding: Exercises and Activities

1. Given the topic of alcohol abuse, how might you develop your speech presentation differently if your audience were made up of (a) high school students, (b) students your own age, (c) bar and tavern owners in your community, or (d) recovering alcoholics? In a short paper, explain how your approach and purpose would differ in each case.

2. Create a model of your belief system, including your core beliefs, authority beliefs, and representative derived beliefs on one of the following topics: gun control, the importance of voting, abortion, civil rights. What does your belief system say about how susceptible you are to being influenced on the topic selected?

3. Interview a student from another country who is studying at your university. What most surprised him or her about American culture? What would Americans be most surprised to know about his or her culture? Write a short paper or give a short talk about what you have discovered.

4. Learn as much as you can about the cultural, demographic, and individual diversity of your classmates. Construct a short questionnaire that will guide you in preparing for an upcoming speech. After obtaining your instructor's approval, write a survey about your chosen topic. You might ask questions about what your audience already knows about the topic, their attitudes for or against your position, and their level of interest in the topic. Distribute the questionnaire to your classmates and collect their responses (anonymously, of course). Tabulate the results. For example, if your topic is banning the sale of handguns known as Saturday night specials, you might report that 60 percent of your classmates were familiar with the term, while 40 percent were not; that 50 percent agreed with a ban, 20 percent opposed one, and the remainder had no opinion; and that 30 percent felt gun violence was a major issue, while 70 percent did not. Based on these results, write a short paper on how you used this information to shape your speech. Also indicate how your plans for your speech may have changed based on the information from your survey.

Notes

1. Carolyn McCarthy, Candidate for the House of Representatives, "Remarks to Democratic National Convention," August 27, 1996.

2. The description of Carolyn McCarthy's story is drawn from several sources: Tamara Jones, "A Candidate's Uneasy Station in Life: Train Massacre Leads to Convention Call," *Washington Post,* 27 August 1996, B01; Michael Daly, "It All Started with 'Why?'" *New York Daily News,* 28 August 1996, 25; Jay Bobbin, "NBC Movie Traces the Aftermath of Commuter-Train Tragedy," *Sacramento Bee on TV,* 3–9 May 1998, 4; Jeffrey Zaslow, "Straight Talk," *USA Weekend,* 1–3 May 1998.

3. Lloyd Bitzer, "The Rhetorical Situation," *Philosophy and Rhetoric* 1 (1968): 5. Bitzer further defines an exigence as "an imperfection marked by urgency; it is a defect, an obstacle, something waiting to be done, a thing which is other

than it should be." In this text we prefer to focus on the speaker's goal, which, strictly speaking, is to *overcome the exigence* present in the rhetorical situation.

4. Aristotle, *Rhetoric*, trans. W. Rhys Roberts (New York: Modern Library, 1954), 24.

5. Bitzer, "Rhetorical Situation," 8.

6. Geert Hofstede, *Cultures and Organizations: Software of the Mind* (London: McGraw-Hill, 1991), 14.

7. Hofstede, *Cultures and Organizations*, 14.

8. Hofstede, *Cultures and Organizations*, 262.

9. Hofstede, *Cultures and Organizations*, 260.

10. Hofstede, *Cultures and Organizations*, 261.

11. Hofstede, *Cultures and Organizations*, 53.

12. Hofstede, *Cultures and Organizations*, 261.

13. Hofstede, *Cultures and Organizations*, 262.

14. Hofstede, *Cultures and Organizations*, 263.

15. Hofstede, *Cultures and Organizations*, 261.

16. Hofstede, *Cultures and Organizations*, 262–263.

17. Hofstede, *Cultures and Organizations*, 15–16.

18. Julia T. Wood, *Gendered Lives* (Belmont, Calif.: Wadsworth, 1994).

19. Jennifer Warren, "Boonville's Sprightly Lingo About to Die Out," *Sacramento Bee*, 21 January 1996, A2.

20. Warren, "Boonville's Sprightly Lingo," A2.

21. Sarah Trenholm, *Persuasion and Social Influence* (Englewood Cliffs, N.J.: Prentice Hall, 1989), 6.

22. Milton Rokeach, *Beliefs, Attitudes and Values* (San Francisco: Jossey-Bass, 1968), 6–21.

23. Martin Fishbein and Icek Ajzen, *Belief, Attitude, Intention, and Behavior: An Introduction to Theory and Research* (Reading, Mass.: Addison-Wesley, 1975), 6.

24. Trenholm, *Persuasion and Social Influence*, 11, based on Rokeach, *Beliefs, Attitudes and Values*.

25. Milton Rokeach, "Change and Stability in American Value Systems, 1968–1971," in *Understanding Human Values: Individual and Societal*, ed. Milton Rokeach (New York: Free Press, 1979), 129–153.

26. Robert Fulghum, *All I Really Need to Know I Learned in Kindergarten* (New York: Ivy Books, 1988).

27. Howard Fineman and Vern E. Smith, "An Angry 'Charmer,' " *Newsweek*, 30 October 1995, 33.

28. Charlton Heston, FOX News Channel, September 15, 1997. (NRA [online]. Available http://www.nra.org/).

CHAPTER 6

Elie Weisel, Nobel
Peace Prize winner,
has been a force for
ethics as he fights
against bigotry and
racism.

Ethical Speaking

OBJECTIVES

After reading this chapter, you should be able to:

- Demonstrate an understanding of the differences among ethical relativism, universalism, utilitarianism, and situational ethics.
- Apply ethical principles to a variety of different public speaking situations.
- Explain plagiarism and the role of attribution in avoiding plagiarism.
- Explain and apply the basic ethical obligations of both speakers and listeners.

KEY CONCEPTS

categorical imperative	plagiarism
cultural relativism	situational ethics
ethical relativism	trustworthiness
ethics	universalism
good reasons	utilitarianism
goodwill	

Logic clearly dictates that the needs of the many outweigh the needs of the few or of the one.

—MR. SPOCK, Vulcan philosopher and Star Fleet officer, 23rd century.[1]

Although Mr. Spock believed that the needs of the many outweighed the needs of the one, his shipmates risked their many lives to save him after his "death" in *Star Trek II: The Wrath of Khan.*

You may remember the climactic scene of *Star Trek II: The Wrath of Khan,* when Mr. Spock enters the warp drive chamber of the *Starship Enterprise* to prevent the destruction of the ship, sacrificing his own life to save those of his shipmates. Of course, thanks to the miracles of science fiction, Spock is reborn in the sequel. By *Star Trek IV* he is back to his normal, logical self. Questioned by his human mother, "Does the good of the many outweigh the good of the one?" Spock replies, "I would accept that as an axiom."[2] His mother then informs him that he is alive because the crew of the *Enterprise* violated that axiom. His shipmates risked their *many* lives to save *one* life—his.

In many senses, this question—Does the good of the many outweigh the good of the one?—is at the heart of ethics. **Ethics** is a system of principles of right and wrong that govern human conduct. Mr. Spock is governed by an ethical principle that is not too far from the philosophy of John Stuart Mill, who believed that one should always choose the action that maximizes happiness and minimizes unhappiness for the greatest number of people.[3] Ethical standards and practices should not be viewed as all-or-nothing propositions. In fact, there are degrees of ethical behavior, from highly ethical to totally unethical.[4]

In this chapter we treat ethics as an important concern of all participants in the public speaking transaction, speakers and audience members alike. The same standards that govern our everyday conduct are applicable to the public speaking transaction. In addition, because speakers can potentially influence a great many people, they have to face some special concerns. Thus, we begin this chapter with a review of some basic ethical questions. Next, we suggest a set of norms, or guidelines, for public speaking. We then focus on ethical issues faced by public speakers, including plagiarism. Finally, we discuss specific ethical obligations of both speakers and listeners.

BASIC ETHICAL QUESTIONS

As a speaker you will often be grappling with topics that involve ethical considerations: Why should you care about ethics? How will you adapt to differences in groups and cultures that have different standards of ethical conduct? Are there some universal principles that simply cannot be compromised? What constitutes the greatest good for the greatest number, and to what extent should some people be asked to sacrifice for the greater happiness? What are the situational constraints that impinge on your ethical decision making? What means are ethically acceptable in seeking to achieve ethical ends? These are some of the questions we address in this section.

Why Care About Ethics?

Perhaps the most basic ethical question of all is "Why care about ethics?" After all, why shouldn't everyone just look out for number one? There is, of course, no way that reading a book or enrolling in a class will make a person who doesn't care about ethics into Mother Teresa. However, we believe that most people are fundamentally ethical and seek to do the right thing. Ask yourself about your own motives. Have you ever sacrificed something you really wanted to help out someone less fortunate than yourself? Have you ever helped a friend through a difficult situation or talked someone out of harming him- or herself or others? If you have done any of these or countless other ethical things, you know the feeling that comes from doing what is right. The next question is, "How do ethical principles apply to the public speaking situation?" Our goal in this chapter is to help you answer that question. It doesn't mean we can give you pat answers for every situation. But we do hope to provide you with guidelines for "doing the right thing."

Is Everything Relative?

Ethical relativism is a philosophy based on the belief that there are no universal ethical principles. This theory goes back at least as far as the Sophists, who believed that truth was relative and depended on circumstances.[5]

The most radical version of relativism asserts that any one person's ethical standards are as good as the next person's. Although this philosophy has the advantage of simplicity, it makes a civilized society impossible. Life would be, essentially, a free-for-all. Even when a group of people holds such a radical view, the consequences for society are potentially disastrous. After all, the Nazis believed they were entitled to enslave and kill Jews and other "undesirables." No doubt the street gangs in many cities believe it is expedient but moral to shoot members of rival gangs. Whatever the rationale, an individual- or group-based ethics is untenable.

On the other hand, many people endorse **cultural relativism,** the notion that the criteria for ethical behavior in one culture should not necessarily be applied to other cultures. This was the position of the Sophist Protagoras, who argued that moral laws are based on the conventions of a given society.

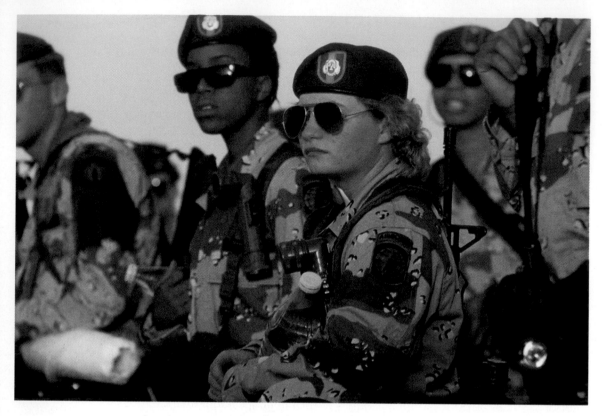

American women played an important role in Operation Desert Storm, which conflicted with the norms for women in Saudi culture.

Examples of such differences among cultures are easy to find. In Western cultures, for example, women are held to be, at least in principle, equal to men. In some other cultures, women are subservient to men; this is a fundamental ethical principle. Differences between two cultures were starkly apparent during the U.S. involvement in the Persian Gulf War in 1991. Female American officers often commanded male soldiers, something unthinkable in Saudi Arabia. Saudi women are not even allowed to drive cars, much less serve in the army or issue commands to men. By what right could either culture claim superiority over the other?

Similarly, there are cultural differences in ethical standards governing communication. One such difference involves the extent to which people should be explicit or "brutally honest" in certain situations. In collectivist cultures, "saving face" is important to the good of all society, so people are often indirect and may stretch the bounds of truthfulness in certain situations. To do either in an individualistic culture such as that of the United States could be regarded as unethical communication. Can either culture claim superiority over the routine communication practices of the other? Not really.

Cultural Relativism and Credit

It is sometimes surprising to speakers who come from a traditional Euro-American background that practices they take for granted as being acceptable are held to be morally wrong in other cultures. For example, taking out a loan for college expenses, a car, or a new wardrobe is routine for most Americans. However, those who practice the religion of Islam may find such practices morally unacceptable. As reporter Fahizah Alim explains in an article about a Sacramento, California, restaurant owner, Khaled Umbashi, many Muslims view the interest charged today by banks as *riba* (usury), which is forbidden by the Koran. Umbashi refuses to borrow money to improve or advertise his restaurant because "his Islamic religion forbids him from borrowing the funds and paying interest on that loan. . . . 'Our Islamic religion prohibits paying or charging compounded interest,' says Umbashi, a native of Libya."

Not all Muslims agree with this interpretation of the Koran. For example, Asghar Aboobaker, a Muslim who has written on the topic, holds that "this is a very complicated issue, and there are many, many camps." On the other hand, Irfan Ul Haq, a Muslim businessman, economist, and author, believes, "Much of the world's financial crisis has to do with the interest based system."

Thus, although most of those raised in a Western culture find nothing wrong with borrowing money, some Muslims consider such a practice not just unwise, but morally objectionable.

We make mention of this story because we have heard countless speeches on topics that involve credit or paying interest on a loan. We actually heard a student boast in a speech how he capitalized on the "bull market" by using money from student loans to purchase stock. This student emphasized that with a rate of return of 22 percent on one stock pick, he was making 14 percent on the $5,000 student loan on which he was being charged 8 percent interest.

Clever as our stock-wise student was, his ethics might be questioned by students in general. Certainly the Muslim students in his audience were given pause by his speech.

Knowing and respecting culturally diverse moral principles is often essential to your success in a culturally diverse society.

Source: Fahizah Alim, "No Credit: For Muslims, Asking for a Loan Is a Question of Religion," *Sacramento Bee*, 29 August 1998, Scene, 1, 3.

At the same time, there are limits to what most people will accept as culturally relative ethics. Even within a society, customs change over time as people reexamine their ethical values. Human sacrifice was once a routine part of some religions, yet no one today would consider such behavior ethical. Less than a century and a half ago, a significant number of Americans believed that slavery was ethical and gave their lives to defend the institution. A mere 50 years ago, during World War II, American citizens of Japanese ancestry were interned in "relocation" camps. And today, female infants are routinely killed or allowed to die in a number of countries around the world. What makes one culture or one time period ethically superior or inferior to other cultures or other times? Or is it all relative?

We need to be careful not to exaggerate cultural differences, however. Philosophy professor James Rachels, for example, points out that different cultures often agree on underlying principles but disagree on how they are to be applied. For example, he notes that even apparently inhumane practices, such as the Eskimos who once left the elderly to die in the snow, are grounded in the need of the family to survive in a harsh environment. Rachels argues that "the Eskimos' values are not all that different from our values. It is only that life forces upon them choices that we do not have to make."[6]

Are There Rules for Every Situation?

An alternative to ethical relativism is **universalism,** the philosophy that there are ethical standards that apply to all situations regardless of the individual, group, or culture. Immanuel Kant, an 18th-century philosopher, developed such a philosophy. He proposed the **categorical imperative:** *"Act only on that maxim through which you can at the same time will that it should become a universal law."*[7] To will the maxim be universally applicable means that you would want everyone to obey the same rule as you are proposing.

Suppose, for example, that you think it's acceptable for anybody to lie at any time, so you propose, as a universal rule, that lying is permissible for any reason. What would the result be? Lies would deceive no one, because lying had become the rule. Thus, a universal law that lying is permissible would in fact make lies ineffective. Consider voting as another example. You might think you don't need to vote, because your own vote doesn't make a difference. But imagine that as a universal rule: "Since individual votes don't matter, voting is unnecessary." If not voting were a universal rule, democracy would collapse. So Kant gives us a test for specific ethical rules. To be an ethical principle, a rule or maxim must be capable of being applied universally.

One of the most important ethical rules that Kant proposed relates directly to the public speaker. Kant proposed the maxim *"Act in such a way that you always treat humanity whether in your own person or in the person of any other, never simply as a means, but always at the same time as an end."*[8] One practical implication of this maxim is that speakers should treat audience members with respect, not simply as a means of achieving their goals. Conversely, audience members should respect and treat speakers as fellow human beings, not as objects of derision. Obviously, then, tactics that deceive or demean either an audience or a speaker would be unacceptable.

Kant's categorical imperative is not without drawbacks. Consider truth telling. If lying is unacceptable in any circumstance, innocent people may suffer as a consequence. Miep Gies, for example, lied to authorities throughout World War II to protect the Jews she was hiding from the Nazis, including a young girl named Anne Frank. And this isn't an isolated example. History is replete with cases demonstrating that it's sometimes better to bend the truth to fit the situation.

Of course, one can reformulate Kant's rule and say people shouldn't lie except under certain circumstances, such as when necessary to save lives. But that creates another problem: How do we know which actions fall under these conditions? Rachels points out a key problem with Kant's universalism: "For any action a person might contemplate, it is possible to specify more than one rule that he or she would be following; some of these rules will be 'universalizable' and some will not. . . . For we can always get around any such rule by describing our action in such a way that it does not fall under that rule but instead comes under a different one."[9] To examine your own principles, see the box "When Is It Acceptable to Lie?"

When Is It Acceptable to Lie?

Read the following scenarios carefully. Put a check mark next to the scenarios in which you think it would be acceptable to lie. Be prepared to present your responses in class and to discuss any differences between your responses and those of your classmates.

_____ 1. You know your best friend is cheating on a lover. The lover is suspicious and asks you, "Is Jane/Joe cheating on me?"

_____ 2. The person seated next to you during an exam appears to be copying your answers. As you turn your exam in, the instructor asks, "Was X copying from your exam?"

_____ 3. A casual friend misses several lectures in a class you both attend. He asks to borrow your notes to copy them. You don't want to hand over your hard work, but you also don't want to appear unsympathetic.

_____ 4. A person repeatedly asks you out on a date. You've run out of excuses, but to be honest about it, you find the person completely unattractive.

_____ 5. Your parents have always trusted you. Over a break from school they ask you whether you've experimented with marijuana. Even though you have used marijuana, you are of the opinion that what your parents don't know won't hurt them.

Does the Good of the Many Outweigh the Good of the Few?

Another ethical standard, utilitarianism, was proposed by English philosophers Jeremy Bentham, John Stuart Mill, and Henry Sidgwick. **Utilitarianism** is based on the principle that the aim of any action should be to provide the greatest amount of happiness for the greatest number of people. Much like Mr. Spock, these philosophers sought the greatest good for the greatest number. And they specifically defined the good as that which creates happiness—"not the agent's own greatest happiness, but the greatest amount of happiness altogether."[10]

This certainly is a useful standard for the public speaker. Most topics on which you will speak are about choices and trade-offs. If we trim social spending to fund a tax cut, some people will suffer while others will benefit. If we crack down on crime and build more prisons, there will be less money for schools and colleges. What constitutes the greatest good for the greatest number? As a speaker, you have an obligation to your audience to thoroughly research your subject to determine what position will ensure the greatest good and to put that greatest good ahead of mere personal gain. If you fail to fully inform your audience of the facts, if you lie to or deceive them, how can _they_ rationally decide what will promote the general good?

Utilitarianism, of course, has its critics. Many would say it promotes ethical relativism. After all, if the greatest good for the greatest number means that some minority of people are oppressed, would not utilitarianism justify that oppression? Could not a Hitler rationalize his extermination of the Jews in the name of the greater good for all of Germany? Certainly that is not what the utilitarians contemplated. But critics of utilitarianism have a point. Seeking the greatest happiness for all does not guarantee that particular individuals will not suffer unjustly.

If you think these issues are mere philosophical musings, think again. Consider the case of a newborn baby who suffers from a genetic abnormality that will cause its death in a short time. The parents want to donate the baby's organs to help other ill children. However, in the process of dying, the baby's organs will so deteriorate that they will not be usable for transplantation. The parents seek to have the baby's life support disconnected, but they are overruled by a judge. Here a utilitarian would have no difficulty justifying "pulling the plug." The baby is brain-dead and can enjoy no happiness. Several other babies can benefit from the transplantation of the organs. But those with other philosophical views might argue that all human life is sacred. They can claim that this is the first step on the road to disconnecting life support from viable infants to save the lives of others. These sorts of dilemmas have led to the emergence of a new field, known as biomedical ethics. Many hospitals now have review boards that deal with ethical dilemmas in medicine.

How Do Specific Situations Affect Ethical Principles?

Another approach to ethics is known as **situational ethics.** According to this philosophy, there are overriding ethical maxims, but sometimes it is necessary to set them aside in particular situations to fulfill a higher law or principle, such as love. As one writer put it, "What acts are right may depend on circumstances . . . but there is an absolute obligation to will whatever may on each occasion be right."[11]

Situational ethics is particularly useful in explaining how what appears to be the same kind of act can be ethical in one case and unethical in another. For example, most people agree that giving a speech in the classroom written by someone else is unethical. The principle that a student should do his or her own work is embedded in American education. At the same time, no one expects Jay Leno to write all of his own jokes or the president of the United States to write all of his own speeches. In those situations, everybody knows that Leno has comedy writers and the president has ghostwriters.

Critics of situational ethics argue that this is just relativism in another guise and thus provides no criteria for ethical judgment.[12] However, situationists do not mean we should abandon all ethical principles. As ethicist Joseph Fletcher writes: "The situationist enters into every decision-making situation fully armed with the ethical maxims of his community and its heritage, and he treats them with respect as illuminators of his problems. Just the same he is prepared in any situation to compromise them or set them aside *in the situation* if love seems better served by doing so."[13]

One problem with situational ethics, however, is that it would allow the use of unethical means to achieve ethical goals.[14] That brings us to our final question.

Do the Ends Justify the Means?

You may have heard the old saying "The ends don't justify the means." This means that it is not acceptable to do something wrong just because it will produce a good result. Of course, some people will use a good result as the justification for behavior normally considered immoral. But to do so raises serious ethical concerns. As a speaker you need to concern yourself with both ends (goals) and the means you use to achieve them.

In terms of ends, many of your topics are likely to be about issues of right and wrong, morality and immorality, the weighing of the good of the many against the good of the few. Understanding how people make ethical decisions is important to your choice of topic and the goals you seek. Obviously, the first and foremost ethical obligation of any speaker is to seek ethical ends, that is, to make sure you are striving to achieve a goal that is ethical and just. So, as you choose your topics, adapt to your audience, and seek to fulfill your goals as a speaker, you should always focus on accomplishing ethical ends.

Not only should your goals be ethically sound, but how you seek to reach those goals should also be ethical. Consider the example of a speaker who wants to raise money for a worthy cause, such as finding a cure for AIDS. Certainly the end is admirable. But suppose the speaker knows the audience is strongly homophobic and so tells them that the money will be used for cancer research. Does the end—raising money to fight AIDS—justify the means—lying about how the money will be spent? Would it not be a greater good to educate the audience about AIDS, letting them know that it is not just a disease that gay men get, rather than giving in to their phobia? Further, once you accept the premise that it's acceptable to lie to raise money for AIDS research, why not for the homeless, for the poor, or for communication majors at the local college? No matter what the goal, the ethical speaker uses ethical means to achieve his or her ends.

ETHICAL NORMS FOR PUBLIC SPEAKERS

Developing standards for ethical public speaking is not an easy task. Probably the closest thing to a code of conduct for public speakers is the National Communication Association's Credo for Free and Responsible Communication in a Democratic Society, reprinted in the following box "Codes of Conduct for Public Speaking." More than any specific code of conduct, however, ethical public speakers are guided by the traditional standards of rhetoric that date back over 2,000 years. As explained in Chapter 5, Sophists were known for their philosophical relativism. Some Sophists carried this philosophy to its logical extreme, arguing that virtually any rhetorical deception was justified if it furthered their cause.[15]

Such philosophical relativism ran counter to the philosophy of Socrates, who taught that absolute truth was knowable through a question-and-answer technique known as dialectic. Socrates' student Plato wrote two dialogues, the *Gorgias* and the *Phaedrus*, that expounded this Socratic view of rhetoric. To Plato, rhetoric, as practiced by the Sophists, was a sham, with no truth to it, designed to deceive

Codes of Conduct for Public Speaking

Although it is not a full-fledged ethical code, such as those found in law and medicine, the National Communication Association's Credo for Free and Responsible Communication in a Democratic Society forms an important touchstone for the ethical public speaker. Other guidelines that may be of help to the public speaker are found in the American Advertising Association's Code of Ethics, the Code of Ethics of the International Association of Business Communicators, and the Public Relations Society of America's Code of Professional Standards for the Practice of Public Relations.[1]

CREDO FOR FREE AND RESPONSIBLE COMMUNICATION IN A DEMOCRATIC SOCIETY[2]

Recognizing the essential place of free and responsible communication in a democratic society, and recognizing the distinction between the freedoms our legal system should respect and the responsibilities our education system should cultivate, we the members of the National Communication Association endorse the following statement of principles:

We believe that freedom of speech and assembly must hold a central position among American constitutional principles, and we express our determined support for the right of peaceful expression by any communicative means available.

We support the proposition that a free society can absorb with equanimity speech which exceeds the boundaries of generally accepted beliefs and mores; that much good and little harm can ensue if we err on the side of freedom, whereas much harm and little good may follow if we err on the side of suppression.

We criticize as misguided those who believe that the justice of their cause confers license to interfere physically and coercively with the speech of others, and we condemn intimidation, whether by powerful majorities or strident minorities, which attempts to restrict free expression.

We accept the responsibility of cultivating by precept and example, in our classrooms and in our communities, enlightened uses of communication; of developing in our students a respect for precision and accuracy in communication, and for reasoning based upon evidence and a judicious discrimination among values.

We encourage our students to accept the role of well-informed and articulate citizens, to defend the communication rights of those with whom they may disagree, and to expose abuses of the communication process.

We dedicate ourselves fully to these principles, confident in the belief that reason will ultimately prevail in a free marketplace of ideas.

[1]Richard L. Johannesen, *Ethics in Human Communication*, 4th ed. (Prospect Heights, Ill.: Waveland Press, 1996), chap. 10.
[2]Used by permission of the National Communication Association.

listeners. In the *Phaedrus*, Plato proposes an ideal rhetoric, one based on philosophical truths. The basic function of this rhetoric is to take the truth discovered through dialectic and energize it for the masses.

The best-known response to Plato came from his student Aristotle, whose *Rhetoric* is probably the most influential book on communication to this day. To Aristotle, rhetoric was not the opposite of dialectic but rather its counterpart. Aristotle did not view rhetoric as either moral or immoral. Rather, it was an art that could be put to both good and bad uses. The moral purpose of the speaker was the determining factor. Aristotle believed that "things that are true and things that are just have a natural tendency to prevail over their opposites."[16] Therefore, he stressed the importance of training in rhetoric. Even arguing both sides of a question was not immoral; rather, it was a way of learning how to refute someone who misstates the facts on the other side of an issue. For Aristotle, in sum, rhetoric was an art, not a sham.

In the 1st century A.D., the Roman orator and rhetorician Quintilian provided an ethical standard that many emulate to this day. To Quintilian, the ideal citizen-orator is a good person, speaking well. As he put it, "Oratory is the science of speaking well."[17] Further, because no one "can speak well who is not good,"[18] the moral quality of the speaker is not irrelevant. Rather, it is central to the ideal orator.

Today, the issue of ethical standards for public speaking has once again become a central concern for communication educators. What constitutes ethical communication? Most of us would agree that speakers should not lie or distort the truth. Beyond that, however, what are the moral obligations of speaker to audience and audience to speaker? Based on the work of the philosophers discussed, as well as several communication scholars, we suggest the following norms or guidelines for the public speaker: (1) Be truthful. (2) Show respect for the power of words. (3) Invoke participatory democracy. (4) Demonstrate tolerance for cultural diversity. (5) Treat people as ends, not means. (6) Provide good reasons. Let's look at each of these more closely.

Be Truthful

James Jaksa and Michael Pritchard of Western Michigan University have developed a set of ethical norms for speakers. Three of these seem particularly relevant to us. The first is the norm of truthfulness, which is fundamental to all communication.[19] The speaker caught in a lie loses his or her credibility and the goodwill of the audience, which are essential to belief. As former presidential spokesman Larry Speakes learned, the loss of credibility can be disastrous. After acknowledging in his 1988 book, *Speaking Out*, that he made up quotations and attributed them to President Reagan, he lost his prestigious position at Merrill Lynch. In retrospect he admitted, "It was wrong—wrong then and wrong now."[20]

Of course one does not have to tell an outright lie to deceive listeners. As we discuss in more detail in Chapter 14, distortions and omissions can sometimes be as harmful to the truth as outright lies. If you doubt that, we invite you to check out the "facts" in many political ads. Although most are based on a kernel of truth, often what's left out changes the whole meaning of the ad. We recall one political challenger who showed a video clip of the incumbent saying, "I'll do anything to get reelected." What the ad failed to mention was that the incumbent was playing the part of the challenger! The video clip was edited to reflect the exact opposite of the meaning intended by the incumbent. Of course the ad didn't lie outright—the words were actually said—but because the context was omitted, the result was the same as a lie.

A speaker who is unsure of the facts must learn the truth before speaking. Even a speaker who is simply misinformed, not consciously lying, can cause considerable harm. One of the authors heard a student speech based on the theory that AIDS is not caused by a virus but is a result of the homosexual lifestyle. That thesis flies in the face of every reputable medical study done on the disease. Documented cases of AIDS transmitted from mother to baby at birth or through blood transfusions clearly disprove the theory. Yet students in the class seemed to believe every word of the speech. Although a guest in the class, the author finally intervened and

Talks shows such as the "Jerry Springer Show" feed on the power of inflammatory language.

questioned some of the student's claims. Such misinformation, if believed, can have serious, even fatal consequences for audience members who come to believe they are immune to a lethal disease because they are heterosexual.

Show Respect for the Power of Words

Another norm cited by Jaksa and Pritchard is respect for the word.[21] The power of words is undeniable. Consider the reaction of people to certain emotionally laden words. Even words and usages that were once acceptable, such as referring to a woman as a "girl," or an African American man as "boy," have come to be viewed as sexist and racist. Emotionally charged words can cause severe damage.

Although freedom of speech is central to our democracy, the courts have recognized that there are limits. As Chief Justice of the Supreme Court Oliver Wendell Holmes, Jr., once said, freedom of speech does not give you the right to shout "fire!" in a crowded theater. Although Justice Holmes was speaking metaphorically, the principle he was expressing is as relevant to the current debate about speech codes as it was nearly a century ago. The fact that you can say almost anything that comes to mind in this country doesn't make the content of what you say either ethical or wise. The old saying "Sticks and stones can break my bones, but words can never hurt me" is incorrect. In fact, words are very powerful and can cause great harm as well as great good. The ethical speaker recognizes that words have consequences.

Invoke Participatory Democracy

Jaksa and Pritchard discuss the importance of participatory democracy, which rests on a foundation of choice and respect for people.[22] Citizens must have accurate and ample information in order to make informed choices. Further, the golden rule of treating others as we would have them treat us applies to public speaking as well as to interpersonal communication. Speakers should put themselves in the shoes of listeners and ask if they are treating them as they would like to be treated. The ethical speaker recognizes the audience as an equal participant in the communication transaction. Similarly, listeners need to show respect and tolerance for speakers, even if their views are different from their own. Shouting down a speaker, for example, infringes on the speaker's freedom of speech and the public's right to hear a full spectrum of viewpoints.

In other words, ethics in communication is a joint responsibility. For example, there have been many complaints in recent years about negative and deceptive political advertising. Yet political consultants say they are only giving the public what it wants. Although that is no ethical defense for their behavior, we must also realize that deceptive advertising succeeds only because voters fail to protest against it and continue to vote for candidates who engage in such practices.

Demonstrate Tolerance for Cultural Diversity

Clearly, what people regard as ethical or unethical depends a great deal on their culture and the set of beliefs that inhere in it. It is difficult for people to avoid using their own culture's ethical standards when judging the behavior of people in another culture. In North America, for example, we generally like people to be "up front" with us, that is, to communicate honestly and directly, even if we don't like the message. We generally don't want people to beat around the bush on matters we personally perceive as significant.

But what we call beating around the bush is the norm in many cultures around the world. Physicians, businesspeople, and even family members may be less than direct or forthright in their transactions with each other. In Japan, physicians and family members commonly hide the truth from a terminally ill patient. They believe that telling the truth in this case will undermine the power of the person's mind to intervene and perhaps divert the disease's course.

Some cultures, groups, and individuals are more tolerant of diversity than others. In general, Americans have historically been intolerant of behavior that runs counter to accepted norms. As our culture grows more diverse, this lack of tolerance becomes more apparent. Immigrants who accede to American norms are quickly assimilated. Those who don't are often singled out for disapproval. Think about this in terms of cultural relativism. Many of the cultural practices recent immigrants have brought with them are outside the bounds of what the majority of Americans regard as ethical. These cultural practices include religious rituals, food choices, and even dress.

Ethical speakers recognize that the customary criteria they use in making ethical judgments may be inappropriate in judging the behavior of people from other cultures. This tolerance guides ethical speakers in both interpreting and responding to the communication behaviors of those who are culturally dissimilar to them. Tolerance is not synonymous with unconditional approval, however. Ethical speakers may tolerate ethical norms with which they disagree, but they may also engage in constructive dialogue with the individuals who follow those norms.

Treat People as Ends, Not Means

To these principles we wish to add one taken from Kant, namely, that people should never be treated as mere means to an end. Their best interests should be the ends sought by the speaker. Using people as objects, manipulating them even to achieve desirable ends, is never justified. Consider the case of the *Jenny Jones Show*, a TV talk show. In 1994, Jones invited people to go on the air and meet their secret admirers. What the producers didn't tell these people, however, was that these secret admirers could be heterosexual, gay, or lesbian. You may recall the tragic results of this attempt to "entertain" the viewing audience. One guest discovered that his secret admirer was gay and later stalked and murdered the admirer.

Of course the guest's tragic overreaction was also unethical and far out of proportion to the deception perpetrated by Jones. Nevertheless, the television show was widely criticized as having gone too far. Embarrassing people on national TV as a means of simply building program ratings is clearly unethical.

Provide Good Reasons

Another principle of ethical speaking has been articulated by Karl Wallace, scholar and former president of the Speech Communication Association (now known as the National Communication Association). Wallace believes that the public speaker must offer his or her audience "good reasons" for believing, valuing, and acting.[23] **Good reasons** are statements, based on moral principles, offered in support of propositions concerning what we should believe or how we should act. Wallace believes that ethical and moral values, as well as relevant information, are the basic materials of rhetoric. Speakers who rely on "good reasons" value all people and the ethical principles to which they adhere. Not only does the use of good reasons help ensure that the speaker uses ethical means, it is also far more likely to be successful in accomplishing the ethical ends sought by the speaker.

SPECIAL ISSUES FOR SPEAKERS

As a public speaker, you face some special issues that might not be as relevant in other communication situations. A speech is a uniquely personal event. Unlike a written essay, for example, in which the author may be unknown to the reader, a speaker stands as one with his or her words. In fact, Aristotle said that character "may almost be called the most effective means of persuasion" possessed by a speaker.[24] Four important issues need to be addressed, therefore, because of their special significance for public speakers: (1) plagiarism and source attribution, (2) building goodwill and trustworthiness, (3) revealing or concealing true intentions, and (4) discussing both sides of a controversial issue.

Plagiarism and Source Attribution

Plagiarism—stealing the ideas of others and presenting them as your own—is highly unethical. What makes it a particular sin for speakers is that they are jeopardizing their most important asset—their character. Few students begin their speech assignment intending to plagiarize. But other pressing assignments, poor time management, sloppy note-taking, or just plain laziness often intervene. Students are tempted to use someone else's words or ideas without credit, assuming that no one will be the wiser. The consequences of such behavior can be severe. An example from the authors' own experience illustrates what can happen.

One of our teaching associates (we'll call him Jack) was ill and asked another TA (Jane) to cover his class. It happened that one of the students in Jack's class was the roommate of a student in Jane's. When Jane heard the same speech in Jack's class that she had heard earlier in the week in her own section, bells went off. Of course, it turned out that one roommate had appropriated the other student's speech. The plagiarizer was caught red-handed, but it didn't end there. The original speech writer was guilty of aiding and abetting the roommate. Both students had to face disciplinary action from the university as well as failure in the class.

Although it's true, of course, that this act might have gone undetected had Jack not become ill, this is not the only way plagiarism is discovered. At our university, and we suspect this is true at others as well, professors often talk about speeches they have heard in class. In fact, every speech at our university is recorded on videotape. Over the years, we have discovered several instances of plagiarism. Each time the students have been shocked and repentant. They have come to realize that they have put their college careers at risk for a few extra points on a speech. The negative consequences of plagiarism are not confined to students. Plagiarism can also destroy a career, as described in the following box "Truth or Consequences: Joseph Biden."

How can you avoid plagiarism? First, you need to recognize that there are varying degrees of the offense. Because plagiarism is a form of theft, we call these variations "the total rip-off," "the partial rip-off," and "the accidental rip-off."

The Total Rip-Off   The case of the roommates who used the same speech is an example of a total rip-off. Here a student simply gives someone else's speech. Usually it is not a speech from a published source, because such speeches don't often fulfill the assignment. Further, if the speech is well known, it is likely to be spotted instantly as a phony. More common is the use of a speech from a classmate who took the class in a previous term or who is in another section. This is clearly academic dishonesty equivalent to cheating on an exam or turning in someone else's term paper. Most universities and colleges suspend or even expel students caught in this sort of dishonesty. If the speech was knowingly given to the plagiarist, the original author can face the same penalties.

Avoiding this type of plagiarism is easy: Don't offer a speech or accept the speech of another person to present as your own. Most students who use other students' speeches do so out of desperation. Our advice is not to put off writing your speech until the last minute. Give yourself as much time to research and prepare as you would to write a paper for an English class. Realize also that giving a speech you don't really know is likely to be a disaster. You will stumble over words and be unable to answer questions. Even if you escape detection, you'll do yourself little good. If you simply cannot get a speech ready to deliver on time, talk to your instructor. Policies will vary, but your own speech, given late, even with a penalty, is far superior to a ripped-off speech given on time.

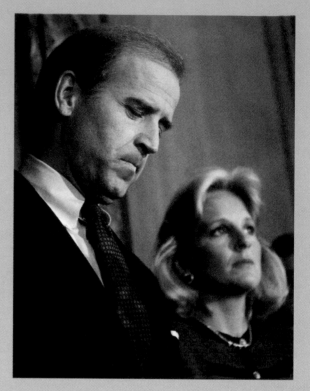
Truth or Consequences: Joseph Biden

Senator Joseph Biden was a leading contender for the Democratic nomination for president in 1988 when he spoke in Des Moines, Iowa, on August 29, 1987. Little did he know that his candidacy was about to unravel.

Biden had seen a videotape of Neil Kinnock, leader of Britain's Labour party, in which Kinnock asked: "Why am I the first Kinnock in a thousand generations to be able to get to university?" Pointing to his wife, he continued, "Why is Glenys the first woman in her family in a thousand generations to be able to get to university? Was it because all our predecessors were thick?" He concluded, "Does anybody really think that they didn't get what we had because they didn't have the talent or the strength or the endurance to the commitment? Of course not. It was because there was no platform on which they could stand."

Biden spoke almost the same words at an Iowa State Fair debate, without attribution: "Why is it that Joe Biden is the first in his family to ever go to a university? Why is it that my wife who is sitting over there in the audience is the first in her family ever to go to college? Is it because our fathers and mothers were not bright?" He concluded: "No, it's not because they weren't as smart. It's not because they didn't work hard. It's because they didn't have a platform on which to stand."

Those purloined words came back to haunt Biden. When newspapers reported the similarities and his political opponents began circulating videotapes comparing the two speeches, his fate was sealed. Soon other instances of Biden's borrowing words from politicians like Robert Kennedy and Hubert Humphrey came to light. Ultimately he was forced to end his quest for the presidency. Although Joseph Biden has remained in the Senate, his hopes for national office appear dead. And it all began when he lifted a few words from Neil Kinnock.

Source: Jack W. Germond and Jules Witcover, *Whose Broad Stripes and Bright Stars? The Trivial Pursuit of the Presidency 1988* (New York: Warner Brothers, 1989), 230–231.

The Partial Rip-Off   More common than the complete rip-off is the partial rip-off. Here a student creates a speech by patching together material from different sources. Rather than quoting the sources, the speaker presents the ideas as if they were original. The irony is that the speaker has done a lot of work. The problem was not that time ran out. Rather, the speaker wanted to be credited with the ideas.

The way to avoid this type of plagiarism is to give credit to your sources orally and to make sure that your speech is only *partially* made up of material from these sources. Rather than simply using the words of another, tell the audience who made the statement or where the idea originated. Interestingly, research has shown that under many circumstances, citing sources in your speech enhances your persuasiveness.[25] Audiences are impressed that you have done your homework. It is important to cite sources as you speak, not just in the bibliography of your written outline. Only by citing sources orally can you inform your audience of where the words, phrases, and ideas came from, which is what you need to do to build your credibility as a speaker.

Citing sources is important for direct quotations as well as for specific facts, statistics, and ideas derived from the work of others. Thus, you might not quote Martin Luther King, Jr., directly, but you would still refer to him as the author of the idea that people should be judged by their character, not their skin color.

The Accidental Rip-Off   Perhaps the most frustrating thing for an instructor who discovers a student's plagiarism is when the student simply doesn't understand what he or she has done wrong. For example, a student may take significant ideas or even quotes from sources listed in a bibliography accompanying the speech, without saying so in the speech. The student sees no problem, responding, "I did cite my sources—they are right there in the bibliography." For the listener, however, there is no way to know which ideas came from outside sources and which are the speaker's own, as mentioned in the previous section. A common variant of this is that the speaker attributes ideas to a source but actually uses a word-for-word quotation without making that clear to the audience. The written version of the speech outline should include quotation marks to distinguish between paraphrased ideas and direct quotations. Further, you should use "oral" quotation marks. Either state that you are quoting someone, or make it clear from your tone of voice that you are in fact quoting someone else's words. Use such phrases as "To quote Martin Luther King, Jr., . . ." or "As Martin Luther King, Jr., said. . . ."

Finally, be careful of letting ideas become disassociated from their source. We've all had the experience of remembering an idea or a quote but forgetting where we heard it. Unfortunately, the tendency in a speech is to just use the words. By taking careful notes as you research your speech, you are less likely to accidentally borrow an idea from another source without attribution.

Whether a full-scale rip-off, an incremental theft, or an accidental violation, plagiarism is a serious ethical offense for the public speaker. Our best advice is to resist the temptation, cite the sources of your ideas for your audience, and take pride in those ideas that are your own. In Chapter 7 we discuss how to record and cite sources in a speech. But the general principle is to let your audience know exactly where your ideas are coming from.

Building Goodwill and Trustworthiness

A speaker's credibility has several components. Two of the most important are goodwill and trustworthiness. **Goodwill** is the perception by the audience that a speaker cares about their needs and concerns. A speaker who truly cares about his or her audience's needs, and who can communicate that to the audience, not only is more likely to be effective but also is much more likely to behave ethically.

There is a huge difference, for example, between the speaker who is trying to put one over on the audience and one who really cares about the well-being of the audience. If speakers apply the principle developed by Kant of treating people as ends and not means to ends, then that is a mark of goodwill.

Trustworthiness is the perception by the audience that they can rely on a speaker's word. A promise made is as good as done. The effect of a broken promise or a revealed lie on a speaker's trustworthiness is devastating. In recent years, there has perhaps been no clearer example of the importance of telling the truth than President Clinton's problems following his categorical denial in January 1998 of having had "sexual relations with that woman, Monica Lewinsky." His subsequent televised admission of an improper relationship following his Grand Jury testimony fell short of an admission that he had lied, and was followed by numerous attempts at public contrition. Clinton ultimately became only the second president ever impeached in the history of the United States, based on allegations of perjury and obstruction of justice. One reason politicians in general are held in such low regard by the public is that so many of them have broken their promises and become untrustworthy in people's eyes.

As a speaker, you need to realize that you rarely can accomplish your purpose in one speech or even a short series of speeches. Often your goals will require a long-term commitment. And your relationship to your audience needs to be one of trustworthiness. If you violate their trust, not only have you behaved unethically, you have jeopardized your chances of achieving your goals as well. The solution to this problem is twofold. First, don't make promises you cannot or do not intend to keep. And second, if circumstances might require you to deviate from prior promises, make it clear what limits there are on your promise.

Revealing or Concealing Intentions

One of the thorniest issues you face as a speaker is whether or not to reveal your intentions to your audience. Sometimes, to begin your speech by announcing a position that you know your audience drastically opposes is to deny yourself the opportunity to be heard. On the other hand, to conceal your true intentions can be unethical, particularly if those intentions violate what the audience perceives as its best interests. In some ways, this decision requires the application of "situational ethics." Consider a couple of examples.

You are speaking to a potentially hostile audience about a controversial issue. Let's say you want to convince a group like the Moral Majority that we should not have state-sanctioned prayer in school. Should you begin by announcing your position? What is the likelihood that your argument would be heard? On the other hand, suppose you begin by describing a scenario in which the state requires everybody in school to study the Koran and pray to Allah. "How would you react?" you ask them. "Well, now reverse the situation," you continue. "What if Muslim students are required to study the Bible and say the Lord's Prayer?" The idea would be to work from a common ground—that Christians should not be forced to pray to a Muslim God—to the logical application of that principle to the issue of state-sanctioned school prayer.

Certainly this approach is no guarantee of persuading the audience of your viewpoint. But it is hard to argue that it is ethically wrong to begin with points of agreement before moving to areas of disagreement. The intentions of your speech are revealed to the audience. When and how those intentions are revealed is a strategic rather than an ethical issue.

On the other hand, consider the case of the person who knocks on your door and asks you if you would be willing to participate in a survey. Sure, you reply, always happy to help out. After going through a series of questions, you realize that the "pollster" is actually a salesperson for an encyclopedia company. Your time has been wasted, and now you have to figure out how to get the person to leave. The clear misrepresentation of intent—pollster as opposed to salesperson—is ethically wrong. And you have been harmed, if for no other reason than the salesperson stole your time. And, as many sellers know, once they get their foot in the door, the likelihood of closing the sale increases.

What makes these two cases different? Both people begin by concealing their intentions, and both eventually do reveal their goals. But in the first case, the speaker does not misrepresent his or her intentions; rather, they are deferred until after some common ground is established. In the second case, a direct misrepresentation is made—there is no poll. While the two cases seem on the surface to be similar, we would argue that the situations are far different and that that difference is ethically relevant.

These types of cases are not always easy or clear-cut. A universal rule—always state your purpose up front—cannot be applied. Speakers must sincerely ask themselves in what ways their interests and those of their audience intersect. They must then decide the best approach to take in any given case, at the same time striving to maintain goodwill and trustworthiness.

Discussing Both Sides of a Controversial Issue

One question with both ethical and practical implications is whether you should provide an audience with only your side of an issue or mention arguments on the other side of the issue as well. For a number of years, speech experts answered this question pragmatically: It depends on the makeup of your audience. If the general level of education in your audience is high school or less, stick to your side only. If the level of education in your audience is beyond high school, introduce the other side as well. Of course this raises some real ethical concerns. It smacks of using the audience as a means rather than treating them as ends. Basically, it says if you can fool enough of the people, no need to worry about fooling all of them.

The authors have never thought much of the recommendation to present only one's own side of an issue. What's more, we now have research on our side. This research, which combined the findings of more than 25 studies done over the past four decades, suggests that speakers should use a two-sided persuasive message regardless of the audience's level of education. Specifically, the most effective persuasive strategy is to present both sides of a controversial issue along with a refutation of the opposing point of view.[26] If you think about it, this makes good sense. Only someone living in a complete vacuum is not going to eventually hear the other side of the story. What does it do to the audience's perception of your credibility if they believe they've not been told the whole truth? Two-sided presentations are not only more ethical, they are also more effective. We discuss the issue of "message sidedness" in more detail in Chapter 13.

ETHICAL NORMS FOR LISTENERS

People who find themselves in the primary role of listeners also need to think about their ethical obligations. Remember, audience members are very much a party to the public speaking transaction. When you are a listener, you too bear some responsibility for the consequences of the speech. Thus, we suggest these norms for ethical listening: (1) Take responsibility for the choices you make. (2) Stay informed on the issues of the day. (3) Speak out when you are convinced that a speaker is misinforming or misleading people. (4) Be aware of your own biases.

Take Responsibility for Choices

The first guideline for listeners is to recognize that unless coerced, they are responsible for the choices they make during and following a communication transaction. This means listeners cannot blame a speaker for the decision to riot following a speech or for violating human rights because they were persuaded to do so by a charismatic communicator. Just as the judges at the Nuremberg trials following World War II concluded that "following orders" was not an excuse for war crimes, audience members cannot excuse their unethical behavior on the grounds that they were complying with a speaker's request.

Stay Informed

A second guideline, which logically follows from the first, is that listeners are responsible for keeping themselves informed on issues of the day. People who are uninformed about important topics and vital issues are easy prey for propagandists. History is replete with examples of people who have tried to attribute unethical behavior to ignorance, real or imagined. They range from the people who said they didn't know the Nazis were sending millions of Jews to their death during World War II to the tobacco company executives who claimed tobacco was not addictive. Simply put, ignorance is no excuse for unethical behavior.

Speak Out

The third guideline for listeners is related to the first two. It involves the audience members' ethical obligation to speak up when convinced that a speaker is misinforming or misleading people. Most of us have been in situations where we knew someone was bending the truth, leaving out pertinent details, or passing off another's ideas as original. Under some unique set of circumstances, keeping this knowledge to ourselves may be justified. In most circumstances, however,

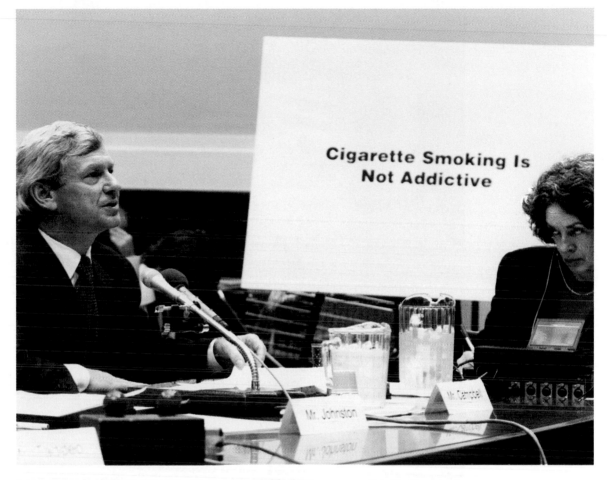

Ethics and economic profit are not always compatible, as the congressional testimony of tobacco industry executives clearly demonstrated.

listeners owe it to themselves and others to speak up. Speaking up can take the form of a question for the speaker following a presentation, asking the appropriate agency for equal time to speak, writing a letter to the editor of a newspaper or magazine, or confronting the speaker one on one. Whatever the appropriate medium, constructive objections are generally preferable to silence.

Be Aware of Biases

The final guideline for listeners concerns their subjective view and the manner in which it biases how they receive and process a speaker's message. Perception is colored by one's experiences, both real and vicarious. Rather than denying the fact, it's much healthier and realistic for us to admit this to ourselves. Only then can we determine how much of our reaction to a speech is based on its content and relational dynamic and how much is attributable to our individual biases.

Is it ethical to stand up in silent protest or to shout another speaker down?

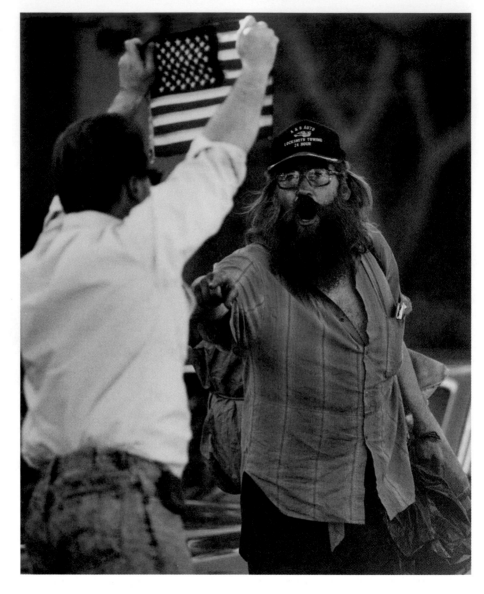

ETHICAL OBLIGATIONS OF SPEAKERS AND LISTENERS: A SUMMARY

Finally, having discussed the ethical principles underlying all human action, as well as norms specific to public speaking, the special issues faced by speakers, and ethical norms for listening, we offer a summary list of guidelines for both speakers and listeners.[27]

Ethical Guidelines for Speakers

- Provide truthful, relevant, and sufficient information to allow audience members to make informed choices.
- Present "good reasons," not just those that may work. Appeal to the best, not the worst, in people.
- Reinforce and be consistent with democratic processes. Recognize the importance of free speech in a democratic society and the right of others to disagree.
- Demonstrate goodwill and trustworthiness toward the audience.
- Put yourself in the position of the listeners and treat them with the same respect you would expect were the roles reversed.
- Recognize that both the means and the ends of a speech should be ethical. Be concerned with the possible consequences of accepting the message as well as with its truthfulness and accuracy.
- Take responsibility for your own work. Plagiarism is the ultimate in intellectual dishonesty.

Ethical Guidelines for Listeners

- Be aware that all communication is potentially influential and that there are consequences to accepting any message. Ask what influence the speaker is seeking to exert.
- Stay informed on important topics so that you can judge the accuracy of the communication provided by others. Be willing to independently confirm information that appears questionable.
- Be aware of your personal biases to reduce your susceptibility to appeals to prejudices. Be willing to listen to opposing views with an open mind.
- Be aware of deceptive communication ploys and work to expose those guilty of fallacious reasoning, propaganda ploys, and outright deception. Be willing to speak out in response to deceptive speech.
- Put yourself in the position of the speaker and treat him or her with the same respect you would expect were the roles reversed.
- Provide constructive feedback to the speaker if the opportunity is given.

SUMMARY

Several basic ethical questions are of concern to speakers: (1) Why care about *ethics?* Most people fundamentally want to do what is right and so turn to ethical guidelines, including those governing the public speaking transaction. (2) Is everything relative? *Ethical relativism* answers that there are no universal ethical principles. *Cultural relativism* is the notion that the criteria for ethical behavior in one culture should not be applied to other cultures. (3) Are there rules for every situation? *Universalism* answers that there are ethical standards that apply to all situations regardless of the individual, group, or culture. (4) Does the good of the many outweigh the good of the few? *Utilitarianism* answers that the aim of any action should be to provide the greatest amount of happiness for the greatest number of people. (5) How do specific situations affect ethics? *Situational ethics* answers that, though there are overriding ethical maxims, sometimes it is necessary to set them aside in particular situations to fulfill a higher law or principle. (6) Do the ends justify the means? The authors argue that speakers should seek ethical ends utilizing ethical means.

Although no codified system exists for speakers, useful guidelines can be found in the National Communication Association's Credo for Free and Responsible Communication in a Democratic Society. A series of ethical norms for public speaking can be derived from both traditional and contemporary sources. Among these norms are (1) be truthful, (2) show respect for the power of words, (3) invoke participatory democracy, (4) demonstrate tolerance for cultural diversity, (5) treat people as ends, not means, and (6) provide *good reasons*.

Public speakers face special issues: (1) *Plagiarism*, the stealing of the words or ideas of another, is considered a serious ethical violation. Audiences, at least in Western cultures, expect speakers to distinguish between their own ideas and those of others through proper source attribution. (2) Building *goodwill* and *trustworthiness* is essential to successful and ethical public speech. (3) Whether to reveal or conceal one's intentions can present an ethical as well as practical dilemma for speakers. (4) Giving a two-sided presentation, rather than concealing one side of the story, is both ethically sound and pragmatically more effective.

There are also important ethical norms for listeners. Listeners should (1) take responsibility for the choices they make, (2) stay informed on the issues of the day, (3) speak out when they are convinced that a speaker is misinforming or misleading people, and (4) be aware of their own biases.

Since public speaking is a transaction between speakers and an audience, both parties have ethical obligations.

Check Your Understanding: Exercises and Activities

1. In a brief speech or short paper, explain the reason you believe the best ethical standard for the public speaker is (a) relativism, (b) universalism, (c) utilitarianism, or (d) situational ethics. Define the version of ethics you endorse, and why you feel it is the best alternative for public speakers.

2. Read the following cases and answer the questions about each one. Depending on your instructor's directions, either write a short paper responding to one or more of the scenarios or discuss one or more of them in a small group.

    Case A: A student in your public speaking class presents a speech that contains glaring factual errors. As an audience member who is familiar with the topic, you realize that the speaker has not done research and has "made up" certain "facts." What should you do? What do you think the instructor should do?

Case B: You are preparing a speech arguing against a tuition increase at your college. In your research, you discover strong arguments against your position. Nevertheless, you still believe the tuition increase is a bad idea. Should you share the arguments against your position with your audience, or present only your side of the story?

Case C: You are required by your instructor to attend a speech outside of class time. You discover on arriving at the lecture hall that the speaker holds views precisely the opposite of your own. What should you do?

Case D: You are assigned by your teacher to speak for a position you fundamentally oppose on a question about which you hold strong moral beliefs, such as abortion. What should you do?

3. In a short paper, discuss the differences and similarities between the ethical obligations of speakers and listeners. As a speaker, how would you deal with listeners who are unwilling to meet their basic ethical obligations? As a listener, how would you respond to a speaker you felt was unethical?

4. In a short paper, discuss whether you agree with Quintilian that "no one can speak well who is not good." Cite some contemporary or historical examples to support your position.

5. In a short paper, consider the question of whether there can be any situation in which it is ethical to "shock people into action" through the use of especially horrifying or unpleasant images. Give examples to support your position.

6. In your view, what modern politician is most successful at eliciting feelings of goodwill and trustworthiness? Why do you think this person is successful in doing so? Be prepared to discuss your example in class.

7. Administrators, faculty, and students on campuses across the United States are trying to come up with speech codes that strike a balance between First Amendment rights and the right of people in the college community to be protected from hateful and demoralizing language. Working either on your own or in an instructor-assigned group, find out if your school has a speech code that prohibits the use of certain types of words and language. If it does, how would you amend it to fit your or your group's thinking? If it doesn't, what would you include in such a code? Write a short paper on your findings or thoughts, or be prepared to discuss them in class.

Notes

1. *Star Trek II: The Wrath of Khan* (Paramount Pictures, 1982).

2. *Star Trek IV: The Voyage Home* (Paramount Pictures, 1987).

3. Nina Rosenstand, *The Moral of the Story: An Introduction to Questions of Ethics and Human Nature* (Mountain View, Calif.: Mayfield, 1994), 100.

4. J. Vernon Jensen, "Ethical Tension Points in Whistleblowing," in *Ethics in Human Communication*, 3rd ed., ed. Richard L. Johannesen (Prospect Heights, Ill.: Waveland Press, 1990), 281.

5. Samuel Enoch Stumpf, *Socrates to Sartre: A History of Philosophy* (New York: McGraw-Hill, 1966), 35.

6. James Rachels, *The Elements of Moral Philosophy* (New York: Random House, 1986), 21.

7. Immanuel Kant, *Groundwork of the Metaphysics of Morals*, trans. H. J. Paton (New York: Harper & Row, 1964), 88.

8. Kant, *Groundwork of the Metaphysics of Morals*, 96.

9. Rachels, *Elements of Moral Philosophy*, 108–109.

10. John Stuart Mill, *Utilitarianism*, in *Essential Works of John Stuart Mill*, ed. Max Lerner (New York: Bantam Books, 1961), 198–199.

11. William Temple, *Nature, Man and God* (New York: Macmillan, 1934), 405, as cited in Joseph Fletcher, *Situation Ethics: The New Morality* (Philadelphia: Westminster Press, 1966), 27.

12. James A. Jaksa and Michael S. Pritchard, *Communication Ethics: Methods of Analysis*, 2nd ed. (Belmont, Calif.: Wadsworth, 1994), 21.

13. Fletcher, *Situation Ethics*, 26.

14. Fletcher, *Situation Ethics*, 121.

15. Stumpf, *Socrates to Sartre*, 36.

16. Aristotle, *Rhetoric*, trans. W. Rhys Roberts (New York: Modern Library, 1954), 22.

17. Quintilian, *Institutio Oratoria*, trans. H. E. Butler (Cambridge, Mass.: Harvard University Press, 1920), 317.

18. Quintilian, *Institutio Oratoria*, 315.

19. Jaksa and Pritchard, *Communication Ethics*, 65.

20. Larry Speakes, *Speaking Out: The Reagan Presidency From Inside the White House* (New York: Avon Books, 1988), 400.

21. Jaksa and Pritchard, *Communication Ethics*, 64.

22. Jaksa and Pritchard, *Communication Ethics*, 74.

23. Karl R. Wallace, "The Substance of Rhetoric: Good Reasons," *Quarterly Journal of Speech* 49 (1963): 239–249.

24. Aristotle, *Rhetoric*, 25.

25. James C. McCroskey, "A Summary of Experimental Research on the Effects of Evidence in Persuasive Communication," *Quarterly Journal of Speech* 55 (1969): 169–176.

26. Mike Allen, "Meta-Analysis Comparing the Persuasiveness of One-Sided and Two-Sided Messages," *Western Journal of Communication* 55 (1991): 390–404.

27. Several of these speaker and listener responsibilities are also derived from Sarah Trenholm, *Persuasion and Social Influence* (Englewood Cliffs, N.J.: Prentice Hall, 1989), 18–20.

Putting Theory
Into Practice

PART THREE

CHAPTER 7

Your classmates can
help you brainstorm
for topics.

Inventing Your Message

Genius is one percent inspiration and ninety-nine percent perspiration.

—THOMAS EDISON

OBJECTIVES

After reading this chapter, you should be able to:

- Explain the benefits of focusing on the audience when you choose an appropriate topic, formulate a specific purpose, and invent a speech.
- Recognize the types of support you can use for a speech.
- Conduct systematic library research to find support for a speech.
- Conduct a search of the Internet to find support for a speech.
- Conduct a meaningful interview with an expert on the topic of a speech.
- Prepare a bibliography for your speech using one of two academic styles (APA or MLA).
- Record information in a usable form for your speech.

KEY CONCEPTS

abstract	fact	online catalog
Boolean operators	index	primary sources
CD-ROM	Internet	research
chat lines	Internet service providers	secondary sources
description		statistics
e-mail	key term	usenet groups
example	narrative	Web browser
expert opinion	narrative fidelity	World Wide Web
explanation	narrative probability	

Thomas Edison understood the essence of his inventive genius. Although all great inventions begin with some spark of inspiration, they come to reality only through hard work. The same is true of speeches. Inspiration may get you started, but it won't see you through the home stretch. Hard work is necessary to create a speech out of an idea for a topic, a problem you want to solve, or a persuasive goal you want to accomplish.

VIDEO FILE

If you have access to the videotape that accompanies this book, view segment 5, which follows a student through the process of creating a speech.

This chapter is about the hard work that is essential to transforming thought into public speech. It looks at the process set into motion when your instructor first explains the nature of the speaking assignment you must complete. The specific topics we'll examine include focusing on the audience, topic, and specific purpose; supporting your speech with examples, facts, statistics, expert opinion, explanations, descriptions, and narratives; finding support, including library resources, the Internet, and interviews; and finally, preparing a bibliography and recording information.

FOCUSING ON YOUR AUDIENCE, TOPIC, AND SPECIFIC PURPOSE

As we discussed in Chapter 5, the rhetorical situation you face as a speaker includes your goals, the audience, and constraints. To successfully invent a speech that fulfills your goals, you need to understand whether your audience favors, opposes, or is undecided about your goals. You need to understand the diversity of your audience, including cultural, demographic, and individual differences. Understanding your audience does not mean simply telling them what they want to hear; it means knowing whether your basic message is likely to fall on receptive ears or to be tuned out.

In addition to an audience's attitude toward your topic, you need to consider their level of knowledge about and interest in the topic. If they already know most of what you are going to say, they are likely to think your speech is a waste of time. On the other hand, if the audience members know nothing about your topic, they may not be able to understand your speech. So you need to meet your audience's level of knowledge—presenting them with something new and worthwhile, yet not going beyond what they can absorb in a short period of time.

As you select your topic, do your research, and construct your speech, always keep your audience in mind. Focusing on the audience is the hallmark of the successful speaker.

As we discussed in Chapter 2, a good speech topic should be interesting to you, interesting to your audience, appropriate to the situation, appropriate to the time available, manageable, and worthwhile. Obviously, a thorough analysis of the rhetorical situation should help you meet these standards. Understanding the needs you share with your audience, the situation, the time available, and your resources should help you in determining a topic your audience is likely to find involving.

The question for many students, though, is "Where do I find the ideas for a speech topic?" As we discussed in Chapter 2, you may begin with your own knowledge or turn to the popular media, the Internet, or a number of other sources available to you.

In an introductory speech class, the *general* purpose of your speech—to inform, persuade, or entertain—probably will be assigned. What you will not be assigned is a *specific* purpose, which, as discussed in Chapter 2, is your goal or objective in speaking to a particular audience. If, for example, your general purpose is to persuade, your specific purpose might be "to persuade the audience to donate blood at the next campus blood drive."

SUPPORTING YOUR SPEECH

You may have decided on a topic and a specific purpose, but a speech involves more than your own opinion. You need to find ways to support the points you make in your speech. Possible types of support include examples, facts, statistics, expert opinion, explanations, descriptions, and narratives. The important thing to recognize is that not all forms of support are equal. Not all examples, for instance, carry equal impact.

Examples

An **example** is a specific instance that represents some larger class. Thus, you might cite a recycling program in your hometown as an example of how curbside recycling can work. The test of an example is whether it is actually representative of the larger category. To test whether an example is representative, ask the following questions:

- *What is the relevance of the example to the larger category?* If you are talking about products that are made from recycled material, then a cardboard box made from new materials, although it could be recycled by the consumer, is not relevant to your point.

- *Are there enough instances to support the generalization?* A few years ago, a disposable-diaper manufacturer ran an ad campaign claiming that its diapers could be turned into compost. However, according to a *Consumer Reports* article, only about a dozen cities had the capability to compost disposable diapers.[1] Thus, if you were listing products that can be set out for curbside recycling, disposable diapers wouldn't be a good example.

- *Is the example typical of the larger category?* One needs to be careful of isolated and atypical examples. Just because your roommate's PC is always crashing doesn't mean that all computers are unreliable.

- *Are there counterexamples that disprove the generalization?* A counterexample is an example that contradicts the generalization. Whereas several examples can only suggest the truth of a blanket generalization, even one example to the contrary can disprove it. If a speaker claims *all* American cars are unreliable, then pointing to just one car line—for example, the Saturn—as having been shown to be reliable disproves that generalization. If counterexamples exist, either the generalization is false or it needs to be reformulated to be less inclusive. Thus, a speaker might say, "Many American cars are unreliable," a generalization that one counterexample would not disprove.

Facts

A **fact** is something that is verifiable as true. It is a fact that there are 50 states in the United States. As former baseball-great Yogi Berra might say, "You can look it up." On the other hand, the statement that Texas is the best state in which to live is not a fact, though it may be widely believed by Texans.

A fact, of course, is only as good as the source of that fact. To evaluate a fact, ask the following questions:

- *Does the fact come from a reliable source?* Encyclopedias, almanacs, authoritative books, and scholarly articles are usually reliable. On the other hand, if the "fact" comes from someone who has a clear bias about the topic, you should be suspicious. For example, many Internet sites claim to contain facts, such as the existence of extraterrestrials or that there are "black helicopters" waiting to take over control of the United States. Just because you find something on the Internet, do not assume that it is true. Later in this chapter we will suggest some specific tests for Internet-based information.

- *Is the fact verifiable?* You should be suspicious of facts that are difficult to verify. For example, there are widely varying estimates of certain types of crime, such as rape. Part of the discrepancy is that many rapes go unreported. Thus, the number of reported rapes is multiplied by some factor assumed to represent the number of unreported rapes for every reported rape. However, these numbers are impossible to verify for the very reason that the unreported rapes are, by definition, unverifiable. Although these estimates may be useful, they are not "facts" in the sense of being verifiable.

- *Is the fact the most recent available?* Until recently, statistics about the federal budget showed a large annual deficit. Yet as this book is being written, the federal government is projecting a modest surplus for the coming years. A speech built around the existence of budget deficits would clearly be out of date in the current economic climate.

- *Is the fact consistent with other known facts?* Facts do not stand alone. You should be suspicious of alleged "facts" that seem to be inconsistent with other known facts. For example, many tobacco manufacturers claim that nicotine is not addictive. However, not only the surgeon general but anyone who has tried to give up smoking can tell you that such a "fact" is suspect. Double-check your sources for possible error. Be particularly careful with **secondary sources,** which rely on another source rather than gathering the information firsthand. It is always better to look at **primary sources,** which are the original sources of information, because there may be honest mistakes in transferring information from one source to another. Finally, keep in mind what facts your audience already knows. If your facts are inconsistent with what the audience believes to be true, you have to first convince them that yours are more reliable if you are to have any success.

Statistics

Statistics are numerical summaries of data, such as percentages, ratios, and averages, that are classified in a meaningful way. Statistics can be a rich source of information. Yet they also can be confusing and misleading. For example, an American automobile manufacturer announced a survey showing that its cars were preferred overwhelmingly to foreign cars. However, it turns out that the company included only 200 people in its survey, none of whom even owned a foreign car.[2]

We are constantly bombarded by statistics that seem authoritative but are of dubious value. Some questions to ask about statistics are the following:

- *Is the source of the statistics reliable and unbiased?* The tip-off to the problem with the survey on foreign versus American cars is that it was sponsored by an American car company. Statistics found on the Internet are often particularly suspect. On the other hand, statistics found in official sources, such as the *Statistical Abstract of the United States,* are less likely to be biased.

- *Were unbiased questions asked?* A poll asking whether disposable diapers should be banned was preceded by a statement that disposable diapers account for only 2 percent of trash in landfills. Not surprisingly, 84 percent of those polled felt disposable diapers should not be banned.[3]

- *Was the sample representative?* A representative sample is absolutely necessary for a statistic to be reliable and valid. A representative sample is one where the people who comprise the sample possess the same attributes as the people in the population from which the sample was drawn. Your speech class, for example, could be representative of the student body at your college. But unless your class was drawn randomly from the entire student body, we do not know for certain.

  There are many ways to obtain a representative sample, but the most common way is to randomly select people from the population in which you are interested: for example, college students between the ages of 18 and 25; all single mothers in the state; or members of your state bar association. Generally speaking, the larger the sample randomly drawn from a population, the more representative the sample.

  The complexities of statistical sampling are beyond the scope of this book, much less a single section of a single chapter. Still we want you to know that the value of any statistic depends on sampling. Thus, at a minimum, you should never accept a statistic at face value; demand from the source of the statistic information about the sample on which the statistic is based.

- *Is the statistic based on a poll?* Polls are statistically driven. A meaningful poll calls you, not the other way around. Based on sophisticated sampling techniques and random selection, a national poll can predict a presidential election with about a four-percentage-point margin of error. But when your local television station or newspaper conducts an "unscientific poll" in which people call in to record their views, the results are meaningless. Only people who are interested in the topic will call, and there is nothing to prevent someone from calling a hundred times. In short, such polls are worse than worthless, because they undermine confidence in legitimate polls.

- *Are the differences in the poll greater than the margin of error?* Good polling results state the margin of error. Keep in mind that the margin of error increases as the sample gets smaller. Whereas the margin of error for a sample of 1,067 people is about 3 percent, for 150 people the margin of error is about 8 percent.[4] Suppose a poll has a margin of error of 4 percent. Thus, if it shows a political candidate ahead of her opponent by 51 to 49 percent, she could be ahead by as much as 55 to 45 percent, or behind by 47 to 53 percent—or any number in between. Subgroups within a sample may have even greater margins of error than the larger group. For example,

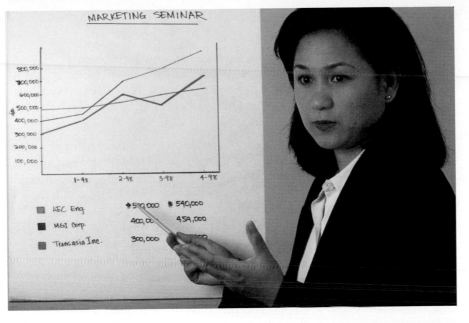

Using a visual aid helps your audience visualize statistics.

large-scale national polls on the Clarence Thomas and Anita Hill controversy showed that most people believed Thomas. An ABC–*Washington Post* poll showed 38 percent of women believed Thomas, whereas 28 percent believed Hill, a 10-point difference. However, the margin of error of this particular subgroup was reported as 12 percent![5]

- What are the percentages based on? There's been a 10-percent increase in the rate of inflation! Sounds pretty alarming, doesn't it? However, unless you know what the underlying rate of inflation is, this is a meaningless figure. Inflation rates are themselves a percentage. Say that inflation is running at 4 percent. That means what cost $100 last year now costs $104. A 10-percent increase in the rate of inflation means that it would cost $104.40—not too bad. On the other hand, a 10-percent rate of inflation means that what cost $100 a year ago now costs $110. Sound confusing? It is. The point is that you need to be sure of what percentages are based on before relying on them to prove a point.

- *What is meant by average?* One of the most frequently reported statistics is the average or mean. Although easily computed, the average or mean is often misleading because it is commonly distorted by numerical extremes.

  Consider a newspaper report that states the average salary for new college graduates is $30,000 a year. That doesn't mean a majority of college graduates are paid $30,000 a year. It simply means that when you add the salaries paid to all college graduates surveyed and divide that sum by the number of graduates in the sample, that's the mean (the arithmetic average) you get. The number likely has been distorted by graduates in engineering, computer science, and information systems management who, though few in number, start at salaries two to three times as much as their more numerous counterparts in the liberal arts and social sciences. The most telling statistic is always the median, which is the midpoint in a distribution of numbers. Knowing the median tells you that half of the numbers in the distribution are larger, and half are smaller. In Chapter 14, we discuss the mean and median in more detail.

This list of questions is not meant to discourage you from using statistics. They can be a powerful form of support. The key is to know what your statistics mean and how they were collected, and to avoid biased sources and questionable sampling techniques. Most important, you need to explain enough about the statistics to your audience so that they will have confidence in the claims you are using the statistics to support. In Chapter 11, we discuss the use of visual aids, which are particularly helpful in explaining statistics to an audience.

Expert Opinion

One very useful source of support is **expert opinion,** a quotation from someone with special credentials in the subject matter. Quotations from experts, whether gathered from a personal interview or from written sources, can be a persuasive way of supporting your points. However, you need to ask three basic questions about expert opinion:

- *What is the source's expertise?* How do you know this person is an expert? Look to biographical sources (such as *Who's Who*) if you do not know who the person is. Look for marks of expertise, such as academic credentials, official positions, or references from other authorities. Finally, make sure your source is an expert in the subject matter of your speech. It is important to explain to your audience why the person you are quoting is an expert they should believe.

- *Does the expert have a reputation for reliability?* How accurate have the expert's previous statements been? If someone has a record of either false or mistaken statements in the past, it is misguided to rely on that person's statements today. For example, many of the spokespeople who defended President Clinton's denial of an affair with Monica Lewinsky found themselves in a difficult position when, in August of 1998, Clinton admitted that he had misled the American people and in fact had had an improper relationship with the former intern.

- *Is the source unbiased?* If a source has a vested interest in one side of a topic, his or her opinions are automatically suspect. Your audience needs to be assured that you are not relying on sources who have an ax to grind.

Explanations

An **explanation** is an account, an interpretation, or a meaning given to something. Detailed explanations may prove useful in a speech. But to be effective, explanations must meet two tests:

Can you find words to accurately describe the beauty of Lake Tahoe?

- *Is the explanation clear?* A complex or unclear explanation may only confuse your audience. One way to clarify an explanation is to use comparisons and contrasts. Thus, someone might explain a nuclear power plant by comparing it to a tea kettle whose source of heat is a nuclear reaction.

- *Is the explanation accurate?* An explanation that is clear is not necessarily complete or correct. You must also make sure that your explanations are as complete and accurate as possible, given the limitations of a speech situation.

Descriptions

A **description** is a word picture of something. For example, you might describe a place you have visited or researched. Consider the following statement from a speech by one of our students, Chalsey Phariss (the entire speech is outlined for you in Chapter 8): "Imagine a place where the rivers are flowing, the sun is shining, and the fun is unlimited, where there is never a dull moment and the freedom of the outdoors will captivate your mind." This description leads into a speech about the "Lake of the Sky," Lake Tahoe.[6]

Descriptions should meet the following tests:

- *Is the description accurate?* Descriptions can be tested for accuracy by comparing them with the thing being described. Thus, for the Tahoe example, looking at pictures of the lake or actually visiting it would help to verify the description.

- *Is the description vivid?* To hold an audience's attention, you need to paint a word picture. Calling Lake Tahoe by its Indian name, "Lake of the Sky," is much more vivid than simply describing the blueness of the water. Photographs and other visual materials, which are discussed in Chapter 11, can sometimes supplement descriptions in a speech.

Narratives

A **narrative** is an extended story that is fully developed, with characters, scene, action, and plot. Narratives sometimes provide an effective way of driving home a point to an audience. An effective narrative builds gradually from the beginning, through conflict, to a climax. The conflict is then resolved, and the ending of the story often ties back into the beginning. For example, consider a story we all remember from childhood, "Little Red Riding Hood." In the beginning Little Red Riding Hood is simply off to deliver a basket of goodies to her grandma. Conflict develops when the girl is confronted by the wolf. The climax occurs at Grandma's house, when she asks the wolf in Grandma's clothes a series of questions and the wolf answers each by saying, "All the better to (hear, see, eat) you with, my dear." The resolution comes when the hunter arrives to rescue Little Red Riding Hood from the wolf. Finally, the story ends with the demise of the wolf and the freeing of Little Red Riding Hood. Often the ending of a narrative ties into the beginning. Little Red Riding Hood has learned a valuable lesson, as have the children who hear the story: Don't trust strangers.

Narratives can be more than a useful supporting tool for a speech; in some cultures, narrative is an organizing principle of speaking. The storyteller in North and Central American culture, for example, is revered. The authors were in the audience when actor-activist Edward James Olmos spoke at our university. His speech was largely a series of stories—about his career, his family, how people of different cultures can come to understand one another. Award-winning rhetorical scholar Walter Fisher has argued, in fact, that human beings are fundamentally storytellers. Fisher believes that reasoning is done in the form of narrative. Even if one doesn't accept his narrative paradigm, it is undoubtedly the case that a well-told story, real or fictional, can captivate an audience. Fisher claims that two basic tests apply to narrative reasoning:[7]

- *Does the narrative have probability?* **Narrative probability** is the internal coherence or believability of a narrative. Does a story make sense in and of itself? One of the hallmarks of the success of Academy Award–winning director James Cameron's movie *Titanic* was his attention to detail, in an effort to make the movie historically accurate.

Although many critics disagreed, The movie *Titanic* had both narrative probability and narrative fidelity to millions of movie-goers.

- *Does the narrative have fidelity?* **Narrative fidelity** is the degree to which a narrative rings true to real-life experience. Even if a story makes sense internally, it may not make sense in terms of the real world. Although many critics applauded *Titanic* writer/director James Cameron's historical accuracy, others pointed out that in 1912 it was highly unlikely that a steerage-class passenger like Jack Dawson would ever have met, let alone developed an intimate relationship with, a first-class passenger such as Rose. Of course, for millions of moviegoers, this relationship was completely believable, as they returned to view *Titanic* again and again, making it the highest grossing movie of all time.

When you tell a story to an audience, you should let them know if it is true or hypothetical. But either type of story needs to ring true to the audience's own experience if it is to have impact. Although we may enjoy hypothetical stories for their entertainment value, we don't find these narratives "real." For a speech to have impact, the narratives need to have probability and fidelity.

FINDING SUPPORT

Examples, facts, statistics, expert opinions, explanations, descriptions, and narratives constitute the supporting materials from which you will construct your speech. The process of gathering these supporting materials is called **research.** There are two basic steps to research. First there is the *search,* whereby you find the sources likely to contain information on your topic. Then there is the *research,* in which you examine these sources for materials you can use. Many people mistakenly rely on the first source they find on their topic, jotting down a few notes and then writing their speech. In other words, they skip to the *research* phase of the process before they have done a thorough search of information available on their topic. To avoid this mistake, which can lead to an incomplete and even deceptive speech, look for as many sources as you can before deciding about the materials on which you'll most rely.

There are innumerable sources from which to gather materials on a topic, including personal experience and knowledge, nonprint media, library resources, interviews, and the Internet. In this section we will focus on three of these sources: the library, the Internet, and interviews with experts. This does not mean that you shouldn't use personal experience or other sources of information. However, to build a well-supported speech, authoritative sources, such as those discussed in the following section, are essential.

The Library

Most research for your public speaking class will involve a trip to your campus or community library. The library is the intellectual center of most universities and colleges—the repository of the history of ideas and thought. Although campus libraries vary in their extensiveness and degree of sophistication, the basic principles of a library search are the same.

The first step in using your library is familiarization. Most campus libraries feature guided tours, handouts, and special seminars for groups interested in a particular area of research. Your instructor also may have your class take a library tour or send you on a library scavenger hunt to familiarize you with the library. Whatever you do, though, don't wait until you are facing a deadline before familiarizing yourself with your library. If you didn't do it during your first few weeks on campus, make it a priority now.

We recommend the following five steps when you do library research.

Tips and Tactics

Five Steps of Library Research

1. Select key terms.
2. Search the library catalog.
3. Search relevant indexes and abstracts.
4. Search computerized databases.
5. Consult reference books.

Although you may not need to use each step every time you do library research, it's useful to know about each step and how they are connected. Let's look at each step in detail.

Select Key Terms   A **key term** is a word or phrase used in library catalogs and indexes to identify a subject. Key terms are like the combination to a safe: If you have the right combination, you can easily open the door; without it, however, your chances of opening the door are slim. Thus, the most effective library search begins with a key term or terms on the topic of interest.

The basis of most university library card catalogs and indexes is the *Library of Congress Subject Headings*, which tells you what a term is used for and lists broader topics, related topics, and narrower topics. For example, if you are interested in the topic of "green marketing," which is the practice of companies' selling their products as environmentally friendly, you might look under the term *recycling*. The *Library of Congress Subject Headings* indicates that the processing of recyclables is found under the term *recycling*, whereas reclaiming and reuse of larger items is listed under *salvage*. Thus, you would begin your search for sources on "green marketing" with the term *recycling*.

Search the Library Catalog   Although some libraries still use a physical card catalog to list their book holdings, an increasing number use computerized online catalogs, which ease your task and allow you to construct more complex searches. An **online catalog** is a computerized listing of library holdings. Some libraries may require you to physically be in the building to search their online catalogs, whereas other catalogs may be accessible from a remote computer terminal or even through the Internet. Whether they use physical cards or a computerized system, library catalogs are built on the same principles.

Catalogs are arranged by subject, author, and title. Some online catalogs may also permit searching by call number or combining all categories in the search. Because you are just beginning a search on your topic, it is unlikely that you will know specific authors, titles, or call numbers. Thus, the subject heading is the most likely basis for your search.

You will have used the *Library of Congress Subject Headings* first, so you already know the key term(s) to search for. Let's continue to use the example of recycling. Using that term alone, you might find 80 or more publications. At this point, you could look through the list of books, noting the call numbers of the most likely sources. Titles may suggest whether the book would be directly relevant to your topic. Also, you would want to select the most recent books.

If you are using an online catalog, one additional advantage is that you can use what are called **Boolean operators.** These are terms, such as *and, or,* and *not,* used to narrow or broaden a computerized search of two or more related terms. For example, using the Boolean operator *or* to find books listed under either "recycling" or "landfills" might yield an additional 27 books. The Boolean operator *and* allows you to narrow the search to only those books that deal with certain aspects of recycling. For example, for the combination "recycling and plastics," there might be only two books dealing with both topics. Finally, you can limit your topic to books

FIGURE 7.1
Boolean Operators

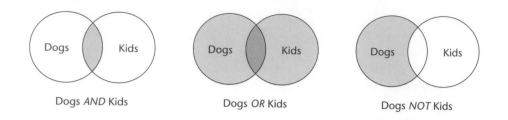

that do *not* deal with a certain topic. Using the Boolean operator *not*, you can find all the books that deal with recycling but not aluminum. Finally, you can also further limit your search by specifying items such as the year a book was published.[8] How Boolean operators can be used to broaden or narrow a search is shown in Figure 7.1.

As you can see, the online catalog provides increased capabilities to expand, limit, and speed up your search. Some online terminals are connected to printers so that you can print out the results of your search and use that to locate the books you need. If you cannot get a printed copy of your search, however, you should note the author, title, date, and call number of each source that appears promising. Simply going into the stacks with a series of call numbers can be confusing; you will soon forget which call number goes with which book.

When you visit the stacks, it is a good idea to do a little browsing as you find the specific books you have noted. Because books are shelved by subject, it is not unusual to find a book closely related to your topic that you overlooked in your search. This serendipitous search for information often turns up better sources than those you originally found.

One great advantage of going to books for information first is that the authors have done much of your work for you. Most books have a bibliography or footnotes that lead to other sources. Obviously, the more recent the books you read first, the more up-to-date their bibliographies. In many ways, a researcher is like a detective looking for clues. A good general book on a topic is like a room full of clues. The author will have left fingerprints all over the place. Follow the leads suggested by general books.

Search Relevant Indexes and Abstracts   An **index** is a listing of sources of information, usually in newspapers, journals, and magazines, alphabetically by topic. An **abstract** is a summary of an article or a report. There are numerous paper or "hard copy" indexes and abstracts that are commonly found in libraries. For example, the *Readers' Guide to Periodical Literature* is an old standby for those seeking articles in general interest magazines. In addition, every topic you can imagine is classified in one or more specialized indexes. A good library has hundreds or even thousands of indexes related to specialized fields. Some indexes both list and abstract articles in journals. On the topic of recycling, for example, a good place to look for information is *Environmental Abstracts*. In addition to abstracting articles from a variety of journals, conferences, and reports, it has a review of the year's key environmental events. In terms of recycling, there are specific listings for recycled products, such as rubber or plastic. Thus, if you were interested in the recycling of plastics, you would find numerous citations in this index.

Of course, not every library has every journal listed in any given index. Thus, you must compare the most promising articles in the index with your library's holding of journals. Some libraries provide listings of the journals they have. The card or online catalog may also list journals. You would look under title, for example, to see if your library had the journal *BioCycle*, which is listed in *Environmental Abstracts*. Even if your library does not have a particular journal, you may be able to use interlibrary loan services to obtain a copy if time permits. Also, some libraries subscribe to special services, such as Carl UnCover, which allow them to have copies of journals not held in their collections faxed to the library for users at a nominal charge.

Major newspapers, such as the *New York Times*, the *Wall Street Journal*, and the *Christian Science Monitor*, provide printed indexes that you need to consult before looking through reels of microfilm for newspaper articles on your topic. The computerized national *Newspaper Index* covers five national newspapers. If this index is available to you, it will make finding relevant newspaper articles much easier than using printed indexes. In addition, as we will soon explain, many newspapers are now available in electronic form and databases exist to help you find what you need.

Because we cannot list every index here that you would be likely to need and some we would list may not be available to you, the best strategy is to ask a reference librarian what indexes would be suitable for a given topic and where they are located. Make sure you have narrowed down your topic to something specific before going to the librarian. For instance, "I have a speech to give tomorrow on recycling, and I need some help" is less helpful than "I'm doing a speech on recycling, and I want to find out how much of our landfill space is being wasted because people don't recycle."

Search Computerized Databases At one time a computerized search for sources was prohibitively expensive. Fortunately, technology has progressed to the point where money is not the deciding factor in taking advantage of computerized databases. Many databases are now available on CD-ROMs. A **CD-ROM** is a compact disc–read only memory, used for storage and retrieval of data. CD-ROM technology has revolutionized computerized searches. Using the same technology as music compact discs, CD-ROMs store information in a compact disc–read only memory format. In addition, there are numerous online databases that can be searched. A couple of examples will indicate the potential of such searches.

A popular database for searching scholarly and professional journals in the social sciences, humanities, sciences, and communication is *Academic Search*. This database contains information on everything from astronomy to religion, law, psychology, and current events. Other databases include *Business Source*, which contains articles on finance, business, and related topics, and *PsycINFO*, which covers areas such as psychology, linguistics, social work, and other similar

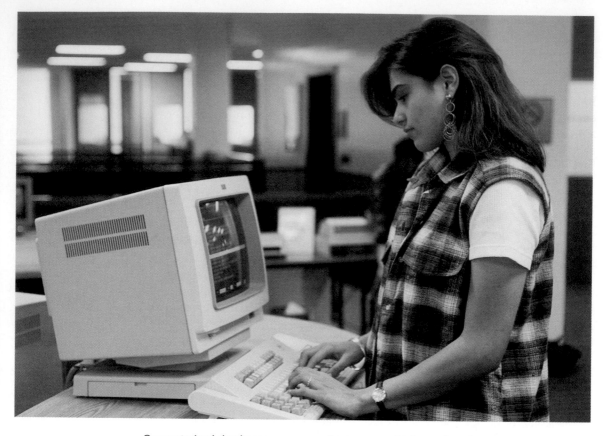

Computerized databases are an excellent source of information about your topic.

topics. Not only are citations and abstracts of articles available, but one may also find full texts for selected publications. To search these databases, you simply follow easy on-screen directions to enter appropriate search terms. These databases also enable you to search files that go back to the early 1980s and to conduct advanced searches by such categories as date, journal, or author's name. The same Boolean operators you would use in an online catalog search can be used with most computerized databases. When you enter your search, a list of citations will be produced and you will be able to mark the ones that interest you for viewing. Depending on your library's facilities, you may be able to print out, copy to a disk, or even e-mail the results of your search to yourself or a classmate.

Another powerful database is Lexis-Nexis, which is widely used in business, publishing, and law. Some universities and colleges have educational subscriptions that allow students to access Lexis-Nexis for academic purposes. (Commercial users pay substantial costs to do Lexis-Nexis searches.) The advantage to Lexis-Nexis is that it includes newspapers, magazines, scripts of televised public affairs programs, newswire reports (such as Reuters), and legal sources. The use of Lexis-Nexis requires some hands-on training, so we will not attempt to explain it here. But, as with other computer databases, by using Boolean operators, as well as limitations on dates, journals, and the like, one can find almost anything published on a given topic in major newspapers or magazines. Furthermore, Lexis-Nexis is a full-text service. It not only looks for the words you search for in titles or subject headings, but anywhere in the text. Thus, if you are looking for a report of a speech in which someone made a particularly memorable statement, you can use Lexis-Nexis to search for that specific phrase in any of the newspapers, magazines, or TV news reports that covered the speech. Unlike subject searches, when you do a search for a word in a text, you are going to get dozens to thousands of "hits" unless you carefully narrow your search. For example, former Clinton advisor George Stephanopolous commented that if you did a Nexis search for the phrase "the economy, stupid" during 1992, you would get thousands of hits. So a full-text database needs to be used judiciously.

Not all libraries have access to the same databases, so you should consult your reference librarian to learn about what is available at your library.

Consult Reference Books   Frequently you need to find a very specific fact—for example, how much plastic was produced in the United States in a certain year. You could search a dozen articles and never find that number. But a good reference book, such as the *Statistical Abstract of the United States*, puts that kind of information at your fingertips. In fact, frequently requested portions of the *Statistical Abstract* are available on the Internet.[9]

Perhaps you need a good quotation to begin or end your speech. Numerous books of quotations are available. In fact, because there are so many, a reference book called *Quotation Location* was written to help you find any of 900 published compilations of quotations.[10]

These are only two of the countless reference books to which you can turn in the effort to track down information. Numerous other reference books are found in most libraries. For example, almanacs and yearbooks, such as *The World Almanac and Book of Facts* and *Information Please Almanac*, are useful sources of statistics and facts. Digests of information, such as *Facts on File* and *Editorial Research Reports*, are useful sources for information on current issues. Biographies, such as the *Who's Who* series, help you find out about the qualifications of various sources. You should not overlook encyclopedias, which are often available on CD-ROM. Although the information in them is likely to be general and dated, encyclopedias can provide a useful source for your early search. There are even subject-specific encyclopedias, such as the *Encyclopedia of Associations*, which provides addresses and phone numbers of relevant groups. Atlases are valuable in learning about the world. By consulting an atlas, you can learn not only where a country is geographically but also important facts about it.

The Internet

One of the most exciting new developments for research is the **Internet**, a collection of computer networks connecting computers around the world. The Internet

Doonesbury

BY GARRY TRUDEAU

is like a highway in that it allows the user to travel electronically to almost any-where in the world. The access to information resources it provides is virtually lim-itless. In this section we give you a brief explanation of the Internet and its use. For a more detailed discussion, see John A. Courtright and Elizabeth M. Perse, *The Mayfield Quick Guide to the Internet for Communication Students,* available from Mayfield Publishers for adopters of this book.

Use of the Internet is increasing rapidly. A survey done by Nielsen Media Research for CommerceNet in 1995 reported that 1 in 6 Americans and Cana-dians over age 16 had access to the Internet.[11] In 1995, only 4 percent of adults used the Internet as a weekly source of news. By 1998 that number had soared to 20 percent.[12] The Internet is the means used to access the **World Wide Web,** a collection of thousands of sites where "server" computers can allow you to access text, graphics, audio, and even video on your "client" computer. Our experience as professors suggests that college students are increasingly using Internet re-sources in preparing their speeches. In the 21st century, there is little doubt that the Internet, or its successor, will be one of the principal resources for speakers in inventing their messages.

What's on the Internet? Among the most important resources for speakers are e-mail, chat lines, usenet groups, and the World Wide Web.[13] **E-mail** (elec-tronic mail) is a message sent from one computer, over the network, to one or more other computers. If you know the e-mail address of a source that interests you, contact that source directly. You can e-mail most government, education, and commercial institutions. Several of our advanced communication students have had success in e-mailing the authors of books or articles that interested them.

Chat lines are real-time discussions with other computer users on topics of common interest. Multiple users can participate simultaneously and respond to each other. Although not necessarily reliable as sources of factual information (unless the participants are experts in the field), chat lines can certainly help you get ideas for speech topics. Or you can bounce ideas off other people interested in the same topic.

Usenet groups are electronic "newsletters" to which subscribers can contribute. In the field of speech communication, for example, there are usenet groups for those interested in communication theory and research and those interested in academic debate, to name just two areas.

Finally, the most useful aspect of the Internet to speakers is the World Wide Web. Within each Web page there are connections to other sites, which can link to even more sites. Sites cover everything from sports to literature. For example, you can find the latest scores of your favorite sports or the entire text of some books on the Web. Even items such as atlases, encyclopedias, government publications, and much more may be available through your computer. In a sense, the Internet can be thought of as a "virtual library."

Connecting to the Internet How does the average person connect to the Internet? First, you need a computer. It does not have to be a particular brand; Windows, Macintosh, or other platforms will do. Second, you need to physically connect your computer to the Internet. Many colleges have computers in their labs or even in dorm rooms that are connected to a local area network, which will provide access to the Internet. Otherwise, you need a modem, a device that connects through ordinary telephone lines. The faster the modem (measured in what is called baud rate), the better. Recently, some cable TV providers have begun offering extremely fast Internet connections through the same cable that is used to receive television programs.

In order to use the Internet, you need to have an account on the network computer (called a server) that you are connected to, whether directly or by modem. Numerous **Internet service providers (ISP),** such as America Online as well as local companies, are commercially available to connect you to the Internet for a monthly fee. In addition to access to the Internet, these ISPs may offer news, entertainment, and advertising. A cheaper alternative for college students is often to obtain an account with the computer network at their college, which means they are using the college's computer system to connect to the Internet. Check this alternative before shelling out the money to join a commercial service. Even if you don't own a computer, most colleges have computer labs students can use for network access.

Finally, you will need a **Web browser,** a program that lets you search for and reach World Wide Web sites from a computer. Most computers come with a Web browser either as part of the operating system or as a separate program. The most widely used programs for searching the Web are Microsoft Internet Explorer and Netscape Navigator. These programs allow you to reach various Web sites with the click of a mouse. On the Web pages are links, which can be words or phrases or pictures. Selecting one will take you to another page, which may be a different site. Like a web, the sites are interconnected in almost infinite ways.

The actual use of the Web browser depends on the software that comes with your computer. For our examples, we will use Netscape Navigator, which is the most popular browser as of this writing (although Internet Explorer has been rapidly increasing its market share because it comes preloaded on most Windows-based machines). The basic layout of the Netscape browser is shown in Figure 7.2.

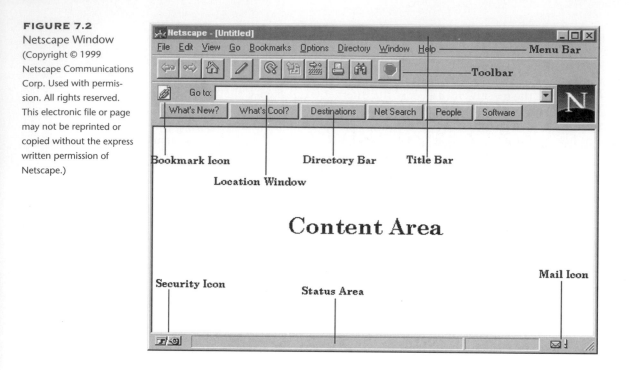

A detailed discussion of how to use the various components of the screen can be found in the *Mayfield Quick Guide to the Internet*. But the basics are pretty simple. To go to a site, you can either type in its address in the location window, or if you have previously saved the site as a Netscape "bookmark" or an Internet Explorer "favorite," you can use Bookmark or Favorites from the menu bar to select that site. One of the first things you'll want to do is to create bookmarks or favorites that will help you find the specific sites you need for your speech or research project. In the next section, we discuss some of the ways to do this.

Navigating the Web   Every Web site has an address, called the URL (Uniform Resource Locator). Most addresses begin with the letters "http://" (which tell you it uses a hypertext transfer protocol). Sometimes you can pretty well guess the rest of the address, called the "domain." For example, if you wanted to read the *New York Times* online, you would go to http://www.nytimes.com/, which is the URL for the newspaper's home page. The ".com" tells you it is a commercial site. To get past the home page, you'll need to actually subscribe to the online newspaper, which, as of this writing, is a free subscription. Other common endings for Web sites are ".edu" for educational, ".gov" for government, ".net" for network, and ".org" for organization. As we shall see later, knowing what type of a site you are visiting may be helpful in evaluating the validity of the information you obtain.

But how do you learn what Web sites exist? One source is friends, including those to whom you connect by e-mail. Usenets frequently provide lists of favorite Web sites. Many computer magazines and even general circulation magazines,

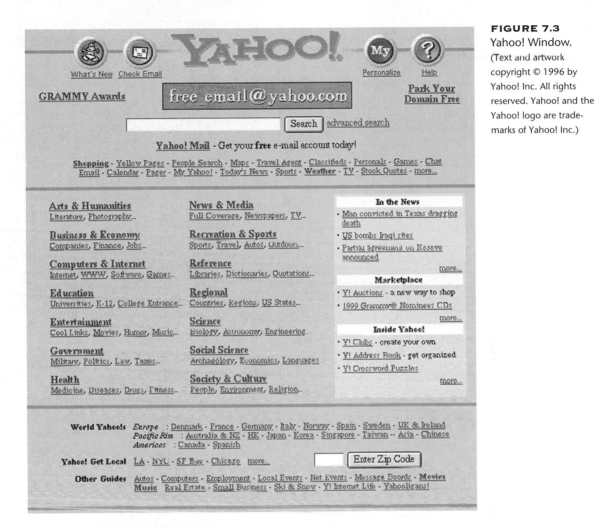

FIGURE 7.3
Yahoo! Window.
(Text and artwork copyright © 1996 by Yahoo! Inc. All rights reserved. Yahoo! and the Yahoo! logo are trademarks of Yahoo! Inc.)

such as *Newsweek*, devote sections to favorite Web sites. If you know the address, you can simply type it into the location window and hit Return (Enter).

However, if you know your subject, but don't have a specific site in mind, you'll want to use online information directories, such as Yahoo!, and search engines, such as Webcrawler. These are much like the library catalogs and online indexes we discussed earlier in this chapter. By entering key words or phrases and using Boolean operators, you can conduct a search for the information you need for your speech. First, we will discuss the use of an information directory, using the example of the popular Yahoo! program, and then the use of a search engine like Webcrawler.

The online information directory Yahoo! (http://www.yahoo.com/) is basically a collection of links to other directories of information. As shown in Figure 7.3 you can search by general subjects, such as arts and humanities, business and economy, and the like. The use of Yahoo! is relatively simple. Basically, you enter search terms in the box next to the Search button, and Yahoo! will locate sites that may be of help to you. However, be aware that broadly worded searches will yield far too much for you to use in a speech. You need to narrow the search down—using specific terms and Boolean logic.

Search engines like Webcrawler (http://www.webcrawler.com/) allow you to search for a specific string of characters (words, numbers, letters) in any of thousands of Web sites. Enter your search words in the box and click on the Search button and you will find a wealth of information. Again, your biggest problem will be narrowing your search. By clicking on the highlighted links you will be able to actually visit the Web sites that seem most promising for your topic. An even more comprehensive search engine is called MetaCrawler (http://www.metacrawler.com/), which actually searches other search engines.

Courtright and Perse suggest several hints on how to narrow your searches using search engines:[14]

- *Use phrases instead of words.* If you type in green marketing, you will get any Web site that contains either word. If you type "green marketing" in quotation marks, then your search will be narrowed to just that phrase.

- *Use specific, not general, words.* "Pollution" is a very general term. "Smog" is still rather broad. "Carbon monoxide" is much more specific.

- *Use Boolean operators like* not, and, *and or to narrow or broaden your search.* The same principles we discussed in library searches apply to Internet searches. *Not* will eliminate items you don't want included (for example, entering *pollution not oil* will exclude examples of oil spills). *And* will limit the search to sites with both terms (*oil and pollution* will only give sites that deal with both topics). *Or* (*pollution or oil*) will give you sites that refer to either term, thus broadening your search.

Keep in mind that computers are stupid beasts. They only look for the *exact* string of characters that you enter. If you misspell a word or use a different form of the word (*pollute* rather than *pollution*), you will often be disappointed in your search results. Always double-check your typing and the spelling of the words.

Saving What You Find   Suppose you conduct your search and have found a number of very good Web sites. Obviously you don't want to copy down the information on little note cards for use in your speech. How can you save what you have found? First, if you are using your own computer, be sure to make a bookmark (or "favorite" in Internet Explorer) to save the site on your browser (in Netscape Navigator this is done by pulling down the bookmark menu from the menu bar and selecting "add bookmark"). Second, you can often physically highlight and cut and paste information into your word processing program. Third, you can print up what you find, but that may leave you with reams of paper and undermine the very reason you want to search by computer—ease of manipulating the information. Fourth, some programs will allow you to e-mail either yourself or someone else the actual Web page as an attachment. Finally, Netscape allows you to save a Web page to your computer or a floppy disk (using the Save command under the File menu). Our recommendation is to save the results of your search electronically and only print out the things you know you need in hard copy. Once you've saved the material, particularly in your word processing program's format, it is easy to later incorporate material from your search into your speech outline. Of course, you will need to keep a full citation of where you found the information, so that it may be properly cited in the speech, a topic we will address later in this chapter.

This brief discussion of how to navigate the Web cannot substitute for actual hands-on practice. Well before you need information for a speech, you should go to a computer lab or log on to your Internet service provider and practice finding Web sites and downloading information.

Evaluating Internet Information   Unlike published books and articles, which are usually subject to editing, fact checking, and peer review, the Internet is unregulated. Anyone can say anything and, short of outright pornography, there's no government regulation. You must also be cautious with information gathered from the Internet because you have no assurance as to its reliability and verifiability. There have been instances of material being altered on the Net. As a speaker you have an ethical responsibility to ensure that such information is accurate, even if this requires tracking down the original source of the information. So, all the tests of supporting materials that apply to published materials apply doubly to computer information. Nevertheless, there is the advantage that because Internet-based information is unedited and uncensored, you can directly read the ideas of others, even controversial or unpopular ones that would never make it into print. In many ways the Internet is the ultimate marketplace of ideas. The following standards and criteria for electronic information are suggested by Courtright and Perse.[15]

- *Who is the source of the information?* Often the source of a Web site is not clear. For example, during the last presidential election, one of the authors found a site that *appeared* to belong to the Republican Party. However, one of his students pointed out that an official Republican Party site would end with .org (organization), whereas the site in question ended with .com (commercial). In other words, someone was masquerading as the Republican Party site. During the election some sites were designed to parody or spoof real sites. So, make sure you know who is the real source of the information. That source can then be subject to all the normal tests of evidence—bias, reliability, and the like.

- *Is the source primary or secondary?* If you go to the White House site, you can obtain primary reports of presidential speeches, proclamations, and important documents. A CNN report of a presidential speech, on the other hand, would be a secondary source. Whenever possible, primary sources are preferable. One of the great advantages of the Internet is

Cultures on the Web

One of the great advantages of the Internet is that it is a global phenomenon. You can literally read newspapers from anywhere in the world. You can send e-mail to and receive it from people on the other side of the globe. In fact, Dr. Madeline Keaveney, a professor at our university, established an e-mail pen-pal program with students in Japan for her intercultural communication class. The possibilities of learning about other cultures and sharing information with people from these cultures is endless.

There are Web sites that deal with Native American, Latino, Asian, and African American cultures.

Any list of these sites would be incomplete and highly selective. Rather, we suggest that you do your own Internet surfing to learn about other cultures and then incorporate that information into your next speech. For starters, we suggest you try Yahoo!, which has numerous links dealing with society and culture (http://www.yahoo.com/Society_and_Culture/). For example, you can learn how different cultures deal with topics such as death and dying, disabilities, families, fashion, food and drink, gender, holidays, mythology and folklore, religion, sexuality, and weddings, just to name a few. So go ahead, reach out globally—from your own computer!

that the average person can visit the sites of almost any organization imaginable, and thus obtain primary information that was previously only available by writing or calling the source—and hoping they would provide the needed material in time for your speech.

- *How old is the information?* Web sites usually have a line at the bottom of the page stating when they were last updated. If a site has not changed in several months, chances are the information is out of date. Furthermore, be very cautious of listings of Web sites found in published books. It often takes close to a year from the date an author writes a book until it is edited, typeset, printed, and distributed. Thus, we have avoided providing extensive lists of Web sites in this book. Those mentioned are well-established government or commercial sites. Many students have been frustrated by trying to find Web sites based on what is in a book. Instead, rely on search engines and Web directories to help you find the appropriate sites for your research. Then pay careful attention to when the site was last updated before using information from it.

Interviews

We put off discussing interviews until now for a reason. Far too often students go into an interview before researching their topic. In a sense, they expect the expert they interview to write their speech for them. Although interviews with experts can offer useful information and may lead you to other sources of information, they cannot substitute for doing your own research. Thus, an interview should be conducted only after you've been to the library and searched the Internet so that you will have done the research necessary to ask the interviewee intelligent questions.

Finding potential interviewees on most topics is not as difficult as you may think. On the topic of recycling, you may be able to arrange an interview with the director of a local recycling center. Community leaders, including members of the city council, also may have information on topics such as recycling, traffic congestion, parking, and growth. At a university, most departments have experts on various topics. Often a call to the department asking if there is anyone familiar with your specific topic will elicit a name. In other cases, you may simply want to consult a department's course offerings. Someone who teaches a class on ecology, for example, most likely is an expert in that subject.

Another strategy is to contact organizations that are related to your topic and ask if someone there would be available to interview. For example, if you are researching the effects of secondhand smoke, the American Lung Association is a likely source of potential interviewees.

Sometimes you may already know a person who can help you. We recall the case of one student who was speaking about a "miracle" weight-loss product. After calling the company's home office and getting the runaround, she contacted her local pharmacist. He informed her that the ingredients in the product were in no way capable of helping a person lose weight—in fact, they were potentially harmful. A brief interview with the pharmacist gave her information she would have had great difficulty finding on her own.

Once you have decided on a person you would like to interview, the following basic guidelines for before, during, and after the interview should help you proceed. For additional advice, read the following box, "The Importance of Interviewing: Professor Rick Rigsby."

Before the Interview

- Contact the potential interviewee well in advance. Explain why you want to meet and how much time you think you'll need. If the person agrees to be interviewed, ask for a convenient time and place for a meeting (usually at the interviewee's place of business). If possible, confirm your appointment in writing. Verify where and when you will meet and how much time you have to spend, which will guide you both in formulating questions and in ascertaining the number of questions you can reasonably pursue.

- Do some general reading on your topic. Read at least a book or two and some recent articles or visit relevant Web sites. This will give you a basis for framing your questions and allow you to concentrate on those things you cannot easily find out for yourself.

- Prepare specific questions in advance. You should attempt to ask open-ended questions, which will allow the interviewee an opportunity to talk at some length. Of course, be prepared to deviate from your question as answers suggest other avenues to follow. But at least you know you won't be wasting time trying to come up with questions on the spot.

The Importance of Interviewing: Professor Rick Rigsby

Dr. Enrique D. "Rick" Rigsby teaches speech communication at Texas A&M University in College Station, Texas. He also serves as a mentor for A & M athletes and is in great demand as a motivational speaker. Before becoming a teacher, he was a television news reporter for 7 years. Not only did Rick use the interview as a principal technique in television reporting, he continues to conduct interviews as part of his research, as he explains below. We asked Rick to explain the importance of interviewing to students of public speaking.

To appreciate the role interviewing performs, one must understand that we humans tend to be storytelling animals. Everyone has a history filled with commendations, successes, and struggles. These stories are marked by significant dates and may include a supporting cast of characters. The stories develop in basements and ballparks, departments and dormitories. We experience life, record dramas, and share the stories when called upon. Thus, our stories contribute to newscasts, government reports, research projects, even speeches in communication classes!

For the college student preparing a speech, interviewing someone with expertise on the subject might produce insights other sources cannot generate. Make sure to avoid this one pitfall: Refrain from interviewing the person most available. Rather, carefully select the individual who will enhance your work. A simple question to ask yourself is "Will the interview I conduct enlighten the audience about the subject and increase my credibility as a speaker?"

I have used the medium of interviewing in both my collegiate and professional careers. When I was a speech communication major in college, interviewing individuals for speeches allowed me to use real-life adventure to help inform, persuade, or entertain my audience. As a television news reporter, I interviewed thousands of people in a variety of situations. Imagine talking to a person who has just won the lottery or thrown the winning touchdown pass! Getting the right interview can make the difference between a presentation that few hear or a speech that few will ever

forget. I continue to use interviewing today. A large part of my job as a college professor is to conduct research. My research focuses on volunteers who participated in the civil rights demonstrations of the sixties. An essential part of my research task is to interview those former protesters and document their stories.

If your future includes the preparation of a presentation, you would be well advised to consider the medium of interviewing as a way of obtaining information. Remember, we're a storytelling culture. But what good is a story if it's never told? You know, interviewing a subject as a part of your speech preparation could make the difference between a mediocre speech and a memorable oration. But don't take my word for it . . . go interview your speech prof!

During the Interview

- Show up on time, dressed professionally, and ready to begin. Introduce yourself and explain how you will use the interview in your speech. If you are planning to tape-record the interview, be sure to ask for permission. If an interview is by phone, you have a legal obligation to inform and gain consent from the other party if you are planning to tape the conversation.

- Using what you've learned about your topic as a guide, begin with general questions and then move to specific ones. Be sure to let the interviewee talk. Don't monopolize the conversation; doing so defeats the purpose of the interview.

- Ask the interviewee if he or she can suggest other sources of information—books, pamphlets, periodicals, or other experts. Often an expert will lead you to sources you never would have thought of yourself. If you are lucky, your interviewee may even loan you some relevant journals or other publications.

- Use the active listening skills discussed in Chapter 4, especially setting goals, blocking out distracting stimuli, suspending judgment, being sensitive to metacommunication, and using paraphrasing and questioning.

- Either tape-record (with permission) or take complete notes during the interview. If you do not get something down, ask a follow-up question to make sure you get the essential points on paper. If you want to use quotes from the interview in your speech, make sure they are accurate.

- When your time is about up, ask the interviewee if there is anything he or she can add to what has been said. Perhaps there is some area you have completely overlooked.

- Thank the interviewee for his or her time and exit graciously.

After the Interview

- A follow-up thank-you letter is common courtesy and may help you get subsequent interviews.

- Transcribe your tape or your notes while the interview is fresh in your mind. Notes that may have been clear at the moment will quickly fade from memory unless you flesh them out soon after the interview.

- Follow up on leads or other interviews suggested by your interviewee.

Interviews not only can provide a rich source of information but also can add credibility to your speaking. The fact that you have taken the time to speak directly to an expert shows your concern for your audience. Further, your own expertise is enhanced by virtue of the interview. And if you use the interview in presenting your speech, be sure to let your audience know why your interviewee is a credible source on your topic.

USING YOUR RESEARCH

Preparing a Bibliography

Before beginning in-depth reading on a topic, you should prepare a preliminary bibliography of the sources you have found. You might, for example, find 20 sources on recycling that look like they will be relevant. Using either your computer word processor or small note cards (4 by 6 inches is a good size) list the following information about each source:

> *For all sources:* author(s), preferably by full name, if an author is listed
>
> *For books:* the exact title and the following facts of publication: location, publisher, and date
>
> *For periodicals:* the article title, periodical title, volume number, date, and pages
>
> *For government documents:* the agency issuing the document, as well as the document's full title, date, and publication information
>
> *For electronic resources:* author, title, publication information, the e-mail address, Web site, or path by which the material was located and the date you found it

Leave space to add additional information to each citation as you read the source.

Because you will need all of this information for your formal speech outline, it is better to list it as you compile it, rather than having to go back to find it later. At the end of this chapter we provide samples of how to correctly cite sources according to the systems developed by the American Psychological Association (APA) and the Modern Language Association (MLA). If you use a computer word processor to prepare your bibliography, you will be able to edit and sort it as necessary for your final speech outline. If you use note cards, it is important to put only one source on each card, because you will need to shuffle their order to obtain an alphabetical listing for the final outline. If you need more space than one card provides for recording the information that you read, give each source a code number or a short title to use on additional cards for the same source.

Recording Information

As you gather materials, carefully record the facts and quotations you discover. It is important to note not only the substance of what was said but also who said it and where. Documenting such information will build your credibility with your audience and enhance your overall effectiveness as a speaker.

If you are doing a computerized search, such as on the Internet, you may be able to download information directly into a computer. For example, transcripts of CNN programs can be found by going to the network's Web site; then follow the instructions of your Web browser for downloading files.[16] Although this technique makes for ease in writing your speech, it does not relieve you from the task of reading and absorbing the material; you will be able to cite or quote only a small portion of the material in a given speech. With this approach, though, you may be able to literally cut and paste quotations from your sources into your own computer files. These can later be edited and incorporated into your speech with proper citation. But if you are using print books or articles, interviews, and the like, you will need to first write the important facts, examples, quotations, and statistics on note cards for easy sorting. Cards need to be large enough to accommodate the information, yet small enough so that you won't be tempted to put more than one fact on each card. The advantage of this technique is that you can organize cards in any way that seems logical when you begin writing your speech.

Another strategy is to photocopy pages from articles or books that seem particularly useful. Then use a highlighter or marker to identify those things you may wish to use in the speech. At this point, cut out the quotations you plan to use and paste or tape them to cards. Again, be sure to note the source and page number on each card. The advantages of this technique over copying information onto note cards are twofold. First, it saves time. Second, it ensures that you will accurately quote the source; handwritten notes can be hard to read or even inaccurate.

Finally, if you have access to a scanner, you may be able to scan articles into computer files and then process them as if you had accessed them from a computerized source directly.

SUMMARY

The process of inventing your speech is like the process of inventing a new product: You need both a source of inspiration and the willingness to engage in hard work.

You begin by analyzing the rhetorical situation and focusing on your audience, choosing an appropriate topic and a specific purpose you wish to accomplish.

Many types of support are effective in speeches. Look for examples, facts, statistics, expert opinion, explanations, descriptions, and narratives to support your specific purpose.

It is important to evaluate supporting material. Ask yourself, are *examples* relevant, of sufficient quantity, and typical, and are there no counterexamples? Are the *facts* from a reliable source, can they be verified, are they the most recent, and are they consistent with other known facts? Are *statistics* from a reliable and unbiased source, were fair questions asked in gathering the data, is the sample representative, do the statistics rely on a poll, and if so, are the differences in the poll greater than the margin of error? What are the percentages based on? Is the average or mean cited exclusively?

Expert opinion depends on the source's expertise, reliability, and lack of bias for its authority. *Explanations* should be clear and accurate. *Descriptions* should be accurate and vivid. Finally, *narratives* must have *probability* (coherence) and *fidelity* to the real world.

Before you can gather the materials for your speech, you need to search for them. Possible sources of information for your speech include library resources, the *Internet*, and interviews. Once you have completed your "search" for sources, you need to *research* the topic, which involves examining the sources you've found for materials you can actually use. Develop a recording system for both sources and data: Download computerized sources, copy information on note cards, use selective photocopying to record information, or scan information directly into your computer.

Check Your Understanding: Exercises and Activities

1. Check your understanding of the American Psychological Association and Modern Language Association guidelines for source citations on pages 196–200. Provide a correct source citation for each of the following hypothetical sources, using both APA and MLA guidelines:

   A book with one author named Jack Smith, titled College Life, published in New York by University Press in 1995. How would your citation change if Smith were the editor of the book? How would you list a second author, John Q. Doe? How would you list a third author, Mary A. Smith?

   An article titled Dorm Life in American Universities, by Peter Chu, published in the scholarly journal Universities and Colleges, volume 31, December 1995, pages 24–56.

   A chapter by Jose Sanchez titled The Nine Lives Myth, appearing on pages 99–109 in the book Cat Stories, edited by Morris T. Katt, published by Feline Press in San Francisco, California, in 1995.

   An article in Canine Magazine titled Snoopy and Me, by Charlie Brown, pages 56–57, on December 14, 1995, in volume 42. How would you list the article if no author were named?

2. A speaker arguing that we should buy American products presents the following example: "I purchased a Japanese car last year. Since I purchased it, I have had nothing but trouble. I think this proves that you should buy American!" Compare this example with the tests of examples discussed in this chapter. Which of the tests does it fail to meet?

3. *Worksheet for speech topic choice.* One way to select an appropriate speech topic is to begin with an inventory of your own interests and those of your listeners as revealed by their self-introductions in class. Under each of the following headings, list at least three things that are important to you and to your audience.

	My interests	Audience interests
Hobbies	_____	_____
	_____	_____
	_____	_____
School	_____	_____
	_____	_____
Work	_____	_____
	_____	_____
Goals	_____	_____
	_____	_____

Situational factors _____

Nature of assignment _____

Time available _____   _____

List of three possible topics _____

_____

_____

4. How would you go about verifying the "fact" that the leading causes of death in the United States are heart disease, cancer, and infectious diseases? What sources would you consult? Are these in fact the three leading causes of death?

5. Obtain a recent poll (one that appears in an article in, for example, *USA Today* or *Newsweek*). Does the poll meet the tests of statistical evidence outlined in this chapter? How large was the sample, and what was the margin of error? Did differences in the poll exceed the margin of error? What, if anything, does the article on the poll not tell you that you need to know to properly test the statistics in the poll?

6. How would you go about determining on what subject Arthur L. Schawlow and Charles H. Townes are experts? (Hint: They won Nobel Prizes for their discovery.)

7. Although the Internet is an invaluable source of information on almost any topic, it is also a notorious source of misinformation. As an exercise, try to locate the Web site of the Central Intelligence Agency (CIA). How many different Web sites did you find before locating the official page? How did you know when you were at the official site?

The following information is based on the *Publication Manual of the American Psychological Association*, 4th ed., 1994.

It is important that you fully document the sources of information you use in preparing a speech outline. Cite the source in parentheses in the actual body of the outline by name and date. Include page numbers for quotations or specific facts, for example, (Jones, 1999, p. 1).

Include a list of "References" at the end of your outline. Always include the author, date, title, and facts of publication. Personal communications, such as letters, phone calls, e-mail, and interviews, are cited only in the text, not the reference list; for example, J. Q. Jones (personal communication, April 1, 1999). The format varies depending on the type of work referenced. Here are some of the most common types of works you may use in a speech. Notice that APA style does not place quotation marks around the titles of articles or book chapters. Also, titles of books and articles are not capitalized, except for the first word, the first word following a colon, and proper names. Periodical titles are capitalized. Authors are listed by last name first, followed by first and sometimes middle initials.

Books

Single Author

Freeley, A. J. (1990). <u>Argumentation and debate: Critical thinking for reasoned decision making</u> (7th ed.). Belmont, CA: Wadsworth.

Multiple Authors

Germond, J. W., & Witcover, J. (1989). <u>Whose broad stripes and bright stars?</u> New York: Warner Books.

Corporate Author

American Psychological Association. (1994). <u>Publication manual of the American Psychological Association</u> (4th ed.). Washington, DC: Author.

Government Document

Department of Health and Human Services. (1989). <u>Smoking tobacco and health: A fact book.</u> (DHHS Publication No. CDC 87-8397). Washington, DC: U.S. Government Printing Office.

Chapter in a Book

Steeper, F. T. (1978). Public response to Gerald Ford's statements on Eastern Europe in the second debate. In G. F. Bishop, R. G. Meadow, & M. Jackson-Beeck (Eds.), The presidential debates: Media, electoral, and policy perspectives (pp. 81–101). New York: Praeger.

Periodicals

Weekly Magazine

Alter, J. (1988, September 26). The expectations game. Newsweek, 112, 16–18.

If the author is unknown, you would list the article as follows:

The expectations game. (1988, September 26). Newsweek, 112, 16–18.

Scholarly Journal Divided by Volume Numbers

Vancil, D. L., & Pendell, S. D. (1984). Winning presidential debates: An analysis of criteria influencing audience response. Western Journal of Speech Communication, 48, 63–74.

[This means the article was published in 1984, in volume 48, on pages 63–74.]

Newspaper

Rosentiel, T. H. (1988, October 14). Minus a Dukakis home run, Bush is called winner. Los Angeles Times, p. A25.

If the author is unknown, you would list the article as follows:

Minus a Dukakis home run, Bush is called winner. (1988, October 14). Los Angeles Times, p. A25.

Pamphlet (published by author)

American Diabetes Association. (1987). Diabetes and you. Alexandria, VA: Author.

Internet

As computer sources multiply, the citation format has been evolving. APA guidelines ask that you include type of medium, the necessary electronic information to permit retrieval, and then the date you accessed the information in brackets. For example:

```
    Clinton, B. (1995, November 27). President's statement
on Bosnian peacekeeping mission. White House Publications
[Online]. Available: http://docs.whitehouse.
gov/white-house-publications/1995/11/1995-11-27-
presidents-statement-on-bosnian-peace-keeping-mission.text
[1996, January 15]
```

All references are listed in alphabetical order, regardless of type, at the end of the speech outline by authors' last names. Works listed by title, where the author is not known, are placed alphabetically by title. For an example of a reference list using APA style, see the outline in Chapter 8 on page 228.

Modern Language Association (MLA) Style

This section is based on Joseph Gibaldi, *The MLA Handbook for Writers of Research Papers*, 5th ed., 1999. Also consult their Web site at www.mla.org.

Although there are numerous similarities between APA and MLA style, there are also many differences. You may cite sources in parentheses in the actual body of the outline, as you do with APA, but you use only the author's name and the page number, not the date, for example, (Jones 1). Notice that in MLA style you do not separate the name and the page number by a comma, nor do you use the letter "p." MLA also allows you to incorporate the name of the author in your text and only cite the pages in parentheses. For example, John Jones tells us that "second-hand smoke is deadly" (1). Notice that the ending punctuation comes *after* the page number in this example.

Include a list of "Works Cited" at the end of your outline. Always include the author, title, facts of publication, and date. Personal communications *are* included in the Works Cited list, unlike in APA style. For example, an interview would be cited as follows: Jones, John Q. Personal interview. 1 Apr. 1992.

Here are some of the most common types of works you may use in a speech. Notice that MLA style does place quotation marks around the titles of articles or book chapters. Also, titles of books and articles and periodicals are capitalized. Authors are listed by last name first, followed by *full* first names and sometimes middle initials. Finally, the date comes at or near the end of the citation, not right after the author's name, as in APA style.

Books

Single Author

```
Freeley, Austin J. Argumentation and Debate: Critical
    Thinking for Reasoned Decision Making, 7th ed.
    Belmont, CA: Wadsworth, 1990.
```

Multiple Authors

Germond, Jack W., and Jules Witcover. <u>Whose Broad Stripes</u>
<u>and Bright Stars?</u> New York: Warner Books, 1989.

Corporate Author

American Psychological Association. <u>Publication Manual of</u>
<u>the American Psychological Association.</u> 4th ed.
Washington, DC: American Psychological Association,
1994.

Government Document

United States. Dept. of Health and Human Services. <u>Smoking</u>
<u>Tobacco and Health: A Fact Book.</u> Washington: GPO, 1989.

Chapter in a Book

Steeper, Frederick T. "Public Response to Gerald Ford's
Statements on Eastern Europe in the Second Debate."
<u>The Presidential Debates: Media, Electoral, and Policy</u>
<u>Perspectives.</u> Ed. George F. Bishop, Robert G. Meadow,
and Marilyn Jackson-Beeck. New York: Praeger, 1978.
81–101.

Periodicals

Weekly Magazine

Alter, Jonathan. "The Expectations Game." <u>Newsweek</u> 26 Sep.
1988: 16–18.

If the author is unknown, you would list the article as follows:

"The Expectations Game." <u>Newsweek</u> 26 Sep. 1988: 16–18.

Scholarly Journal Divided by Volume Numbers

Vancil, David L., and Susan D. Pendell. "Winning
Presidential Debates: An Analysis of Criteria
Influencing Audience Response." <u>Western Journal of</u>
<u>Speech Communication</u> 48 (1984): 63–74.

[This means the article was published in 1984, in volume 48, on pages 63–74.]

Newspaper

Rosentiel, Tom H. "Minus a Dukakis Home Run, Bush Is
Called Winner." <u>Los Angeles Times</u> 14 Oct. 1988: A25.

If the author is unknown, you would list the article as follows:

"Minus a Dukakis Home Run, Bush Is Called Winner." <u>Los</u>
<u>Angeles Times</u> 14 Oct. 1988: A25.

Pamphlet (published by author)

```
American Diabetes Association. Diabetes and You.
    Alexandria, VA: ADA, 1987.
```

Internet

MLA style for online citations is similar to that of APA, in that the online ad-dress and date accessed are included, but the rest of the citation is similar to MLA citations of other sources. (n. pag. indicates no pagination, which is nor-mally the case in computerized sources). The following statement was made on November 27, 1995, but accessed on January 15, 1996.

```
Clinton, Bill. "President's Statement on Bosnian
    Peacekeeping Mission." White House Publications. 27
    Nov. 1995. (n. pag. Online. Internet. 15 Jan. 1996
    <http://docs.whitehouse.gov/white-house-
    publications/1995/11/1995-11-27-presidents-statement-
    on-bosnian-peace-keeping-mission.text>.
```

As with APA, a complete list of sources—called "Works Cited"—in alphabeti-cal order by author (if none, use title) should follow the text. If more than one work by the same author is included, replace the author's name with three hy-phens (---) in all listings after the first.

1. "Selling Green," *Consumer Reports*, October 1991, 687–692.
2. Cynthia Crossen, "Lies, Damned Lies—and 'Scientific' Studies," *Sacra-mento Bee*, Forum, 24 November 1991, 1–2. (Reprinted from the *Wall Street Journal*.)
3. Crossen, "Lies, Damned Lies—and 'Scientific' Studies."
4. Robert S. Erikson and Kent L. Tedin, *American Public Opinion*, 5th ed. (Boston: Allyn & Bacon, 1994), 28.
5. Crossen, "Lies, Damned Lies—and 'Scientific' Studies."
6. Chalsey Phariss, "Lake Tahoe," Speech delivered at California State University, Chico, April 18, 1998.
7. Walter R. Fisher, *Human Communication as Narration* (Columbia: Univer-sity of South Carolina Press, 1987).
8. Based on Meriam Library, *How to Use the On-Line Catalog* (Chico: Cali-fornia State University, 1991).
9. http://www.census.gov/statab/www
10. Patricia McColl Bee and Walter Schneider, *Quotation Location* (Ottawa, Canada: Canadian Library Association, 1990).
11. "Cyberspace Survey Finds That 1 of 6 Uses Internet," *Sacramento Bee*, 31 October 1995, E1.

12. Robert J. Samuelson, "Down With the Media Elite!?" *Newsweek*, 13 July 1998, 47.

13. David Wallechinsky, "Be at Home on the Internet," *Parade Magazine*, 19 November 1995, 6, 9.

14. John A. Courtright and Elizabeth M. Perse, *The Mayfield Quick Guide to the Internet for Communication Students* (Mountain View, CA: Mayfield Publishing Co., 1998), 32–35.

15. Courtright and Perse, *The Mayfield Quick Guide to the Internet for Communication Students*, 44–47.

16. http://www.cnn.com/

Organization is one of the most important ingredients in successful public speaking.

Organizing Your Message

OBJECTIVES

After reading this chapter, you should be able to:

- Develop an organizational strategy geared to your audience.
- Refine the specific purpose of your speech.
- Develop a clear thesis statement for your speech.
- Organize the body of your speech.
- Appreciate organizational patterns from diverse cultures.
- Utilize appropriate signposts to indicate transitions from one point to the next in your speech.
- Construct an effective introduction and conclusion for your speech.
- Prepare a formal outline for a speech to your class.
- Prepare and utilize speaker's notes for a speech to your class.

KEY CONCEPTS

call and response pattern

categorical pattern

causal pattern

extended narrative

formal outline

main points

Monroe's motivated sequence

problem–solution pattern

refutational pattern

rhetorical question

spatial pattern

signposts

spiral pattern

star pattern

subpoint

supporting point

time pattern

wave pattern

Every discourse, like a living creature, should be so put together that it has its own body and lacks neither head nor feet, middle nor extremities, all composed in such a way that they suit both each other and the whole.

—PLATO

203

It is easier for an audience to follow a speech when they know how it is organized.

In everyday conversation, we often speak in a random and seemingly disorganized fashion. Particularly in interpersonal conversation, one idea will trigger another, which will trigger another, and so on. We all have had the experience of wondering how we ended up talking about the latest music video when the conversation began with a question about weekend plans.

When engaged in casual conversation, we have no reason to worry about structuring our message. In fact, part of the fun of such conversations is that they are spontaneous and unpredictable. If we don't understand what someone has said, we can simply ask the person to explain what was meant. Feedback is immediate, verbal as well as nonverbal.

Unfortunately, as we move from engaging in conversation to speaking in public, such random and unpredictable speaking becomes a hindrance to effective communication. Rather than being fun, listening to the random thoughts of a disorganized speaker is frustrating. As listeners we desire structure. We want to know where speakers are going and when they get there. A stream-of-consciousness public speaker is usually an ineffective one.

In this chapter, we assume that you already have a general notion of what you want to communicate in your speech. But, as Plato implied in the quotation at the beginning of this chapter, simply knowing what you want to communicate is not enough. You need to know how to structure that information for maximum effect. There are some specific things you can do organizationally to help you achieve your goals. They include developing an organizational strategy geared to your audience, refining your specific purpose, focusing on your thesis statement, organizing the body of your speech, introducing your speech, concluding your speech, communicating organization through previews and signposts, and preparing the formal outline and/or speaker's notes.

FOCUSING ON YOUR AUDIENCE

Just as with the process of invention discussed in the preceding chapter, the organization of your speech should be grounded in your analysis of your rhetorical situation in general, and your audience specifically. For example, should you put your best foot forward, so to speak, or save your best for last? A lot depends on the audience. Suppose you have an audience that is either disinterested or hostile. If you save your most compelling material until the end, you are likely to lose the audience long before you have a chance to enlighten them or influence their opinion. On the other hand, if your audience already is greatly interested in your topic, you may want to build to a climax so that your best material will be fresh in their minds at the conclusion of the speech. A careful analysis of your audience is also crucial to refining your specific purpose and formulating your thesis statement.

Refining Your Specific Purpose

In Chapter 2, we defined *specific purpose* as a speaker's goal or objective in speaking to a particular audience. Although you will have a specific purpose in mind before you begin to construct your speech, you will need to refine your specific purpose in light of your research and your analysis of the audience. The specific purpose of a speech represents a compromise between the speaker's ideal goal and the constraints of the particular rhetorical situation. Suppose you know the audience is skeptical of your point of view. You may want to refine your specific purpose to a more achievable goal than your ideal. For example, if you want your audience to buy a personal computer, and you know they are largely uninformed and even hostile to the machines, perhaps you should only try to open their minds a little and persuade them to consider trying out a computer.

Focusing on Your Thesis Statement

Recall from Chapter 2 that a *thesis statement* focuses your audience's attention on the central point of your speech. Just as a photographer must clearly focus on the primary subject of a photo, you as a speaker must bring the principal thrust of your speech into clear focus for your audience. Your analysis of the audience may determine when and how you present your thesis statement.

Normally, the thesis statement comes early in the speech, right after the opening. It is frustrating to an audience not to know the central point of a speech early. However, there may be times when presenting the thesis statement early is not the best strategy. For example, a hostile audience may tune you out as soon as they hear your position on a controversial issue. In that case, you may want to hold off stating your position until the end of the speech and instead begin with common ground. Again, audience-focused organization is a key to successful speech making.

Sometimes the thesis statement may be less specific than the specific purpose. For example, if you are dealing with a hostile audience, rather than saying, "Today I am going to convince you that condoms should be distributed at your teenager's school," you might say, "Today I am going to offer some positive steps we can take to prevent the spread of AIDS to your sons and daughters." You must be sensitive to your audience's attitudes, beliefs, and values in formulating a thesis statement that will both express the essence of your speech and allow the audience to give your views a fair hearing.

Once you know your specific purpose and have formulated your thesis statement, it is time to organize the body of your speech. Although you might think that the introduction should be written first, this is rarely the case. Until you have constructed the body of the speech, it is difficult to find an appropriate introduction. Also, in sifting through your ideas and the research you've done for the body of the speech, you might find something that strikes you as ideally suited to a strong introduction.

ORGANIZING THE BODY OF THE SPEECH

As Plato suggested, every speech needs parts that are "composed in such a way that they suit both each other and the whole." Thus, your speech needs not only a strong introduction and conclusion but also a well-organized body to support your thesis statement and achieve your purpose. Carefully thought-out main points, subpoints, and supporting points will provide that organization.

Main Points

Main points are the key ideas that support the thesis statement of a speech. They should fully develop the thesis statement. As a result of understanding these points, your audience should be informed, persuaded, or entertained in accordance with your specific purpose. In developing your main points, keep five guidelines in mind. They are listed below and then described in more detail.

Tips and Tactics

Guidelines for Developing Your Main Points

- Limit the number of main points.
- Focus each main point on one main idea.
- Construct main points so that they are parallel in structure.
- State main points as simply as the subject will allow.
- Give all main points equal treatment.

Number   Every speech needs to be anchored around two or more main points. (If there is only one main point, then that is, in effect, the same as your thesis statement, and what you think are subpoints are in fact the main points.) In our experience, more than five main points is too much for an audience to absorb. Three main points seems to be ideal. The audience (not to mention the speaker) usually can easily grasp three key ideas, especially if they are organized in a memorable fashion. As the number of points increases, each main idea tends to be devalued and the chances of you or your audience forgetting one or more ideas tend to increase. Obviously, there can be no rule in this regard, because some topics do not fit into three neat pigeonholes. But if you find yourself with six, seven, or eight main points, your speech is likely to suffer because either you are trying to cover too much in your speech or what you really have are six to eight subpoints, which could be organized into fewer main points, each with two or three subpoints.

Focus   The main points should clearly relate to the thesis statement. They should fully develop the thesis statement, while not going beyond the focus of the speech. For example, if you are speaking on the structure of the federal government, your thesis statement might be "The federal government consists of three separate branches of government that check and balance one another." An obvious division of this focus into three main points would be

  I. The legislative branch is found in the Congress.

 II. The executive branch includes the president and the Cabinet.

III. The judicial branch includes the Supreme Court and the lower courts.

Imagine, however, that your speech on the branches of the federal government excluded the judicial branch. Clearly, your thesis statement would have to account for the fact. If it didn't, you would most likely leave your audience wondering why you left out such a significant part of your speech. Or, on the other hand, suppose you decided to add another main point to the body of your speech, for example,

IV. Corruption in government is a serious problem.

Although this point is certainly related to the federal government, it is out of the focus suggested by the thesis statement. Thus, you need to reformulate your thesis statement, or rethink your specific purpose, or drop the out-of-focus point.

Think of the thesis statement as limiting the territory covered by your speech. As you construct the body of the speech, include only those items that directly support your thesis statement. At the same time, do not allow your thesis statement to be incompletely supported. By the end of your speech, you should have fulfilled the promise of your thesis statement—no more, no less.

Each main point should be focused on one main idea. For example, consider the potential confusion of this main point

I. Corruption exists in Congress, and laws begin in Congress as bills.

The first part of the main point deals with the problem of members of Congress failing their public trust. The second part deals with the formal process by which our laws are passed. These two ideas should be expressed as separate main points:

I. Laws begin in Congress as bills.

II. Corruption exists in Congress.

Using two separate points does not mean that they are unrelated. Obviously, the method by which a bill becomes law, such as the role of key congressional committees in the process, may help explain why Congress is susceptible to corruption. But the two ideas are clearly different.

Parallel Structure   Your main points form the essence of your speech, so they should be clear, concise, and memorable. One technique to help achieve this is to construct main points in parallel fashion. For example, which of the following is the more memorable way to phrase main points?

I. Congress is corrupt.

II. There are some corrupt members in the executive branch.

III. Some judges take bribes.

or

I. Corruption corrodes Congress.

II. Corruption corrodes the White House.

III. Corruption corrodes the bench.

Obviously, the second example is easier to remember. The repetition of the phrase "corruption corrodes" in all three main points stresses the focus of this speech—that all three branches experience corruption.

Simplicity Versus Complexity   Whereas a reader can reread anything that is complex or confusing, the audience of a speech has only a limited opportunity to process information. If you phrase your main points as complex sentences, you may lose your audience. Concise and simple language will help make the structure of your speech clear. Again, compare two examples of main points:

I. AIDS is transmitted through unprotected sexual relations, including homosexual and heterosexual encounters.

II. AIDS is transmitted when drug users, often desperate for their next fix, share dirty needles.

III. AIDS is transmitted by the exchange of blood, such as in a transfusion or between a mother and her unborn child.

or

I. AIDS is transmitted through unprotected sex.

II. AIDS is transmitted through sharing of needles.

III. AIDS is transmitted by blood.

Which of the two sets of main points do you think the audience will remember? Although you will develop these main points in much more detail as you give the speech, statement of the main points should be as simple as the subject will allow.

Balance   You should aim for balance among the main points of your speech. For example, if one main point composes two-thirds of the speech, audience members may become confused and wonder what they missed. Perhaps they will wonder why you think that one point is so much more important than the other. Or they may suspect that there is another main point you forgot to mention.

Subpoints

Subpoints are to main points what main points are to the thesis statement. A **subpoint** is an idea that supports a main point. Each main point should have at least two and no more than five subpoints. Consider, for example, our speech on the structure of the federal government:

I. The legislative branch makes the laws.   *[Main point]*
  A. The House of Representatives is based on population.   *[Subpoint]*
  B. The Senate provides each state with equal representation.   *[Subpoint]*
II. The executive branch enforces the laws.
  A. The president is the chief executive officer.
  B. The Cabinet consists of the heads of the executive departments.
III. The judicial branch interprets the laws.
  A. The Supreme Court is the final arbiter of the law.
  B. Lower courts must follow the Supreme Court's rulings.

It makes no sense to have only one subpoint under a main point. For example,

I. The legislative branch makes the laws.
  A. The House of Representatives is based on population.

If you wished to talk only about the House of Representatives, then that would be your main point. But if a main point is not subject to division into at least two subpoints, it probably is not of sufficient merit to be a main point. Rather, it is likely to be a potential subpoint under another main point. Like main points, subpoints should be parallel in structure, simply stated, and given equal treatment.

Supporting Points

Sometimes the subpoints within your speech require further support and subdivision. Thus, you might choose supporting points for each subpoint. A **supporting point** is an idea that supports a subpoint. Returning to our example of the federal government, the body of a speech might be organized as follows:

I. The legislative branch makes the laws.   *[Main point]*
  A. The House of Representatives is defined in the Constitution.   *[Subpoint]*

[Supporting point]   1. The qualifications for office are specified in the Constitution.

[Supporting point]   2. The powers of the House are specified in the Constitution.

Obviously, one could further subdivide each of these supporting points. However, such a detailed substructure probably would lose the audience. What's more, for a normal classroom speech, it is unlikely that you will have the time to develop most points beyond this level. If a speech seems to lend itself to further substructure, ask yourself if some of your supporting points are really subpoints, as well as whether some of the subpoints might be better phrased as main points or whether you should narrow your topic further.

If you must further subdivide a supporting point, use lowercase letters in your outline as follows:

[Main point]   I. The legislative branch makes the laws.

[Subpoint]   A. The House of Representatives is defined in the Constitution.

[Supporting point]   1. The qualifications for office are specified in the Constitution:

[Further support]   a. At least 25 years of age

[Further support]   b. U.S. citizen for at least 7 years

[Further support]   c. Resident of the state represented

Patterns of Organization

There are a number of different patterns you can use to organize the body of your speech. In Chapter 2, we introduced four of those patterns. We now will add four traditional patterns of organization, for a total of eight: time, extended narrative, spatial, categorical, problem–solution, refutational, causal, and Monroe's motivated sequence. In addition, we will introduce four nontraditional patterns common in the diverse cultures of our contemporary society: wave, spiral, star, and call and response.

Time   Many topics lend themselves naturally to a temporal sequence. A **time pattern** is a pattern of organization based on chronology or a sequence of events. Topics of a historical nature are likely to follow a time sequence. Suppose you were speaking about the history of the U.S. space program, as did Tom Wolfe in his book *The Right Stuff*. You might divide the speech into the following main points:

I. The race begins in the 1950s with the launch of *Sputnik*.

II. The U.S.S.R. puts the first men into space in the 1960s.

III. The United States sets the goal to land on the moon by the end of the 1960s.

IV. Neil Armstrong is the first human to land on the moon in July 1969.

Topics that deal with a process, such as how-to speeches, can frequently be ordered by a time pattern as well. You might sequence a speech on learning to ski in these terms:

I. Select the right equipment.

II. Invest in lessons.

III. Practice!

Extended Narrative   An **extended narrative** is a pattern of organization in which the entire body of the speech is the telling of a story. In Chapter 7, we introduced narrative as a form of support for a speech. As support, one main point of a speech might be a narrative, but the other main points might be in the form of statistics, expert opinions, facts, and the like. However, an extended narrative means the whole speech is one story. In this case you tell a story in sequence, with a climactic point near the end of the speech. This organizational pattern is often very useful, for example, in speeches to entertain. Thus, if you were to tell the story of your first blind date, you might pattern your speech after the following:

I. I am asked to go out on a blind date.

II. I meet the date.

III. Disaster follows.

Sometimes a persuasive speech can also be built around an extended narrative of some incident that dramatizes the problem you are addressing in your speech. An example of an extended narrative in a persuasive speech might be the following:

I. Jim had too much to drink at a fraternity party.

II. His frat brothers dared him to hop a moving freight train.

III. Jim attempted to jump onto the moving train.

IV. He lost his balance and fell under the train; both of his legs were severed.

V. Jim lived and has dedicated his life to fighting alcohol abuse.

Notice that a story needs not only a plot line but also characters, including a central character with whom the audience can identify. In this particular story, the speaker would seek to create a sympathetic portrayal of Jim, who becomes the protagonist. Of course, each point would be developed in detail, and the audience should be held in suspense as the story unfolds. The moral of the story should not have to be stated explicitly but should be apparent to the audience. This is one of those speeches in which stating the thesis at the beginning would actually undermine the effectiveness of the speech. By the end of the speech, however, no one would doubt the speaker's central idea.

Spatial   A **spatial pattern** is a pattern of organization based on physical space or geography. Some topics lend themselves to a spatial or geographic order. Suppose you want to discuss weather patterns in the United States. You might divide your topic geographically into east, south, north, and west. If you were trying to explain how a ship is constructed, you might do so in terms of fore, midship, and aft. Or if you were giving a tour of your hometown, your points might look something like this:

I. The east side is mostly residential.

II. The central part of town is the business district.

III. The west side is largely industrial.

Categorical   A **categorical pattern** is a pattern of organization based on natural divisions in the subject matter. Many topics naturally fall into categories. The

TV meteorologists often use a spatial pattern to explain the weather.

federal government, as we've shown, can be naturally divided into the legislative, executive, and judicial branches. The essential principle is that you divide your topic along its natural boundaries. Thus, a speech advocating solar energy might be organized as follows:

I. Fossil fuels pollute the atmosphere.

II. Nuclear energy creates radioactive wastes.

III. Solar energy is nonpolluting.

When using this pattern, however, be careful that you don't create false categories. Although it may be categorically convenient to cast people into some specific groups, for example, it also can be highly misleading or even offensive. Much social and ethnic prejudice is rooted in the stereotyping of people into arbitrary categories.

Problem–Solution   Sometimes we speak to propose a solution to an ongoing problem. This is frequently the case when we speak persuasively. One way to approach this type of speech is to use the **problem–solution pattern,** a pattern of organization that analyzes a problem in terms of the stock issues of (1) harm, (2) significance, and (3) cause, and proposes a solution that is (1) described, (2) feasible, and (3) advantageous. A specific example of this pattern might be a speech about the need for better health care. In this case, you might organize the speech in the following way:

I. Millions of Americans are denied access to adequate health care.   *[Problem]*

    A. People suffer and die without this care.   *[Harm]*

    B. More than 37 million Americans lack basic health insurance.   *[Significance]*

    C. There is a gap between government-sponsored health care (Medicaid and Medicare) and private insurance.   *[Cause]*

II. We need a program of national health insurance to fill the gap.   *[Solution]*

    A. All businesses will be taxed to provide national health insurance.   *[Description]*

    B. Similar programs exist in almost every other industrialized country in the world.   *[Feasibility]*

    C. No longer will people be denied access to medical care simply because they cannot pay.   *[Advantages]*

The relationship between harm and significance is important. Harm has to do with the bad consequences of the problem—in this case, potential suffering and death. Significance has to do with the extent of the problem. If 100 people in a nation of 250 million were at risk of suffering or death because of an inadequate health-care system, this would be unfortunate, but it would not be a significant problem relative to the population of the nation. If millions were at risk, then the problem would be significant.

You also need to recognize that there can be numerous different solutions to the same problem. Thus, it is important to stress both the feasibility and the advantages of the solution you propose, if you hope to have it adopted by your audience.

Refutational   Sometimes you are in a position to answer the arguments of another speaker. Perhaps you are involved in a debate. Alternatively, you may read or hear something with which you disagree. The **refutational pattern** is a pattern of organization that involves the following steps:

I. State the argument you seek to refute.

II. State your objection to the argument.

III. Prove your objection to the argument.

IV. Present the impact of your refutation

For example, if you wanted to refute the proposed national health insurance in the previous illustration of the problem–solution method, you might proceed with the following points:

I. The proponents of national health care say the government should control health care.   *[States the argument you seek to refute.]*

II. Government bureaucrats, not physicians or patients, will control medical choices.   *[States your objection to the argument.]*

III. People from Canada, which has national health insurance, often have to come to the United States for medical care they are denied by their government-run program.   *[Presents proof for your objection.]*

IV. The quality of American health care will decline in a program run by government bureaucrats.   *[Presents the impact of your objection.]*

Causal   The **causal pattern** is a pattern of organization that moves from cause to effect or from effect to cause. In cause-to-effect speeches, you are dealing with some known activity and showing your audience that it will produce certain effects. If these are desirable effects, you would be endorsing the activity. If they are undesirable, you would be suggesting that your audience avoid the activity. To illustrate this organizational pattern, suppose that you wanted to convince your audience to quit smoking:

[Cause]
I. Cigarette smoke contains a number of harmful chemicals.
 A. Carbon monoxide reduces the body's ability to absorb oxygen.
 B. Nicotine is an addictive substance.
 C. Tar is made up of thousands of chemicals.

[Effect]
II. Cigarette smoking leads to significant health problems.
 A. Carbon monoxide has been linked to low-birth-weight babies.
 B. Nicotine makes quitting smoking difficult.
 C. Tar is the principal source of cancer-causing chemicals in tobacco.

On the other hand, if you wanted to convince your audience of the need to reduce the power of special interests in Washington, you might argue from various effects back to finding the cause:

[Effect]
I. The country is in economic trouble.
 A. Real wages are declining.
 B. Many industries are moving overseas.
 C. Our trade deficit is growing.

[Cause]
II. We have a system of government that is too tied to special interests.
 A. Lobbyists influence Congress to make bad economic decisions.
 B. Politicians are more interested in getting reelected than in solving problems.
 C. Only by breaking the power of special interests can we get our economy back on track.

Whether you move from cause to effect or from effect to cause, you need to provide proof of the causal links asserted in your speech. Simply because two things occur one after the other does not prove one caused the other. For example, just because a car breaks down doesn't mean the last person to drive it is responsible for the breakdown.

Monroe's Motivated Sequence   A five-step organizational scheme developed by speech professor Alan Monroe, and thus termed **Monroe's motivated sequence,** is another pattern by which a speech can be structured.[1] These five steps overlap somewhat with the introduction and conclusion of a speech, as well as the body. They are as follows:

[Introduction]
I. *Attention:* Gain your audience's attention.

[Body]
II. *Need:* Show the audience that a need exists that affects them.

III. *Satisfaction:* Present the solution to the need.   *[Body]*

IV. *Visualization:* Help the audience imagine how their need will be met in the   *[Body]*
future.

V. *Action:* State what actions must be taken to fulfill the need.   *[Conclusion]*

To see how this motivated sequence might work, consider the earlier example concerning national health insurance:

I. *Attention:* A child dies because her parents couldn't afford to take her to the doctor.

II. *Need:* You could become one of millions of uninsured Americans who face financial ruin if they become seriously ill.

III. *Satisfaction:* National health insurance would guarantee all Americans the right to health care, regardless of their income.

IV. *Visualization:* The United States would join nations like Canada, where no one fears seeing a doctor because of the cost.

V. *Action:* Write your senator and representative today, urging the passage of national health insurance.

Obviously, the motivated-sequence pattern is most directly suited to persuasive presentations. However, an informative presentation could use at least some of these steps, because informative speaking typically is the first step in a persuasive campaign. In an informative presentation, it is important to show your audience why they need to learn the information you have presented and, of course, to satisfy that need. Helping an audience visualize how they will use the information is also valuable. And often you will then want them to put what they have learned into action.

These eight patterns of organization are primarily linear in nature and are well suited to audiences rooted in a Western European tradition. However, as the following box "Organization and Culture" shows, there are other organizational patterns that are well suited to other cultures. We briefly discuss four of these patterns: wave, spiral, star, and call and response.

In constructing the body of your speech, choose one of the basic patterns of organization. As a reminder, we list them here.

Patterns of Speech Organization

Time	Causal
Extended narrative	Monroe's motivated sequence
Spatial	Wave
Categorical	Spiral
Problem–solution	Star
Refutational	Call and response

Organization and Culture

Not all cultures and groups within a larger culture prefer the kind of linear organization patterns commonly discussed in public speaking classes. Cheryl Jorgensen-Earp has suggested that women and some ethnic speakers use less linear, more organic patterns. For example, one pattern found in the speeches of many women and African Americans is the **wave.** Much like a wave cresting, receding, and then cresting again, a speech following this pattern continually returns to the basic theme, repeating a phrase again and again throughout the speech. Perhaps the most familiar example is Dr. Martin Luther King, Jr.'s "I Have a Dream" speech, which gets its title from the constant repetition of the phrase. In addition, King uses the theme "Let freedom ring" repeatedly as he brings the speech to its dramatic conclusion.

Other patterns suggested by Jorgensen-Earp include a **spiral** pattern, which repeats points as does the wave, but with each point growing in intensity as the speech builds to its pinnacle at the conclusion. A third pattern she suggests is the **star,** in which all of the points of the star are of equal importance. Thus a speaker can present the points in any order in support of the common theme that encircles the star and holds the speech together.

A fourth pattern is the **call and response.** In this pattern, commonly found in African American churches, a call by the speaker is followed by a response from the audience. For example, the preacher might say, "Sinners repent, the day is at hand," and the congregation would respond, "Amen." Or the speaker might ask a real question, to which an audience response is expected. For example, a labor leader might ask, "What do we want?" to which the audience responds, "Jobs." "When do we want them?" "Now." Not only may a speech be organized around the call and response pattern, even speeches organized in another fashion can use this technique as a stylistic device to heighten audience involvement.

As a speaker, you should carefully consider both your audience's cultural background as it affects their organizational preferences as well as your own cultural affinity for certain patterns of organization. Although cultural diversity provides the opportunity to expand the ways in which speeches may be organized, it should not be used as an excuse for a lack of any coherent organizational pattern.

Source: The first three of these patterns are cited in Clella Jaffe, *Public Speaking: A Cultural Perspective* (Belmont, CA: Wadsworth, 1995), pp. 187–192. They are based on a telephone interview by Jaffe with Jorgensen-Earp, as well as the latter's unpublished works.

When constructing your speech, try to avoid mixing types of patterns. It is confusing to an audience to begin listening to a time sequence and then find themselves in the middle of a problem–solution speech.

Signposts

In addition to constructing the actual body of the speech, it is important for you to help your audience follow your pattern of organization. A useful way to do so is through the use of signposts. As Chapter 2 explained, **signposts** are transitional statements that bridge your main points. They tell your audience where you have been and where you are going in your speech. By telling listeners where you are in the speech, signposts help those who have become lost or inattentive pick up the thread of your speech.

Signposts such as those listed in Table 8.1 tell your audience you are about to make or already have made a shift in direction. Signposts also serve to verbally link

TABLE 8.1 Transitional Words and Their Functions	
Adding a point:	furthermore, besides, finally, in addition to
Emphasis:	above all, indeed, in fact, in other words, most important
Time:	then, afterwards, eventually, next, immediately, meanwhile, previously, already, often, since then, now, later, usually
Cause and effect:	consequently, as a result, therefore, thus
Examples:	for example, for instance
Progression:	first, second, third, furthermore
Contrast:	but, however, in contrast, instead, nevertheless, on the contrary, on the other hand, though, still, unfortunately
Conclusions:	therefore, to sum up, in brief, in general, in short, for these reasons, in retrospect, finally, in conclusion

Source: E. Hughes, J. Silverman, and D. R. Wienbroer, *Rules of Thumb* (New York: McGraw-Hill, 1990), 99. Reprinted with permission of McGraw-Hill.

your thoughts as you speak. It's always a good idea to let your audience know that there is a sequence to your message—"Let's consider three important issues"—and then to remind your audience where you are in that sequence—"Having covered the first issue, let's now look at the second."

Techniques for Signposting

- *Refer to preceding and upcoming ideas:* "Now that you know what computer viruses are, I'll discuss how to prevent their spread to your computer."
- *Enumerate key points.* If you number your points in the preview, stick with that numbering plan in the signposts. For example: "First, never assume that a program from a friend or computer bulletin board is virus free."
- *Give nonverbal reinforcement.* Frequently, you can emphasize verbal signposts nonverbally. Changes in vocal inflection signal a change is coming. Movement can signal a signpost: Some speakers physically move from one place to another while speaking in order to emphasize that they are moving from one point to the next. Others hold up fingers to indicate number of points.
- *Use visual aids to reinforce signposts.* Moving to a new page on your flip chart or putting up a new slide or transparency clearly signals to your audience that you are moving on. It's also a way to help you remember the sequence of your speech.
- *Use words that cue your audience that you are changing points.* Words and phrases like the following suggest a signpost: *next, another, number, moving on, finally, therefore, in summary.* Don't be afraid to be explicit about signposts. More speeches suffer from a lack of clear signposts than from being overly signposted.

It's also a good idea to let your audience know that your speech is close to the end by using transitional words and phrases such as "finally," "in sum," "in conclusion," and "to close." Far too many times we've watched audiences guess whether they're hearing the end of the speech; the sign of their uncertainty is premature clapping.

After organizing the body of the speech, you can begin to construct your introduction and conclusion.

INTRODUCING YOUR SPEECH

You may recall from Chapter 2 that an introduction should do four things: open with impact, focus on the thesis statement, connect with the audience, and preview the rest of your speech. Let's look at each of these functions in turn.

Open With Impact

A speech should immediately grab the audience's attention. Within a few seconds, we begin forming impressions of others who come into our view. When you are speaking, your audience will form an immediate impression of you. One way to control this impression is to open your speech with impact. Of the numerous ways to do this, some of the most common are a story; a quotation; a startling statement; a reference to the audience, the occasion, or a current event; appropriate humor; a personal experience; or a thought-provoking question.

Story   A brief story, real or hypothetical, is often a good way to begin your speech. For example, a student in one of our classes began her speech by describing the strange behavior of a person who was staggering and incoherent, and who finally collapsed. The quick conclusion most of her audience drew as she was describing the person was that he was drunk. Not only was this conclusion wrong, the truth startled the class. The person had diabetes and was suffering from insulin shock. Needless to say, the class became far more interested in hearing the speech about diabetes than if the speaker had simply begun, "Today I'm going to tell you about diabetes."

Quotation   As we pointed out in Chapter 7, there are numerous anthologies of quotations, usually organized by topic. If you are having trouble deciding how to begin your speech, consider looking for a quotation that will captivate your audience and reinforce your main ideas.

Startling Statement   Humans are attracted naturally to surprising, startling, and unusual events. If you can tie the introduction of your speech to a surprising or startling statement, you will be assured of your audience's undivided attention. For example, we had a student in class who began her speech by announcing that her sister had died of toxic shock syndrome, which was the subject of the speech. Needless to say, her audience was startled and paid rapt attention to the speech that followed.

THE WIZARD OF ID   Brant parker and Johnny hart

By permission of Johnny Hart and Creator's Syndicate, Inc.

Reference to the Audience, Occasion, or Current Events Professional speakers often tailor their speeches to a specific audience and situation, saying such things as "I'm so happy to be here at [fill in the blank] college" or "I join with you in praising your football team's come-from-behind victory last night."

Another possibility is to refer to a previous speaker. Consider an instance in one class when two students chose to speak on gun control, each taking the opposite side of the topic. The second speaker wisely incorporated reference to the prior speech into her introduction. To ignore a speech on the same topic, particularly one at odds with your own speech, is likely to turn off an audience. Without attempting to refute the other speaker, she acknowledged those opposing views but also stated that she would present the other side of the issue.

Finally, current events often spark interest and controversy. If you are speaking on a topic of current interest, it is often a good idea to lead off with the most recent happenings. If you are speaking on terrorism, and a hostage has just been released from captivity, that would be a good place to begin your speech.

Appropriate Humor A classic *Far Side* cartoon shows Abraham Lincoln delivering the Gettysburg Address. His speech, however, begins with a joke, "And so the bartender says, "Hey! That's not a duck!" After a pause for laughter, Lincoln continues, "Fourscore and seven years ago. . . . "

Obviously, one would not begin a serious speech such as the Gettysburg Address with a joke. Humor, if not used properly, can backfire. It is best used on occasions when the audience will find it appropriate. An after-dinner speech, for example, is frequently an opportunity to employ humor.

However you use it, though, humor should be tied to the substance of your speech. Telling an irrelevant joke can detract from the main idea of your speech, rather than enhance it. It can also make you look foolish.

Finally, you need to be sensitive with regard to humor. Ethnic, sexist, and off-color jokes, for example, can get a speaker into justifiable trouble. The reputation of golfer Fuzzy Zoeller was deservedly damaged when he made a racially insensitive remark about the food preferences of golfer Tiger Woods after he won the Master's Tournament in 1997. Speakers need to err on the side of caution when they treat sensitive subjects with humor.

Writing humor is not as easy as it seems. Thus, we asked for the advice of an Emmy- and Golden Globe–winning professional comedy writer for shows such as *Murphy Brown*. You'll find his advice in the box "On Writing Comedy: Russ Woody." In addition, portions of a commencement address given by Russ Woody are found in Appendix B.

Personal Experience   Often there is no other more compelling testimony on a topic than your own personal experience. Not only can a personal experience draw in your audience and get their attention, it also can serve to build your own credibility. For example, the speaker on diabetes referred to earlier had a brother who was diabetic. However, she did not mention this fact until she had finished her speech. Had she begun with her own experiences with a diabetic brother, she would have enhanced her credibility for the remainder of the speech.

Thought-Provoking Question   Sometimes you can use a question to open your speech. A **rhetorical question** is one that the audience isn't expected to answer out loud. For example, one student began a speech on secondhand smoke this way: "How many of you have ever returned home smelling as though you were a stand-in for the Marlboro Man?"[2] The attention-getting language worked well. However, beginning with a question can be ineffective if the question is not thought-provoking. For example, beginning a speech with "How many of you would like to learn to snow ski?" isn't likely to have much impact on your audience. Also, with rhetorical questions, audiences are sometimes unsure whether the question is meant to be answered out loud. On the other hand, we have seen speakers who effectively begin their speeches by asking audience members to respond to a series of questions with a show of hands. Questions, rhetorical or real, should be used only if they add impact to the opening of the speech.

Focus on the Thesis Statement

The central idea you want to convey to an audience should be captured by your thesis statement. Although you should have developed a thesis statement before writing the body of the speech, now is a good time to reflect on its phrasing. Have you really focused on the essential theme of your speech? Be sure your thesis statement is broad enough to incorporate all of your main points. At the same time, do not make your thesis statement so broad that your speech seems to leave something out.

As noted earlier, there may be situations, such as with a hostile audience, where you will not be ready to explicitly state your thesis early in the speech. In the introduction in these situations, indicate the general topic area of the speech, focusing on an area of common agreement, rather than the thesis, if it might provoke a defensive or hostile reaction from the audience. The thesis would then emerge toward the end of the speech, after you had made your case.

On Writing Comedy: Russ Woody

As a college student, Russ Woody excelled in an event called "Speech to Entertain." Not only was humor Russ's hobby, it became his profession. Russ began his writing career at MTM productions, where he wrote episodes for shows such as *Newhart, St. Elsewhere,* and *Hill Street Blues.* For two years he was a producer and writer for *Murphy Brown,* for which he received an Emmy in 1990. He received a Golden Globe as co-executive producer of *Cybill.* He has also served as a consulting producer for *Foxworthy,* and is co-executive producer of *Becker,* currently airing on CBS. He is also working on a pilot called *Berkeley* for TriStar and writing a novel. We asked Russ to do the impossible: explain writing humor in 250 words or less. Here is the result.

WRITING HUMOR?
by Russ Woody

Two-hundred fifty words on how to write humor! Gee, can't I just whack myself in the forehead with a ball peen hammer? Trying to explain humor is a little like trying to wrest a ripe banana from an immense and bitter gorilla. If not handled correctly, you can end up looking rather foolish.

With that in mind, "Hello, Mr. Gorilla . . ."

The fact of the matter is, humor is more difficult to write than drama. Because, while both humor and drama rely heavily on emotional content, humor is much more difficult to break down mechanically. Therefore it's more difficult to construct initially. It's relatively easy to figure out what makes a person sad or angry or uneasy or embarrassed or happy. Yet it is, for the most part, difficult to say why a person laughs.

So I guess the first thing you've got to do is figure out what type of humor appeals most to you. Monty Python, Andrew "Dice" Clay, The Naked Gun, Murphy Brown, Full House, Spy Magazine, Mad Magazine, Saturday Night Live. Whichever it is, find it. Then—study it. Watch it, read it, take it apart, figure out how it's constructed, how it's set up, how it pays off—figure out the dynamics of humor. (Which will make it terribly unfunny when you do, but that's the perpetual hell comedy writers live in.)

For instance—one of my favorite jokes of all time is in one of the Pink Panther movies where Peter Sellers goes into a hotel and approaches a man at the desk who has a dog sitting beside him. Sellers says, "Does your dog bite?" The guy says no. So Sellers reaches over to pat the little pooch, and it tries to rip his arm off. Sellers then looks to the guy and says, "I thought you said your dog didn't bite?" The guy says, "It's not my dog."

I love that joke because every element of it is real, and nobody involved thinks it's funny. The man was quite correct in his literal interpretation of Sellers's question. Sellers is more than a little annoyed at the man for misunderstanding what seemed to be a logical and straightforward question. And the dog is just pissed off. In a more general sense, one person becomes a victim because the other is a stickler for precise wording. It is extreme focus on one character's part and vulnerability on the other character's part. In a way, it's like the movie The In-Laws, with Peter Falk and Alan Arkin. Falk is intensely focused on his job with the government, which, in turn makes Arkin's life a living hell. (If you've seen the movie, you know what I'm talking about—if you haven't, go see it, because I'm coming up on two-fifty pretty fast here, so I can't get into it.)

When you've taken enough jokes and stories apart, you may start to get an idea of how to construct your own. That's when it gets really tough. Just be sure you always remember the one, underlying key to writing humor— oops, outta time.

Connect With Your Audience

No speech should be constructed without asking yourself, "What's in it for the audience? What needs or desires will be fulfilled by listening to my speech?" The introduction is an opportunity to make the link between your speech topic and audience members. If you make this link in your introduction, you are much more likely to gain your audience's collective ear.

The introduction is another opportunity to build your credibility. Link your topic not only to your audience but to yourself as well, stressing your similarity to the audience. The student who spoke on toxic shock syndrome used her family's tragedy to stress that the same thing could happen to any woman. She not only made a connection with her classmates, she established her personal credibility by virtue of her experience and her subsequent research on the topic.

Although connecting with the audience is an important part of the introduction to your speech, the connection should not be made only once. In fact, throughout your speech you should draw a connection between your message and your audience whenever possible.

Preview Your Speech

Although no one knows who first said, "Tell 'em what you're going to tell 'em; tell 'em; and then tell 'em what you told 'em," it is a saying with more than a grain of truth. As we noted in Chapter 2, a *preview* is a forecast of the main points of a speech. It simply tells your audience members what they are going to hear. In many ways, it is a summary before the fact. By telling audience members what will follow, a preview helps them put your statements into a coherent frame of reference.

The way to preview a speech is rather simple: Cue the audience to the fact that you are previewing the main points of your speech, and then state the points in the same sequence they will be presented. A brief preview might be "In today's speech, I would like to share the definition, transmission, and prevention of computer viruses." Or you may want to enumerate your main points, saying, "Today, I want to first define computer viruses; second, explain how they are transmitted; and third, offer a way to prevent them from infecting your own computer."

It is not always necessary, however, to be so explicit. There are often subtler ways of previewing your speech. For example, "All computer owners need to know what computer viruses are, how they are transmitted, and how to detect and prevent them."

CONCLUDING YOUR SPEECH

The conclusion of a speech should be brief and memorable. The last thing an audience wants to hear after "In conclusion . . ." is a 10-minute dissertation on some new aspect of the topic. When you say those magic words "in conclusion" or "to wrap up," be prepared to conclude. Avoid introducing points that were not covered in the body of the speech. If you have another main point to cover, then it belongs in the body of the speech, not the conclusion. There are, consequently, only two basic things to do in concluding your speech: summarize and close with impact.

Summarize

Tell the audience, very briefly, what you have told them in the speech. This is where clear, concisely developed main points pay off. Going back to an earlier example, you might conclude the speech on corruption in the federal government with "We have seen, therefore, that all three branches of government—the Congress, the executive, and the judicial—are vulnerable to the corrupting influence of money." Sometimes you may wish to explicitly number the main points in your summary: for example, "Remember there are three types of bikes you'll see on campus. First, there are cruisers; second, there are mountain bikes; and third, there are touring bikes."

Close With Impact

The final words of your speech should be memorable. The close is your last chance to make an impression on your audience. As with the opening, it should be relevant to the main thesis of your speech. A few of the common techniques for closing are a short, memorable quotation, an anecdote or a brief story, a direct appeal to action, and a return to your opening theme. If you have delayed presenting your thesis statement for strategic reasons, it should be incorporated just prior to this point (right after the summary). If you stated the thesis earlier, it should be reiterated here.

Quotation   The same principles apply to a closing quotation as to an opening one. You want to capture the essence of your talk in a few words. If someone has said it better than you, then it is perfectly appropriate to quote that person. In the conclusion, it probably is best to state who you are quoting and then state the quotation. For example, it is less effective to say, " 'I have a dream,' said Martin Luther King, Jr.," than to say, "As Martin Luther King, Jr., once stated, 'I have a dream.'"

Anecdote   The key in the closing is to be brief and to the point. A long, drawn-out story will undermine the effectiveness of the rest of your speech. A concluding anecdote should highlight your main focus, not detract from it. As with opening stories, such anecdotes can be real or hypothetical but should be clearly identified as such to your audience.

Direct Appeal to Action   Concluding with an appeal to action is typical of a persuasive speech and is an explicit part of the motivated sequence. It involves telling your audience members specifically what they can do to fulfill their needs or solve a problem—for example, sign a petition, write to Congress, or change their own behavior. A direct appeal to your audience is often the most appropriate way to conclude a persuasive presentation.

Return to Opening   One of the most effective ways to close a speech is to return to where you began. Not only does this remind the audience of your introduction,

Jesse Jackson utilizes a direct appeal to action when seeking to register new voters.

it also gives your speech a sense of closure. It takes both you and your audience full circle. For example, the speech that began by describing a person suffering from insulin shock ended by telling the audience that they would now know how to recognize when someone was in insulin shock and would be able to get that person the help he or she needed. If you can find a way to tie your opening and closing together, you can intensify the impact of both.

PREPARING THE FORMAL OUTLINE

Once you have a rough structure of your speech, including the body, introduction, and conclusion, your instructor may recommend that you prepare a formal outline of the speech. A **formal outline** is a detailed outline used in speech preparation but not, in most cases, in the actual presentation. Usually, such an outline should be typed or prepared on a computer, depending on your instructor's requirements. Such outlines help you put your ideas down in a clear and organized fashion. If submitted in advance of a speech, it also allows instructors to give you feedback and make suggestions.

There are two basic types of outlines. *Phrase* or *key word outlines* are meaningful to the speaker but probably would not make a lot of sense to anyone else. For example, a speaker might prepare the following outline for her own use:

Intro: Tell story
    I. Rock music
    II. Volume
    III. Deafness
Conclusion: Same story 10 years later

Because this outline probably would make sense only to the speaker, beginning speakers are frequently expected to prepare a *full-sentence outline*. In this type of outline, you include a full statement indicating what each main point and subpoint cover. All the parts of the speech are included, even signposts. Generally, a formal outline should include the following:

- Your specific purpose, phrased as an infinitive phrase (to . . .), describing exactly what you want your speech to accomplish.
- Three sections—labeled introduction, body, and conclusion—each separately outlined and beginning with the roman numeral "I."

  The introduction, including your opening, focus on thesis statement, connection with the audience, and preview.

  The body, including main points, subpoints, supporting points, and further support, and, if your instructor requires them, signposts (in parentheses) between the main points.

  The conclusion, including a summary and a close.

- A bibliography of "References" or "Works Cited" (depending on whether you use APA or MLA style). Specific quotations or facts drawn from a source, as discussed in Chapter 7, should also be cited in the main outline. Of course, you should check with your instructor about the specific outlining requirements, if any, for your class. Some instructors prefer a different source citation system, for example, than the ones discussed in Chapter 7.

Outlines typically use a standard outline notation, which indicates the levels of subordination of points:

I. Main point
  A. Subpoint
    1. Supporting point
      a. Further support

Any subdivision should include at least two matching points. Thus, if you have an "A" subpoint under a main point, there should also be at least a "B." Supporting point "1" should be matched by at least a "2," and further support "a" should be followed by at least a "b."

Many instructors prefer that outlines be written in complete sentences, at least through the level of subpoints. This provides a clearer idea to both you and your instructor of what you are going to say. Use only one sentence per point and divide separate ideas into different sentences. If you outline using paragraph form, what you really have is an essay with outline notation scattered throughout. Thus, the following is not really in outline form:

I. The first men on the moon were Americans. Neil Armstrong stepped out first. He was followed by Buzz Aldrin. At the same time, Michael Collins orbited the moon.

This paragraph could be turned into the following outline:

I. The first men on the moon were Americans.
   A. Neil Armstrong stepped out first.
   B. He was followed by Buzz Aldrin.
   C. At the same time, Michael Collins orbited the moon.

Notice how each sentence is placed in a separate point. The more general statement is the main point, and the specific instances are subpoints.

Some aspects of an outline do not need to be in complete-sentence form. For example, a speaker who wants to list the components of a larger whole, such as ingredients or tools, could use an outline like this:

   1. Cigarette smoke has three components:
      a. carbon monoxide
      b. nicotine
      c. tar

You need to use judgment, therefore, when you are asked to write a complete-sentence outline. Use complete sentences for your main points and subpoints and anywhere the meaning would not be clear if not expressed in complete-sentence form. The box "Sample Speech Outline: Lake Tahoe by Chalsey Phariss" follows the suggested format. Remember, however, to check with your instructor for specific requirements in your class.

PREPARING SPEAKER'S NOTES

Of course, the outline is a preparation tool. When you are presenting a speech, we recommend that you use **speaker's notes,** which are brief notes with key words, usually written on cards. Your final notes should be meaningful to you as a speaker, but not necessarily to anyone else. However, you should rehearse until you don't need to look at the note cards frequently. It is especially important

VIDEO FILE

If you have access to the videotape that accompanies this book, view segment 6, which shows the speech "Lake Tahoe" by Chalsey Phariss, and compare the experience of seeing the speech with that of reading its outline.

Sample Speech Outline

LAKE TAHOE
by Chalsey Phariss

Specific purpose: To inform my audience about the history, the statistics, and the recreation available in one of the most desirable resorts in the United States.

Title of speech.

This is the goal the speaker seeks to accomplish.

Introduction

I. **Open with impact:** Imagine a place where the rivers are flowing, the sun is shining, and the fun is unlimited, where there is never a dull moment, and the freedom of the outdoors will captivate your mind.

II. **Focus on thesis statement:** Lake Tahoe is one of the most desirable destination vacation spots in the United States.

III. **Connect with audience:** If you've never visited Lake Tahoe, now is your chance to learn about what this beautiful place has to offer.

IV. **Preview:** First I will discuss the physical characteristics and statistics about Lake Tahoe; second, I reveal the historic background of the area; and finally, I will explain the recreation that Lake Tahoe has to offer.

Speech is divided into introduction, body, and conclusion.

Introduction opens with impact, focuses on the thesis statement, connects with the audience, and previews the remainder of the speech.

Body

I. **Main point:** First, the statistical information regarding the beautiful lake is surprising:
   A. Lake Tahoe's original Indian name was "Lake of the Sky."
   B. Lake Tahoe is the highest alpine lake of its size in the entire United States at 6,229 feet above sea level.
   C. The lake is 72 miles around—longer than the English Channel is wide.
   D. Two-thirds of the lake rests in California and the other third in Nevada.
   E. The average depth is 1,000 feet, and the deepest part is believed to be 1,645 feet deep
   F. Although the water is clean and clear, its average temperature is 68°F, which is so cold cowboys who have drowned have been found perfectly preserved.
   G. There are over 40 trillion gallons of water in Lake Tahoe, enough to cover California with 14 inches.

(**Signpost:** Now that you know all of the facts and statistics about Lake Tahoe, I will move on to my second point: the historical background of the "Lake of the Sky.")

Main points begin with roman numeral I.

Signposts are indicated by parentheses.

II. **Main point:** Many important events have shaped the historical background of Lake Tahoe.
   A. The discovery was accidental when, on their way to survey a new road to Mexico, John C. Fremont and Christopher (Kit) Carson discovered the "Lake of the Sky" on February 14, 1844.
   B. For many years prior to the discovery by Fremont, the Washoe Indians had been occupying the land.
   C. Two and a half years later in December of 1846, the famous Donner Party ran into trouble 15 miles north of Lake Tahoe.

continued

Sample Speech Outline (*continued*)

    D. Eventually, as more people started expanding westward, silver was discovered in the mountains of the upper Nevada portion of the lake.

    E. The forests were almost wiped out, but luckily the silver ran out first.

    F. Thirsty westerners tried to tap the waters for their own use.

    G. In 1906, houses began to appear.

    H. Rich visitors came to rusticate in high style.

    I. By 1942, approximately 3,000 people visited on weekends.

Sources are cited within parentheses in APA style; see Chapter 7.

    J. As many as 50,000 people came to the North Shore alone on weekends (Miller, 1997, p. 2).

(**Signpost:** Rich with history, Lake Tahoe also has many forms of recreation and entertainment.)

III. Main point: Summer or winter, it doesn't matter when you visit Lake Tahoe.

    A. If you decide to visit in the summer, the freedom of the outdoors will captivate you.

    B. The snow brings an amazing beauty to its surroundings.

    C. After a long day in the sun or snow, it's time to realize what Lake Tahoe's night life is all about.

(**Signpost:** To summarize, there is never enough time at the "Lake of the Sky.")

Conclusion

Conclusion summarizes speech and closes with impact.

  I. Summarize: Today I have shared as much as possible about the statistics, history, and vacation opportunities of the beautiful lake called Tahoe.

  II. Close with impact: Now, imagine all of this fun and excitement, but imagine that you are there and you are having the best experience of your life.

References

References are listed alphabetically by author at end following APA style presented in Chapter 7.

Carter, C. (1983). *There are so many I wish I'd asked my father.* Truckee, CA: Learning Opportunities.

James, G. W. (1956). The lake of the sky: Lake Tahoe. Chicago: Powner Co.

Miller, S. (1997, November 18). Ski season crowds. *Sierra Sun,* p. 2.

to know your introduction and conclusion very well. The best open or close to a speech can be undone by a speaker who reads it from cards, rather than making direct eye contact with the audience.

Cards about 4 by 6 inches in size seem to work best. Larger cards are too obtrusive; smaller cards require you to strain to see your notes and to constantly be shuffling cards. The following are some helpful hints for preparing note cards.

Tips and Tactics

Tips for Preparing Note Cards

- *Use bright colors and large, bold lettering.* This will make your notes easier to see.

- *Use no more than five or six lines per note card.* If you cram too much on one card, you'll end up confusing yourself.

- *Put each part of a speech on a separate card.* For example, your introduction might go on one card, the body on another, and the conclusion on a third. That way you won't have trouble finding your main points after you complete your introduction nor will you confuse your conclusion with a main point.

- *Number your cards.* It is easy to lose track of your place while speaking. One way to help prevent this from happening is to number each card. That way, even if you inadvertently get your cards out of order, you can quickly recover.

- *Write on only one side of a card.* If you try to write on both sides, you compound the chances of losing your place.

- *Highlight main ideas.* Just as you highlight key passages in books, highlight the points you wish to emphasize.

- *Use note cards to make comments to yourself.* It is perfectly appropriate, for example, to write prompts to yourself on your notes. For example, you might write "O.H." to remind yourself to show an overhead at that point in your speech.

- *Don't try to write out your speech word for word.* This will only encourage you to read your speech, rather than present it in a conversational manner. The only exception to this rule would be exact quotations, facts, or statistics, which obviously you need to write out. It is best to keep lengthy quotations to a minimum in speeches, however, as they inevitably lead to loss of eye contact with your audience.

Speaker's notes contain all the same ideas as the complete outline, but the words are designed to cue you to what comes next. Only with practice can you speak from these notes and still be assured of covering all the ideas in the original outline. And this is the final point we wish to make: Successful speakers practice prior to an actual presentation. No matter how good your organization seems, it is only as good as your ability to deliver it. That takes practice. And practice doesn't mean running through your speech the night before or, even worse, the morning of your presentation. It means devoting significant amounts of time to practicing your speech until you have internalized its basic organization.

OVERHEAD TRANSPARENCIES

Finally, you also can use overhead transparencies to guide you through your speech. Instead of note cards, you record the main points of your speech on transparencies and use them as prompts. You may also want to record subpoints that support the main points. As was the case with note cards, you do not want to outline your entire speech on overheads. Only the skeletal features of your speech should be included. Although we'll have more to say about using overheads in Chapter 11, here are some tips for making overheads and using them as prompts.

Notice how this speaker has used highlighting to emphasize key points on these note cards.

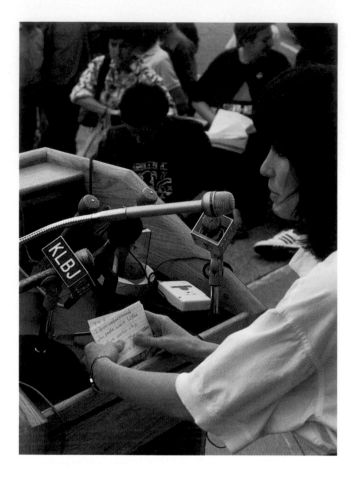

Tips and Tactics

Preparing Overhead Transparencies as Prompts

- Dedicate one transparency to previewing your main points.
- Use one transparency for each main point and, possibly, supporting subpoints if their number is few.
- Follow the guidelines beginning on page 303 in Chapter 11 for preparing and using overhead transparencies effectively.

SUMMARY

Organization is vital to effective public speaking. As with all aspects of speech making, you should focus on your audience when organizing your speech. A well-organized speech refines the specific purpose, which describes what you want to accomplish in your speech. Next, you must create a clear thesis statement, which captures the essence of your speech.

Organize the body of the speech before tackling the introduction or conclusion. Two to five focused *main points* should fully develop the thesis statement.

Use parallel structure, simplicity, and balance to help your audience remember your main points. Develop main points by using *subpoints, supporting points*, and further support. Organize the speech body in one of several patterns: *time, extended narrative, spatial, categorical, problem–solution, refutational, causal, motivated sequence, wave, spiral, star*, or *call and response*. Use *signposts* as transitional statements to help your audience follow the organization of your speech.

The introduction to a speech should have impact, focus on the thesis statement, connect with the audience, and preview the body of your speech. Effective openings may include a brief story; a quotation; a startling statement; reference to the audience, the occasion, or a current event; appropriate humor; a personal experience; or a thought-provoking question.

The conclusion to a speech should summarize the main points of the speech and close with impact. Ways to close include a quotation, a brief anecdote, a direct appeal to action, or a return to the opening theme.

A *formal outline* is sometimes required of beginning speakers. Many instructors prefer students to use standard outline notation and write a complete-sentence outline. Speaker's notes, usually placed on small cards, can be used when presenting the speech, as can overhead transparencies.

Check Your Understanding: Exercises and Activities

1. Consider the following speech introductions. Rewrite them to fit the "open, focus, and connect" model suggested in this chapter.

   Today, I'm going to talk to you about pit bulls. I got attacked last week by a pit bull, and I think they are really dangerous. Something's got to be done!

   Have any of you ever thought about going snowboarding? I really like to snowboard, and that's what my speech is going to be about.

   I think capital punishment is wrong. What if somebody who was innocent got killed? I'm going to persuade all of you that life without parole is a better way to go.

2. View a speech on videotape (either the tape that accompanies this text or a tape of a well-known public speaker). If no tape is available, consult an audiotape or a printed transcript of a speech. Using the format described in this chapter, construct a complete-sentence outline of the speech. How closely did the speech seem to follow the steps indicated in the chapter? Was the speech easy to outline? If not, how could the speaker have made the organization clearer?

3. Analyze a print ad in a magazine or newspaper, to see whether it uses a problem–solution, causal, or motivated sequence. If so, explain how each step is fulfilled. If not, discuss how the ad might be modified to fit one of these organizational patterns.

4. On the following pages is an outline of a speech, followed by a list of points in scrambled order. Your task is to match up the appropriate sentence from the scrambled list with the points in the outline. This may be done as an individual or a group exercise, depending on your instructor's preference.

Specific purpose: _____

Introduction

   I. Open with impact: _____

  II. Focus: _____

 III. Connect with your audience: _____

 IV. Preview: _____

Body

   I. Main point: _____

     A. _____

     B. _____

     C. _____

(*Signpost:* _____)

  II. Main point: _____

     A. _____

     B. _____

     C. _____

(*Signpost:* _____)

 III. Main point: _____

     A. _____

     B. _____

     C. _____

Conclusion

   I. Summarize: _____

     A _____

     B. _____

     C. _____

  II. Close with impact: _____

Scrambled list:

1. Use fresh bread, preferably whole-grain.
2. Use a quality jelly or jam, made without artificial additives.
3. Use either plain or chunky peanut butter.
4. You must have the necessary ingredients.
5. Fold the wax paper neatly around the sandwich.
6. Place the sandwich in a paper bag.
7. Use a biodegradable wrapper, such as wax paper, rather than plastic wrap.
8. You need to package the sandwich to take to school.
9. Put the two slices together.
10. Spread the first slice with peanut butter.
11. Spread the other slice with jelly or jam.
12. You need to assemble the sandwich.
13. To inform the class how to make a peanut butter and jelly sandwich.
14. First make sure you have the necessary ingredients.
15. Finally, wrap the sandwich.
16. Second, assemble the sandwich.
17. Enjoy your lunch and go to a movie with the money you've saved.
18. You can save money and eat better.
19. Today you will learn how to make the perfect peanut butter and jelly sandwich.
20. Are you tired of spending $5 for a greasy hamburger and fries?
21. Making a peanut butter and jelly sandwich involves three basic steps: having the ingredients, assembling the sandwich, and packaging the sandwich.
22. After you have the ingredients, you need to make the sandwich.
23. Unless you are eating it immediately, the sandwich must be wrapped to stay fresh.
24. To review, there are three steps:

Notes

1. Alan Monroe, *Principles and Types of Speech* (New York: Scott, Foresman, 1935). See also the most recent edition: Bruce E. Gronbeck, Raymie E. McKerrow, Douglas Ehninger, and Alan H. Monroe, *Principles and Types of Speech Communication*, 12th ed. (New York: HarperCollins, 1994).

2. Deidra Dukes, "The Right to Breathe," speech delivered at California State University, Chico, 1992.

CHAPTER 9

The disabled
are a powerful
voice against
marginalizing
language.

Language: Making Verbal Sense of Your Message

OBJECTIVES

After reading this chapter, you should be able to:

- Construct examples that illustrate the relationship between language and thought.
- Describe the role language plays in relating to cultural, demographic, and individual diversity.
- Describe the "different voice" that characterizes women's and men's speech.
- Differentiate between denotative and connotative meaning.
- Use rhetorical devices such as metaphor and simile to vary language intensity in your speeches.
- Use concrete language, as well as contrast and action, to reduce uncertainty on the part of your audience.
- Use verbal immediacy and transitional devices in your speeches.
- Avoid marginalizing and totalizing language, using inclusive language instead.
- Avoid sexist and stereotypic language.

KEY CONCEPTS

competence-enhancing language

connotative meaning

denotative meaning

inclusive language

language intensity

linguistic relativity hypothesis

marginalizing language

sexist language

totalizing language

verbal immediacy

verbal qualifiers

How can I tell what I think until I see what I say?

—EDWARD MORGAN FORSTER[1]

235

Mary Shapiro and Thomas Donovan have always had a rocky relationship. Shapiro is the former chief of the Commodities Futures Trading Commission, the federal agency that polices the volatile commodities market. Donovan is president of the Chicago Board of Trade, which promotes the busiest commodities exchange in the United States. When Shapiro learned that Donovan had told his board members during a closed-door meeting that he wouldn't be "intimidated by some blond, 5-foot 2-inch little girl," their relationship took a turn for the worse.[2]

To suggest that Shapiro was displeased about the content of Donovan's speech would be an understatement. She quickly let the financial press know that she wouldn't be bullied by people "lobbing verbal grenades through the window."[3] For the record, Shapiro added that she was also 5-feet, 5-inches tall and, at age 39, no longer a little girl.

This example points to an incontrovertible fact: Language is not neutral. The words we choose to express ourselves and to describe others can elicit the full range of human emotions. This chapter is about language and its role in giving meaning and impact to our ideas. It is also about the power of words and how they affect the way we think about ourselves, our experiences, and the people with whom we come into contact.

On one level, our goal in this chapter is to assist you in appreciating the larger role language plays in our lives. On another level, our goal is to show you how you can use your appreciation of language to construct messages that will be appropriate to both your speech's purpose and the audience with whom you share it. We'll explore the relationship between words and the objects they are meant to represent, how language influences experiences, how language relates to audience diversity, and how you can use language to enhance how you and your speech are perceived by your audience.

LANGUAGE, PERCEPTION, AND EXPERIENCE

Just as a map is not the territory it represents, a word is not the object it is intended to describe. Words are simply spoken sounds or written characters that symbolize or communicate meaning. People use them to refer to the persons, places, and things with which they come into contact. Their meaning depends on the set of experiences people associate with the words when they use, see, or hear them. This fact that meaning depends on experience applies to the members of your audience.

Words have a dramatic impact on the process of perception. When we are told something is "good" or "bad" before we see or experience it, we are likely to rate it the same way. In experiments where subjects have been shown pictures of people described as popular, the subjects rate them as highly attractive. Subjects who are told the same people are unpopular rate them as significantly less attractive. Thus, the words you choose when you speak will influence how your audience perceives your message.

What is true of individual words is even more true of the language one speaks. Whether you speak English, French, Spanish, or Russian makes a differ-

A map represents a territory, but it is not always accurate, as this 16th-century map shows.

ence in how you experience the world. Just as perception influences the meaning assigned to words, language influences the meaning people assign to everything they experience. According to the **linguistic relativity hypothesis,** introduced more than 40 years ago by cultural anthropologist Benjamin Whorf, what we perceive is influenced by the language in which we think and speak. Different languages lead to different patterns of thought.[4]

Whorf formulated this hypothesis while studying the Native American language of the Hopi. He discovered there are no words in their language for the concept of incremental time: no seconds, no minutes, and no hours. Thus, it would never occur to the Hopi that someone could be half an hour early or late for a visit, because they have no words for the concept.

Each language has certain concepts that cannot be easily expressed in other languages. Thus, the expression "something was lost in the translation" doesn't mean part of a statement was literally lost as it was translated from one language to another. It means an equivalent idea couldn't be found in the second language, so part of the statement's original meaning was diminished. In constructing a speech, the first thing you'll want to do is choose words and sentences that you believe will lead people to perceive and think about your speech as you intend them to.

LANGUAGE AND AUDIENCE DIVERSITY

Having seen that words and language color our perception and experience, we can now examine the relationship between language and the three types of diversity (cultural, demographic, and individual) introduced in Chapter 5. Understanding the connections between language and diversity is crucial to effective speaking, since today's audience is more diverse than ever.

Language and Cultural Diversity

The United States is a multiracial, multiethnic, multicultural nation. With the exception of Native Americans, 98 percent of the population can trace its ancestry to another country.

Recall from Chapter 5 that *cultural diversity* is multidimensional, including audience characteristics such as individualism/collectivism, and masculinity/femininity. Knowing something about the dimensions of culture reflected in your audience is essential to choosing appropriate language for your speech.

One of us, for example, had the opportunity to attend an IBM recognition event where former NFL quarterback and ESPN announcer Joe Theismann was one of the keynote speakers. Theismann's audience included many people from IBM operations in the Far East and Latin America, both of which are largely collectivistic in outlook. Although most North Americans in the audience responded positively to Theismann's speech, not everyone did. His remarks were perceived as egotistical and self-aggrandizing by people from such places as Japan, Taiwan, Singapore, Argentina, and Venezuela. As one person from Buenos Aires remarked, "You would have thought American football was an individual sport listening to him [Theismann]—that he won the Super Bowl single-handedly. Does he know a word other than I?"

All too often speakers choose language appropriate to their culture, but not necessarily the cultures of their audience members. Like Theismann, they naively assume that what is good enough for their culture is good enough for everyone's. Of course, this kind of thinking is not only inaccurate, it is arrogant.

Even commonplace language choices, such as what name to call a person, can be influenced by culture. For example, in many cultures, such as those that use the Spanish language, strangers are not addressed informally, and certainly not by their first names. A salesperson, for example, who addresses a potential client by his or her first name may, unintentionally, offend that person. The best advice is to ask people how they prefer to be addressed, rather than automatically assuming that they want to be on a first-name basis.

At the same time, listeners should understand that speakers may be unfamiliar with their cultural background, and not attribute malice to them for a linguistic faux pas. We all have "hot buttons," words that offend or annoy us, and these can sometimes be difficult for others to discern. For example, people of the World War II generation sometimes refer to people of Japanese ancestry in ways that are today felt to be offensive. Yet they may mean nothing by the words, which in their formative years were considered commonplace and inoffensive. Thus, although we should all be respectful of cultural diversity, we need to recognize our responsibilities not only as speakers, but as listeners as well. It is impossible in today's multicultural society for speakers to be familiar with everyone's linguistic preferences. If a speaker's intentions are honorable, an ill-chosen word or two should not be allowed to obscure the underlying message.

Language and Demographic Diversity

You will recall from Chapter 5 that *demographic diversity* is reflected in the groups to which people belong and with which they identify. This includes such characteristics as nationality, race and ethnicity, gender, and religion. Demographic diversity also includes social and economic class, the region of the country that people call home, and the generation to which people belong.

Demographic diversity, although always an important consideration of a speaker's audience analysis, has become even more so. Today's college classroom is likely to be populated by people with a variety of different demographic backgrounds. Race and ethnicity, as cases in point, are often an important part of today's audience diversity.

How you refer to a specific racial or ethnic group can have a strong impact on the individual members of that group in your audience. For example, when Anglos speak to a gathering of English-speaking people of Mexican descent, they need to choose the appropriate language in referring to the audience. Scholars Mario Garcia and Rodolfo Alvarez suggest that people of Mexican descent in the United States constitute several rather than a single demographic group.[5] Two such reference groups are Mexican Americans and Chicanos/Chicanas. The Mexican American group comprises people who immigrated from Mexico to border states, such as California and Texas, following World War II. According to Garcia and Alvarez people who consider themselves Mexican Americans are generally older and more conservative than those who identify themselves as Chicanos or Chicanas, who are generally younger and more militant.

Chicanos and Chicanas came of age in the 1960s and gained some attention in the 1970s. They perceived Mexican immigrants who wanted to assimilate with the predominant Anglo culture as sellouts. To distinguish themselves from the Mexican American group, Chicanos and Chicanas adopted specific patterns of behaving, including their own code words. The list of code words included *vendido* (sellout) and *socios* (the old boy network). Today, members of this demographic group sometimes refer to each other as *veteranos* (veterans). Thus, referring to Chicanos/Chicanas as Mexican Americans in a speech would be inappropriate. As a speaker, you need to learn as much as possible about the

Edward James Olmos's film *My Family, Mi Familia* did an excellent job of showing how people who share the same culture use language differently depending on their generation.

language preferences of your audiences. Otherwise, you may inadvertently offend at least some of them.

The varied preferences of Spanish-speaking people also apply to many other demographic groups as well. Some African Americans prefer being referred to as Black. And though they may be too polite to tell you so, the Chinese, Hmong, Japanese, Korean, Laotian, Taiwanese, and Vietnamese prefer being referred to by their nationality rather than being categorized as Asian.

As a speaker, you cannot afford to overlook the demography of your audience in choosing language. How you refer to people who identify themselves with specific demographic groups and the words you use in talking about the demographic groups themselves will influence not only how the content of your speech is received but audience perceptions of your credibility as well.

Language and Individual Diversity

Choosing appropriate language for a speech doesn't stop with a consideration of cultural and demographic diversity. You also must consider and evaluate *individ-*

Pola Lopez's graphic powerfully demonstrates how words can alter perceptions.

ual diversity, which reflects such factors as personal views on the meaning of gender, sexual orientation, and religious beliefs. The fact that someone is Catholic, Jewish, Muslim, Hindu, or Protestant, for example, doesn't tell you much about the diversity of beliefs held by people who consider themselves members of one of these religious groups. Moreover, religious beliefs are only one element of the individual diversity of your audience. Consequently, before choosing the language with which you'll construct your speech, you also will have to explore other individual beliefs, attitudes, and values of the people in your audience.

As a case in point, think about an audience of people who describe themselves as Christians. Such people are extraordinarily diverse in what they believe individually. Some think the Bible is to be taken literally as the word of God; others believe the Bible should be interpreted metaphorically. Knowing this kind of information in advance is essential for speakers who want the language of their speech to be audience appropriate.

Remember, the words and sentences with which you construct your speech will influence the meaning of your speech in the minds of the audience members.

You want to control this process as much as possible. Thus, doing your homework about the relationship between language and diversity as it reflects your speech transaction is a matter of common sense.

USING LANGUAGE EFFECTIVELY

Let's assume that you have thoroughly analyzed the speech situation, including how audience diversity should be reflected in your choice of words to construct your speech. You are now ready to begin writing the outline of your speech with language that will enhance your credibility with your audience and create a high degree of mutual understanding. There are a number of guidelines you will want to follow in this process. The first rule concerns choosing language that makes every member of your audience feel included in your message. This is known as inclusive language, as opposed to marginalizing or totalizing language, concepts we will explain shortly. The second rule concerns choosing language that will enhance rather than undermine audience perceptions of your competence as a speaker.[6] Finally, the third rule concerns using language to its fullest potential to involve your audience in your speech.

Use Inclusive Language

The first rule in choosing the words of your speech is to use language that is inclusive. **Inclusive language** helps people believe that they not only have a stake in matters of societal importance, but also have power in this regard. Inclusive language doesn't leave people out of the picture because of their gender, race, ethnicity, age, religion, sexual orientation, or ability. At the same time, however, it avoids defining people on the basis of such characteristics.

Remember the example with which we opened this chapter? Thomas Donovan, president of the Chicago Board of Trade, referred to Mary Shapiro, former chief of the Commodities Futures Trading Commission, as a "5-foot 2-inch little girl." Are his words an example of inclusive language? Of course not. His statement illustrates two types of language you'll want to avoid in constructing your speech. The first type is called *marginalizing*. The second type is called *totalizing*.

Marginalizing language diminishes people's importance and makes them appear to be less powerful, less significant, and less worthwhile than they are. Marginalizing language also appeals to biases audience members may hold consciously or subconsciously. When Thomas Donovan called Mary Shapiro a little girl, for example, his language was more than sexist or politically incorrect. He was using language to make Mary Shapiro appear a powerless child incapable of directing powerful adults like himself.

Totalizing language defines people on the basis of a single attribute, such as race, ethnicity, biological sex, or ability. In a speech, the following statements would exemplify totalizing:

"The disabled in this audience . . ."

"As a woman, you've got to learn to assert yourself."

"As a victim of racism . . ."

"Because you are Latino . . ."

"This is really a guy book."

Each of these statements could be well-meaning and intended to demonstrate the speaker's sensitivity to people with disabilities, women, Latinos, and men. Yet, what each statement does in reality is call attention to a single attribute among audience members and treat the attribute as if it were the only thing about audience members that truly counts. Disabled people are more than their disability, women and men are more than their biological sex, and people discriminated against by racists are more than simply victims. Speakers need to use language that acknowledges that people are complex individuals. The late Barbara Jordan spoke eloquently of the need to include *all* people in our vision of America (see the following box " 'We, the People': Barbara Jordan").

Use Competence-Enhancing Language

A number of researchers have documented that there is a difference between "powerful" and "powerless" speech.[7] Powerless speech is characterized by the use of language such as hedges (I *kind of* agree with you), qualifiers (I *could* be wrong), hesitations (uhs and ums), and tag questions (That's right, *isn't it?*). On the other hand, powerful speech is fluent and direct and avoids these types of phrases. Messages containing a significant amount of powerless language produce lower ratings of communicator power, attractiveness, and competence, whereas powerful speech produces higher ratings on these dimensions.

Therefore, the second rule to follow in constructing the text of your speech is to use powerful, **competence-enhancing language,** words that emphasize rather than undermine audience perceptions of your competence. Language that enhances perceptions of competence avoids verbal qualifiers.[8] **Verbal qualifiers** erode the impact of what you say in a speech.

Beginning speakers often use verbal qualifiers without thinking of them as such. They say, for example:

"It's just my opinion, but . . ."

"You'll probably disagree, but . . ."

"This is my belief, but you may think otherwise."

"I'm pretty sure, though I could be wrong in stating . . ."

"Of course, your opinion counts at least as much as mine."

Competence-enhancing language emphasizes the significance of what you say in a speech. Whether giving an informative, persuasive, or testimonial speech, you should be the expert on the subject or person. Not only does this require that you do your homework, it also requires you to choose language that illustrates the fact. Using language such as the following is one way of accomplishing this without appearing to be a "know-it-all" to your audience.

"Ten years of research demonstrates that . . ."

"For the past four summers, I've been involved with . . ."

"We, the People": Barbara Jordan

The late Congresswoman and scholar Barbara Jordan was one of the most impressive and eloquent speakers of the second half of the 20th century. Not only did she possess a powerful voice and impeccable diction, she used language in a way that few could match. Many compared her speeches to those of Winston Churchill and Franklin Roosevelt. Here is a brief excerpt of her statements during the debate on the impeachment of President Nixon in 1974:

We, the people. It is a very eloquent beginning. But when that document was completed on the 17th of September in 1787, I was not included in that "We, the people." I felt somehow for many years that George Washington and Alexander Hamilton just left me out by mistake. But through the process of amendment, interpretation and court decision I have finally been included in "We, the people." [1]

Two decades later, Jordan was asked to head the United States Commission on Immigration Reform. Testifying before the very congressional committee of which she was once a member, Jordan echoed her words from long ago:

I would be the last person to claim that our nation is perfect. But we have a kind of perfection in us because our founding principle is universal—that we are all created equal regardless of race, religion or national ancestry.

When the Declaration of Independence was written, when the Constitution was adopted, when the Bill of Rights was added to it, they all applied almost exclusively to white men of Anglo-Saxon descent who owned property on the East Coast. They did not apply to me. I am female. I am black. But these self-evident principles apply to me now as they apply to everyone in this room. [2]

[1] "Barbara Jordan: A Passionate Voice," *Sacramento Bee*, 18 January 1996, A16.
[2] Jerelyn Eddings, "The Voice of Eloquent Thunder," *U.S. News and World Report*, 29 January 1996, 16.

"Having lived all my life in the United States, . . ."
"Scholars tell us . . ."

Each of these statements begins with a phrase that emphasizes the speaker's competence. They imply that through either research or experience, the speaker knows his or her subject well. You should not exaggerate your claims beyond what you know to be true, but you should take full credit for the facts as you know them.

Use Language to Its Fullest Potential

The third and final rule is to use language to its fullest potential in your speeches. There are many ways to do this. The ones we encourage you to use involve denotative and connotative meaning, grammar, pronunciation, uncertainty reduction, immediacy, and expressiveness.

Denotative and Connotative Meaning   Words have two general types of meaning.[9] The first is **denotative meaning,** which is the generally agreed upon meaning for a word that you find in a dictionary. The second is **connotative meaning,** which is a secondary meaning, usually carrying an attitudinal or emotional component. This meaning will depend on the speech situation and the composition of your audience. Under most circumstances a speech will include words with both types of meaning. On occasion, though, a speaker may choose to emphasize words he or she believes are high in one or the other types of meaning.

In a speech before a group of people who speak English as a second language, for example, speakers will want to use words in a manner consistent with their denotative meaning. This is because the audience probably will translate words literally rather than figuratively. Imagine the difficulty non-native speakers of American-style English would have in translating a statement such as "How many of you have lived with a roommate who bogarts the phone?" Their only reference for the word *bogart* (hoard or fail to share) might be Humphrey Bogart, the star of classic films such as *Casablanca* and *The African Queen.*

On occasion, however, speakers may want to use words that have special meaning to the context in which the speech will take place and to the audience members who will share in the transaction. In a creative writing class, for instance, the instructor wants to encourage people to think about how they can evoke multiple images in the minds of readers. Thus, the teacher might ask class members to rewrite the sentence "The sky is blue" so that it will stimulate the readers' imagination. As a result, students might write, "The azure sky on a cloudless day" or "The sky had turned to the color of blue ice."

The point is that as a speaker, you need to think in advance about the denotative and connotative meanings of the words with which you construct your speech. Don't leave the issue to chance or assume that your audience will "know what you mean" when you use a word.

Grammar   In the effort to use language to its fullest potential, speakers need to consider the rules of grammar. Some common mistakes are double negatives, incorrect subject–verb agreement, and inappropriate slang.

A double negative occurs when someone uses a negative to modify another negative. As in mathematics, a negative times a negative is actually a positive. Thus, "No one never works around here" really means that there is no person who "never works." That suggests people really do work, the opposite of what the speaker intended.

Incorrect subject–verb agreement occurs when a plural subject is matched with a singular verb or vice versa. Thus, you want to avoid such sentences as, "We is going to the movies."

Finally, unless they are essential to the speech, certain expressions common in everyday conversation are inappropriate in a speech. Many speech teachers object in particular to the overuse of "you know" and "like." It is irritating to hear, "You know, like, I really mean it."

This is far from a complete list of grammatical pitfalls for the speaker. And a speech is not as formal as written English. Although you are not supposed to

Last year, people skied on champagne powder, windblown pack, groomed, corn snow, cold smoke, frozen granular, firm, good crud, bottomless powder, sugar, machine tilled, crust, hero powder, buffed snow, man made, corduroy, ball bearings, velvet, cut up powder, spring snow, ballroom, and acre after acre of virgin powder.

[*Eskimos may have more words for snow, but we have more lifts.*]

THE ASPENS
SNOWMASS • BUTTERMILK
ASPEN MOUNTAIN

Aspen Central Reservations 1-800-262-7756 Snowmass Central Reservations 1-800-332-3245.
The Aspen Skiing Company Hotels: The Little Nell, The Snowmass Club 1-800-525-6200.

This ad uses terms for snow that are meaningful to skiers and snowboarders. The language is unique to their sports and enhances the images that come to mind when they think about the cold white stuff that is simply "snow" to the rest of us.

end a sentence with a preposition, it is not uncommon to hear someone in a speech say, "I know what it's all about." The best advice we can give is that if you are in doubt about any grammatical issues, consult someone who is knowledgeable and ask his or her advice or check a grammar handbook, such as Strunk and White's *Elements of Style*.

Pronunciation   Anyone who thinks pronunciation doesn't count is sorely mistaken. Every time we hear someone say "nukular" instead of "nuclear" or "expresso" instead of "espresso," we grit our teeth. And as the box "Common Irritants Grate on the Ears," a reprint of a Dear Abby column, so well illustrates, we aren't the only ones who react negatively to mispronounced words. However, even Dear Abby can get it wrong. She suggests that *jewelry* should be pronounced "jool-uh-ree." If you check your dictionary, you'll discover that she has misplaced

Common Irritants Grate on the Ears

DEAR READERS:

I recently wrote a column on the misuse of words, grammatical goofs and assorted speech irritants, and invited my readers to send me their pet peeves concerning same. Well, here's Collection No. 2:

The most annoying speech irritant is still all those "you knows?" and a close second is beginning every sentence with "basically." People who say, "I could care less" mean to convey that they care so little they could *not* care less—which is what they should have said in the first place.

Most people, even those in the jewelry business, pronounce "jewelry" as "jool-ree" instead of "jool-uh-ree."

And many people in the real estate business pronounce "Realtor" as "reel-a-tor"; it's "reel-tor," really it is.

If you think "epitome" means the ultimate, the tops or the height of—go stand in the corner. "Epitome" means a person or thing that is typical of, or possesses to a high degree the features of a whole class.

The word "arthritis" is correctly pronounced "arth-right-us" (three syllables); so why do so many people insist on pronouncing it "arthur-ri-tis"? The same for the word "athlete"—not "ath-a-leet."

My pet peeve is the lawyer or journalist who uses the word "gentleman" as follows: "According to the police report, a masked gentleman knocked the elderly woman to the ground and fled with her purse." (Some gentleman!)

The word "nauseous" is often misused, even by well-educated professionals, instead of the word "nauseated." Here's a way to remember the distinction: If you are nauseated, you are sick. If you are nauseous, you make other people sick.

Regardless of what you read in the ads, "Where it's at" is incorrect. "Where it is" is correct. Forget "at."

Do you know what an asterisk is? Of course you do. It's the little starlike symbol used in print to indicate the omission of letters or words. But why do most people pronounce it "ass-trick"?

The confusion with "lie" and "lay" is still baffling to many. I explained that people lie down and chickens lay eggs. A reader now informs me, "People lay money on the counter, dogs lie by the fire, and magazines are found lying on the table. All last summer, I lay in my hammock and didn't produce a single egg."

Prominent newscasters have said "most unique" and "partially destroyed." "Unique" and "destroyed" are absolute terms and cannot be qualified, any more than "pregnant" or "dead."

Please do not confuse "momento" and "memento." A momento is a unit of time (Spanish: "uno momento"). A memento is a souvenir, a memory.

Finally, the misplaced "only" is a common gaffe. For example, the one-time popular song, "I Only Have Eyes for You" is meant to say, "I have eyes for you only." For a lover to croon, "I only have eyes for you," is to say: "I have no lips, no arms or anything else—only eyes—for you," which would be a grave disappointment for both of them.

Never say, "It's a true fact." If it's a fact, it's true. Also forget "old antique." If it's an antique—it's old.

In closing, for heaven's sake—never say, "for heaven's sakes." Some people do, so for heaven's sake, watch your language. And if you have a pet peeve I haven't mentioned, please send it to me.

the "l." The proper pronunciation is "joo-uhl-ree." Perhaps that's worth 10 lashes with a wet noodle.

Mispronunciation of words can lead to a number of problems. Two of the most significant involve meaning and how you are perceived. Frequently, for example, people say "assure" when they mean "ensure." Assuring your child that she is safe is not the same as ensuring the safety of your child. *Assure* and *ensure* mean two different things. Mispronouncing words may also lead audience members to form an unfavorable impression of you. Although saying "I'd like to go wid' chew" may be acceptable in conversations with friends, it won't enhance your credibility in the eyes of most audience members.

Uncertainty Reduction   You'll also want to choose language for your speeches that reduces feelings of uncertainty among audience members. Uncertainty-reducing language is concrete rather than relative and ambiguous, varies in its level of intensity, invites contrasts, makes use of words that suggest action, and makes effective use of signposts. Although there are exceptions, people prefer messages that reduce rather than increase uncertainty, whether the message is meant to inform people about a problem-solving strategy, teach them about principles of accounting, or alleviate their fears about catching a deadly disease.[10]

Concrete Language   Language that is concrete is less likely to increase audience uncertainty than language that is ambiguous or relative. The more concrete language is, the less the listener has to mentally stretch to understand it. The word *cat*, for example, is less concrete than the phrase "blue-eyed, long-haired Persian cat." The word *cat* requires us to come up with our own image of a cat. The phrase supplies us, at the least, with a specific kind of cat with which to build a mental image.

Ambiguous words generally are abstract. As a result, how audience members interpret them depends largely on their individual experience. Consider the word *pornography*. As we know all too well, what one person considers a work of art another person may dismiss as filth. To simply describe something as a piece of pornography, then, takes control of the meaning of the word out of the hands of the speaker and puts it in the hands of individual audience members. Relative words, such as *pure* and *a lot,* suffer from the same problem. What is pure to you may not be pure to us. And while one person may think 10 is "a lot," another may think it's "a little." The more ambiguous or relative your language is, the more likely your speech will have an effect other than what you intended. Use concrete language as much as possible.

Language Intensity   A second suggestion for reducing uncertainty is to vary the intensity of your language as you speak. **Language intensity** is the degree to which words and phrases deviate from neutral. The intensity of the words we use varies along a continuum ranging from relatively neutral to highly intense. For example, "savory and delicious" is more intense than "tastes good." By the same token, the phrase "I find you attractive" is not nearly as intense as the phrase "I wanna rock your world."

Care needs to be exercised to avoid words so intense they may cause people to react negatively—to turn off to what we are trying to say in a speech. Language that is threatening or highly fear arousing, for example, tends to turn people off. So does language generally regarded as obscene or off-color.

Contrast and Action   A third way you can reduce uncertainty is to use contrasting phrases and words that suggest action. In discussing the irrationality that of-

John Madden's use of action words has made him a fixture as a sports announcer.

ten grips the minds of people when going to war, German philosopher Friedrich Nietzsche wrote, "How good . . . bad music and bad reasons sound when we march against the enemy."[11] Nietzsche's simple contrast between good and bad is much more effective in making war seem illogical than any extended discussion would have been. And this would have been especially true had Nietzsche delivered the line in a speech.

As you know from your own experience, public speaking is ill suited to extended and convoluted language. The simpler and more active your language, the better. Although we do not approve of the way advertisers abuse grammar, we have to admit that copywriters can be masters at expressing ideas simply and powerfully. The ad slogan "Got Milk!" for instance, is much more effective in getting the point across than "Have you ever thought about how much better a peanut butter and jelly sandwich or Oreo cookies would taste with a cold glass of milk?"

Try to use words that are exciting and action oriented. For example, which do you find more involving, "The speech was well received" or "The speech was a 10"? What about "He got mad" versus "He went ballistic"? To hear examples of action words, listen to sportscaster John Madden. His speech is liberally sprinkled with action words such as "whack," "annihilate," and "wham."

Signposts   The fourth and final technique you can use to reduce audience uncertainty is to make effective use of signposts, which we explained in Chapter 8.

We've repeatedly emphasized how important it is to let your audience know where you are going with your speech. You know from your own experience taking lecture notes that it's much easier to follow an instructor who uses verbal signposts that alert you to changes in direction or clearly link one thought to another. You need to do the same for the members of your audience.

Signposts are transitional words and phrases, such as those discussed in Chapter 8, that tell your audience you are about to make or already have made a shift in direction. Signposts also serve to verbally link your thoughts as you speak. It's always a good idea to let your audience know that there is a sequence to your message— "Let's consider three important issues"—and then to remind your audience where you are in that sequence—"Having covered the first issue, let's now look at the second."

It's also a good idea to let your audience know that your speech is about to end by using transitional words and phrases such as "lastly," "to summarize," "to conclude," and "in closing." Audiences are likely to grow impatient if they think a speech will never end.

Immediacy   A sage once said that speakers need to recognize that there's a fine line between teaching and preaching to an audience. When you teach, you involve your audience as co-participants in the transaction. Immediate language is more likely to encourage this feeling than is language that emphasizes "I'm up here and you're down there."

Verbal immediacy is the use of language that promotes the perception of closeness between speaker and audience. Words high in immediacy suggest closeness between people and imply that a speech is a transaction *between* one person and many people, rather than a one-sided event in which one speaks *to* people.[12]

Some evidence suggests that women are more inclined to use immediate language than are men. Psychology professor Carol Gilligan suggests in her groundbreaking book, *In a Different Voice,* that women tend to think in terms of "we" whereas men tend to think in terms of "me."[13] The words women typically choose to express themselves reflect their more immediate, "we" orientation. The words men often choose, on the other hand, reflect their less immediate orientation, creating unnecessary and not always desirable distance between themselves and their audience. As a general rule of thumb, speakers should try not only to think in terms of "we" but also to avoid using the pronoun "I."

Another way speakers can increase immediacy is to phrase assertions in the form of questions. For example, instead of saying, "I think," it's more immediate to say, "Wouldn't you agree?" Along the same lines, instead of saying, "I'm going to tell you," it's much more immediate to say, "Let's look at. . . ." Table 9.1 compares less and more immediate ways of using language.

Expressiveness   Finally, good speaking demands expressive language that keeps an audience involved with the transaction. This kind of language includes traditional rhetorical devices, such as metaphor, simile, alliteration, parallel structure, and repetition.

TABLE 9.1 How to Say It More Immediately

LESS IMMEDIATE	MORE IMMEDIATE
I Me You Them	We Us
I think It's my opinion I know	Wouldn't you agree? How many of us believe . . . ?
Tell Show Explain	Share Look at
Talk from	Talk between

Metaphor is one of the most powerful sources of expressive language. A metaphor is a figure of speech in which a word or phrase literally denoting one kind of object or idea is used in place of another to *suggest* a likeness or an analogy between them. It's one thing, for example, to say that a corporation is "polluting the environment." It's quite another to say that the same corporation is "raping virgin timberland." To say that "freedom is an open window" or that "music unshackles the mind and spirit" would be metaphorical. Metaphors provide an audience with a kind of linguistic break from the expected. Thus, just when audience members may be losing interest in a speech, a phrase or word can grab them by the lapels.

Metaphors should fit the topic. For example, "sports" metaphors are often used in the popular media to describe political contests. Thus, a political candidate who does well in a debate "hits a home run," whereas a less successful candidate "strikes out." Sometimes a desperate politician is said to "throw a Hail Mary pass," while the favored candidate is said to "sit on a lead." Be careful, however, not to mix metaphors. It sounds odd to say, "He scored a touchdown while steering the ship of state through troubled waters." Metaphors can add spice and interest to a speech, but they must be used appropriately.

Simile is a form of figurative language that invites a direct comparison between two things that are quite different. A simile usually contains the words *like* or *as*. "Sharp as a tack," "tight as a snare drum," and "pointed as an ice pick" are examples of simile. Similes can be used effectively to vary the intensity of your speech.

Similes differ from metaphors in that they *explicitly* state the comparison, whereas metaphors imply it. Similes are useful, therefore, in making a comparison very clear to the audience. For example, a speech on preventing sexually transmitted diseases might use a simile such as "Having unprotected sexual relations is like playing Russian roulette." On a topic such as drunk driving, one might say, "A car driven by someone under the influence of drugs or alcohol is like a loaded revolver."

Alliteration is the repetition of the same initial sound in a series of words. Jesse Jackson is famous for using alliteration to make his speeches more expressive and memorable. Instead of saying, "People need to be given a purpose," for example, Jackson might say, "Empower people with pride, and purpose is sure to follow."

One of the most famous alliterations of American political history came from former Vice President Spiro Agnew, who called his opponents in the media "nattering nabobs of negativism." The power of alliteration comes from the way it sticks in the audience's minds. The danger is that if the alliteration seems forced, it may be memorable, but ineffective.

Parallel structure is the use of the same structure for each main point of your speech. It provides a way to help your audience remember your key points and at the same time serves as a verbal cue that you are presenting a main point. For example, when John F. Kennedy ran for president, he used the phrases "I am not satisfied . . . we can do better" to highlight each of his major criticisms of the Republican administration.

In developing your speech outline, look for a consistent refrain or phrase that can serve as the touchstone for the structure of the speech. For example, a speech on gang violence might be built around several main points that each begin, "We can only stop gang violence if we all. . . ." The use of parallel structure helps the audience anticipate the points to come and remember them when the speech is over. However, one must be careful that the parallel structure really fits the speech. If not, it will seem forced and artificial.

Repetition is the use of the same words repeatedly in a speech to drive home a point. Unlike parallel structure, in which the same phrase is used only to build each main point, repetition uses a word or phrase repeatedly throughout the speech to emphasize the essential point that the speaker seeks to convey. If you recall the speech by Barbara Jordan in the box on page 244, you will note that the phrase "We, the people" is repeated three times in one short excerpt. The theme of that speech is clearly conveyed by that one phrase, taken from the U.S. Constitution.

Use Visual, Kinesthetic, and Auditory Involvement

Not all people process information in the same way. Research shows that some people need to see a lesson, others need only to hear it, and still others need to become immersed in the subject matter. These three styles of learning are technically called *visual*, *auditory*, and *kinesthetic*. The obvious way for a speaker to deal with these three is to augment a speech with visual aids, speak audibly and clearly, or involve the audience in demonstrations or other hands-on experiences. Yet, sometimes options one and three are impossible for a speaker.

To get around this fact, author and corporate trainer Loretta Malandro encourages her clients to connect metaphorically with the varied learning styles present in most audiences. Table 9.2 suggests a number of specific vi-

TABLE 9.2 Words Linked to Vision, Hearing, and Touch

VISUAL WORDS

Focus	Graphic	Watch	Colorful
Bright	Illustrate	Vision	Glimpse
Show	Color	Brilliant	Look
Pretty	See	Evident	Sight
Envision	Picture	Sketch	Shining
Draw	Hazy	Oversight	Hidden
View	Peek	Clearly	Notice
Clear	Imagine	Perspective	

AUDITORY WORDS

Listen	Ringing	Compliment	Pardon
Hear	Resonate	Loud	Sound
Discuss	Yell	Silent	Request
Declare	Told	Shout	Whispering
Implore	Call	Talk	Quiet
Acclaim	Assert	Noisy	Ask
Harmony	Profess	Orchestrate	
Petition	Noise	Address	

KINESTHETIC WORDS

Feel	Terrified	Hunger	Contact
Pressure	Burdensome	Doubt	Nurture
Hurt	Firm	Shocking	Emotion
Get the point	Tense	Heavy	Graceful
Experience	Touchy	Touch	Sensual
Longing	Pushy	Concrete	Weighty problem
Wait	Shatter	Irritated	

Source: Excerpted from: *Twentieth Century Selling.* © Dr. Loretta Malandro. Taught in her program "Speak With Impact," offered by Malandro Communication Inc., Scottsdale, Arizona.

sual, auditory, and kinesthetic words that help your audience better process your speech.

Although you may not be able to literally "show" your audience members prejudice, you can connect with visual learners by

- asking them to envision a world free of hate,
- drawing a picture of racism or sketching out an example for them, or
- making a hazy concept such as affirmative action crystal clear so that they can see the problem.

Although you may not be able to let them literally "feel" your thoughts, you can connect with audience members who need to experience some things by asking them to imagine

- what racism feels like,
- a problem as a giant weight pressing down on them, or
- how oppressed people hunger for freedom.

And though you may not be able to literally produce the "sound" of abused children for your audience members, you can connect to auditory learners by asking them

- whether they hear what you're trying to say,
- to imagine what it's like to live in a world where you cannot speak out for yourself
- to imagine the mournful sound of children crying.

The point is simple. Not everyone in your audience will respond in a like manner to the words you speak. Thus, to maximize audience members' receptivity to what you say, you must make every effort to use expressive words that reflect their different styles of information processing.

In this section we have discussed a number of guidelines for the effective use of language. They are summarized in the list that follows.

Tips and Tactics

Guidelines for Using Language Effectively

- Use language that reflects the multiracial, multiethnic, multicultural audience of today.
- Use language that includes all members of your audience. Avoid language that marginalizes or excludes some people. Also avoid language that defines people by a single attribute, such as a disability.
- Use language that enhances your audience's perception of your competence. Avoid language that undermines their confidence in you.
- Take advantage of all the potential inherent in language. Choose words carefully, with your audience in mind. Use correct grammar and pronunciation. Make your audience comfortable—reduce their uncertainty—by using concrete words, by varying the intensity of the words you choose, by using contrasting and action-oriented words, and by using signposts to signal where you are in your speech. Use language that makes your audience feel closer to you, rather than more distant. Finally, involve your audience by using rhetorical devices to make your language more expressive.
- Connect with the different styles of processing information that the members of your audience may have. Use visual, auditory, and kinesthetic words to help them process your speech.

USING LANGUAGE APPROPRIATELY

We conclude this chapter with a discussion of two issues that are not so much a matter of right and wrong but, rather, of rhetorical sensitivity. The use of language appropriate to your rhetorical situation is not just a matter of effectiveness; it is also one of being ethically sensitive to the detrimental effects stereotypic and biased language can have on people. We look at two specific types of problems caused by inappropriate language; first, the use of language that stereotypes people; second, the use of language that stereotypes people on the basis of their biological sex.

Avoid Stereotypes

Do you see anything wrong with the following references?

"John's a victim of cystic fibrosis."

"Don't forget that Susan's wheelchair bound!"

"It's okay, Lupe, there's plenty of disabled seating in the new auditorium."

"The Howards' baby is physically challenged."

According to the Disabled Student Services on our campus, each of these statements is constructed with inappropriate language. If you're surprised, then please know that so were we. We've heard terms like *victim of* and *physically challenged* used by people in all walks of life, including student speakers.

The fact that we think we know what constitutes appropriate language doesn't excuse us from researching the subject. Language is dynamic and in a continuous process of change. What's more, words such as *victim* or terms such as *wheelchair bound* once were acceptable. Today, however, people with disabilities are defining their own terms on their own grounds. Further, in doing so, those with disabilities have said they prefer the following descriptors to the first set we listed for you:

"John has cystic fibrosis."

"Don't forget that Susan's in a wheelchair."

"It's okay, Lupe; there's plenty of seating in the new auditorium for people in wheelchairs."

"The Howards' baby has a disability."

Thus, we want to remind you of the old adage "It's better to remain silent and be thought a fool than to open your mouth and prove it." When in doubt about words and their consequences, consult an authority. If that's not possible, then when in doubt about a word, leave it out.

Of course, it is not just people with disabilities who are stereotyped. People in different professions, of different ethnicities, and with different sexual orientations, to name just a few categories, are frequently the subject of stereotypic language. The speaker who is sensitive to language avoids such stereotypes. One particular type of stereotype deserves discussion in its own right, sexist language.

How Does Language Marginalize People?

A 53-year-old cabdriver is facing vehicular manslaughter charges in the hit-and-run accident that killed a Silicon Valley executive and critically injured his companion, a state trade official, police say.

Arthur Alan Smith of San Francisco, a driver for DeSoto Cab Co., was arrested at the Hall of Justice Thursday after a police inspector investigating the Friday night accident asked him to come in for additional questioning.

"We talked to him at the scene the night of the accident," Inspector Jeff Levin said. "He told us that another car hit the couple and threw them onto the hood of his cab. We have since been able to determine that was not what happened."

Calvin Threadgill II was killed instantly, and his companion, Tina Frank, was seriously injured when they were struck at about 9:30 p.m. last Friday as they crossed the Embarcadero near Mission Street.

Threadgill, 45, of Castro Valley, was recently appointed vice president of marketing for Zapit, a Silicon Valley environmental technology company.

Frank is the director of the Bay Area regional office of the California Trade and Commerce Agency. . . .

Investigators say the pair were walking in a marked crosswalk when they were struck.

Levin said a reconstruction of the accident by Sgt. James Hughes, evidence gathered by the police crime lab and new information from two eyewitnesses had led them to Smith.

Source: John D. O'Connor, "Cops Hold Cabbie in Hit-Run Death," *San Francisco Examiner,* 12 August 1994, A4. Reprinted by permission.

Avoid Sexist Language

Sexist language is language that stereotypes gender roles, for example, *housewife* and *fireman*. Why is sexist language a problem? Because it conveys, intentionally or not, a stereotype of certain roles and functions, based on sex. When the head of an academic department is referred to as a chair*man*, a member of the U.S. House of Representatives is called a Congress*man*, and a flight attendant on an airplane is known as a steward*ess*, it is clear which roles are held to be "male" and which ones "female." A sensitive public speaker needs to avoid sexist language.

One of the easiest ways to unintentionally convey sexism is to use singular pronouns in the masculine form. For years, speakers and writers excluded women from their examples involving a single person, saying such things as

"If a person is strong, he will stand up for himself."

"When someone believes something, he shouldn't be afraid to say so."

"An individual should keep his promise."

If you have no other choice in constructing examples to illustrate your speech, you can do one of two things with regard to singular pronouns. First, you can say "he or she" in conjunction with a singular verb. Second, you can use "she" in some cases and "he" in others. Yet both of these alternatives are awkward, and neither is likely to please everyone in your audience. Thus, we suggest a third alternative: Use plural nouns and pronouns when constructing examples to make your speech more vivid, involving, and inclusive. Instead of saying, "If a person is strong, he will stand up for himself," say, "Strong people stand up for themselves." Instead of saying, "When someone believes something, he shouldn't be afraid to say so," try, "When people believe something, they shouldn't be afraid to say so." And instead of saying, "An individual should keep his promise," simply say, "People should keep their promises."

Finally, be on the lookout for the subtle ways the news media can reinforce the use of sexist language in their reporting. As the article reprinted in the box "How Does Language Marginalize People?" illustrates, even journalists can perpetuate the misconception that *executive* is a masculine word and *companion* is a feminine one.

SUMMARY

Language is central to effective speaking. The words that make up language are symbols of the objects they are meant to describe. Words influence the process of perception. Language not only influences perception but the process of thinking as well, as expressed in the *linguistic relativity hypothesis*. The language of a speech should reflect the cultural, demographic, and individual diversity characteristic of today's audiences. Consequently, the language of a speech should be *inclusive* rather than *marginalizing* or *totalizing*. Language should be appropriate and nonsexist.

To make full use of language, speakers should use *competence-enhancing language*, which means eliminating unnecessary *verbal qualifiers*. Using language effectively also involves differentiating between *denotative* and *connotative meaning* and using words that reduce uncertainty. To make their speech vivid, speakers should use rhetorical devices such as metaphor, simile, alliteration, parallel structure, and repetition. Effective speaking also demands sound grammar and correct pronunciation. In addition, the language of a speech should connect metaphorically with the varied learning styles present in most audiences. Finally, speakers should choose appropriate language. Special care should be taken to avoid stereotypic and *sexist language*.

Check Your Understanding: Exercises and Activities

1. Rewrite the following paragraph using inclusive language:

   When a speaker begins his speech, the first thing he must do is thank the chairman of the group for the opportunity to speak to his group. As we know, the quality that separates man from the animals is the ability to speak. Regardless of his job, a man must know how to speak clearly. Similarly, a woman must know how to impart language skills to her children. Thus, every speaker is urged to use language to the best of his ability.

2. Write five transitional statements (signposts) without using the following words:

   first (second, third, etc.)

   therefore

   next

   finally

   in conclusion

3. Company X has an internal policies manual that is written in marginalizing language. As an employee of the company, you find the language disturbing and believe the language in the manual should be changed. Write a letter to the head of the documents division explaining why you believe such changes are necessary and why you believe the changes will enhance the image of the company. (Thanks to Dr. Madeline Keaveney for suggesting this exercise.)

4. Exclusive language is marginalizing and biased. Provide an inclusive-language alternative for each of the following, or state under what conditions the term might be appropriately used in a speech. (Adapted from Rosalie Maggio, *The Bias-Free Word Finder: A Dictionary of Nondiscriminatory Language* (Boston: Beacon Press, 1991).)

actress	meter maid
airline stewardess	mother
businessman	majorette
craftsmanship	Mrs. John Doe
doorman	old wives' tale
executrix	waitress
goddess	

Notes

1. W. H. Auden and L. Kronenberger, *The Viking Book of Aphorisms* (New York: Dorsett Press, 1981), 238.

2. "This Boss Is No Girl, She's Just Stunned," *Sacramento Bee*, 10 October 1995, C2.

3. "This Boss Is No Girl," C2.

4. Benjamin Lee Whorf, *Language, Thought, and Reality* (New York: Wiley, 1956).

5. Earl Shorris, *Latinos: A Biography of the People* (New York: Norton, 1992), 95–100.

6. Julia T. Wood, ed., *Gendered Relationships* (Mountain View, Calif.: Mayfield, 1996), 39–56.

7. See, for example: W. M. O'Barr, *Linguistic Evidence: Language, Power, and Strategy in the Courtroom* (New York: Academic Press, 1982); James J. Bradac and Anthony Mulac, "A Molecular View of Powerful and Powerless Speech Styles: Attributional Consequences of Specific Language Features and Communication Intentions," *Communication Monographs* 51 (1984): 307–319.

8. H. Giles and J. Wiemann, "Language, Social Comparison, and Power," in *Handbook of Communication Science*, ed. C. R. Berger and S. H. Chaffee, (Newbury Park, Calif.: Sage, 1987).

9. Tom McArthur, ed., *Oxford Companion to the English Language* (Oxford: Oxford University Press, 1992).

10. Charles R. Berger and R. J. Calabrese, "Some Explorations in Initial Interaction and Beyond: Toward a Developmental Theory of Interpersonal Communication," *Human Communication Research* 1 (1975): 99–112.

11. Auden and Kronenberger, *The Viking Book of Aphorisms*, 359.

12. L. A. Malandro, L. Barker, and D. A. Barker, *Nonverbal Communication*, 2nd ed. (New York: Random House, 1989).

13. Carol Gilligan, *In a Different Voice* (Cambridge, Mass.: Harvard University Press, 1982).

CHAPTER 10

How you say
something may
be as important
as what you have
to say.

Delivery: Engaging Your Audience Nonverbally

OBJECTIVES

After reading this chapter, you should be able to:

- Define nonverbal behavior and distinguish between verbal and nonverbal behavior.
- Describe the relationship between delivery and the eight basic dimensions of the nonverbal system.
- Display nonverbal behaviors characteristic of effective delivery, including control of the speaking environment; proper attire; eye contact and expressive facial cues; vocal variation in pitch, range, rhythm, and tempo; clear and distinct vocal articulation; and gestures and movements that serve as emblems, illustrators, and regulators.
- Control distracting self-adaptive behaviors.
- Use time to enhance your credibility and communicate urgency, drama, humor, and the like during your speech.
- Explain the guidelines for developing a proactive, rather than reactive, delivery.
- Display nonverbal examples of complementing, contradicting, and repeating the message; substituting for a verbal cue; increasing the perception of immediacy; exciting the audience; and delivering a powerful speech.

KEY CONCEPTS

delivery	proactive delivery
emblem	regulators
environment	self-adapting behaviors
illustrators	zone of interaction
nonverbal behavior	

> *What people do is frequently more important than what they say.*
>
> —EDWARD T. HALL, Anthropologist[1]

People often presume too much about a person based on nonverbal behavior in general, and appearance specifically.

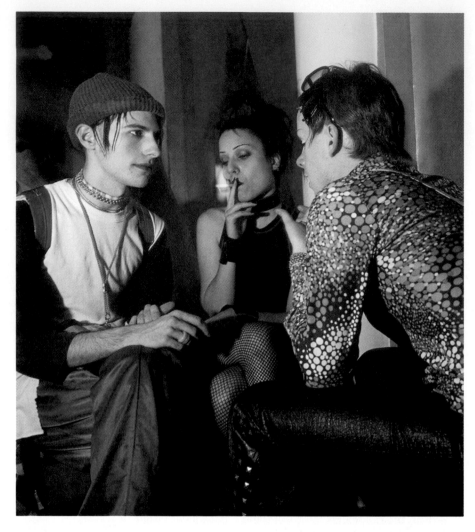

Diana Griego Erwin is a syndicated newspaper columnist who writes about everyday experiences, including lessons she's learned from her day-to-day encounters with people. In one column, Erwin related a lesson about the degree to which you can read a person based on nonverbal behavior. She recounts how a teenage boy boarded the commuter train on which she and her young daughter were riding:

> He looked nervous, and that is what scared me. . . . If a director needed a jittery type for a movie such as "Speed," this is the guy they would cast. By the time he sat down, beads of sweat had popped up on his nose and brow, and he pulled at one side of the black and red woolen cap he wore. He'd look over his shoulder, then look outside. In the space of about 30 seconds, he adjusted his coat twice.[2]

Erwin continues in this vein and tells the reader that she not only was frightened by the boy's appearance and "suspicious" behavior but also was prepared to protect herself should the boy move on her and her daughter. Then Erwin reveals the rest of the story. Just before the next stop, Erwin says,

> The boy-man looked frantically outside. Just before [the train] stopped, he looked at me; made eye contact. "Will you save these seats?" he asked.
>
> He hurried to the doorway where a bent, aging woman struggled to climb the stairs. . . . He took her arm to help her. "Grandma," he said, "I worried the whole time we split up. I never should have let you talk me into leaving you there like that."[3]

All of us are at least a little like columnist Diana Griego Erwin. We presume much about a person based on nonverbal behavior, even though we probably shouldn't. The same also is true of speakers and audiences encountering each other for the first time.

This chapter focuses on the relationship between nonverbal behavior and delivery of a speech. The chapter is designed to complement the previous chapter's discussion of the role language plays in constructing your message. Audiences will arrive at conclusions, both right and wrong, about you on the basis of your nonverbal delivery. Our goal is to show you how you can shape nonverbal behavior to your advantage. We begin by looking at ways of focusing your delivery on your audience and the rhetorical situation you face. We next focus on the differences between verbal behavior, or the content component of your message, and nonverbal behavior, which dominates the relational component of your message. Then we discuss the interdependent dimensions that define the overall nonverbal system, and demonstrate the functional role these dimensions play collectively in the effective delivery of your speech.

VIDEO FILE

If you have access to the videotape that accompanies this book, view segment 7, which shows the ways nonverbal communication can function in the delivery of a speech.

FOCUSING YOUR DELIVERY ON YOUR AUDIENCE

Never forget that public speaking is a transaction between you and your audience. Just as the language you choose for your message should reflect the nature of your audience, so too should your delivery. As a result, we begin our discussion with some audience-related factors you will want to consider while thinking about the delivery of your message. Specifically, we discuss choosing an appropriate method of delivery, adapting to diverse audiences, and adapting delivery to the speech occasion.

Choosing an Appropriate Method of Delivery

Recall from Chapter 2 that there is more than one way to deliver a speech. We discussed four different methods of delivery. As you review your analysis of your audience and rhetorical situation, one of your most important decisions will be an appropriate method of speech delivery.

Manuscript Delivery As you'll recall from Chapter 2, manuscript delivery involves writing out the speech completely and reading it to the audience. This method may be the best choice when your audience requires precise information from you. When you are speaking about highly technical matters before a group of engineers, for example, the precision with which you deliver the information may be extremely important. Similarly, if you expect your words to be quoted by others, having a manuscript of your speech helps ensure accuracy.

Anytime you use a manuscript, however, the dynamics of delivery are restricted. As we show later in this chapter, eye contact, movement, and gesture are important dimensions of nonverbal behavior that may enhance your delivery. Tying yourself to a manuscript interferes with each of these. Manuscript speaking also impedes spontaneity between you and your audience because the manuscript restricts opportunities to survey and creatively respond to audience feedback. Further, a manuscript demands a lectern, which can stand as a barrier between a speaker and the audience. Finally, this method of delivery can sound stilted and artificial because the language of a written message generally is more formal than spoken language.

If you must utilize a manuscript, therefore, learn it well. Practice repeatedly so that you do not have to look down often. Mark up your manuscript with notes to yourself and underline main ideas. Also, be sure pages are numbered so that they will not get out of order. Use a large typeface and double or even triple spacing. Manuscript speaking is far more difficult than most people realize. Its success depends on practice and skill in converting words on a page into a living speech.

Memorized Delivery A speaker using memorized delivery writes out the speech and commits it to memory before presenting it to the audience without the use of notes. Most audiences don't expect a memorized speech, unless they are watching a professional speaker who is highly paid, an actor delivering a soliloquy in a play, or a student competing in a speech tournament. In fact, in a typical speech class, an obviously memorized speech would probably strike most students and the instructor as odd. Although memorization allows you to concentrate on eye contact, movement, and gesture, it does so at a price. You may forget parts of your speech and it requires a greater investment of time than any other method.

When writing a speech to be memorized, keep the organization simple so that you will not confuse one point with another. A good rule of thumb is to memorize the speech in small chunks. Learn a paragraph, then move on to the next one, and so on. Practice reciting your speech from the beginning through as far as you have it memorized. The repetition of earlier parts will help fix them in your mind. Finally, don't panic if you forget a part of the speech. Try to ad-lib for a bit and often the next section will come to mind.

Impromptu Delivery Impromptu delivery is a spontaneous, unrehearsed method of presenting a speech. Usually, these short speeches are given in response to someone who asks you to say a few words, make a toast, or respond to an inquiry. Although an audience is always appreciative of an eloquent impromptu speech, an organized and confidently spoken message is normally enough to fulfill any audience's expectations.

Impromptu speaking eliminates any impediments to using the full range of nonverbal behaviors available to speakers. This can be both good and bad, depending on the comfort level of the speaker. Speakers who are comfortable in an impromptu situation may benefit because their delivery will strike the audience as relaxed and genuine. Uncomfortable speakers, however, are likely to appear rigid, awkward, or distracted.

Extemporaneous Delivery   For most students who are still learning to give a speech, extemporaneous speaking remains their best choice of delivery method. Recall from Chapter 2 that extemporaneous delivery combines careful preparation with spontaneous speaking. The speaker generally uses brief notes rather than a manuscript or an outline. Extemporaneous speaking enables you to maintain eye contact, move, gesture, and spontaneously adapt to audience feedback. You may choose not to use a lectern, depending on how extensive your notes are and how comfortable you are moving freely before the audience.

Today's audiences are more likely to expect and appreciate the extemporaneously delivered speech than other methods of delivery. Just as it allows the speaker to remain in contact with the audience, so does it allow the audience to remain connected to the speaker. Audiences not only can give feedback to someone speaking extemporaneously but also can assess the degree with which their feedback registers with the speaker.

This doesn't mean that extemporaneous speaking is without drawbacks. Note cards can restrict the range of gestures used when you refer to them, and they can also be distracting when waved about while you're speaking. Finally, you can get carried away with note cards, writing down so many of your thoughts that the note cards become almost a manuscript.

Delivering Speeches to Diverse Audiences

Both the method and style of delivery should reflect the diversity of your audience. Throughout this chapter we offer numerous specific examples of cases in which a particular nonverbal behavior means one thing to one culture and something entirely different to another. For example, consider how three different audiences might respond to the same speech. As you speak, a North American audience returns your eye contact and nods in agreement with you. A British audience also returns your eye contact, but heads remain motionless. And a West African audience avoids making direct eye contact with you altogether. What should you make of their feedback in each situation? Before you decide, perhaps it would help to know this: When the British agree with a speaker, they sometimes blink rather than nod their head. Further, the more direct the eye contact of West Africans, the less they respect the person to whom it is directed. Knowing the typical patterns of nonverbal behavior in a given culture is essential if you are to accurately interpret the nonverbal behaviors of your audience members.

Informal situations such as this one invite a conversational delivery style.

Another example of differences among culturally diverse audiences concerns your voice. Almost from birth, the norm for the North American culture is "to speak up and let yourself be heard." What is normative here, however, may be loud in Japan or among the upper class in Great Britain. And much as we may want to be heard, we don't want to be perceived as loudmouths.

Adapting Delivery to the Speech Occasion

Last, how you present your speech depends on the specific rhetorical situation you face and the kind of delivery your audience is likely to expect. A speech commemorating or honoring a person calls for a formal and dignified delivery. Other speech situations call for an energetic, dynamic delivery. A motivational speaker, for example, usually dispenses with the lectern and moves about the stage, perhaps even into the audience. A lively style is expected and rewarded. Then there are situations that call for a lighthearted, comic style of delivery. For example, "roasts" honoring someone often are punctuated with good-natured joking at the honoree's expense. Unlike a commemorative speech, a delivery at a "roast" should be informal and lively. The key is to understand what the audience expects in a given situation and match your delivery style to those expectations.

NONVERBAL CHARACTERISTICS OF DELIVERY

Delivery involves the nonverbal behaviors by which speakers convey their message to an audience. Delivery is what brings mere words to life in the public speaking transaction. **Nonverbal behavior** is a wordless system of communicating. What makes a behavior nonverbal as opposed to verbal? Is it the absence of sound? That cannot be the case, because sign language is considered a form of verbal communication, with signs merely substituting for written or spoken language. Although scholars argue about the exact definition of nonverbal behavior, most agree that it is distinct from verbal behavior in at least three ways: It is continuous, uses multiple channels simultaneously, and is spontaneous.

The Continuous Nature of Nonverbal Behavior

Verbal behavior, composed of words, is discrete. This means verbal behavior can be divided into distinct elements, as was the case when you first began to learn about nouns, verbs, and adjectives. These elements of composition are governed by complex rules, dictating how they should be combined in your speech to form phrases, clauses, and sentences. Each word has a denotative meaning that can be found in the dictionary. Words must be arranged in a precise manner to convey the intended meaning. For example, the words "I am happy" must be arranged in that order to convey the intended meaning. To say, "Am I happy" changes the statement to a question. To say "Happy am I" seems odd to English speakers. When words with agreed-on meaning are used in a specified order, the meaning of the verbal behavior is apparent as in this example. This is not so with nonverbal behavior, which is continuous rather than divisible.[4]

Consider the expression of happiness as you speak. What the audience sees is a complex message that involves the entire face. The muscles of the face contract, affecting the eyebrows, the corners of the mouth, and the corners of the eyes. Unlike verbal behavior, these involuntary movements cannot be broken down into compositional elements. The eyes, for example, do not convey "I," while the eyebrows say "am" and the mouth represents "happy." You cannot rearrange the components to convey a different meaning, as you can with "I," "am," and "happy." There are no rules of grammar to explain the meaning conveyed by these facial expressions. Only the total, continuous combination of these elements can constitute the nonverbal expression of happiness.

The Simultaneous Use of Multiple Channels

Returning to the example of expressing happiness, nonverbal behavior also involves the simultaneous use of multiple channels.[5] For example, try conveying an emotional expression, such as happiness, anger, sorrow, or bewilderment, through a single channel of communication, for example, your mouth or eyes or hands. You'll soon see that it is difficult if not impossible. At the same time, you'll recognize that we use these multiple channels simultaneously rather than sequentially. When happy, we express the emotion all over our face, not with our eyes first, mouth second, eyebrows and forehead third and fourth.

The Spontaneous Nature of Nonverbal Behavior

As each of the preceding characteristics might lead you to believe, the final distinguishing characteristic is that nonverbal behavior is spontaneous. With the possible exception of so-called Freudian slips, when people unintentionally say what they really mean, verbal behavior is planned behavior.[6] We consciously think about the words we speak and write, though we do so with such speed it may not occur to us.

Smiles, gestures, and body language occur at a subconscious level. This doesn't mean that people never plan or orchestrate gestures when they speak. Sometimes they do, and their nonverbal behavior is likely to look phony. Most of us learn to distinguish between authentic and phony nonverbal behaviors by the time we reach our teens. Unless nonverbal behavior is rehearsed to the point it becomes habit, therefore, planned gestures especially will be recognized as insincere. This is a major reason for people putting so much stock in the meaning they infer from nonverbal behavior.

DELIVERY AND THE NONVERBAL COMMUNICATION SYSTEM

Recall that a system is a collection of interdependent and interrelated components. A change in one component will produce changes in them all. The nonverbal system has as its components several interdependent dimensions of behavior that profoundly affect the delivery of a speech. The specific dimensions we discuss in this section are the environment, appearance, the face and eyes, the voice, gestures and movement, posture, touch, and time. As a speaker intent on delivering a message effectively, you need to approach these dimensions systematically. Further, the verbal language with which you construct your speech should take into account what you've learned from your systematic assessment of the nonverbal dimensions.

The Environment

For our purposes, **environment** refers to our physical surroundings as we speak and the physical distance separating us from our audience. Both our surroundings and our physical space have an undeniable impact not only on our delivery but also on how the speech is perceived by our audience.

The physical characteristics of the room in which you speak—for example, lighting, temperature, comfort, and aesthetics—will influence both you and your audience physically and psychologically.[7] A bright, aesthetically neutral room, which is neither sterile nor plushly decorated, and in which the temperature is 68 degrees will have a much different overall impact on the speech transaction than a room that is dimly lit, richly furnished, and 75 degrees. Whereas in the first both you and your audience are likely to be alert and attentive, the second might prove so comfortable that neither you nor your audience are sufficiently aroused for your transaction. Thus, you would have to plan your delivery accordingly. Whereas your "normal" pattern of delivery probably would be appro-

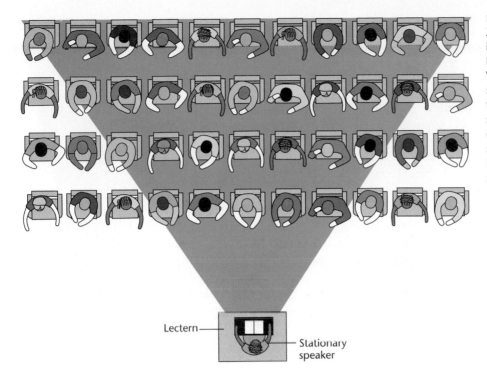

FIGURE 10.1
Zone of Interaction in the Traditional Room Setting. Where people are seated in rows and the speaker is stationary, eye contact between speaker and audience is limited to the shaded area.

Lectern

Stationary speaker

priate in the first environment, you likely would need to put extra energy and enthusiasm into the delivery to succeed in the second.

A second environmental consideration is the physical layout of the room. We have been in situations where student presentations were hindered by pillars supporting the roof, by the width and length of the room, and by immovable objects such as tables. Sometimes you have no alternative but to do the best you can in such situations. As a result, you move more than you had planned as you speak, abandon visual aids that would prove impossible for your entire audience to see, or make gestures larger and more exaggerated than is customary for you.

At other times, however, you will have the opportunity to physically arrange the room in which you will speak. This may include the position of a lectern, elevation of a stage, and configuration of an audience. Given this opportunity, experienced speakers will arrange the environment in concert with their style of delivery. Speakers who have a traditional style of delivery may prefer a lectern, perhaps an overhead projector immediately to their side, and an elevated stage from which to speak. Speakers who are much less formal in their style of delivery may want the room to be arranged so that they can move from side to side or even up and down its length.

Both the traditional and informal styles of delivery can be equally effective. However, the room layout consistent with the traditional style is more restrictive than its counterpart in two ways. The first way concerns the **zone of interaction,** the area in which speakers can easily make eye contact with audience members (Figure 10.1). The second way concerns the amount of space physically separating speakers from their audience.

FIGURE 10.2
Shifting the Zone
of Interaction With
Movement.
Changing positions
can increase the
perception of
inclusiveness as
well as add energy
to your speech.

The zone of interaction is limited to the range of your peripheral vision. The immediate zone of interaction between speakers and their audience diminishes as a room gets larger. To compensate for this fact, speakers have two choices. Either they can shift the zone of interaction by looking from side to side or they can physically move from one point to another when they deliver their speeches. This latter choice is illustrated in Figure 10.2. Obviously, in a very large room the traditional style of delivery limits you to looking from side to side in the attempt to shift the zone of interaction. This means that you cannot help but ignore part of your audience part of the time.

The traditional style of delivery allows less flexibility in manipulating the physical distance separating speakers from their audiences. Whereas a speaker who moves about the room can reduce or increase distance physically as well as psychologically, a relatively stationary speaker is restricted to the latter. Thus, for those who prefer this style of delivery, eye contact becomes their primary agent for managing how immediate they are perceived to be by their audience, a point which we discuss shortly.

To summarize: The relationship of the speaking environment to delivery is a significant one. Not only does it influence your style of delivery, it also influences how you are perceived by your audience. Experienced public speakers try to plan the delivery of their speeches accordingly. When faced with a "tough room," for example, they know that the arousal level of their delivery will need to increase if they are to reach their audience. Inexperienced speakers, on the other hand, all too often play "victim" to their speaking environment. Instead of

Seating Arrangements

Can the physical seating arrangement have an impact on both your speech and the manner in which it is perceived? A very dramatic one. As a result, you should think about your goals as a speaker and the physical layout of the room in which you speak. Traditional rows will focus attention exclusively on you. A horseshoe arrangement, however, allows audi-ence members to make eye contact with each other. And speaking at the head of a conference table not only narrows the zone of interaction but also puts a physical barrier between you and your audience. Which of these arrangements do you think would most likely encourage audience feedback and partici-pation? Why?

Traditional rows   Horseshoe   Conference table

surveying and planning for the environment, they simply deliver their speech as if the environment were of no consequence to them. As a student of public speaking, you know what's good and bad about the layout of the classroom in which you must speak. Thus, you too should plan your delivery accordingly. The box "Seating Arrangements" discusses another factor you should consider when planning your delivery.

Appearance

Appearance often has a disproportionately significant effect on audience per-ceptions of a speaker's message and delivery.[8] Speakers never get a second chance to make a first impression with an audience. First impressions are based largely on appearance, including body type and height, skin and hair color, and cloth-ing and accessories.

The significance of appearance to public speaking can be measured in at least two ways. The first involves audience members' first impressions. The second involves how people perceive themselves as a result of their appearance and the impact this perception has on their self-confidence and delivery.

According to communication expert Dale Leathers, "Our visible self functions to communicate a constellation of meanings which define who we are and what we are apt to become in the eyes of others."[9] These "others" are the people with whom we come into contact, including the members of our audiences.

Audience members use appearance to initially make judgments about a speaker's level of attractiveness. The consequences of this judgment are far-reaching for speakers. Research tells us that speakers perceived as attractive by audience members also are perceived as smart, successful, sociable, and self-confident. As a result, speakers who fall into this category enjoy an audience whose initial impression of them is favorable.

Yet appearance influences more than an audience's initial impression of a speaker. Appearance also can have a very real effect on a speaker's self-confidence. Research tells us that speakers who feel they appear attractive report greater self-confidence than those reporting otherwise.[10]

Although some facets of your appearance and their impact on audience perception are outside your control—for example, body type and height—there is one facet you can easily control: your dress. Simply said, your dress should be appropriate to the situation. Obvious as this advice may seem, it is frequently ignored by students in public speaking classes. All too often they show up to speak dressed as if they had thought little about the appropriateness of their attire. Their attitude, as reflected in their dress, seems to be saying, "It's just a speech class."

Consider an analogy. Good students know what the research suggests about the relationship between the appearance of a term paper and the mark it receives. Frequently, it's the difference between a minus or a plus in their grade. Good students, therefore, go to some length to make sure that their papers not only conform to the requirements but "look" impressive as well.

The same relationship may exist between appearance and the marks students receive on their speeches. Although an Armani suit may not turn a mediocre speech into an outstanding one, it certainly won't cause the speaker to lose points. Inappropriate attire or careless grooming will never add points to a speech; moreover, there is a chance they will unnecessarily detract from such things as the speaker's perceived competence.

The Face and Eyes

In the previous chapter, we advised that in your speeches you use immediate language, that is, language that promotes the perception of "closeness" between you and your audience. We said that immediate language can reduce the undesirable feelings of distance that sometimes separate speakers from audiences. Immediate language also can lead people to regard you as friendly and approachable, stimulating, open to dialogue, and personable. What is true of immediate language is even more true of nonverbal behavior. The face and eyes are very useful in com-

Can you identify the meaning of these different facial expressions?

municating friendliness to an audience and reducing undesirable feelings of distance between the speaker and audience.

Yet making the delivery of your speech more immediate is only one of the roles the face and eyes play in enhancing your delivery. The face and eyes, for example, can communicate happiness, surprise, fear, anger, disgust, contempt, sadness, and interest. The face and eyes also can modify the intensity of any of these nonverbal expressions of emotion.[11]

Just as we can use rhetorical devices such as metaphor to manipulate language intensity, we can use the face and eyes to intensify our delivery. In most cases, we intensify what we say in this manner with little or no conscious thought. As we grow angry, for example, the muscles in our face tense and our eyes narrow spontaneously. The purveyor of bad news can make things even worse by accentuating it with the face and eyes.

You also can use your face and eyes to neutralize the message you deliver. Based on an analysis of your rhetorical situation, you may know that at least some members of the audience will disagree with your views. Suppose you are in a class situation that requires you to deliver a persuasive speech. If your topic is a truly controversial one, you can reasonably predict that not everyone in your audience will agree with everything you say. Although you may not be able to win them over, you also don't want to alienate them. As a result, you may want to use your face and eyes to neutralize some of the more contentious and evocative points you wish to make.

In a sense, what we give an audience in our face and eyes will determine what we can expect to get back from that audience. Thus, an intensely worded argument accompanied by the delivery of an equally intense message in the face and eyes invites the same from those who differ with us. On the other hand, using the face and eyes to neutralize the message improves your chance of a more favorable response from your audience.

This brings us to eye contact, specifically. In the North American culture, eye contact is perceived as a specific message. Speakers who are respectful, trustworthy, friendly, and interested in our well-being make eye contact with us. What's more, the best speakers don't simply make eye contact with the audience, but with individual members of the audience as they deliver their speech. This makes it appear to the audience member that he or she is engaged in dialogue with the speaker.

Remember, though, this kind of eye contact is a North American norm, not a universal one. In many cultures, the focus and sustained eye contact North Americans expect would be frowned upon. Such eye contact is viewed by members of many Asian cultures, for example, as rude and even hostile. As both a speaker and an audience member, you should keep this in mind. As a speaker, recognize that when international students appear uncomfortable with or don't return your attempts to make eye contact, it may be the result of their culture. As an audience member, realize that your expectancies about eye contact may be at odds with the norms of the international student who is speaking.[12]

The Voice

Try reading out loud this familiar nursery rhyme under three different conditions. In the first condition, your goal is to make your audience sad. In the second, your goal is to make your audience happy. And in the third, your goal is to make your audience anxious about the well-being of the characters.

Mary had a little lamb,
Its fleece was white as snow;

FIGURE 10.3
Physiology of the Voice

And everywhere that Mary went,
The lamb was sure to go.

Much of the emotional impact of your delivery is conveyed in your voice.[13] Consider an emotion such as excitement. We've heard many speakers unconvincingly tell an audience that they were excited about both their topic and the opportunity to speak. What betrayed their true feelings was not their language, but the absence of appropriate emotion in their voice.

To suggest that we can use our voices in a number of ways to enhance the delivery of our speeches would be an understatement. Drama, irony, sarcasm, and urgency are but a few of the emotions we can convey vocally.

To gain maximal control of your voice you need to know two things: the mechanics of the voice, and the importance of finding your own voice rather than imitating the voice of someone else.

Vocal Production   The production of sound in the voice is fairly straightforward. We take in air and expel the air through the trachea across our vocal cords, which are contained in the larynx, and then across our teeth, tongue, and lips (Figure 10.3). Variations in the amount of air expelled, the positioning of the vocal cords, or the placement of the teeth and tongue and position of the lips will result in variations in the sounds we produce. Shallow breathing and the rapid expulsion of air across the vocal cords, for example, will produce a much different sound than breathing deeply and then slowly expelling the air. In the first case, your voice is likely to be described as feminine and in the second masculine, even though neither is necessarily true. The placement of the tongue and the shape of the lips affect how sounds are articulated. The mechanical operation of the voice is not as important to our purpose as are the mechanical characteristics of the voice. These include volume, pitch, range, rhythm, tempo, and articulation.

Volume   Volume is how loudly you project your voice. It is a consequence of both the amount of air you expel when speaking and the force with which you expel it. Some examples of people with "big" voices, capable of speaking with great volume, are actor/talk-show host Rosie O'Donnell, conservative broadcaster Rush Limbaugh, actor James Earl Jones, and the late congresswoman and distinguished professor Barbara Jordan. Some people, on the other hand, are naturally soft-spoken. Examples include former President Jimmy Carter, actor Liv Tyler, and singer/songwriter Jakob Dylan.

As a public speaker, you need to have enough volume to be heard by your audience. Too soft a voice will simply not be heard. On the other hand, shouting at the top of your lungs can turn off your audience. The key is to speak loudly enough to be heard, while not speaking too loudly for the room. Of course, if you have the use of a microphone, you can be heard even if you speak relatively softly. It is also useful to vary your volume during the speech, using either an increase or decrease in volume as a means of emphasis. If the entire speech is delivered at the same volume, nothing will stand out as most important.

Pitch   Pitch refers to the degree our voices are high or low. A person who sings bass has a low pitch, whereas a person who sings soprano has a high pitch. The pitch of blues singer B. B. King's voice is low, whereas the pitch of pop diva Mariah Carey's voice is relatively high. Effective speakers vary their pitch during their speech. One must be careful, however, because an excitable voice can often assume a higher-than-normal pitch. At the same time, one should not attempt to artificially alter the pitch, since it will appear unnatural and may strain the voice.

Range   Range is the extent of the pitch, from low to high, that lies within a person's vocal capacity. Just as a piano, for example, has a tremendous range in pitch, some speakers have a great vocal range. On the other hand, some speakers are like an electric bass guitar, which no matter how well played, does not have much range. As a speaker, you need to make the fullest use of your normal conversational vocal range. Raising or lowering the pitch of your voice can emphasize a particular word or phrase in your speech. Avoid a monotone delivery, which can lull your audience to sleep.

Rhythm   Rhythm is extremely important to the delivery of your speech. It involves the characteristic pattern of your volume, pitch, and range. Perhaps you have heard someone describe a speaker's voice as "singsong." What this means is that the speaker's voice is consistently going up and then down in pitch in a predictable and sometimes irritating pattern. Although variation in the rhythm of your voice is certainly to be encouraged, the exact pattern of variation shouldn't be completely predictable as your speech begins to unfold.

Tempo   Tempo is the rate at which you produce sounds. How quickly or slowly you speak will influence how you are perceived. Tempo also tends to vary across and even within cultures. In the Deep South, for example, tempo is relatively slow. In the East, tempo is accelerated. This is readily apparent if you compare the tempo of southern actress Holly Hunter's delivery with that of eastern actress Marisa Tomei.

Because tempo varies, you have to use good judgment in terms of how quickly or slowly you speak. Doing either to the extreme can turn off your audience. An excessively rapid pace can be perceived as a sign of nervousness. An excessively slow pace may suggest a speaker is not well prepared. Researchers have found that moderate to fast rates of speaking tend to be associated with increased perceptions of a speaker's competence on the part of the audience.[14] Other researchers have noted a ceiling to that effect, however, meaning that too fast a rate of speaking can backfire.[15] In addition, when audiences perceive speech rates as similar to their own, they are more likely to find speakers socially attractive and to comply with their requests.[16] The best advice, therefore, is to moderately vary your tempo. Not only will this accommodate the different preferences of individuals in your audience, it also will enhance the overall effect of your message.

Your tempo is also affected by pauses. Sometimes a brief moment of silence can convey much to an audience. Pausing just before delivering a crucial word or phrase helps grab the audience's attention. Pausing after you've made an important point gives it time to sink in. Don't be afraid to use pauses when appropriate. It also is better to pause a moment than to fill the air with "ums," "uhs," and "you knows," which are really "vocalized pauses."

Articulation   Articulation refers to the distinctness with which we make individual sounds. We've all experienced the frustration of listening to someone who sounds "mushy," failing to distinctly vocalize sounds. A common articulation problem comes from either running together differing sounds or dropping parts of a word: "goin' " instead of "going," "wanna" instead of "want to," or "whatcha doin'?" in place of "what are you doing?" If you expect an audience to understand what you are saying, you need clear articulation. A good way to test your articulation is to tape-record your speech and listen critically to yourself. If you find a consistent articulation problem or set of problems, you may want to find out if your college or university offers a course in voice and articulation. Sometimes drama or theatre departments have courses in voice for performers that can also be of assistance. Severe articulation problems are often best treated by a speech pathologist. But for most students in public speaking classes, exercising care, practicing, and slowing down are the keys to being understood by the audience.

In the final analysis, judgments about the relationship between the qualities of your voice and the quality of your delivery will depend on the preceding

Tips for Improving Your Voice

Like it or not, people will make judgments about you on the basis of the way you sound. George Bush, for example, was criticized for sounding "shrill" near the end of the presidential campaign in 1992. Evidently, this meant he was beginning to sound desperate—which is not the way an incumbent president wants to be perceived. On the other hand, Bill Clinton so overused his voice that it became hoarse and raspy. Near the end of the campaign, Hillary Rodham Clinton was forced to speak for her husband because he had completely lost his voice.

Although we want you to be comfortable with your voice, the following tips may help you if you think something about your voice needs to be changed.

- *Relaxation:* More than one problem with voice can be solved by monitoring tension in your vocal apparatus. Nasality, shrillness, or screeching, and excessive rate of speech often are a consequence of tension/stress. The same relaxation techniques discussed in Chapter 3 can be used to alleviate the impact of tension/stress on your voice.

- *Vocal variation:* Tape-record yourself or have someone tape you when you speak. If you find as a result of monitoring your audiotape that greater vocal variation is needed, pick out someone whose vocal characteristics you admire and repeatedly listen to the person. Then try to model the vocal variation in which the person engages. Repeat this process while using a tape recorder.

- *Being heard:* Have a friend monitor your speaking volume. When you speak too softly, tell your friend to raise an index finger within your view. Use this signal to increase the volume of your voice. The goal is to be easily heard, even in the back of the room.

characteristics operating in concert. Important as pitch or tempo may be on their own, it is their collective impact with range and rhythm that most counts.

Finding Your Own Voice   With this in mind, let's now turn to your voice specifically. Are you pleased with the way it sounds and complements your overall delivery? No matter how you answer this question, it is just as important for you to find your own voice as a speaker as it is for authors to find their own voice when they write. We mention this need to find your own voice with good reason. When public speaking students are advised to make better use of their voice in their delivery, all too often they take this to mean they must change their voice to some ideal. The ideal, moreover, is usually thought to be the voice of a television or radio personality.

We don't encourage you to imitate the vocal delivery of someone who hosts a game show, reads the news, or introduces music videos. Instead, we encourage you to experiment with your voice; for example, record your attempts to convey varying emotions in your voice, listen to yourself, and then repeat the process. This kind of exercise will let you hear what your vocal strengths and weaknesses are. In the process, be realistic but not unfairly harsh about how you think you sound. Chances are, what you think you hear is much different than what others hear.

Finally, recognize that important as it is, your voice is but a single nonverbal component of your overall delivery. Not all good speakers have tremendous "pipes." For example, Diane Sawyer's and Geraldo Rivera's voices may be interesting, but they would hardly be described as rich in timbre. Further, if you were

Late-night talk-show host Jay Leno uses a gesture to add emphasis to his verbal message.

to listen to a number of paid speakers, you would see that this is the case. All of us tend to underutilize the full potential of our voices. What ultimately counts, then, is whether we're willing to do the hard work necessary to rectify this fact. If you think something about your voice needs to be changed, see the box "Tips for Improving Your Voice."

Gestures and Movement

You've heard the expression "different strokes for different folks." Nowhere is it more applicable than it is to the subject of gestures and movement relative to delivery. Although Ronald Reagan neither moved nor gestured very much when he spoke, he was a consummate public speaker. And though you practically have to nail Elizabeth Dole's feet to the floor to keep her from moving, she too is a public speaker of notable achievement. Thus, before we say a single word about how much or how little you should gesture or move as you speak, we want to say this: Your gestures and your movements as you grow as a public speaker should be a refined reflection of what you do naturally.

As is the case with the face and eyes, gestures and movements also can be used to intensify or lessen the emotional impact of our verbal messages. Many gestures, for instance, serve as *affect displays*; that is, they visibly communicate feelings. Placing both hands near the heart at the same time we explain how important a subject is to us is an example. So too are clenched fists, open palms held face up, or lightly slapping the side of the face.

Given the preceding caveat, gesturing and moving can complement your delivery in several ways.[17] These include making your delivery more emblematic, making your delivery more illustrative, and regulating the speech transaction.

Emblems   The speeches of the best public speakers are usually rich in emblems. An **emblem** is a nonverbal behavior that can be directly translated into words and phrases and may replace them.[18] For example, Winston Churchill's "V" was an emblem for victory. Thus, emblems must meet the following criteria:

1. The emblem means something specific to the audience members.
2. The emblem is used intentionally by the speaker to stimulate meaning.
3. The emblem can be easily translated into a few words.

Gestures are defined by the culture in which they are learned. As a case in point, when Richard Nixon was Dwight Eisenhower's vice president, he incited an embarrassing protest while deplaning at a South American airport. He greeted the crowd with arms outstretched above his head, the thumb and first finger of each hand joined together in what North Americans take to mean "A-OK." In many South American countries, however, this nonverbal emblem was then synonymous with what we call "giving the finger" or "flipping someone off."

Illustrators   **Illustrators** are nonverbal behaviors that accompany speech and "show" what is being talked about. Although a lot like emblems, they are more general and seldom translate into a few words. The most common way we nonverbally illustrate is with our hands. Verbal directions or descriptions beg for the use of our hands. Try giving someone directions or describing an object—say, a spiral staircase—without using your hands.

At the beginning of the semester, we usually ask a student to describe the shapes in Figure 10.4 to other students without showing them or using the hands to illustrate the shapes. Students listening attempt to reproduce the shapes on paper. Not only do both groups find the task next to impossible, most also consider it frustrating.

Regulators   **Regulators** are gestures that influence the amount and type of feedback received from the audience. If you hold up your hand when asking audience members whether they've ever felt frustrated waiting in line, for example, you are much more likely to prompt them to raise their hands as well. If you are stationary throughout a speech, your audience will give you much different feedback than if you were to move and periodically change the zone of interaction.

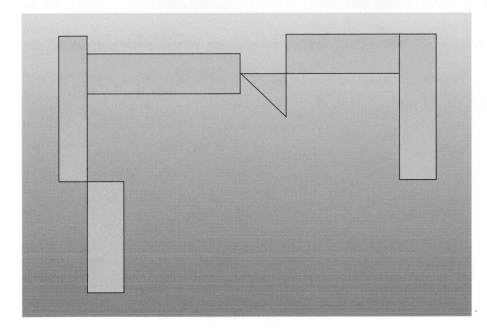

FIGURE 10.4
Communication Challenge.
Can you instruct a classmate on how to draw an identical set of geometric shapes without using nonverbal expressions or referring back to the figure itself?

Using gestures and movement to regulate feedback, however, requires planning and rehearsal. An unplanned or inappropriate gesture or specific movement may elicit a response from the audience that you don't expect.

Regulating audience feedback is particularly important when a speaker answers audience questions. Without regulation, such question-and-answer sessions can turn ugly. The box on page 282, "Handling the Q&A" provides some practical advice on how to handle audience questions.

Posture

This dimension is obviously related to movement, gestures, and your overall appearance. Posture is very important to your delivery and the manner in which it is received. People make all kinds of attributions about speakers on the basis of their posture, ranging from how confident a speaker is to how seriously the speaker takes the topic and the situation. At the least, consequently, you will want to guard against an audience making an incorrect attribution about you because you slouched, folded your arms across your chest, stood with one hand on your hip, or put your hands in your pockets.

Because the norms governing appropriate posture vary across cultures, there are no hard-and-fast rules for speakers to follow. Still, given what we know generally about the culture of the beginning public speaking class, there are some steps you can follow to achieve a good posture for delivering your speeches. Remember that the more you slouch and shrink posturally, the less powerful you are likely to be perceived. Remember as well that posture influences the mechanics of your voice. Standing with shoulders back stretches the diaphragm and opens

Handling the Q&A

Frequently after a speech, you will be expected to take questions from the audience. You should not be fearful of this situation, as it is actually an opportunity to gain important feedback from your audience as well as to clarify points that may not have been completely understood. Successfully answering questions, even hostile ones, can add to your credibility as a speaker. The key is to regulate that feedback in a constructive manner. Some basic guidelines for handling the question-and-answer period following a speech are given below.[1]

- *Announce at the outset that you will take questions at the end of your speech.* Under no circumstances take questions during the speech, as it will cause you to lose control of the situation. When audience members know they will have the opportunity to ask questions at the end of the speech, they will be able to think about them as you speak.

- *Overprepare for your speech.* You need to know more than you cover in the speech if you are to take questions. If you expect a hostile audience, it is a good idea to anticipate their toughest questions and prepare answers in advance.

- *Restate questions if they cannot be heard by all.* If you are speaking with a microphone, someone asking a question from the audience probably cannot be heard. Restating the question not only allows everyone to hear what was asked, it also allows you time to think of an answer. If a question is wordy, hostile, or imprecise, try to rephrase it in a way that neutralizes some of the problems with the question.

- *Answer questions directly with facts to back up your answers.* This requires you to be fully prepared. However, if you don't know the answer, just say so. You can always promise to obtain the facts and get back to the questioner at a later date. It is better to admit you don't know an answer than to be proved wrong because you tried to bluff your way through an answer.

- *Take questions from different audience members.* Don't let yourself get into a debate or an argument with one audience member. Insist that everyone

Gestures frequently assist speakers in regulating their transaction with an audience.

who has a question gets a chance to ask it before you return to a previous questioner. Choose questioners from different parts of the room as well so that everyone feels they will get their chance.

- *Be brief.* Answer questions as succinctly as possible and move on to the next question. Overly long answers bore the audience and frustrate others who want to ask questions.

- *Announce when you are near the end of the Q&A.* When you sense the audience growing restless, the questions have become repetitive, or you are near the end of your allotted time, simply announce that you can take only one or two more questions.

- *At the end of the Q&A, restate the focus of your speech and summarize its essential points.* This is your chance to get in the last word and remind the audience of the basic theme of your speech. Depending on the situation, you may want to make yourself available for informal discussion after the speech.

[1]Some of these guidelines are based on a pamphlet by Robert Haakensan, *How to Handle the Q&A* (Philadelphia: Smith Kline & French Laboratories, Department of Public Relations, n.d.).

the air passages. That's one reason opera singers invariably have good posture. It helps them use their voice to full effect.

Guidelines for Posture While Delivering a Speech

- Find your center of balance. Usually this means standing with your feet apart at about shoulder width.
- Pull your shoulders back, sticking your chest out and holding your stomach in.
- Keep your chin up and off your chest.
- Initially let your arms rest at your sides with palms open, which will allow you to gesture easily as you speak.

Touch

Touch, which is by far the most intimate and reinforcing of the nonverbal dimensions, can affect your delivery in at least two ways.[19] The first involves **self-adapting behaviors,** which are distracting touching behaviors that speakers engage in unconsciously.

Frequently in arousing situations, we touch our face, hair, or clothes without realizing it. Just as frequently we touch some convenient object. We may squeeze the arm of a chair, roll our fingers on a tabletop, trace the outside edge of a glass with our fingertip, or mistake the top of a lectern for a conga drum. We do these things unconsciously.

Because public speaking is arousing, it too can provoke these self-adaptive forms of touch. Further, they can needlessly detract from your delivery. Tugging at an earlobe, rubbing the outside of your upper arm, or jingling the change in your pocket won't help your delivery. Neither will pounding on the lectern with the palms of your hands or rocking it from side to side.

The second way touch can affect your delivery concerns people. At some point, it's likely your presentations will involve other people. Corporate trainers spend much of their lives giving informative presentations that involve audience participation. The same can be said for sales managers, teachers, attorneys, and practitioners of public relations. Touch very often comes into play in these scenarios. Sometimes it's as simple but as important as shaking a person's hand. At other times, however, it may involve guiding someone by the hand, patting someone on the back, or even giving a more demonstrative tactile sign of approval. At the same time, one must avoid touch that can be interpreted as inappropriate. For example, there have been several widely reported cases of schoolteachers accused of inappropriately touching students. Unwelcome touching can, in fact, be grounds for accusations of sexual harassment.

Time

The final nonverbal dimension to think about relative to delivery is time. As journalist Michael Ventura writes

Time is the medium in which we live. There is inner time—our personal sense of the rhythms of time experienced differently by each of us; and there is imposed time—the regimented time by which society organizes itself, the time of schedules and deadlines, time structured largely by work and commerce.[20]

First, time varies from one individual to the next. Research confirms what you no doubt long ago suspected. The internal body clock each of us has regulates not only when we sleep but also peak performance when we're awake. Some people perform best from early to mid-morning, some during the middle of the day, and others late at night. What is true of performance in general, moreover, is true of public speaking specifically. During our time awake, there are periods when our speaking abilities peak, depending on our individual body clock. Most of us know from our own experience that we either are or are not very alert in the early morning or late afternoon. To the extent that one can arrange speaking times, attempt to schedule a time when you know your mind and body will be alert.

Time affects our delivery in other ways as well. For example, the time limits you face as a speaker can have an impact on your delivery. As a result of attempting to cover too much material, for example, time limits may cause you to "hurry" your delivery. Conversely, if you find that you're about to finish your speech under the minimum time requirement of an assignment, you may slow down the delivery of your speech in the attempt to meet the time requirement.

The audience's perception of your delivery also will be affected by your "timing," a term frequently used in reference to actors and comics. Just as their timing of a joke or dramatic monologue can spell the difference between success and failure, so too can your timing. Rushing a punch line or dramatic anecdote, for instance, may negate its intended effect. Telling a story too slowly may do likewise.

Because the norms that govern the use of time vary across cultures, how fast or how slowly you deliver your speech may be a consideration. Whereas a relatively speedy style of delivery may be well received in New York City, it may be received as evidence of the "little time" you have for an audience in parts of the South and Southwest. Conversely, a slow rate of speech, which some mistakenly confuse with the speed at which a person thinks, may prove irritating to audience members whose culture is fast paced.

Finally, whether you are "on time" or late, not only for a speech but just in general, affects your credibility in our North American culture. People who are on time are perceived as efficient and courteous, both of which affect perceptions of competence and trustworthiness. People who are routinely late give the impression they are disorganized and not especially considerate of the time needs of an audience. This is very true of both your classmates and your instructor.

THE FUNCTIONS OF NONVERBAL BEHAVIOR IN DELIVERY

The eight dimensions of nonverbal behavior we've been talking about perform a number of important functions in speech delivery.[21] As we've discussed, these dimensions interact to make our speeches more emblematic and illustrative.

They also can help us regulate audience feedback and intensify or lessen the emotional impact of what we say during a speech. Other ways that nonverbal dimensions such as the face, eyes, and voice function to facilitate the delivery of our messages include complementing, contradicting, and repeating the message; substituting for a verbal cue; increasing the perception of immediacy; exciting the audience; and delivering a powerful speech.

Complementing Your Message

A complementary nonverbal cue serves to reinforce what you verbally share with your audience. A genuine smile on your face as you thank your audience for the opportunity to speak, for example, carries more weight than either message standing on its own. There are many ways to complement the delivery of your message nonverbally. Changing the expression on your face, raising the pitch of your voice, or even breaking off eye contact are just a few of them.

Contradicting Your Message

Often, people contradict themselves nonverbally while communicating interpersonally. Forcing a smile and saying "I had a great time" is a classic example. While the smile may have covered up how they really felt, chances are it only served to contradict what they said but didn't mean.

Usually we try to keep the preceding from happening. In the case of public speaking, however, we can use contradiction to enhance our delivery, for example, by rolling our eyes, shrugging our shoulders, or having a sarcastic expression. Certainly, Shakespeare knew that contradiction could enhance delivery. He frequently wrote speeches for his characters that invited actors to contradict their verbal statements with nonverbal cues. For example, in Marc Antony's eulogy of Julius Caesar, the line "But Brutus was an honorable man" is usually delivered by an actor in a sarcastic voice that says exactly the opposite. Because it is an attention-getting device, this kind of antithesis in a speech can enhance the impact with which the verbal message is delivered.

Repeating Your Message

Repetition is one of the most common ways speakers manipulate their message nonverbally. It's also one of the easiest ways to do this as well. Raising three fingers as you say you have three points to make doesn't require the oratorical skill of a Colin Powell.

Repetition differs from complementing in a significant way. Whereas a complementary nonverbal cue reinforces the message, a repetitious one serves to make it redundant. The classic example is when *Star Trek's* Mr. Spock makes the Vulcan V sign while saying "Live Long and Prosper." Other examples include nodding your head up and down while communicating agreement and shaking your head from side to side when communicating disagreement.

Substituting for a Verbal Cue

Have you ever seen entertainers and politicians raise their hands and motion in the attempt to stop an audience's continued applause? They are using a nonverbal cue as a substitute for a verbal one. In many circumstances, such a nonverbal cue is both more appropriate and more effective than a verbal one. An icy stare shot in the direction of someone talking as you speak is likely to be less disruptive, for example, than politely asking the person to be quiet. Shrugging your shoulders, reaching out with open palms, and raising your eyebrows, moreover, may more clearly communicate your bewilderment than to actually say you're puzzled by something.

Increasing the Perception of Immediacy

As we said in the discussion of the face and eyes, nonverbal behavior can also increase the perception of immediacy between you and your audience. Again, immediacy concerns how psychologically close or distant people perceive each other, as well as the degree to which they perceive each other as approachable.[22]

Generally, the perception of immediacy between people is desirable. This is because people who are perceived as immediate are also perceived as friendly and approachable, stimulating, open to dialogue, and interpersonally warm.

Because public speaking normally takes place in a setting that arbitrarily puts physical distance between speakers and their audiences, speakers usually have to reduce this physical distance psychologically. We can do this in at least two ways. The first, which we discussed at length in Chapter 9, involves the use of immediate language. The second is to make our delivery more nonverbally immediate.

The easiest and most effective way to make the delivery more immediate is through nonverbal channels. Eye contact is the perfect case in point. Even when people are separated by substantial physical distance, eye contact enables them to bridge this distance in a psychological sense. The best public speakers, for example, are often the ones who seem to be speaking to us, and only us, with their eyes as well as their voices.

Eye contact is not the only medium, however, through which we can achieve greater immediacy with our audience. Immediacy can also be achieved with facial expressions such as a smile, with a conversational rather than condescending tone of voice, and by standing beside the lectern instead of appearing to hide behind it.

Exciting the Audience

One way we gauge the effectiveness of a speech is the degree to which it stimulates us. The best speakers are the ones who make us think, provoke us to laugh, or motivate us to act. Generally, an audience's degree of excitement can be traced to the degree of excitement the audience senses in the speaker.

The level of excitement of public speakers is most noticeable in their delivery. This includes rate of speech, volume of speech, and vocal as well as facial expressions. Excited speakers, the research tells us, speak faster and louder than speakers unaroused by their topic or by the transaction between them and their audience.

Excited speakers, the research also tells us, reveal more of themselves as they speak through changes in facial expressions as well as changes in the pitch of their voice.

Does this mean that someone who simply is excited also is a good speaker? Of course not. Too much excitement can be as distracting as too little excitement can be boring. The idea, then, is to moderate your excitement for your topic or audience rather than to inappropriately exaggerate it with your delivery.

Delivering a Powerful Speech

When it comes to public speaking, the power of words depends mightily on the manner in which they are delivered. No doubt many speech writers have suffered as the power of the words they so carefully crafted was wiped out by the person delivering them. This shouldn't and needn't be the case. With care and practice, you can capitalize on the varying dimensions of nonverbal behavior to make the delivery of your speech powerful. Some of the ways you can do this are obvious; others are more subtle.

Posture is an obvious way you can control the power of delivery. Standing tall and self-assured, in and of itself, communicates power. When combined with movement away from the lectern, this is even more the case.

You also can enhance the power of your delivery with your eyes, with your voice, and through movement and gestures. In North America, at least, powerful speakers make eye contact, speak in a controlled and confident tone of voice, reduce the distance between themselves and their audience by moving closer to it, and gesture as a natural extension of their spoken message. In stark contrast, speakers whose delivery lacks power avoid eye contact, fail to speak up, and usually try to tie up their hands by sticking them in their pockets, gripping the side of the lectern, or hiding them behind their back.

TAKING A PROACTIVE APPROACH

Knowing something about the nature and functions of nonverbal behavior should assist you in making your speech delivery proactive rather than reactive. To engage in **proactive delivery** means that the speaker takes the initiative and anticipates and controls for as many variables as possible, rather than merely reacting to them. Reactive delivery is like the boxer who only counter-punches. This wait-and-see attitude is rarely the mark of a championship boxer, and it can be disastrous for even the most seasoned public speaker. The guidelines that follow should assist you in making sure that your nonverbal behavior enhances—rather than detracts from—the delivery of your speech.

Guidelines for Proactive Speech Delivery

Tips and Tactics

1. *Familiarize yourself with your speaking environment.* **This is important because it will influence the quality of your delivery. Know well in advance and plan for such things as seating arrangement, availability and location of**

lectern, availability and location of overhead screen and projector or easel for displaying poster boards or charts, and lighting.

2. *Take control of your appearance.* Dressing appropriately is one of the easiest ways to enhance initial impressions of you as the medium of your message. Think about the possible effects of apparel, such as the baseball cap that seems to be attached to your scalp, the baggy shorts you prefer, or the saying on your favorite T-shirt.

3. *Increase your nonverbal immediacy.* Practice using your face and eyes to increase immediacy with your audience. Specifically, practice making eye contact with individual members of the audience. If possible, videotape your practice session and review the tape for immediate facial expressions. On the day of your speech, smile at your audience and establish eye contact before speaking.

4. *Use natural gestures.* Review your practice tape to check on your gestures. Do they appear natural and complement your delivery, or do they appear forced and detract from your spoken message?

5. *Work to improve your voice.* Review the box "Tips for Improving Your Voice." Don't be afraid to experiment with your voice. At the same time, remember to be true to your own voice.

6. *Time your speech.* Do this more than once and on videotape if you can. Note your timing and the degree to which the rate at which you speak facilitates the mood you want to communicate to your audience. Also, remind yourself that your practice time probably will be longer than when you actually speak before your audience.

7. *Avoid self-adapting behaviors.* During practice, watch out for self-adapting behaviors such as playing with your hair, tugging on a finger, cracking knuckles, licking your lips, and hiding your hands. Self-adapters such as these will call attention to themselves and undermine perceptions of your power and self-confidence.

8. *Work on your posture.* Check out your posture and what it conveys about your comfort and level of confidence. Remember, good delivery is next to impossible without good posture.

SUMMARY

Effective speech *delivery* begins by focusing on your audience. Choosing among manuscript, memorized, impromptu, and extemporaneous delivery methods depends on the audience and the rhetorical situation you face. Nonverbal behaviors may carry different meanings depending on the cultural, demographic, and individual diversity of an audience. The appropriate style of delivery depends also on the speech occasion.

Unlike language, *nonverbal behavior* is a wordless system of communicating. Nonverbal behavior is continuous, uses multiple channels simultaneously, and is spontaneous.

The system of nonverbal behavior is composed of eight interdependent dimensions: the environment, appearance, the face and eyes, the voice, gestures and movement, posture, touch, and time. The *environment* includes such things as the seating arrangement, physical layout of the room, temperature, and lighting. Appearance includes how you dress and what your attire communicates to your audience. The face and eyes are very expressive, communicating emotional states such as joy, anger, and sadness. The voice also influences audience emotions through such characteristics as volume, pitch, range, rhythm, tempo, and articulation. Gestures and movement, including *emblems*, *illustrators*, and *regulators*, complement verbal behavior and regulate the speech transaction, including the kind of feedback you receive from an audience. Good posture is important to effective delivery and can affect your audience's perception of you. Touch is often used to compensate for nervousness when you speak and includes distracting *self-adaptive behaviors* such as slapping the top of the lectern. Time is important to public speaking in terms of how your audience perceives you and in terms of the "timing" of your speech.

The eight dimensions of nonverbal behavior function to enhance the delivery of speeches. These functions include complementing, contradicting, and repeating the message; substituting for verbal cues; increasing the perception of immediacy; exciting the audience; and delivering a powerful speech. Guidelines for *proactive delivery* include familiarizing yourself with your speaking environment, taking control of your appearance, increasing your nonverbal immediacy, using natural gestures, working to improve your voice, timing your speech, avoiding self-adapting behaviors, and working on posture.

Check Your Understanding: Exercises and Activities

1. Observe a speaker outside of your class. Keep track of the number of times the speaker (a) changes the zone of interaction, (b) moves away from the lectern, and (c) gestures. On a scale of 1 to 10, with 10 being the high end, rate the speaker in each of these areas. Compare and discuss your observation and ratings with those of other students. See if a pattern emerges.

2. Differences in nonverbal norms, as well as differences in communication styles and patterns, are common across cultures. Choose two or three North American norms for nonverbal behavior—for example, eye contact, gesturing, and time. Interview a student or faculty member from a culture other than North American about how these communication behaviors differ in his or her culture. Write a short paper summarizing your findings.

3. Explain why sign language is a *verbal* behavior whereas vocal variation in pitch, rate, tempo, and the like are *nonverbal* behaviors, even though sign language is not vocalized and vocal variation is.

4. Explain why nonverbal behavior is continuous, uses multiple channels simultaneously, and is spontaneous and how these characteristics distinguish it from the language of your speech.

5. Review the eight guidelines for proactive delivery. Before your next speech, develop a plan to use at least four of these guidelines to improve your delivery skills in that speech.

6. Ask a classmate to apply Exercise 1 to your next speech. Talk with the classmate afterward about the relationship between his or her observations and the overall effectiveness of your delivery.

Notes

1. Edward T. Hall, *The Silent Language* (Greenwich, Conn.: Fawcett Publications, 1959), 15.

2. Diana Griego Erwin, "Signs Were There; Facts Were Missing," *Sacramento Bee,* 17 December 1995, A2.

3. Erwin, "Signs Were There; Facts Were Missing," A2.

4. J. Burgoon, D. W. Buller, and W. G. Woodhall, *Nonverbal Communication: The Unspoken Dialogue,* 2nd ed. (New York: Harper & Row, 1989). See also M. Knapp and J. A. Hall, *Nonverbal Communication in Human Interaction,* 3rd ed. (Fort Worth, Tex.: Harcourt, Brace, and Jovanovich, 1992).

5. L. A. Malandro, L. Barker, and D. A. Barker, *Nonverbal Communication,* 2nd ed. (New York: Random House, 1989).

6. V. P. Richmond and J. C. McCroskey, *Nonverbal Behavior in Interpersonal Relationships* (Englewood Cliffs, N.J.: Prentice Hall, 1991).

7. R. Sommer, "Man's Proximate Environment," *Journal of Social Issues* 22 (1966): 60.

8. Ellen Berscheid and Elaine Walster, "Beauty and the Best," *Psychology Today* 5, no. 10 (1972): 42–46.

9. D. Leathers, *Successful Nonverbal Communication: Principles and Practices* (New York: Macmillan, 1986).

10. Malandro, Barker, and Barker, *Nonverbal Communication.*

11. P. Ekman and W. V. Friesen, *Unmasking the Face: A Guide to Recognizing Emotions from Facial Expression* (Englewood Cliffs, N.J.: Prentice Hall, 1975). See also P. Ekman, W. V. Friesen, and S. Ancoli, "Facial Signs of Emotional Expression," *Journal of Personality and Social Psychology* 39 (1980): 1125–1134.

12. P. Ekman, *Telling Lies* (New York: Norton, 1985). See also Bella M. DePaulo, Miron Zuckerman, and Robert Rosenthal, "Humans as Lie Detectors," *Journal of Communication* 30 (1980): 129–139; R. E. Kraut, "Verbal and Nonverbal Cues in the Perception of Lying," *Journal of Personality and Social Psychology* 36 (1978): 380–391.

13. K. R. Scherer, H. London, and J. J. Wolf, "The Voice of Confidence: Paralinguistic Cues and Audience Evaluation," *Journal of Research in Personality* 7 (1973): 31–44; J. Thakerar and H. Giles, "They Are—So

They Spoke: Non-Content Speech Stereotypes," *Language and Communication* 3 (1981): 255–261.

14. George B. Ray, "Vocally Cued Personality Prototypes: An Implicit Personality Theory Approach," *Communication Monographs* 53 (1986): 266–276.

15. Richard L. Street and Robert M. Brady, "Evaluative Responses to Communicators as a Function of Evaluative Domain, Listener Speech Rate, and Communication Context," *Communication Monographs* 49 (1982): 290–308.

16. David B. Buller and R. Kelly Aune, "The Effects of Speech Rate Similarity on Compliance: An Application of Communication Accommodation Theory," *Western Journal of Speech Communication* 56 (1992): 37–53.

17. Judee Burgoon, "Nonverbal Communication Research in the 1970s: An Overview," in *Communication Yearbook 4*, ed. D. Nimmo. (New Brunswick, N.J.: Transaction Books, 1980), 179–197.

18. Joseph A. Devito, *The Communication Handbook: A Dictionary* (New York: Harper & Row, 1986), 105.

19. Stephen Thayer, "Close Encounters," *Psychology Today* 22, no. 3 (1988): 31–36. See also A. Montague, *Touching: The Significance of the Skin* (New York: Harper & Row, 1971).

20. Michael Ventura, "Trapped in a Time Machine With No Exits," *Sacramento Bee*, 26 February 1995, C1.

21. Burgoon, Buller, and Woodhall, *Nonverbal Communication: The Unspoken Dialogue*; E. T. Hall, "System for the Notation of Proxemic Behavior," *American Anthropologist* 65 (1963): 1003–1026.

22. Malandro, Barker, and Barker, *Nonverbal Communication*.

CHAPTER 11

Visual aids must be used carefully, as Microsoft's Bill Gates learned when he presented Windows 98 to the public.

Presentational Aids

OBJECTIVES

After reading this chapter, you should be able to:

- Explain the advantages of using presentational aids in your speeches.
- Select the types of presentational aids that are appropriate to the purpose of your speech.
- Select the appropriate materials for constructing your presentational aids.
- Use the principles of simplicity, visibility, layout, and color in constructing and using visual aids.
- Practice setting up and using your presentational aids before your speech.
- Effectively use presentational aids in your speech.

KEY CONCEPTS

audio aids	organizational chart
audiovisual aids	overhead transparency
bar chart	pie chart
flip chart	presentational aids
flow chart	visual aids
line graph	

Seeing is believing.

—ANONYMOUS

When billionaire Microsoft co-founder Bill Gates (pictured in the opening photograph of this chapter) introduced the media and industry opinion leaders to Windows 98 not long ago, it's a safe bet he didn't expect a glitch in the presentational aids he planned on using to complement his speech. Yet, when Gates initially tried to call up the software-driven visuals programmed for his speech, a glitch is exactly what he got. Nothing appeared on the giant monitor above and behind him.

Because Gates is a polished and well-practiced public speaker, he was able to continue as his army of support people scrambled to fix the problem. He remained calm and even made light of what a less-seasoned public speaker might have found to be an insurmountable obstacle.

Bill Gates's example makes a valuable point about the subject of this chapter. It's a point, moreover, that contradicts the notion that today's technology has minimized the role of the speaker in the contemporary speech transaction. Of course, nothing could be further from the truth. Aside from the fact that the hardware necessary to drive today's presentational software to full effect is very expensive, Murphy's Law applies as much to contemporary technology as to yesteryear's. To rely excessively on technology when speaking, therefore, or to assume that it is more important than the skill level of the speaker is folly.

This chapter focuses on the functions and appropriate use of presentational aids, including presentational software such as Microsoft PowerPoint. We introduce you to: (1) the reasons for using presentational aids, (2) the types of presentational aids commonly used in public speaking, and (3) the criteria you need to follow in selecting and constructing the presentational aids you plan to use.

WHY PRESENTATIONAL AIDS?

Presentational aids—visual, audio, and audiovisual—have the potential to increase the selective attention of your audience, which, as we pointed out in Chapter 4, is a necessary step if they are to listen to what you have to say. This is because, among other things, presentational aids can help make your verbal message more concrete or more intense. It is much easier to explain the workings of an internal combustion engine, for example, using a scale model than relying on words alone. Showing your audience an enlarged photograph of children victimized by war is likely to intensify the effect of the words you speak while showing the photo.

Presentational aids also can serve some of the same functions as nonverbal communication in the process of speaking. Visual media in particular can be used to complement or even substitute for your verbal message. Presentational aids can add information to your message and direct the focus of your audience.

So, you see, presentational aids are not simply "add-ons." They are extensions of the verbal message you share with your audience. Used wisely, research shows that presentational aids also can actually:

- increase your speech's persuasive effect
- enhance audience perceptions of your credibility

- facilitate audience attention and comprehension, and
- make your audience more agreeable.[1]

ADAPTING PRESENTATIONAL AIDS TO YOUR AUDIENCE

Whether you should use presentational aids depends on the rhetorical situation, particularly on the audience and their goals and expectations. For example, visual aids would usually seem out of place in a sermon or eulogy. On the other hand, a teacher who never used any kind of visual aid would be unusual. Classrooms are designed with writing boards and sometimes overhead projectors and video monitors for a reason.

Always keep in mind how your audience will process the presentational aids you use in your speech. For example, how large will charts, posters, and objects need to be in order to be seen from the back of the room? If you are using sound, will you be able to amplify it sufficiently for the audience to hear? If you must darken the room for slides, will this present a problem for audience members who need to take notes? As with all other aspects of public speaking, if you design your presentational aids with the audience's needs in mind, you are much more likely to achieve your purpose.

TYPES OF VISUAL AIDS

Visual aids are presentational media that convey a message visually. There are numerous types of visual aids that you may want to consider for your speech. Five basic types are objects; models; photographs; diagrams and illustrations; and charts, graphs, and maps. Let's consider each type of visual aid in turn.

Objects

In some cases, the object you are discussing in your speech is perfectly suited to your needs. A speech about the bagpipe might call for you to demonstrate on the instrument itself. A demonstration of karate or judo almost demands that you use people to show how the moves are done; in this case, people are your presentational aids.

The keys to using objects are to make sure they are easily visible to your audience and that they are appropriate to the situation. A speech on auto repair could not use a real car, because it would be too big for most classrooms. A small but visible part from an automobile engine could be used to illustrate how to repair it, however. The use of inappropriate objects can create problems. For example, almost every semester we have students who wish to do speeches on some aspect of firearms. However, firearms are prohibited on our campus (except for those of campus security officers) for obvious reasons. Wine tasting is another popular topic we must veto, because alcohol is also prohibited on our campus. Thus, before you plan a speech using actual objects, be sure to ask your instructor what is appropriate and permissible on your campus.

VIDEO FILE

If you have access to the videotape that accompanies this book, view segment 8. It shows how a number of visual aids can be used to enhance your speech.

This speaker's use of the actual object that is the subject of the speech helps makes the speech more vivid for the audience.

Models

Often a three-dimensional model of an object can be used when it is impractical to use the actual object. We recall a speech on the common American cockroach. Bringing live cockroaches to the classroom would have been disconcerting, to say the least. However, the student cleverly constructed a large-scale model of a cockroach that she kept hidden in a box until just the right instant, when she revealed the topic of her speech. Not only was her speech informative and entertaining, it was also enhanced by her ability to explain her subject vividly with her model.

Photographs

A photograph of an object or your subject matter can be a very useful visual aid, as long as it is clearly visible to everyone in the audience. Thus, you must either enlarge the photo to poster size or show it through a slide or overhead projector. For example, a speech on art history would be greatly enhanced by slides or enlargements of photographs of various periods and styles of painting.

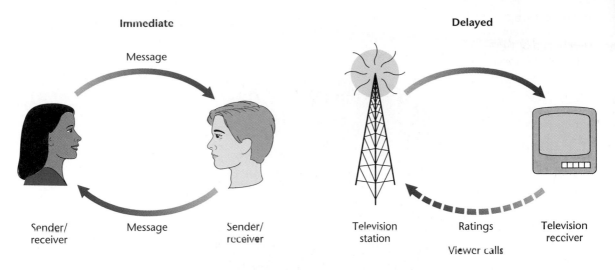

Immediate

Message

Sender/
receiver   Message   Sender/
receiver

Delayed

Television
station   Ratings   Television
receiver

Viewer calls

FIGURE 11.1 Diagram Illustrating an Abstract Concept. This illustration explains communication feedback.

Diagrams and Illustrations

Sometimes an illustration or a drawing will serve your purpose better than a photograph. Diagrams are a good way to represent the parts of an object. For example, a cutaway drawing of a firearm can be used to explain its functional parts, and the diagram—unlike a real gun—is neither illegal nor dangerous. Figure 11.1 illustrates an abstract concept, communication feedback, through use of a diagram.

Charts, Graphs, and Maps

Often a speech calls for a particular kind of visual representation of numbers and statistics through charts or graphs. Three of the following types of charts and graphs are particularly useful for depicting statistical information: pie charts, line graphs, and bar charts.

Pie Charts A **pie chart** is a circular chart that divides a whole into several parts, each represented by a slice of the circle proportional to its share of the whole. Figure 11.2 shows a typical pie chart, which represents the percentage distribution of state lottery proceeds in a specific year. The advantage of pie charts is that they simplify and dramatically illustrate the relative proportions of parts of a whole. Pie charts are not of much use, however, in demonstrating trends over time because several pie charts would need to be displayed simultaneously, one for each unit of time. That would make each chart smaller and more difficult to see.

Line Graphs A **line graph** shows numerical data as a series of points connected by a line. Line graphs are well suited to showing changes over time, such as

FIGURE 11.2
Pie Chart: Percent
Distribution of 1993
State Lottery Proceeds

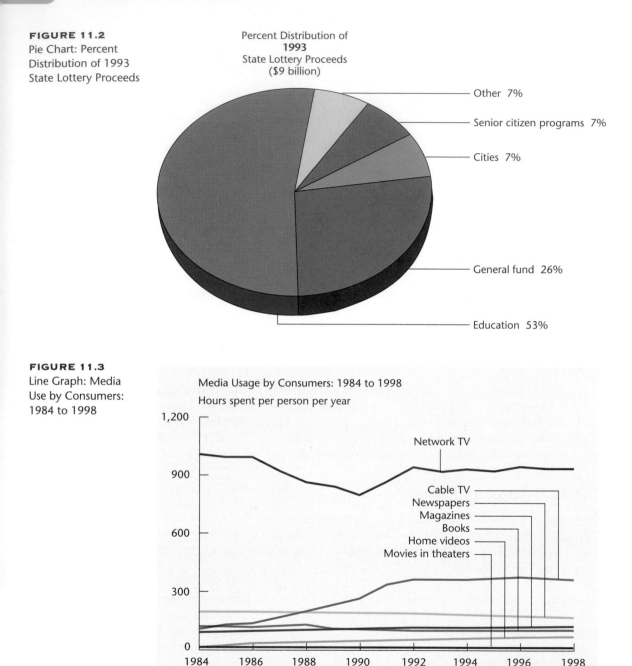

Percent Distribution of
1993
State Lottery Proceeds
($9 billion)

Other 7%

Senior citizen programs 7%

Cities 7%

General fund 26%

Education 53%

FIGURE 11.3
Line Graph: Media
Use by Consumers:
1984 to 1998

Media Usage by Consumers: 1984 to 1998

Hours spent per person per year

Network TV

Cable TV
Newspapers
Magazines
Books
Home videos
Movies in theaters

changes in media use by consumers over a 15-year period, as in Figure 11.3. By using more than one line (each can be in a different color), you can show how two or more things compare across the same time period. Thus, if you wanted to compare spending on schools with spending on defense over the past 10 years, a line graph with two lines would work well.

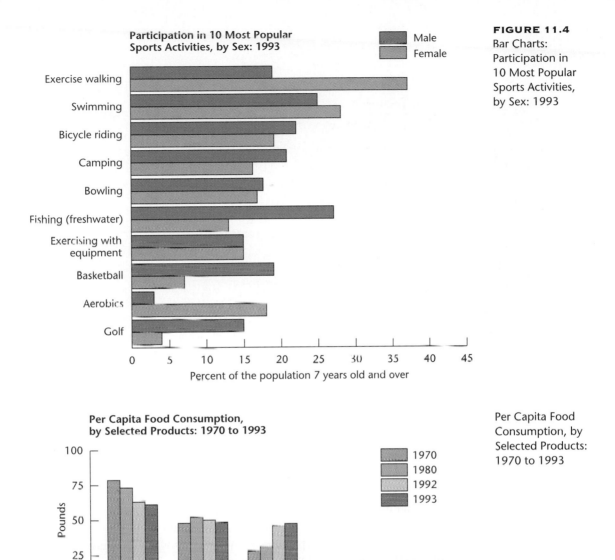

FIGURE 11.4
Bar Charts:
Participation in
10 Most Popular
Sports Activities,
by Sex: 1993

Per Capita Food
Consumption, by
Selected Products:
1970 to 1993

Bar Charts A **bar chart** uses filled-in vertical or horizontal bars to represent various quantities, as shown in Figure 11.4. By grouping two or more bars or by color-coding them, you can compare two or more categories. For example, the first bar chart in Figure 11.4 compares the participation of men and women in the 10 most popular sports in a given year. The other chart shows how per capita food consumption has changed over the period between 1970 and 1993. You can readily see that consumption of beef has declined, while consumption of chicken and turkey has increased.

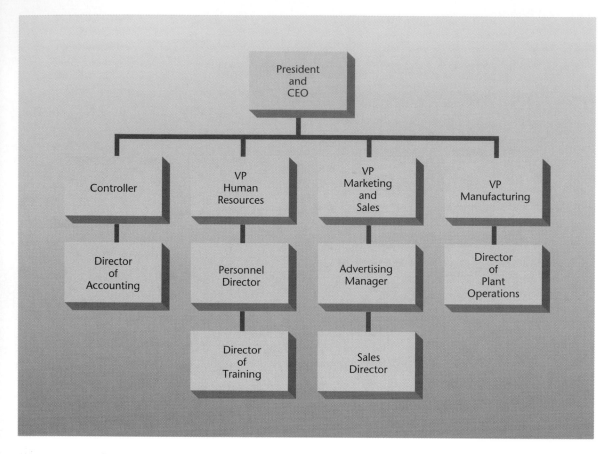

FIGURE 11.5 Organizational Chart

Organizational Charts   An **organizational chart** represents the structure of an organization, using boxes and lines to convey hierarchy and lines of authority. Figure 11.5 is an example. Such charts are useful in business, industry, or governmental organizations. For example, they can illustrate the organization's structure for new employees or be part of an annual report to shareholders.

Flow Chart   A **flow chart** uses boxes and arrows to represent the relationship of steps in a process. In other words, a flow chart shows how a process is carried out. For example, you might construct a flow chart like the one in Figure 11.6 to illustrate the steps necessary in preparing a speech.

Text-Only Charts   Sometimes a visual aid will consist exclusively of text. For example, a speaker might list on a visual aid textual material such as main points of a speech, the steps involved in a process, or important information for audience members to remember. Teachers commonly chart their lectures on overheads for students to follow. This textual material clues students to the major topics the teacher plans on covering.

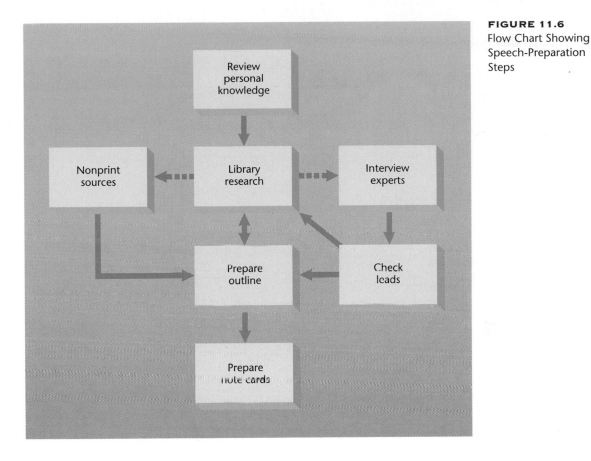

FIGURE 11.6
Flow Chart Showing
Speech-Preparation
Steps

Maps Maps are useful for speeches describing the spatial layout of an area, whether a dangerous intersection in your hometown or the disputed border between hostile nations. Maps can also be used to describe a dynamic process, such as a battle. At the site of the historic Civil War battle of Gettysburg, for example, numerous maps display various stages of the battle. One large-scale map uses embedded lights to show the daily progress of the battle.

MATERIALS FOR VISUAL AIDS

Visual aids can be made from a number of different materials. The same concept—say, a pie chart—might be expressed on a poster, a transparency, or a slide. Typical media for visual aids include poster board, flip charts, overhead transparencies, slides, handouts, and chalkboards.

Poster Board

Poster board is one of the most common materials used by students for their visual aids. You can draw illustrations, diagrams, or charts on it with colored marking pens.

It is important to support posters and flip charts on an easel.

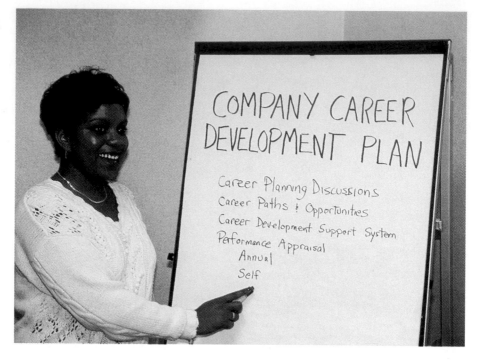

Or you can paste enlarged pictures on it or emphasize key words with rub-on letters or other prepared materials. Colored poster board may be visually more interesting than white board, as long as it contrasts markedly with the lettering.

Use a pencil to lightly sketch in the words or diagram, and then use felt-tip markers in various colors to finish the poster. Permanent markers are preferable, because posters prepared with water-based marking pens can be easily ruined by rain or a clumsy roommate. Use poster board that is thick enough to stand up without folding over. During the presentation, put the poster on an easel. Otherwise, you will have to either hold it while you talk or lean it up against the wall or lectern. This makes for a hard-to-see and wobbly visual aid.

If you are using a series of posters, prepare and place them in the order you will need them in the speech. Use a blank poster to cover posters that are not in use. As you begin talking about each poster, remove the blank and place it behind the poster you are discussing. When you are finished talking about that poster, remove it, revealing the blank poster. When you are ready to talk about the next poster, move the blank sheet behind it, and so on, until you get to the last poster.

Flip Charts

A **flip chart** is a series of drawings, charts, or graphs, usually attached at the top by a binding and supported on an easel. Speakers use flip charts to present a series of visual aids in a predetermined order. As with poster board, rough out your visual aid in light pencil and then fill in appropriate symbols with permanent

FIGURE 11.7
A PowerPoint
Template

OUR RELATIONAL SYSTEM

- *People Buy People*

- *Buying Is a Perceptual Process*

- *What People Perceive Determines
  What People Buy*

- *Business of Managing Perceptions*

marking pens. Be sure that the ink does not bleed through to the next sheet of paper. Leave blank sheets between visual aids if you will not be using one immediately after another.

Overhead Transparencies

An **overhead transparency** is a plastic sheet that can be drawn on or used in a photocopier to produce an image that is then projected on a screen for an audience to see. Overhead transparencies are a popular visual aid in business and classroom presentations. They have the advantage of low cost and ease of preparation, and they can be used without dimming the lights too much. Many classrooms and business conference rooms have overhead projectors, but you should always check in advance to make sure a projector is available. Also be sure to check out the equipment in advance, since machines operate differently.

Anything you can put on a poster or flip chart you can also put on an overhead transparency. You can write or draw directly on the transparency with a special pen, or you can use a computer to create text or graphics and then transfer that to a transparency using a photocopier. For example, software now exists that not only makes it easier to create overheads, but to create much more attractive overheads as well. Microsoft PowerPoint, which is available for both PCs and Macs, is very easy to use to make simple but visually powerful overheads. PowerPoint, for example, includes templates you can open and modify to suit your specific needs (Figure 11.7). PowerPoint also includes "wizards," which guide you step by step through the process of creating not only overheads, but also speaker's notes to accompany the overheads (see Figure 11.8).

This is just the beginning of what PowerPoint offers you as a speaker. You can add graphics to a template, add clip art, and even animate the graphics and clip art. You can scan images and include these as well, depending on your purpose. Finally, you can make color overheads using PowerPoint or color slides that you can store and link to a projection device with a laptop computer.

FIGURE 11.8
Overhead Made From
PowerPoint Wizard

Opinion Leadership
NSAA Michael Scott

OPINION LEADERS IN PROFILE

- *Knowledge*

- *Community Membership*
   Appearance
   Background
   Values and Lifestyle

- *Communication Skills*

Of course, PowerPoint isn't your only alternative for producing visually ap-pealing overheads. One easy way to make a transparency is to take a chart or graph from a book or magazine, enlarge it on a photocopier, and then copy the enlarged version onto the transparency. It may take you several tries to get ex-actly the image you want, so don't try to enlarge directly onto the plastic sheet. Enlarge on plain paper and then copy your final version onto the transparency. When using a photocopier, be sure to use transparency stock designed for plain-paper copiers; otherwise, the transparency can melt inside the copier!

It is also possible to print text or graphics directly onto a transparency with some computer printers. Again, be sure to use the transparency stock designed for your printer.

It is always a good idea to use color, and there are several techniques for adding color to your overhead transparencies.[2] The first and easiest is to use a computer and a color printer that can print directly on a transparency. If you do not have a color printer but do have a computer, you also can store the image planned for your overhead on a floppy disk, and then have the overhead made for you at a copying shop.

If you have a black-and-white printer connected to your computer, you can either print your overhead onto a transparency and then color it, or print it on paper, copy the information onto a transparency, and color it. Use water-based color pens in either case.

Finally, if none of the above works for you, you can make a color photocopy of an image you want to share, for example, a photograph from a book. You can then photocopy the image onto a transparency using the color photocopier.

The following guidelines should help you with your overheads.

Guidelines for Creating and Using Overheads

- **Make the text large enough to be seen when projected on a screen. A simple rule of thumb is that the smallest image on the screen must be at least 1 inch high for every 30 feet of viewing distance. To check for size, stand 10 feet** away from your transparency and read the text unprojected with the naked eye. If your vision is normal and you can't read it from that distance, it is too small and needs to be enlarged before it is copied onto a transparency.[3] Most photocopiers have an enlargement feature.

- Place the projection screen high enough for those in the back of the room to see clearly, with the bottom at least 48 inches from the floor. To avoid a keystone effect, where the top of the image is wider than the bottom, angle the screen so that the bottom is pulled back toward the wall. Ideally, the screen should be to the right of a right-handed presenter so that the speaker can write on the transparency without blocking the light.[4] Be sure to consider the audience's line of sight. Depending on where you are standing, you may be blocking the view of some of the audience members. Move away from the machine at times to give all of your audience members a clear view. Don't hesitate to ask if everyone can see.

- When using the overhead projector, don't turn your back on the audience to point to something on the screen. Instead, use a pointer or a pencil to point to the plastic sheet on the projector. This technique enables you to maintain eye contact with your audience and yet point to things on the overhead.

- Consider using special water-based marking pens to underline or otherwise highlight points on overheads as you go along. For example, a black-on-clear overhead could be intensified by using a red pen to underline key words. You can also use colored pens in advance to add color to black-on-clear outlines on charts or graphs.

- Just as you cover a poster board or flip chart when it's not in use, turn off the overhead projector when you are not using it. Don't leave an old overhead up on the screen, and never just project a bright light with no content on the screen. On the other hand, make sure you leave the overhead on long enough for the audience to read it and, if necessary, copy pertinent information. The amount of time will vary with the amount of material on the overhead.

- Use a piece of paper to cover the parts of the overhead you haven't discussed yet.[5] Covering part of an overhead and revealing points as you go along—a technique known as revelation—keeps your audience on track with you. It also allows you to control the pace of your presentation and prevents audience members from reading ahead.

- Keep a printed copy of each transparency on the lectern so that you can refer to it without having to stare into the glare of the projector's light or turn your back on your audience to read the screen.

Slides

Slides are a useful way to project a picture or other image onto a screen to ensure that everyone in the audience can see it. However, because slides require a darkened room, it's best to present them all together. You don't want to speak in the dark between segments of your speech that use slides.

As mentioned earlier, you can make color slides with Microsoft PowerPoint and store these slides sequentially on a floppy disk or the hard drive of a laptop computer. You can then link the laptop to a projection machine to display your slides.

You also may use traditional 35mm slides using a carousel projector. Be sure to organize your slides in advance. Make sure you load the slides properly, usually upside down, so that you're not embarrassed by an upside-down or reversed slide during your speech. Having to right an improperly loaded slide will disrupt your entire presentation.

Most slide projectors have a remote control so that the speaker can control the pace of the slides. If this is not the case, someone must sit at the slide projector and advance the slides for you. Be warned, however, that it is distracting to have a speech interrupted by constant calls for "next slide, please."

If you plan to use slides, rehearse their use carefully. If you must use a colleague to advance the slides, work with that person so that he or she knows roughly when to expect slide changes.

Although a slide presentation can be highly effective when done professionally, most beginning speakers should stick to simpler visual aids. Photographs that can be enlarged and placed on poster board, for example, often work just as well as slides and do not require any special equipment.

Handouts

Handouts create special problems for speakers. If they are distributed prior to the speech, your audience is likely to be reading the handout, not listening to what you say. Distributing them during the speech will disrupt the flow of your presentation and take up valuable time. If you wait until after the speech to distribute them, they cannot be an integral part of the speech.

The major use of handouts is to give your audience something to take with them from the speech. Perhaps you want your audience to write letters to members of Congress, so it is appropriate to give them addresses to take away from your speech. If you do not plan to directly use the handouts in the speech, by all means pass them out after you are finished speaking. If you have a recipe or formula that you want to distribute to the audience, you could put it on an overhead transparency or poster board and leave it on display long enough for it to be copied, or you could announce in advance that you will distribute copies after the speech.

Sometimes, however, you have a handout that should be used during the speech. Perhaps there is a self-administered questionnaire that your audience is expected to fill out and refer to during the speech. In cases where you do need to use a handout during the speech, distribute it at the beginning of the speech and ask your audience to turn it over and not look at it until you call on them to do so. Of course, not everyone will comply, but at least you will minimize the number who are looking at the handout rather than listening to you.

In general, use handouts only when no other type of visual aid will serve your purpose. Handouts are a distraction and allow the audience, not the speaker, to control the focus of attention. In all cases, avoid passing a single handout around the audience while you are speaking. This is the worst possible situation, as every member of the audience will see it at a different time, and there will be a distraction from your speech every time the handout moves to the next person.

Writing Boards

Writing boards, such as chalkboards or erasable marker boards, are sometimes useful for putting up brief information. For example, a phone number, an address, or a few key words can be quickly placed on the board. However, using a writing board as your sole or major visual means of support is not wise. For one thing, you have to turn your back on the audience in order to use the board. Anything more extensive than a few words will take longer to write than you would need for a prepared visual aid, such as an overhead transparency.

Even classroom teachers should consider alternatives to the writing board. Overhead projectors with a roll of acetate film can be used by math teachers, for example, to work through sample problems. Rather than turning their back on the class, teachers can do the problems while still facing their class.

In short, the writing board is of limited use to most speakers. Erasable marker boards have one advantage: Their white background and the availability of multicolored markers make them more interesting to use than the traditional black or green chalkboard. However, you still have to turn your back on the audience in order to use these boards effectively.

GUIDELINES FOR CREATING AND USING VISUAL AIDS

Once you have decided on the type and function of a visual aid, there are four basic guidelines you need to keep in mind in its construction: simplicity, visibility, layout, and color.[6] Let's consider each of these in turn.

Simplicity

There is a common tendency to try to put too much information on any one visual aid. We have seen people simply take a page from a magazine and copy it onto an overhead transparency. Some students try to save a few dollars by putting two or three ideas on one poster. These tendencies undermine the effectiveness of visual aids. The best advice we can give you is to keep it simple.[7]

Tips for Simplicity

- Limit yourself to one idea per visual aid.
- Use no more than six or seven words per line.
- Use no more than six or seven lines per visual aid.
- Use short, familiar words and round numbers.
- Keep charts and graphs simple enough to be sketched easily by your audience.

Visibility

Any visual aid is only as good as it is visible to your audience.[8] If they can't see it easily, it will hinder your presentation as your audience members strain or ask a neighbor what's on the screen.

Tips for Visibility

- Make your images at least 1 inch high for every 30 feet of viewing distance.

- Create transparencies that are readable by the naked eye at 10 feet. Use type no smaller than one-quarter inch, which is known as 18-POINT TYPE.

- Make sure you do not block your audience's view of your visual aid as you show it during the speech.

Layout

An organized, consistent, and uncluttered layout is necessary for an effective visual aid.[9]

Tips for Layout

- Place images near the top of your visual aid to ensure maximum visibility.
- Accentuate key points with bold type, underlining, or color.
- Write horizontally, not vertically. Vertical writing is hard to read.
- Leave generous margins, larger on top than bottom and equal on the sides.
- Present information from left to right and from top to bottom. For example, a chart showing progression over time should have the oldest year on the left and the most recent year on the right, not vice versa. If the information is presented vertically, the oldest should be at the top and the most recent on the bottom.

Color

Research has shown that the proper use of color helps your audience pay attention, comprehend, and remember your visuals.[10]

Tips for Color

- Use primary colors—red, blue, and yellow—which have been shown to create the strongest impact.
- Use contrasting but complementary colors so that your audience can see clearly. Yellow lettering on a white background, for example, is almost invisible.

- Use colored backgrounds, as long as the color is not so dark that the message is hard to see. Colored backgrounds are more visually soothing.
- Don't use clashing or confusing colors. For example, don't use red to show profits and black to show losses.

AUDIO AND AUDIOVISUAL AIDS

Although most people think only of visual aids, there are other ways to enhance a presentation. Some presentational aids add only sound, whereas others combine sound and pictures.

Audio aids are presentational aids that use sound only, such as tape recordings. Some speeches cry out for sound, such as one on different styles of music. A speech discussing different dialects obviously would be enhanced by samples of speech from different regions. A speech on old-time radio shows might use a few snippets from *The Lone Ranger*.

The most obvious way to prepare audio aids is with a tape recorder. Because you are unlikely to have time in a five- or ten-minute speech to completely present a song, let alone a symphony, you will want to edit your tape to include only the brief portion of the sounds you need. You can do this on any recording equipment that permits you to dub from tape to tape or from CD to tape. You could also use sophisticated and expensive recording equipment, but for most student speeches, a simple tape deck will do the job.

Audiovisual aids are presentational aids that combine sound and sight, such as film, videotape, filmstrips, and slide/tape presentations (we'll talk about computers separately). Film and videotape offer sound and motion, whereas filmstrips and slide/tape presentations combine still photos with sound.

Videotape has several advantages over film. Unlike film, videotape does not require a darkened room. Also, you can much more easily search a videotape for a particular segment to show to your audience. With two VCRs and audio and video cables to connect the machines, you can even edit videotape presentations. Usually, however, speakers have their videotapes cued to the points they plan to use. For example, we recall a student who was speaking against the colorization of old black-and-white movies. She brought in two versions of Frank Capra's classic, *It's a Wonderful Life*. In about a minute, she was able to compare a scene originally shot in black and white with the colorized version of the same scene. Her audience could clearly see for themselves the differences colorization had made.

With either film or videotape, the big danger is that you will cease to be a speaker and become merely a projectionist or button pusher. Any use of video or film should be brief (no more than a minute or so for a 10-minute speech) and central to the speech. With video, also consider the use of slow motion or freeze frame to emphasize your point. For example, a speaker explaining gymnastic scoring might want to freeze the tape or use slow motion to call attention to mistakes that warrant a deduction in points.

Filmstrips or slide/tape presentations basically involve prerecording the speech, which is then presented in coordination with still photos projected on a

Computer-assisted presentations can still fall prey to human error. FOXTROT © 1988 Bill Amend. Reprinted with permission of Universal Press Syndicate. All rights reserved.

screen. For most speech classes, this is not an appropriate method, because it replaces your speech with the mediated presentation. However, the slide/tape technology is often useful for sales presentations, as a teaching device, and in situations where a speaker will follow up with a speech. Because the time limits for most speech classes do not allow for this technology, we will not go into it in detail here. Suffice it to say that, with the right equipment, one can prepare an effective slide/tape presentation at a reasonable cost.

COMPUTER-ASSISTED PRESENTATIONAL AIDS

As we pointed out in the discussion of visual aids, computers and presentational software now can be used to enhance our public speaking transactions visually and aurally. In fact, the use of this technology is now commonplace in most business settings. To use this technology effectively, however, meticulous planning is required. You cannot simply try to dazzle your audience.[11]

Further, while the presentational software about which we speak is readily available, even to students, the laptop computers and video projection machines necessary to use the software to its best effect are less so. It's best not to forget, therefore, that even the most sophisticated presentational technology out there is best viewed as a complement to the substance of your speech and the skill with which you deliver it.

Because presentational software and hardware are being improved upon daily, what we recommend to you today could be obsolete tomorrow. Thus we are not going to attempt the impossible and try to teach you the ins-and-outs of Microsoft PowerPoint or Adobe Persuasion here. We simply want to alert you to the existence of this technology and encourage you to explore its appropriate use in your presentations.

The advantage of using specifically designed presentational software is that many programs will create appropriate charts or graphs once you enter your information. To reiterate, there also usually are prepared templates that you can use in preparing your own graphics. Templates are particularly helpful because they include restrictions that limit the number of words and lines to ensure that the visuals will be easily understood by the audience. Clip-art images are typically part of the package, allowing you to pick and choose images that fit your needs. A scanner will allow you to store pictures in your computer for use as graphics. In short, the computer can help you in the creative process of producing graphics to be displayed on the traditional media of visual aids.

Because the screen on a computer is too small to be seen by an audience, you need a way to project your visual aids on a large flat screen, just as you would an overhead transparency or a slide. There are thin, transparent display units, called liquid crystal display pads, made for this purpose. The pad is placed on top of an overhead projector and connected by a cable directly to your computer. At the same time an image is displayed on your computer screen, the pad on the overhead displays the image on a thin panel through which the light from the overhead projector can pass. This projects the image on the screen for your audience to see. Even animation and sound are possible with the right hardware and software. You should be aware, however, that many of the projection units that are placed on an overhead projector are not bright enough to project slides without turning out or dimming the lights. Thus, you should check such equipment in advance so that you will not be surprised by a lack of visibility of your overheads.

There also are several brands of stand-alone projectors that can be linked to a laptop computer so that the sounds and images stored on a floppy disk or the computer's hard drive can be displayed on a screen for your audience. Should you want to rush out to buy one, their prices range from a low of a few thousand dollars for a portable tabletop model to a high of tens of thousands for a projector capable of projecting a large image to an auditorium-sized audience.

Of course, besides cost and availability, the downside to this technology is that the speaker risks becoming secondary to the equipment. And if you do not know how to correctly operate the computer or if there is an equipment failure, you risk embarrassment. Thus, for beginning students, we recommend computers primarily for the creation of more traditional visual aids. However, the range of computer-assisted presentations is ever increasing and will likely become more common throughout your lifetime.

Hints for Using Presentational Aids

Tips and Tactics

Before Your Speech

- Check the room and your equipment.
- Practice, if possible, with the same equipment in the same room where you will give your speech.
- Double-check your presentational aids immediately before the speech. For example, make sure posters, overheads, or slides are in proper order, right-side up, and ready to go.
- Allow ample time for setup and takedown.

Computers not only help speakers create visual aids, they may also be used to display them.

During the Speech

- Avoid distractions—cover or remove visual aids and turn off projectors when not in use.
- Do not block the audience's view.
- Allow the audience enough time to process the information. Then remove the aid.
- Talk to your audience, not to the visual aid.

No matter how much you plan, things can still go wrong. For some tips on how to cope with the unexpected, see the box "Murphy's Law."

SUMMARY

Presentational aids can make the difference between a successful speech and a failure. People learn more, remember longer, and are more likely to be persuaded by speeches with effective presentational aids.

As with all other aspects of your speech, begin by analyzing the rhetorical situation and the audience in deciding whether to use presentational aids and which ones to use. Be sure that visual aids will be visible to the audience and appropriate to the occasion.

Basic types of *visual aids* are objects; models; photographs; diagrams and illustrations; and charts, graphs, and maps. The media commonly used for visual aids include poster board, *flip charts, overhead transparencies*, slides, handouts, and writ-

Murphy's Law

Murphy's Law is the well-known adage "If anything can go wrong, it will." Unfortunately it applies as much to the use of presentational aids in public speaking as to your car battery on a cold morning. Although you can prepare your visual aids thoroughly, there is no way to be completely prepared for the "unexpected." The best defense is to anticipate problems and prepare alternatives. Here are a few of the things that can go wrong that you need to prepare for. (At one time or another, they have all happened to the authors of this book.)

Problem: The battery in your equipment (tape recorder, microphone, or whatever) is dead.

What to do: Test the equipment the morning of your speech and carry a spare battery.

Problem: There is no overhead projector, even though you reserved one.

What to do: Make sure you call to confirm your reservation on the morning of your speech. Physically check out the projector if possible.

Problem: The overhead projector's lightbulb is burned out.

What to do: Most overheads have a spare lightbulb. Make sure you know where it is beforehand.

Problem: The slide projector (film projector, VCR, etc.) does not work.

What to do: Again, check it out in advance if possible. If it unexpectedly fails, you will need to verbally describe what is on your slides. We recall one case where a person simply stood in front of a blank screen, pre-

tended to show slides, and described them in elaborate detail as he went along ("As you can clearly see from this slide . . ."). It turned a frustrating situation into a humorous one.

Problem: Your visual aids are out of order or upside down, or some are missing.

What to do: An ounce of prevention is worth a pound of cure. Check and double-check them before the speech. If you run into this problem, try not to get flustered. Make a joke while you look for the missing visual; if you can't find it, verbally describe the visual or skip a part of the speech.

Problem: There's no chalk for the chalkboard or no dry erase markers for the white board.

What to do: Bring extra chalk or dry erase markers with you.

Problem: It takes a lot longer than you thought to demonstrate a process using your visual aids.

What to do: First, always practice with your visuals so that you know how long it will take. Second, if you are demonstrating a multistep process, have various steps along the way already prepared.

Remember, nothing can happen to you that hasn't already happened to someone else. Most audiences are sympathetic to speakers who are obviously prepared and yet encounter technical difficulties beyond their control. At the same time, audiences have little sympathy when Murphy's Law strikes someone who is just winging it. And keep in mind, "Murphy was an optimist."

---

ing boards. Other presentational aids include *audio aids*, such as tape recorders, and *audiovisual aids*, such as films, videotapes, filmstrips, and slide/tape presentations.

Computer-assisted graphics enable you to prepare professional-looking charts, graphs, and visual depictions that can be printed directly on overhead transparencies or paper. These graphics can be converted into everything from slides to posters. Computers can also be used during a presentation, although there is a danger of letting the computer steal the show from the speaker.

Four basic guidelines for creating and using visual aids are simplicity, visibility, well-planned layout, and effective use of color. Before your presentation, check your equipment and presentational aids. Rehearse if possible with the exact equipment you will be using. Allow time for setup and takedown. During the speech, avoid distractions, do not block your audience's view, allow the audience time to process the information, and talk to your audience, not your visual aids.

Check Your Understanding: Exercises and Activities

1. Check on your campus or at local copying shops to find out where you can have the following made: black-on-clear overhead transparencies, color overhead transparencies, enlarged photographs, slides, videotapes.

2. Find out where on campus you can obtain an overhead projector, and find out who can answer questions about its operation. Learn how to turn it on and off, how to focus it, and what to do if the bulb burns out.

3. Find an example of a bar chart, a pie chart, a line graph, and a map in *USA Today* or your local newspaper, and describe whether each one would make a suitable visual aid for a speech. Evaluate them in terms of *simplicity, visibility, layout,* and *color.*

4. Contact the computer center at your college or university. What, if any, services are available to help you prepare computer graphics for your speeches? If you own or have access to a computer, go to a computer dealer or consult a software catalog, and find at least three presentation-graphics programs available for your computer.

5. Consider the following speech situations: an informative speech on the Impressionist Movement in art; an informative speech on the Persian Gulf War; a persuasive speech about health insurance in the United States; a speech to entertain on the topic of traveling by train, plane, or automobile. What types of visual aids would be most appropriate for each speech situation, and why?

Notes

1. Donald R. Vogel, Gary W. Dickson, and John A. Lehman, "Persuasion and the Role of Visual Presentation Support: The UM/3M Study," commissioned by Visual Systems Division of 3M, 1986, cited in John J. Makay, *Public Speaking: Theory Into Practice* (Fort Worth, Tex.: Harcourt Brace Jovanovich, 1992), 172–173.

2. Minnesota Western, *Visual Presentation Systems* (Oakland, Calif.: Minnesota Western, 1988–1989), 181.

3. Minnesota Western, *Visual Presentation Systems,* 180.

4. Minnesota Western, *Visual Presentation Systems,* 170–171.

5. Minnesota Western, *Visual Presentation Systems,* 177.

6. Minnesota Western, *Visual Presentation Systems,* 180–181.

7. Minnesota Western, *Visual Presentation Systems,* 180.

8. Minnesota Western, *Visual Presentation Systems,* 180.

9. Minnesota Western, *Visual Presentation Systems,* 181.

10. Minnesota Western, *Visual Presentation Systems,* 181.

11. Margaret Y. Rabb, ed., *The Presentation Design Book: Projecting a Good Image With Your Desktop Computer* (Chapel Hill, N.C.: Ventana Press, 1990).

Contexts for Public Speaking

PART FOUR

CHAPTER 12

Jaime Escalante
motivated his
students to achieve
through the power
of *ganas,* the desire
to succeed.

Informative Speaking

OBJECTIVES

After reading this chapter, you should be able to:

- Explain how to adapt your informative speech to audiences with diverse learning styles.
- Explain the relationship between informative speaking and learning.
- Use the message attributes—novelty, compatibility, comprehensibility, relative advantage, observability, and trialability—in your informative speeches.
- Prepare informative speeches that explain, instruct, demonstrate, or describe processes, concepts, and skills.
- Illustrate how informative speaking can be used in your other classes, at work, and in your community.

KEY CONCEPTS

compatibility	novelty
comprehensibility	observability
ganas	relative advantage
informative speaking	trialability

Determination plus hard work plus concentration equals success, which equals ganas.

—JAIME ESCALANTE[1]

Jaime Escalante, whose picture you see in the opening photograph, is not simply a gifted teacher. He is a remarkable person. He immigrated to the United States from Bolivia in 1969, where he had taught mathematics and physics. He spoke not a single word of English. But Escalante had what he called **ganas**—that is, a desire to succeed regardless of the odds against it. Thus, at age 30, he reentered school to work toward his teaching credential, even though it meant subjecting his out-of-shape body to a required course in P.E.

The rest of the story, of course, is probably well known to you. Escalante's life became the subject of the critically acclaimed film *Stand and Deliver*. In the movie, actor Edward James Olmos portrays Escalante, who took East Los Angeles barrio students who could barely do simple math and, in two years of intensive work, prepared them for the Advanced Placement Test in Calculus. His students were so successful that all 18 who attempted the test in 1982 passed, the most from any high school in Southern California. Each year, more students passed; by 1987, 87 of his students passed the exam. Remember, these were students who were not expected to attend college, let alone receive college credit for calculus while still in high school. But as Escalante says, "Students will rise to the level of expectations." When students wanted to quit, Escalante would challenge them by saying, "Do you have the *ganas*? Do you have the desire?"[2]

Although there are many reasons that Escalante was able to overcome odds others would have perceived as insurmountable, we think his success in life as well as in the classroom can be found in that word of his: *ganas*. Not only did Escalante have it when he needed it, but also his life is testimony to the fact that he has instilled it in many of his students. As a result, they too have succeeded.

In a sense, this chapter is about *ganas*. Like Jaime Escalante, the best informative speakers do more than simply pass on information to an audience. With their words and actions, they create a desire in their audience to put the information to constructive use. In the case of Escalante, the desire involved a subject that many students prefer to avoid: mathematics. In yours, it may involve anything from how we treat our environment to the kind of foods we eat.

Informative speaking is the process by which an audience gains new information or a new perspective on old information from a speaker. Put another way, the goal of informative speaking is audience learning. In order to be an effective informative speaker, you need to master several skills, which we will look at in this chapter. These skills include

- focusing on your audience and appealing to their various styles of learning;
- understanding the relationship between informative speaking and learning;
- learning to utilize various attributes of messages in informative speaking;
- putting theory into practice in speeches that explain, instruct, demonstrate, or describe; and
- understanding the differences and similarities among the forums in which you are likely to give informative presentations, namely, the classroom, the workplace, and the community.

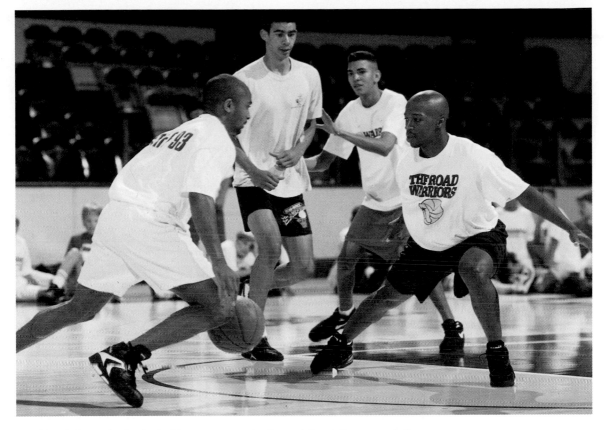

Teaching kids to play basketball is an opportunity for an informative presentation.

FOCUSING ON YOUR AUDIENCE: ADAPTING TO DIFFERENT STYLES OF LEARNING

Consider the following scenarios. In the first, the president of the United States goes on national TV to explain a foreign-policy situation that could lead to the commitment of our armed forces. In the second, a police officer visits a local elementary school to instruct children about bicycle safety. In the third, an NBA pro at a basketball camp demonstrates to high school students the proper techniques for accurate free-throw shooting. And in the fourth a NASA spokesperson describes findings from the latest Hubble space telescope transmissions.

Each of these scenarios can be viewed as a speaking situation. Further, each involves a speaker publicly *informing* an audience. In each case, the speaker must focus on relating the information to the needs and goals of the audience members. Jaime Escalante had to first reach out to and connect with his students before he could really begin to teach them calculus. So too must every informative speaker reach out to and connect with his or her audience before presenting them with information.

Informative Speaking and Styles of Learning

One important consideration in focusing on your audience is recognizing that not everyone has the same style of learning. Not everybody thinks in a linear or "logical" fashion. Some people can simply read a book and absorb the information, whereas others need to hear and see to learn. Still others learn best by doing. Good public speakers recognize these differences and appeal to as many styles as possible. Here is one listing of diverse learning styles:[3]

- *Auditory linguistic:* Learning by hearing the spoken word.
- *Visual linguistic:* Learning by seeing the printed word.
- *Auditory numerical:* Learning by hearing numbers.
- *Visual numerical:* Learning by seeing numbers.
- *Audio-visual-kinesthetic combination:* Learning by hearing, seeing, and doing in combination.
- *Individual:* Learning when by oneself.
- *Group:* Learning in collaboration with other people.
- *Oral expressive:* Learning by telling others orally.
- *Written expressive:* Learning by writing.

At first, such a long list of diverse learning styles may be intimidating. How in the world can one speech or even a series of speeches adapt to all of these different ways of learning? Of course, you cannot be all things to all people. But teachers confront this variety of learning styles every day. Many teachers use a combination of methods—individual and group work, written and oral assignments, print and visual materials—in an effort to adapt to the variety of learning styles in their classrooms.

Rather than trying to guess which one style of learning is most widespread in an audience and focusing on that, it is better to use multiple channels and modes of learning. That way, you are likely to reach most of your audience members with something that suits their style of learning. In any given audience, there are likely to be individual learners as well as group learners, those who respond best to oral instruction and those who need to read it, and so on. Using visual aids, for example, is an excellent way to reinforce visually what you say orally. Distributing a handout after a speech can help visual learners retain what was said. Provide your audience with an opportunity to use as many senses as possible to process your message. If parts of your presentation can be seen, heard, and even touched, you will increase the odds that your message will sink in.

One speech we heard, for example, was about using acupressure to relieve stress. By instructing the class to press on certain points on their bodies, the speaker allowed the audience to use their sense of touch to understand what was being said. Other speakers appeal to the sense of taste. We frequently have international students speak about a food unique to their culture and bring samples for the audience to try. Further, the active involvement of some audience members will help reach those who need group reinforcement to learn. Audience involvement is a technique used by Jonathan Studebaker, who we introduced in Chapter 2. He frequently talks to children at elementary schools about dealing with disabilities and tries to involve them by asking them questions and responding to their answers. A speech by Jonathan is not a one-way transmission, but a true transaction between him and the audience.

Informative Speaking and Learning

Whether your speech is aimed at explaining a process such as photosynthesis, describing the alignment of the planets in our solar system, or demonstrating the uses of the wok in Chinese cooking, informative speaking is basically about learning. As your own experience tells you, exposure to new information or a new perspective doesn't guarantee that you will learn it. No matter how convinced a teacher is of the importance of his or her subject matter, there is no guarantee students will share the teacher's conviction. Jaime Escalante, for example, first had to convince his students that calculus was worth knowing before trying to teach it to them.

So it is with you and your informative speeches. Before you attempt to explain, describe, or demonstrate something to your audience, you must first connect its value with the self-interest of your audience. Then, and only then, will your audience be sufficiently motivated to listen to what you have to say.

SIX ATTRIBUTES OF EFFECTIVE INFORMATIVE SPEAKING

What makes one speaker's presentation so informative and stimulating that you want to learn more about what you initially thought was a boring topic? And why does another speaker's presentation leave you cold from beginning to end? Is the reason (a) the speaker, (b) the topic, (c) the message, (d) your perceptions, or (e) all of the above? Because the public speaking transaction is an interdependent system, the answer, of course, is (e) all of the above.

However, if an informative speech is seen as personally or professionally relevant, it can be successful in spite of being delivered by a marginally skilled public speaker. The reverse is not always true; that is, we may not find an entertaining speaker personally or professionally informative.

Research over the past two decades suggests that the likelihood of an audience's perceiving information as relevant and conducive to learning depends significantly on six message attributes: novelty, compatibility, comprehensibility, relative advantage, observability, and trialability.[4] These attributes represent the criteria people use to decide whether a speaker's information is worth the time and effort necessary to pay attention and learn from it.

Novelty

Novelty is the quality of being new and stimulating. Just as plants are heliotropic, we human beings are stimulitropic. Whereas plants continuously orient themselves to the sun to activate the process of photosynthesis, we continually orient ourselves to new sources of stimulation.

Although novelty alone is not enough to sustain an informative speech, it certainly can make your speech more effective. Research has time and again documented the fact that the perception of novelty heightens selective exposure, selective attention, and selective retention of information. In other words, people are likely to seek out, pay attention to, and remember novel information. The most obvious way to get the benefit of novelty in an informative speech is to choose a topic that is novel for your audience. You're much more likely to initially captivate the attention of audience members with the unfamiliar than with the mundane. Novelty, however, shouldn't be confused with the obscure. For example, whereas computer software for accountancy probably would be an obscure topic for most audiences, the fact that the software could save you money on your taxes might be a novel topic.

Another way to use novelty to your advantage is in the construction of your message. Even though the rule of thumb is to structure your speech so that the audience can predict what comes next, this is not an unbending rule. Sometimes it is to your advantage to violate the expectancies of an audience. Writers, for example, sometimes begin with a story's end and then backtrack. Similarly, a skilled speaker could start a speech with what normally would be considered its conclusion and build backward.

Finally, novelty in your delivery can work to your advantage when speaking informatively. Audiences, for instance, generally are accustomed to speakers who are relatively stationary. Movement may add needed novelty to your presentation. In addition, if you review some of our suggestions about the nonverbal dynamics of delivery in Chapter 10, you'll find other ways to introduce novelty to your presentation.

Compatibility

Early in this book we said that communication is perceptual and that the process of perception is selective. Basically, people perceive what they choose to perceive. In the effort to reach your audience with an informative speech, a second message attribute you'll need to take into account is compatibility. **Compatibility** is the audience's perception that a message is consistent with their belief systems—their attitudes, beliefs, values, and lifestyle. All too often, speakers fail to take compatibility into account when choosing a topic and then constructing their informative speech.

For example, we've heard several informative speeches on sexually transmitted diseases (STDs) and their prevention. We've also had students approach us after class and tell us they were offended or made to feel unjustifiably uncomfortable as a consequence of (1) the information in some of these speeches, (2) their perception that these speeches promoted a lifestyle with which they disagreed, and (3) the use of visual aids they didn't perceive to be in good taste. To a large degree, we were surprised by these reactions to a topic we believe needs to be openly discussed. We don't feel that student speakers should altogether avoid sensitive topics such as this one. However, they do need to consider the question of compatibility so that they can soften or qualify the information so that it is appropriate for the audience.

Consider how you might approach an informative speech on the constitutional rights of accused felons for two different audiences. The first audience is composed of law school students. The second is a group of veteran police officers. Both audiences need the information you have. Would you give an identical speech to both of them? Probably not. For the police officers, you most likely would have to qualify the information in your speech with such statements as

"I realize some of you take exception with the courts' rulings on the rights of the accused."

"Putting our personal feelings aside, the Constitution is clear . . . "

"Before I begin, I want you to put the shoe on the other foot; assume that you are the accused."

The point is that information that is potentially incompatible with audience members can be made palatable if it is presented in a way that acknowledges the audience's point of view.

Comprehensibility

Jaime Escalante understood that no matter how simple or complex your topic, your audience needs to perceive it as something they can understand. **Comprehensibility** is the perception that a message is not too difficult or complex to understand. Research tells us that one of the quickest ways to turn off an audience is to complicate a topic. You don't have to avoid complex topics for your informative speeches. In fact, they are likely to be both novel for your audience and interesting for you to research. The goal is to make complex topics comprehensible and compelling.

Jaime Escalante's calculus classes in *Stand and Deliver* are models of the presentation of complex information. He broke the lessons into easy-to-digest bits, what he called "step by step." In fact, he would say to his students, "This is easy." It's not so much the complexity of the topic as the complexity of a speaker's explanation that makes a topic difficult for an audience to understand.

An excellent way to reduce the complexity of a speech is through analogies or comparisons. Explain a complex process, for example, by comparing it with a common process based on the same principle. One speech we heard explained nuclear power plants by using an analogy to the steam produced by heating water in a teakettle.

Visual aids can also be helpful in reducing complexity. For example, we recall a speech about a complex carbon molecule in which the speaker used a "Tinkertoy" model to show what the molecule looked like. The speaker also used an analogy, calling the molecule a "soot ball," to help the audience visualize what it would be like.

Relative Advantage

When we introduced the tools you need to get started on your first speech, we talked about the importance of connecting with your audience. If they are to learn, audience members need to know explicitly why it is in their interest to listen to what you have to say.

When we connect with our audience, we are in effect saying, "My topic and message hold some relative advantage for you." The audience's **relative advantage,** or their perception that a message will benefit them, can be a more informed view on some topic or an improved way of behaving. Don't think that just because you have a good idea, people will necessarily see the advantage in adopting it. History is replete with good ideas, the proverbial better mousetrap, that are collecting dust for want of the public's attention. Consider two examples from Everett M. Rogers's classic work, *The Diffusion of Innovations*.[5]

If you have studied the history of science, you may recall that the disease scurvy, caused by a deficiency of vitamin C, was a serious problem for sailors on long voyages. As early as 1601, it was found that sources of vitamin C effectively inhibited scurvy. Yet it took almost 200 years for the British navy to put this finding to use on its ships, and almost 75 years more for sources of vitamin C to be made available on commercial ships.

The second example concerns the arrangement of the keyboard on typewriters and personal computers. If you have ever thought the keys were illogically arranged, you are not alone. A far better method of arrangement of keys has been available since 1932. The Dvorak method is more efficient than the system almost everybody uses and is more easily mastered. So why weren't you taught the Dvorak method in the beginning? Because the one you use was invented in 1873 and has been designed into almost all keyboards ever since. One of the reasons for staying with the less logical keyboard was that the metal keys of early typewriters stuck when the typist worked too quickly. Thus, the keyboard we use today on computers and electric typewriters was originally invented to *slow down* typists on mechanical typewriters.

All too often, speakers assume that audience members will recognize they have something to gain personally or professionally from a speech. What may be perfectly obvious to the speaker, however, may be just the opposite for the audience. Consider a case with which you already have some experience—college classes. Regardless of the subject matter of their classes, most college professors believe that the information they have to share is absolutely essential to every student's intellectual well-being. So secure are they in this belief, in fact, some seldom spend any time convincing students that there are "good reasons" for their being in the professor's class.

Occasionally, this oversight doesn't much matter—for example, when students are taking a course in their major. Students listen because they know they "have to learn" what is being taught, regardless of how well it's being taught. This is seldom the case, though, when they find themselves in a required course outside their major. "Why do I need a course in art history?" complains the computer science major, while the chemistry major asks, "Why do I need a class in public speaking?" To motivate students in math classes, Jaime Escalante put together a video called *Who Needs Math?* starring people like Bill Cosby.

Just as teachers have an obligation to connect their course to the professional aspirations of students, so do speakers have the same kind of obligation to

Observability is an important attribute of speeches that explain.

their audiences. It's not enough that their information is perceived as novel or compatible by their audience. Their information—their speech—also must be readily perceived as something that will benefit their audience.

Observability

Seeing is believing, or so the saying goes. Information that can be made observable for your audience can work to your advantage. **Observability** is the degree to which information can be seen. For example, in and of themselves, statistics such as gross national product, median income, the consumer price index, and the rate of inflation can ring very hollow in the ears of an audience. Yet such information very often is the stuff of which informative speeches are made. One way to breathe life into statistics is to augment the speech with creative visual aids, such as those discussed in Chapter 11. In fact, this kind of augmentation may be what makes your audience nod in understanding instead of staring back at you with blank expressions.

Clothing designer Diane von Furstenberg uses the principle of observability on QVC as she wears the shirt she is selling on the air. Like other on-air salespeople, she also employs the principle of trialability by offering a money-back guarantee.

The need for observability is not limited to statistical information. A working model of an internal combustion engine certainly would help a mechanically disinclined audience understand an informative presentation on automotive engineering, a detailed cross section of the human eye would help a group of biology students understand the role of the cornea, and even a visually appealing list of the daily diet of the American teenager might help a group of nursing students relate to an informative speech on nutrition.

Although visual aids may be the most obvious way to give pictorial life to your informative speech, you also can provide word pictures for your audience. For example, in the effort to assist your audience in visualizing your information you can ask the audience to imagine a situation; use examples for which the audience is likely to have a visual referent, such as the Statue of Liberty, a landmark at your school, or a national park; and use descriptive adjectives, action words, and visual metaphors. Regardless of how you give visual life to your informative speech, however, the objective is the same: You want your audience to "see" what it is you are talking about.

Trialability

The final message attribute we want to share with you is most relevant to informative presentations that require some demonstration. **Trialability** is the opportunity to experiment with an idea, a product, or a practice without penalty.

Simply put, people prefer to "try something on for size" before deciding on its personal or professional worth.

In the business world, for instance, when the PC began to replace the typewriter, and the fax and e-mail began to replace letters, trialability was essential to informative presentations on the uses of these new technologies. One of the lessons learned in the process of computerizing the workplace was that people were quicker to respond favorably to innovations when provided with an opportunity to try them out in a nonthreatening environment.

Of course, it is often not realistic to have an entire audience "try out" something as you speak. Sometimes the solution is to provide the audience with information on where they can go to try out what you have discussed in your speech. For example, a speech on CPR should include specific information on where to get hands-on training. On other occasions, you can invite a few audience members to the front of the room and have them try out the process in front of everyone else, showing how it can be done. Then you can urge audience members to try it out on their own. In any case, if some kind of trial experience can be incorporated into a speech, it will enhance the audience's understanding of the subject matter.

At some point in either your educational or professional life, you can reasonably expect to provide some demonstration for an audience. It may be something as simple as explaining your job, or it may be assisting people in the solution of a complex problem. Whether simple or complex, the best demonstrations are those that involve the people with whom you are speaking. After all, it's much easier to relate to information with which we have hands-on experience than to relate to information that has been conveyed passively.

PUTTING THEORY INTO PRACTICE

Now that you know some of the principles related to conveying information to an audience, it's time to plan your own informative speech. This section offers some practical suggestions for how to give an informative speech. We discuss four ways to inform an audience: explanation, instruction, demonstration, and description. Informative speeches may employ more than one of these modes of informing. And the list is not exhaustive. Nevertheless, these four categories should be a useful way of thinking of how to translate the principles of informative speaking into an actual speech.

Speeches That Explain a Process

One of the primary functions you may wish to accomplish in an informative speech is to explain a process. Technically, a *process* is a continuous phenomenon without an obvious beginning or end. Examples of processes are plentiful in science and include photosynthesis, erosion, and osmosis. Because true processes are complex and often hidden from our ordinary senses, their explanation requires genuine creativity from a speaker. At a minimum, the speaker must break down the process into increments that the audience can readily comprehend. If the process involves a specialized vocabulary, the speaker also needs to define terms for the audience. Because the process also may be invisible, the speaker may have to create visual aids that approximate the process.

The key to explaining a process is to find the right complement of language and visual media for your audience. This involves finding the best analogies, metaphors, and similes to start. You can then complement these elements of language with static visual media such as overheads or dynamic visual media such as videotape or CD-ROM.

Speeches That Explain a Concept

Although not as difficult to explain as a process, a concept demands care on the part of the speaker who chooses to explain it. A *concept* is a symbolic abstraction that pulls together a class of objects that share common attributes. The word *ball*, for example, is also a concept that can be applied to baseballs, basketballs, footballs, golf balls, racketballs, squash balls, and volleyballs. Although different in size and purpose, these types of balls share at least one common attribute: They are round.

The key to explaining a concept is to describe the criterial attributes that distinguish it from other concepts. How is a democracy different from a republic? The United States is a republic, yet most people refer to it as a democracy. A good informative speech would not only explain why this is the case, but also point out the specific attributes that distinguish a republic from a democracy.

In selecting a topic for a speech that explains a process or a concept, keep in mind that the topic should be relevant to the audience, something they are capable of understanding, and something you can explain in the time allotted. Although the theory of relativity is highly relevant, explaining it in a 5- to 10-minute speech is a tall order.

The message attribute of comprehensibility is particularly important in speeches that explain. Recall that one way to reduce complexity for an audience is to use an analogy. Consider the use of analogy in this excerpt from a speech by Jonathan Studebaker explaining a process, namely, the progressive disease he has:

> Like I said, I'm a nice person. I'm cheerful, I'm energetic. Okay, so I have a disability. I was born with osteogenesis imperfecta, a disease which causes my bones to be fragile. Have you ever accidentally dropped a glass on the floor? What happens? It breaks. Well, my bones kinda break like glass, which is why I tell people, when you carry me, treat me like your best crystal.[6]

The use of a simple analogy of bones to glass helps the audience understand a disease most of us cannot even pronounce. For Jonathan's purposes, which are to introduce himself and explain his disability, that is the extent of the technical information his audience needs to know.

A second attribute that is important in speeches that explain a process or a concept is observability. One of the best ways to make something observable is with visual aids. They can make an abstract concept concrete and thus easier to understand.

During your college career, you will undoubtedly be called on to explain something to an audience, if not in your public speaking class, then in another setting. Similarly, in the professional world, it is common for people to be called on to explain everything from a new product idea to why the last quarter's sales were so bad. Using the principles of comprehensibility and observability can help you enhance your explanations.

Speeches That Instruct

Informative speaking can also be used to instruct an audience. The key to instruction is to provide new information the audience can put to use, or a new perspective on old information. Modern educational theory emphasizes observable behavioral objectives; that is, after receiving instruction, students should be able to show that they have mastered the subject, either by answering questions or by engaging in some activity.

The message attributes of novelty and relative advantage are particularly relevant to speeches that provide instruction. First, consider novelty. Unless the information in your speech presents *new* information or a *fresh perspective* to your audience, all you have done is bore them with what they already know. For example, speeches on how to ride a bike or how to pack your suitcase are unlikely to provide anything new to an audience. However, even new topics can be perceived as irrelevant or of no relative advantage by large portions of an audience. For example, a speech on how to wax your skis is old news to experienced skiers, but irrelevant to nonskiers in the class.

So, the key to speeches that instruct is to provide new yet relevant information to your audience, or at least a new perspective on such information. That means using the novelty of your topic to gain interest while pointing out the relative advantage of learning the information to at least the majority of listeners.

Speeches That Demonstrate How to Do Something

Speeches that demonstrate how to do something are closely related to those that provide instruction, but they use the message attributes of observability and trialability. In a speech that demonstrates, the speaker actually shows the audience how to do something. Further, a good demonstration allows the audience to try out what is being demonstrated, if not during the speech itself, then later on their own. A good example of speeches that demonstrate are the late-night infomercials you see on TV. From food dehydrators to onion slicers, the product is demonstrated for the audience. Viewers at home and in the studio can clearly see how to use the product. Audience members are often given a chance to try the product. Viewers are urged to order the product and try it at home, with a no-risk, money-back guarantee. The combination of observability and trialability has made infomercials highly successful.

Failure to properly prepare for a demonstration is the hallmark of Tim Allen's comedy on *Home Improvement,* but it can lead to disaster in an informative speech.

Whatever a speaker is demonstrating, he or she needs to provide audience members with enough information to do the activity on their own, or with information on where to obtain further instruction, so that they can try out the activity. For example, although no one can master karate from just listening to a single speech, or even a series of speeches, a demonstration of karate moves can spur an audience member to seek out individual instruction in the martial arts. In fact, many martial arts studios make a practice of giving demonstrations in schools and at public events as a way of recruiting new students.

Topics for speeches that demonstrate need to be chosen with care. A complex, difficult task cannot be adequately demonstrated in a few minutes. There can even be the danger of making people think they know how to do something based on a speech when in fact they do not. Few of us could do CPR, for example, based on simply watching a speaker demonstrate the activity. We need the opportunity to try it out (perhaps on a life-size doll) before we can know whether we can do it. On the other hand, another lifesaving technique, the Heimlich maneuver, is often the subject of demonstration and can be learned in a reasonably short time.

The key to making your demonstration effective is careful planning. For example, if you have ever watched the show *Home Improvement,* you know that

Tim (The Tool Man) Taylor rarely has practiced what he is doing. If you plan to demonstrate a process in your speech, rehearse it carefully. Also, it is sometimes useful to prepare various steps of the process in advance. Watch any cooking show demonstration on TV. The onions are already chopped, the flour is already sifted and measured, and an example of the finished product is near at hand. You don't want the audience drifting off as you measure ingredients or sift the flour. Providing a written recipe in a handout or as a visual aid will save you a lot of time and let the audience focus on watching your demonstration. In short, a demonstration requires extra preparation.

In addition, be sure that the demonstration is an accurate re-creation. If you misinform an audience, you have done more harm than good. Depending on what you are demonstrating, you might even be inviting injury to the audience member or someone else. Make certain, therefore, that you can accurately demonstrate the process in the time allowed.

Finally, make sure the demonstration is visible to the audience. We recall a student who was an expert fisherman and wanted to demonstrate the art of fly tying. Because fishing line is almost invisible and a fishhook is very difficult to see, he used a large-scale fishhook (made from a coat hanger) and colored yarn to tie his fly. Only by enlarging the actual objects was he able to give the audience a meaningful demonstration.

Speeches That Describe

Another function of informative speeches is description. Observability is the key to descriptive speech. Not only can visual aids be useful; you may also want to provide a word picture of your subject. Consider the following description of a familiar character, Mickey Mouse, provided by student speaker Jennie Rees:

> They designed him using a circle for his head and oblong circles for his nose and snout. They also drew circles for his ears and drew them in such a way that they appeared to look the same any way Mickey turned his head. They gave him a pear-shaped body with pipe-stem legs, and stuffed them in big, oversized shoes, making him look like a little kid wearing his father's shoes.[7]

Can't you almost picture Mickey from that description? Visual language is key to effective description.

Description can be used not only for physical objects but also for scenes or events. Consider the briefings given by General Norman Schwarzkopf during the 1991 Persian Gulf War. He used a variety of maps and charts to explain every move. He used terms from football and other sports, calling the American troop movements a "Hail Mary pass." Further, rather than merely telling the audience about the success of U.S. smart bombs, he used a video to show the accuracy with which targets were destroyed. In one memorable incident, he pointed to a vehicle passing through the crosshairs of the bomber just before the target was hit. He called the driver "the luckiest man in Iraq."

Putting It All Together

VIDEO FILE

If you have access to the videotape that accompanies this text, view segment 9. It shows Suzanne Mifsud's informative speech "How to Be a Friend to a Rape Victim."

Whether your speech is primarily explanation, instruction, demonstration, or description, it is important that you incorporate as many of the six attributes of effective informative speaking as possible. Regardless of the type of speech, keep in mind that compatibility is an important factor. If your audience sees the topic as incompatible with their needs, beliefs, attitudes, or values, they will view your speech as a hostile persuasive attempt, rather than an informative speech.

What, then, does an effective informative speech look like? For one example, see the box on pages 334–335, "Sample Informative Speech Outline: How to Be a Friend to a Rape Victim, by Suzanne Mifsud." This outline and the accompanying annotations should help you put together the concepts discussed in this chapter as you plan and prepare your own informative speech.

FORUMS FOR INFORMATIVE SPEAKING

Informative speaking is probably the form of public speaking you're most likely to be called on to do at some point in your life. One of the chief reasons is that informative speaking is used in so many settings, including the classroom, the workplace, and the community.

Informative Speaking in the Classroom

Two time-honored traditions in the college classroom are the term paper and oral report. Although most students have at least passing familiarity with the elements of a good term paper, many students don't make the connection between the elements of a good oral report and the process of informative speaking.

Undergraduate speech majors are usually pleased to see that an oral report is required in a course outside their major. They know that an oral report basically is an informative speech. Thus, by putting to use what they know about informative speaking, they usually are able to give oral reports that are both substantively and stylistically more effective than those of their classmates.

Viewing the oral report as an opportunity to speak informatively has several advantages. First, it provides you with an organizational framework for constructing your report. Second, it reminds you that you have an audience for your report whose background and perceptual reality must be taken into account. Finally, it forces you to think about how relevant the information in your report is to both your instructor and student colleagues.

Informative Speaking in the Workplace

All the people we have profiled in this book realize now what they didn't necessarily realize as undergraduates: Regardless of major or career, the ability to stand up and speak publicly is a skill both admired and rewarded in the real world.

No matter what you plan on doing to make a living, the odds are great that you will need to make informative presentations. Although you won't necessarily have to speak informatively to large numbers of people, you can reasonably expect to speak informatively to your immediate co-workers, perhaps your entire department, or in a meeting with people to whom you're subordinate. It is common in the workplace to make informative presentations before groups. For some presentations you will have to stand and speak; other presentations may be delivered from your seat.

Although the different situations require adjustments in your style of delivery, the substantive elements of your informative presentation are the same. You will still need to follow a cohesive organizational sequence, analyze your audience carefully, and consider the message attributes described earlier in this chapter.

All too often, speakers get trapped into thinking that the smaller their audience, the more informal their delivery and content can be. Instead, they need to make the relational features of the message more interpersonal without sacrificing the content of the message. They can increase nonverbal immediacy, for example, while protecting the formal structure of the speech.

Informative Speaking in the Community

You can reasonably expect to speak informatively with members of your community in at least one of two capacities: as a representative of your employer or as a concerned citizen. Private, as well as public, enterprises are justifiably concerned about their image within their local community. Opinion poll after opinion poll shows that the public is increasingly suspicious of the motives of private enterprise and increasingly dissatisfied with the performance of public agencies in particular. It's not uncommon, therefore, for these organizations to make themselves available to service groups, such as Rotary International, the general public, or a citizens' group organized around a specific cause.

Some businesses have a person whose job is company spokesperson; large corporations may even have whole departments dedicated to public relations. Many organizations, however, have come to expect anyone in management to serve as an informative speaker to the community. In fact, private corporations, such as IBM, and public agencies, such as the police or fire department, may actually write such community service into their managers' job descriptions. Thus, just because you currently perceive your intended career as low profile, that doesn't necessarily make it so.

Finally, remote as the possibility may seem to you now, you may one day want or need to speak informatively as a private citizen. If you live in a community where cable television is available, your city council meetings probably are televised on your community access channel. If you tune in, you will see ordinary citizens making informative presentations at these meetings. Topics can range from the environmental impact of a new housing development to excessive noise from student housing. If you watch several of these presentations, you probably will conclude that very few of the speakers have much training in public speaking; people who do have training are easy to spot.

Your days as a public speaker will not be over once you've completed this class. Given what we've said here, in fact, you should now realize they are just beginning.

Sample Informative Speech Outline

HOW TO BE A FRIEND TO A RAPE VICTIM
by Suzanne Mifsud

Specific Purpose: To teach my audience how to be helpful to a rape victim.

Introduction

I. **Open With Impact:** My friend from the dorms came to me about being raped early in the school year.
   A. I didn't know what to say and I didn't know what to do.
   B. I ended up convincing my friend to talk to our Dorm R.A.
   C. Fortunately my friend did just this, and she got the help she needed from our R.A.

II. **Focus on Thesis Statement:** You may be approached by a loved one after she has been raped, and I hope that after today, you'll be able to help her through her time of need.

III. **Connect With the Audience:** One in four college women have experienced rape or attempted rape since the age of 14 (American College Health Association, 1992).
   A. The majority of victims of rape are between the ages of 15 and 24.
   B. These statistics may sound alarming because they deal with our age group.
   C. The rape victim could be your roommate, your friend, your daughter, your co-worker, or maybe even your lover.
   D. You need to be prepared to know how to help the victim through this very tough time in life.

IV. **Preview:** Today I will teach you how to deal with the aftermath of a rape and how to be a friend to someone by learning (1) how to identify a rape victim, (2) how to talk to the victim about the incident, and (3) where to find other help for the victim.

Body

I. **Main Point:** The first step to helping a rape victim is knowing how to identify one.
   A. A friend who has been raped may confide in you 10 minutes or maybe 10 years after the attack (American College Health Association, 1992).
   B. A person who has been raped may have major feelings of depression, low self-esteem, and may even be acting as though she doesn't feel there is a place for her in this world.
   C. Most women experience major mood changes (Tobin, 1997).
   D. They may be uncomfortable around others or be experiencing feelings of shame or guilt.
   E. Months later, signs such as nightmares, anger, depression, fear, and guilt mean that outside help is needed (Tobin, 1997).

(**Signpost:** Now that I've told you how to identify a rape victim, let me teach you how to talk to a rape victim about the incident.)

Title of speech.

Specific purpose is to teach audience how to deal with a situation the speaker has faced herself.

Speaker begins with a story of her own experience with a rape victim, building her credibility to speak on the subject.

Thesis statement is clearly labeled and focuses on relative advantage to audience.

Statistics are used to show that this is a much more common problem than most students might think.

Age of victims is compatible with ages of audience members.

Speaker shows the audience that they could be placed in the same situation.

Preview of speech is provided to help audience follow its organization.

Body of speech is labeled.

Main points begin with roman numeral I.

Signposts are transitional statements between main points and serve to aid the comprehensibility of the speech.

II. **Main Point:** The second most important thing to learn is how to communicate to the victim just how much you are there for her.

    A. Be a good listener.

    B. Realize that each victim's reactions will be different.

    C. Tell her over and over it wasn't her fault; no one asks to be raped and no one deserves to be raped.

    E. A rape will cause a disturbance in her life for 1 to 2 years or more, but she will get through it (Tobin, 1997).

    F. We should be there for her, but also help her get the extra help she wants and needs (Tobin, 1997).

(Signpost: When helping a rape victim, you should also be aware of where to get additional help, which brings me to my final point.)

III. **Main Point:** You need to know where to find other help for the rape victim.

    A. Counselors or private psychologists can be very helpful to rape victims.

    B. Locally there is a Rape Crisis Intervention Center.

    C. I will have fliers with the numbers available at the end of my presentation for anyone who is interested.

> *Speaker gives audience specific information on where to go to get help. Use of fliers contributes to observability.*

Conclusion

I. **Summarize:** I hope that all of you have gained a better knowledge of what to do in a situation where you may be approached by a rape victim by knowing:

    A. how to spot a rape victim,

    B. how to talk to a rape victim, and

    C. how to get that extra help when it is needed.

> *Speaker gives a summary of main points, aiding the comprehensibility of the speech.*

II. **Close With Impact:** Had I known then what I know now, I would have been able to help my friend a lot better earlier in the year.

    A. Rape is a very serious crime affecting people of our age.

    B. The only way to help is to be educated on how to help someone in the aftermath.

    C. A friend may confide in you 10 minutes or maybe even 10 years after the incident.

    D. So if, and when, you are told, you should be well aware of how to help your friend.

> *Speech closes with impact. Ask yourself if it matches the impact with which the speech opened*

References

American College Health Association. (1992). <u>Acquaintance Rape.</u> Baltimore: Author.

Tobin, S. (1997). <u>Rape on Campus.</u> Chico, CA: Campus Wellness Center.

Warshaw, Robin. (1998). <u>I Never Called It Rape.</u> New York: Sarah Lazin Books.

> *Speaker lists references at end of speech with full bibliographic citation.*

SUMMARY

To be successful, informative speakers must do as Jaime Escalante did, instill *ganas*, the desire and the motivation to succeed, into their audiences. Speakers must also adapt their informative speeches to audiences with diverse learning styles. One way to do so is to incorporate multiple methods and channels of learning into their speeches.

Informative speaking is the process by which an audience gains new information or a new perspective on old information from a speaker. Informative speaking is related to learning in that the speaker's goal is to explain, instruct, demonstrate, or describe something to the audience. But before an audience can learn, they must be motivated to do so. Successful informative speakers motivate their audience by identifying the audience's self-interest, by showing them why the information they are about to hear is valuable to them.

Informative speakers should use the message attributes *novelty*, *compatibility*, *comprehensibility*, *relative advantage*, *observability*, and *trialability* in their informative speeches. Informative speeches may explain, instruct, demonstrate, and/or describe. Each of these types of speeches employs one or more of the six attributes of effective informative speaking.

Informative speaking is by far the most common type of public speaking and routinely occurs in the classroom, the workplace, and the community.

Check Your Understanding: Exercises and Activities

1. Develop an outline for a 1- to 2-minute speech in which you inform an audience about a topic with which you are personally very familiar. Then show how you would adapt that speech to at least three different learning styles: auditory linguistic, visual linguistic, and audio-visual-kinesthetic.

2. Come up with at least two possible topics each for speeches that explain, instruct, demonstrate, and describe. Do some topics seem to fall naturally into one category? Are there other topics that might be used for more than one type of speech?

3. Reread Suzanne Mifsud's outline for her speech "How to Be a Friend to a Rape Victim," presented on pages 334–335. (If you have access to the videotape that accompanies this book, you may also view the speech in segment 9.) To what extent does this speech incorporate the attributes of novelty, compatibility, comprehensibility, relative advantage, observability, and trialability discussed in this chapter? To what extent would the speech benefit from further use of any of these message attributes?

Notes

1. Jay Mathews, *Escalante: The Best Teacher in America* (New York: Henry Holt, 1988), 191.

2. *Stand and Deliver*, director Tom Menendez, with Edward James Olmos, Lou Diamond Phillips, Rosana De Soto, and Andy Garcia, An American

Playhouse Theatrical Film, A Menendez/Musca & Olmos Production, Warner Bros., 1988.

3. P. Friedman and R. Alley, "Learning/Teaching Styles: Applying the Principles," *Theory Into Practice* 23 (1984): 77–81. Based on R. Dunn and K. Dunn, *Teaching Students Through Their Individual Learning Styles: A Practical Approach* (Reston, Va.: Reston Publishing, 1978).

4. Michael D. Scott and Scott Elliot, "Innovation in the Classroom: Toward a Reconceptualization of Instructional Communication" (paper presented at the annual meeting of the International Communication Association, Dallas, Texas, 1983).

5. Everett M. Rogers, *Diffusion of Innovations* (New York: Free Press, 1983).

6. Jonathan Studebaker, "Speech of Self-Introduction: Who Am I?" The full text appears in Appendix A.

7. Jennie Rees, "Informative Speech: Mickey: A Changing Image," California State University, Chico, 1992.

Persuasive speaking often requires the speaker to take a stand on controversial issues.

Persuasive Speaking

OBJECTIVES

After reading this chapter, you should be able to:

- Describe how your assessment of the rhetorical situation is important to persuasive speaking.
- Describe the four goals persuasive speeches are designed to achieve.
- Analyze the audience of a persuasive message in terms of cultural, demographic, and individual diversity.
- Define ethos, logos, and pathos.
- Achieve persuasiveness through the use of speaker credibility.
- Describe the process of elaborated thinking in relationship to persuasion.
- Demonstrate how to use first-, second-, and third-order data as evidence in a persuasive speech.
- Explain the rationale for presenting a two-sided persuasive message, and construct a two-sided persuasive message.
- Demonstrate how certain types of persuasive appeals are linked to audience members' emotions and primitive beliefs.

KEY CONCEPTS

behavioral intention

elaboration likelihood model

ethos

first-, second-, and third-order data

logos

opinion leader

pathos

persuasion

source credibility

> *Character may almost be called the most effective means of persuasion.*
>
> —ARISTOTLE[1]

The House Judiciary Committee appeared to have closed minds on the issue of Bill Clinton's impeachment as they voted along party lines.

As the impeachment hearing and subsequent trial of William Jefferson Clinton so vividly illustrated, persuasion is complicated. It is not always a matter of people objectively presenting the facts of the matter and others then weighing those facts. Some members of the House and Senate had made up their minds on the fate of the Clinton presidency well in advance of the presentations of evidence before the House Judiciary Committee, the House managers' presentations before the Senate of the case for removing Clinton, or those of the lawyers who followed to speak in Clinton's defense. For such closed-minded individuals, no amount of evidence, no matter how eloquently presented, could have changed their minds. At the same time, some Senators appeared to have had genuinely open minds about the matter, and they sought to forge a bipartisan solution to the impeachment trial. Simply put, persuasion is not always the outcome of rational discourse, nor is it automatically an irrational process. Evidence, argument, emotional appeals, and even personal prestige may all affect the outcome of any persuasive effort.

Ironically, President Clinton's State of the Union addresses in both 1998 and 1999 bracketed the Lewinsky scandal. His 1998 address was delivered as the affair was first made public, and his 1999 address occurred in the midst of his Senate trial. Although both speeches carefully avoided any mention of the crisis, both were positively received by the public and political pundits and raised his standing in the public opinion polls. Thus, even persuasive efforts outside the formal trial process were important to the persuasive efforts taking place in Congress.

With that in mind, this chapter is about **persuasion,** the process by which a speaker influences what audience members think or do. The topics covered in this chapter include

- the relationship between persuasive speaking and the rhetorical situation;
- factors to take into account in your attempts to reinforce what an audience believes, inoculate an audience against counterpersuasive speeches, change audience attitudes, and prompt an audience to act;
- the relationship of persuasive speaking to the concepts of opinion leadership, ethos, pathos, and logos; and
- how you can use these concepts to construct an effective persuasive speech.

FOCUSING ON YOUR AUDIENCE: ASSESSING THE SITUATION

Audience-focused persuasive speaking begins with an assessment of the rhetorical situation, which we first talked about in Chapter 5. You will need a clear understanding of your goals as a speaker, knowledge about your audience, and an assessment of the constraints facing you, including the ethical boundaries you must respect.

The Four Goals of Persuasive Speaking

There are four common, and sometimes interdependent, goals we can achieve through persuasive speaking. The first is to *reinforce* the attitudes, beliefs, and values an audience already holds. Keynote speeches at national political conventions, for example, are usually designed to bolster the common core of beliefs, attitudes, and values to which members of a political party subscribe. Much of the persuasive posturing about whether President Clinton committed impeachable offenses, for example, was designed to reinforce rather than try to change what Clinton's supporters and detractors believed.

The second goal of persuasive speaking is to *inoculate* an audience against counterpersuasion, that is, persuasive messages opposed to the speaker's views.[2] Although it is possible to bolster an audience member's attitudes, beliefs, and values through straight reinforcement, it takes more to make them truly resistant to counterpersuasion. Anti–drug use messages aimed at children, for instance, are most effective when they give sound reasons not to use drugs, rather than telling kids to "just say no." Children can then use these reasons to defend

Schoolchildren are often subjected to anti–drug persuasive speakers, but do these messages really help prevent later drug use?

their anti–drug use behavior when confronted with peer pressure to experiment with illegal substances.

The third goal of persuasive speaking is to *change attitudes*. This is a difficult task, because the audience is often one that disagrees with or is even hostile to your position. For example, a speaker calling for the complete legalization of marijuana needs to realize that most audiences do not share that point of view. Changing people's attitudes requires incremental change over time. Taking small steps, such as first convincing an audience that marijuana should be legalized for medical purposes, is more likely to achieve success than trying to change people from total opposition to total support in a short time.

Attitude change may also occur with an audience that is apathetic or disinterested in your topic. To convince an audience that they should care about a problem, rather than be unconcerned, is itself a change of attitude. Thus, many campaigns for political offices or on ballot initiatives are targeted toward "undecided" voters, those usually least interested in the political process. For example, the initiatives recently passed in several states to legalize medicinal marijuana focused on motivating undecided voters by stressing the need to relieve the suffering of cancer, AIDS, and other patients, an argument that many undecided voters found persuasive.

The fourth goal of persuasive speaking is to prompt an audience to *act*. This is the most difficult goal to achieve. People are seldom moved to act as a result of a single persuasive speech. A foundation must first be laid that will make the audience likely to act. That takes time and repetition of the message. When it appears that people are responding to a single message, the persuasive speech

Does Drug Education Really Work?

Remember elementary school and the "just say no" campaign to discourage drug use? It is just one part of a massive drug education campaign, ranging from Drug Abuse Resistance and Education (DARE) to Red Ribbon Weeks, designed to inoculate youngsters against being persuaded to try drugs. Billions of taxpayer dollars are spent nationally on such programs, and the State of California alone spends about $400 million annually on drug education. To determine if the programs were worth the cost, the California Department of Education commissioned educational research consultants at the University of California at Berkeley to study the state's drug education programs. The results of the 3-year study, completed in 1995, were so controversial that the Department of Education refused to release them. They were finally published 2 years later, in 1997, in the academic journal *Education Evaluation and Policy Analysis*. The results were shocking to drug educators. Only 15 percent of students found drug education persuasive. Nearly 70 percent of the 5,000 students surveyed were either neutral or even negative toward the programs.

According to the study's lead author, Joel Brown, "Not only are the programs ineffective, but for many youth they have an effect counter to what is intended." Among the comments from students about such programs, a typical one was "I don't think handing someone a ribbon saying 'Drug Free Is for Me' is going to make someone stop using drugs." In contrast, many students praised presentations by people suffering from AIDS as something that "really gets to you."

Brown's study has not been without its critics, however, including the California Department of Education, which rejected the findings as "significantly flawed." Nevertheless, the facts are that drug use among teens has risen in the past 5 years, despite the expenditures of billions on drug education programs.

If you experienced drug education programs such as these during your elementary and secondary education, what did you think about their effectiveness? As attempts to inoculate youth against the temptation of drugs, were these efforts persuasive to you and your peers? If not, how could they have been made more persuasive?

Source: Peter Hecht, "School Anti-Drug Programs Bashed," *Sacramento Bee*, 19 March 1997, A1, A12.

usually is the most recent in a long line of catalysts that have been building momentum for action. Consider the people who respond to an evangelist's call to get out of their seats, move to the stage, and orally proclaim their faith. The fact that these people voluntarily chose to be in the audience means they probably were predisposed to act. Thus, the evangelist's persuasive sermon was a catalyst rather than the sole cause of their action.

Which of these four goals you will pursue in a given speech depends largely on the audience you are addressing. If they already share your attitudes and values, then a speech of reinforcement is warranted. On the other hand, if they are likely to be the subjects of counterpersuasion or if their commitment to your point of view is shaky, then inoculation is likely to be your goal. If you face an audience opposed to your views, you will need to attempt to change their attitudes, usually a time-consuming incremental process. Finally, if the audience is primed by prior persuasive messages to behave in accordance with your goals, then prompting them to action may be your best approach. Although these goals are related, any given persuasive speech is likely to focus primarily on one outcome.

Analyzing Audience Diversity

The realization of any of the four persuasive speaking goals depends on how well you have analyzed your audience. Audience analysis starts with an assessment of the relationship between the audience and the goal you hope to achieve. Not all audiences are capable of acting to help you achieve your goals, even if they desire to do so. For example, people who are not U.S. citizens or who are under age 18 cannot vote in elections. The candidate who directs a persuasive campaign to either of these groups is just wasting time and money. Preparing and delivering a persuasive speech intended to induce action to a specific group makes sense, therefore, only if that group is capable of acting.

Once you are sure your goal makes sense in relation to your audience, the next step is to analyze audience diversity. Remember that we live in a multicultural, multiracial, and multiethnic society. There are three levels of audience diversity you'll need to consider: cultural, demographic, and individual. Cultural diversity concerns collective ways of thinking and acting. Demographic diversity reflects the attributes according to which people can be grouped, for example, the generation to which people belong. Finally, individual diversity is revealed in people's most deep-seated beliefs, attitudes, and values.

Simply put, the more you know about audience diversity, the better you will be able to predict how the audience is likely to respond to issues and the people associated with them, as well as the kind of message likely to prove resonant with the audience. A persuasive speech about product safety delivered to the National Association of Manufacturers, for example, would be quite different from one delivered to a group of personal-injury attorneys. In either case you would have to construct your persuasive message on the basis of what you knew about each demographic group.

Cultural Diversity   As you may recall, cultural diversity refers to the differences among people in language, beliefs, and customs. In Chapter 5 we introduced you to five dimensions of cultural diversity: power distance, collectivism versus individualism, femininity versus masculinity, uncertainty avoidance, and long-term versus short-term orientation to life. Knowing the cultural background of your audience can be very important in deciding on the best strategies for persuading them to your point of view. For example, appeals to rugged individualism, which might be expected to work well with a traditional North American audience, are likely to fall flat with an Asian audience.

Demographic Diversity   As we pointed out in Chapter 5, demographic diversity involves differences related to basic and vital data regarding any population, including age, socioeconomic status, occupational roles, geographic origin, ethnicity, gender, religion, and language. Some of this information may be readily available to you, either by direct observation of your audience or by making relatively simple inquiries. For example, age and gender are often directly observable. Speaking to a group of senior citizens about the future of Social Security is very different from speaking to a group of Gen-Xers. Socioeconomic status and occupations may or may not be known to you. If possible, try to learn as much about these characteristics as possible before speaking. For example, a sales presentation geared toward a high-income audience of software entrepreneurs is probably very different from one presented to an audience of unionized assembly line personnel. Finally, characteristics such as religion and geographic origin may be difficult to determine. If they seem relevant to your presentation, you should make an effort to find out as much as you can about these aspects of your audience.

Individual Diversity   Recall from Chapter 5 that individual diversity involves audience members' beliefs, attitudes, values, motives for being at the occasion, and expectations for the speech. Recall that *beliefs* are assertions about the properties or characteristics of an object, *attitudes* are predispositions to respond in a consistently favorable or unfavorable manner with respect to an object, and *values* are more general and enduring than attitudes and hold that some ways of behaving and some goals are preferable to others. An individual's motives for being at a speech are important to audience analysis, as are individual expectations of your speech. In addition to these factors, two others should be considered in preparing a persuasive speech: behavioral intentions and people's level of involvement with a topic.

Behavioral Intentions   A **behavioral intention** is a person's subjective belief that he or she will engage in a specific behavior.[3] Behavioral intentions usually can be inferred from a person's beliefs, values, and attitudes. Intentions are just that: intentions! Not everyone behaves in accordance with their attitudes, beliefs, and values. For example, most Americans oppose sex discrimination in the workplace and report in polls that they endorse equal opportunity for women. Yet reality does not reflect these attitudes. Women in America still make only "72 cents for every dollar a man takes home," and only 3 percent of top executive jobs are held by women.[4]

The important point for you as a speaker is that it is not enough simply to obtain a statement of behavioral intentions from an audience. Ideally, you want to empower your audience to behave in accordance with their stated intentions. Although this is not always easy, one technique for doing so involves having audience members make public commitments. At the end of his sermons, for example, the Reverend Billy Graham doesn't conclude with, "Having said that, I hope all of you will consider accepting Jesus Christ as your personal savior." Instead, he calls on people to rise from their seats and join him at the platform to convert. Graham recognizes what the research repeatedly demonstrates: Commitments made in the presence of others are even more difficult to break than private ones. Thus, the more speakers encourage audience members to publicly commit to a certain behavior, the more likely their goals will be achieved.

Involvement in the Topic   Two persons may hold roughly the same beliefs, attitudes, and values regarding a topic and yet be quite different in how easily they are influenced. When Carolyn McCarthy, profiled in Chapter 5, spoke to families of those killed by handguns, these people had direct personal involvement with the topic. You would expect them to respond more favorably to her message than someone who only empathized on an intellectual level with her views on

FIGURE 13.1
Latitudes of
Acceptance,
Rejection, and
Noncommitment

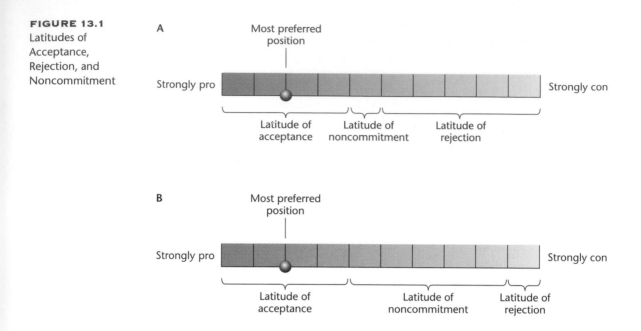

the topic. It is not just a matter of what attitude people express on a topic, then. You also need to assess how involved they are with the topic. The more involved people are, the more they interpret messages that disagree with their own position as discrepant from their own. This is known as a *contrast effect*. On the other hand, people also *assimilate*, which happens when they perceive messages that are reasonably close to their own as more similar than they actually are. Thus, highly involved persons tend to polarize views: You are either with them or against them. Attempts to change the views of highly involved people even a little are likely to be rejected out of hand.[5]

Highly involved persons normally have a very narrow latitude of acceptance of positions different from their own, and they have wide latitudes of rejection. In fact, they may well perceive positions different from their own as more extreme than they really are. On the other hand, persons with low levels of involvement have large latitudes of noncommitment and small latitudes of rejection. Simply put, they are much more likely to listen to opposing views than to reject them out of hand. In Figure 13.1, person A tends to have very little room for noncommitment and probably is highly involved in the topic. Person B, on the other hand, while holding the same most-preferred position as A, has a much bigger latitude of noncommitment and is thus more open to different ideas on this topic. Often, for example, people may not have a lot of information about an issue. What they initially think they believe, therefore, can easily change as they learn more about it.

Often speakers need to make uninvolved audiences feel more involved in their topic. By using real and even hypothetical examples, speakers can bring life to an abstract subject. By bringing in personal experiences, speakers can help audience members appreciate the reality of a topic. Whatever the audience's initial level of involvement, successful persuaders need to make the topic come alive and seem directly relevant to their audience.

Ethical Constraints

Finally, audience-focused persuasive speaking is bound by ethical constraints. The realization of your persuasive goal shouldn't come at the expense of your audience. Selling worthless swampland may help the speaker achieve the goal of making money, but only at the expense of gullible audience members who may lose their life savings. The end you hope to achieve must reflect not only your interests but those of your audience as well. Along the same lines, you need to thoroughly think through the persuasive means you plan on using to achieve your goal. Noble ends do not justify ignoble means. As a case in point, we happen to believe that the remaining stands of giant sequoias should be protected from logging. We also would be happy to assist someone in preparing and delivering a speech that suggests reasonable means to achieve this end. This doesn't mean, however, that we would help someone who, as a part of his or her persuasive message, plans to advocate tree spiking, placing metal spikes in trees to keep them from being cut down. Such activity can lead to serious injury to or even death of loggers.

THE SPEAKER: BECOMING A MODERN-DAY OPINION LEADER

An **opinion leader** is a person who routinely uses principles of persuasion to shape people's beliefs about ideas, products, practices, and each other.[6] To become an opinion leader, a speaker must understand the dimensions of perception on which he or she will be evaluated.

Two thousand years' worth of theory and research suggests that whether an audience regards a speaker as an opinion leader depends on two interdependent dimensions of perception. The first dimension involves the degree to which the audience perceives the speaker as similar to them. The second, and most important, of the two perceptions involves the speaker's **ethos,** that is, the degree to which the audience perceives the speaker as credible.

Similarity

To begin with, people are suspicious of people they perceive as dissimilar to themselves. How can an outsider, for example, understand their needs? By the same token, however, people are not likely to follow the advice of those they perceive to be their clones. What can they learn, after all, from someone whose background, education, and experience is nearly identical to their own.

The key, then, is to be perceived by an audience as a member of the community who is similar in terms of background and values, but who is also uniquely qualified to shape opinions about relevant matters. This is where credibility comes into the picture.

Ethos (Credibility)

Any discussion of the concept of credibility begins with Aristotle's concept of ethos. Aristotle defined rhetoric as "the faculty of observing in any given case the available means of persuasion,"[7] and he identified three means of persuasion—ethos, logos, and pathos—which were briefly introduced in Chapter 5. Aristotle believed that to be persuasive a speaker must be not only competent but also a person of substantial character. Aristotle described this combination of competence and character as *ethos*. He believed that ethos was a personal attribute and was essential to a speaker's chances of persuading an audience. In fact, as the opening quotation in this chapter suggests, he viewed ethos as the most important aspect of a speaker's persuasiveness.

Modern communication researchers have substantiated Aristotle's thinking about the importance of ethos. Today's scholars use the term **source credibility,** which is the audience's perception of the believability of the speaker.[8] It is a quality your audience gives to you rather than one with which you are born. Thus, a speaker might be truly competent in a particular subject matter, but if the audience does not know this, the speaker's expertise will not increase his or her credibility. Similarly, a speaker may be of good character, but if the audience does not believe it, the speaker will suffer low credibility.

Components of Credibility   Credibility is rooted in audience perceptions of believability. Researchers have shown that credibility consists of two primary components. Although researchers label these differently, the two perceptions that lead audiences to confer credibility on a speaker are competence and character.[9] Although both competence and character are necessary to sustain the perception of ethos, neither is sufficient by itself to do so. To perceive you as credible, your audience must believe that you are not only competent and knowledgeable about your topic but also a person of character who can be trusted.

Competence   If you are largely unknown to your audience, how your audience perceives you as a speaker in terms of your knowledge, intelligence, and expertise on the topic of your speech is critical to your success. If you have special expertise or first-hand experience, by all means let your audience know. If you have done extensive research on your topic, this will help your audience appreciate your newly acquired competence on the subject. Use facts, statistics, and quotations from experts to help your audience know that you are well informed on the subject.

Character   Even an expert can lack credibility with an audience, if he or she is perceived as untrustworthy. For example, attorneys frequently call on expert witnesses to bolster their cases. Illustrations include scientists who testify about DNA evidence, forensic pathologists who testify to matters such as time and cause of death, and accident investigators who testify about such things as driver negligence. The trouble with such experts is that they are usually paid hand-

How Similar or Dissimilar Are You and Your Audience?

Fill out this form prior to your first persuasive speech. Compare your appearance to that of your audience. In what ways are you similar and in what ways dissimilar? Do the same for your cultural, demographic, and individual factors. In what ways can you use your similarities to build your credibility? How can you overcome or even positively utilize your dissimilarities?

Factors to Assess Prior to Persuasive Speech	*Similar to Audience*	*Dissimilar to Audience*
Appearance _____	_____	_____
Cultural Factors _____	_____	_____
Demographic Factors _____	_____	_____
Age _____	_____	_____
Socioeconomic status _____	_____	_____
Geographic origin _____	_____	_____
Ethnicity _____	_____	_____
Gender _____	_____	_____
Religion _____	_____	_____
Language _____	_____	_____
Factors Relating to Your Speech Topic		
Attitudes [toward it] _____	_____	_____
Beliefs [about it] _____	_____	_____
Values [regarding it] _____	_____	_____
Behavioral intentions [toward it] _____	_____	
Other Factors _____	_____	_____

somely for their testimony. This calls their character into question in the minds of many, including jurors. This can and often does undermine perceptions of their overall credibility.

Enhancing Audience Perceptions of Credibility   There are three points in time when a speaker can help to enhance audience perceptions of his or her credibility. These include the time before the speech; during the speech; and perhaps one you didn't expect, after the speech.

Because it is a perception, credibility is dynamic and changeable. The fact that a speaker is perceived as credible going into a persuasive speech doesn't guarantee that he or she will still be perceived as credible afterward. Similarly, the speaker who begins with little credibility can build credibility in the process of speaking. One of your goals is to build and maintain your credibility as you speak. You want it to be at least as high—and preferably higher—when you conclude as it was when you began.

Credibility Before the Speech   Often, speakers' reputations precede their appearance before an audience. In fact, reputation may be what prompts the audience to attend, especially when the speaker is famous, an expert, or has new or unusual information about the topic. For example, a recent speech on our campus by actor Edward James Olmos was so well attended that there was standing room only. His fame and reputation as a powerful speaker and crusader against gang violence had ensured a degree of credibility with his audience before he spoke a single word.

Of course, most of us are not experts, and may not even be known to our audience. One way to build your credibility before you speak is to have someone introduce you to the audience. In Chapter 15, we will talk about how to present a speech of introduction that will enhance an audience's perception of the speaker's credibility. If you do not have an introduction, you will have to establish your own credibility by what you say in your speech and how you say it.

Credibility During the Speech   Under most but not all conditions, the speaker's level of credibility at the outset of the speech is insufficient to sustain the audience's perception of believability. Credibility by way of reputation can be negated as a result of the speaker's appearance, message, and delivery. Audience members can become quickly disenchanted and may even turn on a speaker whom they feel is just going through the motions or resting too much on his or her laurels.

On the other hand, even speakers with little initial credibility can build perceptions of competence and character during their speech. As a case in point, students in an introductory public speaking course may have little initial credibility with each other because they don't know each other and don't know each other's qualifications to speak on various topics. Practically speaking, then, these students begin to build their credibility with their first speeches. Their appearance, the care with which they've prepared their message, and their delivery can begin to establish their competence and character with their fellow students and their instructor.

To make certain you are perceived as a credible speaker in a persuasive transaction, though, you'll need to provide your audience with proof of your credibility through the reasoning and evidence in your message. The reasoning and evidence you present in your persuasive speech should not only support the arguments you make but also support the audience's perception that you are competent and a person of high character. Also, if you have special expertise or credentials that are relevant to your topic, you'll want to share the fact with your audience.

Credibility After the Speech   Speakers whose persuasive message bolstered their credibility with an audience cannot rest on their laurels. Just as initial credibility can suffer from a poor speech, the credibility you've established during your speech can be negated as well. No one knows this better than President Clinton. After denying for seven months that he had had an improper sexual relationship with intern Monica Lewinsky, he was forced to recant his denials before a grand jury and the public at large. His forceful denial had initially quelled the public outcry. However, when it was later learned that he had not been fully truthful, his presidency suffered as a result, and he became only the second American president in history to be impeached.

Never lose sight of the fact that perceived credibility is dynamic. Once gained, credibility needs continued nourishment. The following list provides some reminders and tips for maintaining credibility.

Tips for Speaker Credibility

- Ask yourself about the degree to which your audience already perceives you as credible. Also ask yourself whether your classroom behavior could have lowered your credibility in the eyes of the other students. For example, coming to class late and interrupting a speaker, not being ready to speak when it was your turn, or delivering speeches that were hastily put together tells other students about your competence and character. If this is the case, you'll need to work harder to establish your credibility.

- Dress appropriately for the occasion. Persuasion is serious business and should be approached seriously.

- Incorporate any special expertise or experience you have with your topic into the body of your speech. This information will enhance the audience's perception of your competence.

- Use evidence to support the claims you make. The facts and logical arguments you provide will help enhance your ethos.

- Engage your audience nonverbally, using the characteristics of effective delivery described in Chapter 10.

- Use powerful language (which research suggests is linked to persuasive effects), as described in Chapter 9.

- Use inclusive language, discussed in Chapter 9, to make certain all audience members believe they have a stake in the topic of your persuasive speech.

THE MESSAGE: PERSUASION THROUGH LOGOS

Aristotle's Concept of Logos

Aristotle also recognized the power of words (*logos* is Greek for "word") in the process of persuasion. As a result, he spent considerable time theorizing about both the nature of words and the manner in which they are arranged to form a message. **Logos** is the proof a speaker offers to an audience through the words of his or her message. Aristotle believed speakers should use logical proof. Consider two examples. In the first, the speaker claims without any proof that Socrates is mortal. In the second, the speaker makes the same point in the form of a syllogism, that is, a conclusion plus the premises supporting it. Specifically, the speaker tells the audience: "All men are mortal. Socrates is a man. Therefore, Socrates is mortal." In this case, the speaker not only has stated a conclusion the audience can either accept or reject but also has communicated proof in support of the conclusion.

Aristotle believed that there are several ways to prove a point. A syllogism follows the rules of formal logic, and Aristotle claimed that rhetoricians actually use an abbreviated syllogism (called an enthymeme) in speaking. He also believed that speakers could prove their case through the use of examples and signs. In the next section, we discuss a research-based model of persuasion that explains how audiences respond to the messages they hear. We then discuss two specific message strategies: the use of evidence and the use of two-sided messages.

The Elaboration Likelihood Model and Persuasion

Like any speech transaction, the persuasive transaction involves active participation by both the speaker and the audience. In some persuasive transactions, the audience engages actively in thinking critically about a complex topic. In other situations, the audience responds almost without thinking. Social psychologists Richard Petty and John Cacioppo offer the **elaboration likelihood model** of persuasion to explain why audience members will use an elaborated thinking process in some situations and not in others.[10]

To illustrate these differences in how a message is processed, consider the topic of gun control. The causes of violence in America, the statistics on whether guns are more likely to kill the gun owner or the criminal, and the correct interpretation of the Second Amendment are all complex issues. Fully developed arguments on the topic of gun control invite the audience to engage in what Petty and Cacioppo call *elaboration* of the message, or "central route processing." On the other hand, some messages about gun control do not provoke much thinking. "When guns are outlawed, only outlaws will have guns" and "Stop the violence—ban handguns" are both examples of messages that are designed to avoid an elaborated thinking process. Petty and Cacioppo term this "peripheral route processing."

The questions for a public speaker are (1) what factors are likely to lead an audience to engage in either central or peripheral message processing, and (2) which of these processes is most likely to lead to the achievement of speaker goals?

The second question is the easier to answer. In most situations, the speaker wants the audience to use the elaborated, or central, processing route. The reason is that if the argument presented by the speaker is accepted by audience members, they are more likely to undergo long-term attitude change. The audience member who thinks through the various arguments about violence in America, the likelihood of a gun killing the owner rather than the criminal, and the purposes of the constitutional right to bear arms is likely to form a strongly held attitude on gun control. Those who later seek to change that attitude will face a difficult task. On the other hand, the audience member who reaches an opinion through the peripheral route, based on slogans such as "People—not guns—kill people," is likely to be easily persuaded to another position by subsequent speakers. Thus, the public speaker who wants his or her message to "stick" needs to provoke audience members into an elaborated method of thinking using the central processing route.

To reiterate, then, the first question speakers should ask is "What factors in this rhetorical situation will increase the likelihood of elaboration on the part of an audience member?" If audience members are motivated and able to understand a message, they are more likely to engage in elaborated thinking. On the other hand, if they find a message irrelevant or are unwilling or unable to understand the message, they are more likely to follow the peripheral route. Some factors are beyond the speaker's control. For example, individual listeners differ in their "need for cognition," that is, their need to process information centrally.[11] There's not much a speaker can do to make people who don't like to think about messages do so. On the other hand, a speaker can take steps to make the topic relevant to the audience and to provide understandable and strong arguments that will be persuasive to those who are motivated to process the message centrally.

The elaboration likelihood model is depicted in Figure 13.2 on the next page. Let's walk through this model to further explain the process. As you can see from the route on the left side of the model, an audience member must be *motivated* and *able* to process your message to engage in elaborated thinking. Depending on their *initial attitude*, the *quality of your argument*, and similar factors, an audience member may have either *favorable* or *unfavorable* thoughts about the topic. If the message isn't sufficient to stimulate such thoughts, audience members won't engage in elaborated thinking. If new ideas are *adopted and stored in memory*, and these are more *salient* (relevant) than what the audience member previously thought, then *attitude change* (favorable or unfavorable) will occur and be relatively enduring. These attitudes are also more likely to *predict future behavior*.

On the other hand, if the peripheral route is followed because audience members are *not motivated* to engage in elaborated thinking, *cannot understand the message*, or find the message *ineffective*, then attitude shifts are relatively *temporary* and *susceptible to further persuasive efforts* for the other side. Future *behavior is not predictable* from such attitude shifts.

The first step in applying the elaboration likelihood model to your own persuasive speech is selecting an appropriate topic. We have repeatedly emphasized the importance of this deceptively simple step because your audience must be motivated to pay attention to your topic. Not only must you choose a topic that your research tells you the audience should find stimulating, but you also must connect the topic to the personal and professional needs of your audience. For example, a speech on the Americans With Disabilities Act might not be directly linked to the needs of an audience without disabilities. But pointing out that each of us is only one accident or serious illness away from disability can make the connection clear.

The second step is making your topic and message comprehensible for your audience. As discussed in Chapter 12, audiences tend to turn off to messages perceived as too complex for their information-processing abilities. An audience whose nonverbal feedback says "Huh?" is not likely to favorably evaluate your persuasive message.

Now comes the hard part. The third step has to do with the audience's initial position regarding your message. Even if your topic is stimulating and your message is comprehensible, there is no guarantee people will respond favorably to it.

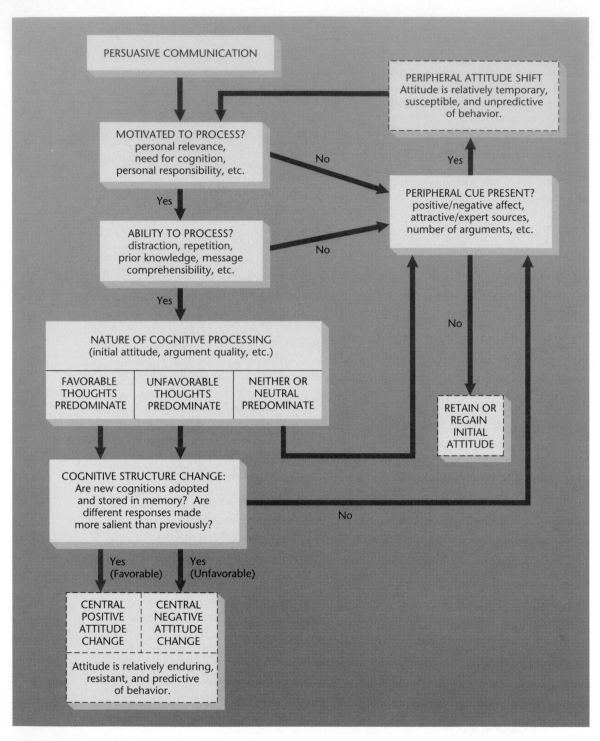

FIGURE 13.2 Model of Elaboration Likelihood

Members of your audience may disagree with the position(s) taken in your message. The degree to which they disagree is likely to vary as well. Whereas a group of businesspersons may be very receptive to the argument that environmental regulations are too restrictive, costing jobs and economic growth, the local Sierra Club chapter may have an opposite reaction that they hold passionately. This fact reemphasizes, then, just how important it is to learn as much as possible about your audience prior to constructing your persuasive message. Simply put, if you craft a persuasive message without sufficient knowledge of what your audience already believes regarding your topic, the message is destined to fail. Audience members will incorporate their own preexisting knowledge and attitudes into their processing of your message, overwhelming the arguments you have provided them. A persuasive message is not simply a narrative that reflects its author's point of view. A persuasive message is based on factors known to affect audience beliefs, attitudes, and occasionally values.

To summarize: Elaboration likelihood clearly suggests an active role on the part of the audience you hope to persuade. This active role includes (1) seeing your topic as relevant to their needs, (2) understanding and comprehending your message, and (3) centrally processing the nature and quality of the information you offer in terms of their preexisting knowledge and beliefs.

Evidence and Persuasion

For many years, it was believed that social scientific research on the value of evidence in persuasion was conflicting and inconsistent. In 1988, however, communication scholar John Reinard published a thorough analysis of 50 years of research on the persuasive effects of evidence.[12] Unlike many previous researchers, Reinard did not rely solely on the conclusions of other studies; he went back to the original works and reinterpreted the data using comparable definitions. He found that the research was surprisingly consistent. Further, he found that evidence, under most conditions, did in fact enhance the likelihood of persuasive effects. As Reinard writes: "After fifty years of research on the persuasive effects of evidence, the claims for the persuasiveness of evidence emerge as quite strong."[13] Some of his most important findings follow.[14]

Testimonial assertions (the judgment and opinions of people other than the persuader) are most effective when the sources are identified and their qualifications explained to receivers. Mere "name-dropping," however, has not been found to be persuasive.

Reports (a type of factual information that describes events as seen by either participants or observers) are persuasive, especially when they are believable, specific, and the receivers are intelligent. It is also important that the reporter's qualifications be explained for receivers.

Statistics, somewhat surprisingly, tend not to be very persuasive in the short term, although results are better in the long term. To be most effective, statistics should be preceded by a specific example, which is then shown to be representative through the use of statistics. It is also important to explain how statistics were gathered for them to be persuasive. Research has demonstrated that when examples and personal anecdotes conflict with statistics, people are more likely to be persuaded by the examples.

Source credibility—that is, the believability of the person delivering a persuasive message—has an important impact on the persuasiveness of evidence. Using evidence tends to build a persuader's credibility. However, a source that is already highly credible is not likely to become more persuasive through the use of evidence in the short term (although long-term persuasiveness is enhanced). This is because of a "ceiling effect," which means the persuader has already reached the maximum persuasive potential through his or her source credibility. With or without evidence, the persuader cannot become more persuasive.

Although the mode of presentation (video, tape, live, etc.) doesn't seem to make any difference, a poorly delivered presentation will not be persuasive no matter how good the evidence.

One very consistent research finding is that the most persuasive evidence comes from highly credible sources, found to be believable by receivers. The overall finding of the body of research is that high-quality evidence is more persuasive than low-quality evidence, especially for receivers who have a personal stake in the issue, who are trained in reasoning, who find the topic novel, who are not biased about the issue, and who have attended college.

Reinard's analysis supports the traditional view that it is important to use credible, high-quality evidence in seeking to persuade others. Furthermore, he provides specific guidance as to the best evidence in specific situations. One of his most interesting findings is that statistics alone are not likely to be very persuasive. Persuaders need to bring the statistics to life by first presenting a vivid example. Statistics then serve to bolster the specific case, rather than replace it.

Technically, there are three types of evidence. They are called first-, second-, and third-order data.[15]

First-order data is evidence based on personal experience. When a person whose life was almost destroyed by drugs speaks to a high school audience about the dangers of drugs, this is first-order data. It not only carries with it logical force, but helps enhance the credibility of the speaker.

Second-order data is evidence based on expert testimony. When those who debate the wisdom of our current drug laws cite professors, public officials, and other experts on the wisdom or folly of our current policy, they are presenting the audience with second-order data.

Third-order data is evidence based on fact and statistics. The number of drug arrests each year and the percentage of teenagers experimenting with drugs are examples of third-order data.

The Importance of a Two-Sided Message

To be most effective, you also need to carefully order the arguments in your persuasive message and include an acknowledgment of the other side of the issue. Whereas the research once was not consistent in this regard, it now shows that whenever possible, you'll want to make sure your persuasive speech is two-sided rather than one-sided.[16]

Statistics Versus Examples

Suppose you have to choose between presenting a mountain of statistics to an audience or giving them a few well-chosen examples. On the one hand, scientifically there is no question that properly gathered statistical evidence is far more meaningful than a few examples. Yet, for persuasive effect, the example is superior to statistics, according to communication researcher Daniel O'Keefe. For example, when future high school teachers were presented with information about a certain type of science curriculum, the report of a single teacher on the success of the curriculum in an actual class was more persuasive than statistics that summarized the experience of numerous teachers. Similarly, prominent examples of the life-saving benefits of mammograms, such as the widely publicized cases of former First Ladies Nancy Reagan and Betty Ford, had more impact on visits to breast cancer detection clinics than well-publicized statistics about the same topic.

Furthermore, persuasion based on examples is less vulnerable to being refuted by later messages than is persuasion based on statistics. Attitudes that result from persuasive messages using examples endure over time better than those resulting from statistics. O'Keefe concludes that "the example seems to be a particularly powerful form of information, especially when compared to information in statistical summary form."

What does this suggest to you, a potential designer and presenter of persuasive messages, about the use of examples compared with statistics in your message design? Does this suggest any special caution that you, a critical thinker about the persuasive messages created by others, should exercise in evaluating those messages that rely primarily or solely on specific examples for proof?

Source: Daniel J. O'Keefe, *Persuasion: Theory and Research* (Newbury Park: Calif: Sage, 1990), 168–169.

Whereas a one-sided persuasive speech offers only evidence in support of your claim, a two-sided persuasive speech makes use of a brief statement of the other side of the issue and your response to it. Let's say, for example, that you want to persuade your audience to support the claim that the war on drugs is a failure. In a standard, one-sided persuasive speech you would only present evidence and appeals you believe will prove effective with your audience.

In a two-sided speech, you would do all of this and more. After making the argument, you would indicate what the other side might have to say, as well as present your answer to those arguments. Of course, this does not mean you abandon your point of view. Rather, this means you acknowledge counterarguments to it. You would then go on in your speech to point out the weaknesses in the other side's point of view. You simply tell the audience that there are reasonable people who don't support your position and then give the audience an example of the kind of evidence these reasonable people have given for not supporting your side. You then refute this example with a further argument or show that in spite of their argument, your overall claim is more credible.

Not only is a two-sided message more persuasive than a one-sided message, but research suggests at least two other benefits from its use. First, a two-sided message enhances the audience's perceptions of the speaker's credibility. Second, because it gives audience members arguments to rebut those arguments most commonly associated with the opposing view, a two-sided message also makes audience members more resistant to counterpersuasion.

Culture and Persuasion

As a society, we value a reasoning process that is more likely to produce true than false beliefs, likely to produce a large number of truthful arguments and statements, and likely to do so with a fair amount of speed. Through our collective experience we learn that certain types of reasoning work well. We internalize these and use them as templates for evaluating communicators and their messages.

Some cultures value reasoning more than others. Western culture tends to value rational argument and view anything labeled fallacious with suspicion. As Rodney A. Reynolds and Michael Burgoon point out, "Logical explanations are typically rewarded and con-

tradictions or absurdities punished as children develop."[1] Another culture, such as that of Japan, may place greater emphasis on tradition and appeal to authority than does the North American culture. Thus, operating in a system that values rationality requires a persuader to at least appeal to reason and evidence in order to be successful.[2]

[1]Rodney A. Reynolds and Michael Burgoon, "Belief Processing, Reasoning, and Evidence," in *Communication Yearbook 7*, ed. Robert N. Bostrom (Beverly Hills, Calif.: Sage, 1983), 88.

[2]John C. Reinard, *Foundations of Argument: Effective Communication for Critical Thinking* (Dubuque, Iowa: W. C. Brown, 1991), 171.

THE AUDIENCE: PERSUASION THROUGH PATHOS

Aristotle's Concept of Pathos

Aristotle recognized the role of the audience's emotions in the process of persuasion. He reasoned what modern researchers have demonstrated again and again: People are persuaded not simply by cold logic but also by emotional appeals. **Pathos** refers to the emotional states in an audience that a speaker can arouse and use to achieve persuasive goals. These methods are not inherently unethical, but they can be abused by unscrupulous persuaders.

Aristotle catalogued the many emotions a speaker can evoke in the attempt to persuade people. Specific emotions he mentions in his writings about persuasion include anger, fear, kindness, shame, pity, and envy.[17] Sometimes the speaker may choose to appeal to audience members' emotions or primitive beliefs. Because of social conditioning from the earliest years of childhood, people respond to some messages in specific, predictable ways. Whereas logical proofs are designed to induce elaborated thinking on the part of the audience, emotional appeals are designed to provoke audience members to respond without elaborated thought. These appeals are linked to emotions such as anger, fear, kindness, calmness, confidence, unkindness, friendship, shame, pity, enmity, shamelessness, and envy.[18] To illustrate the way appeals to the emotions operate, we will review one of the most researched: fear.

Appealing to Emotions: Motivating Through Fear

Common sense tells us that we sometimes do things as a result of fear; for example, we obey the law because we are afraid of the penalties we could suffer should we break it. Yet the research suggests that when it comes to persuasive speaking,

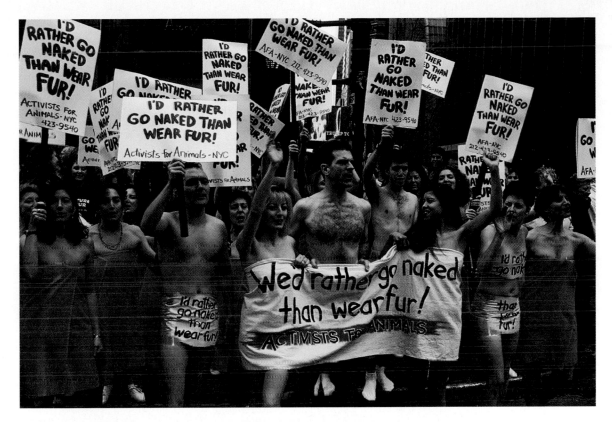

Animal-rights groups often base their persuasive messages on strong appeals to their audience's emotions.

fear has its limits. Whether your goal is to encourage the use of shoulder and lap belts while driving, demonstrate how flossing your teeth can prevent gum disease, or convince people everyone needs a gun for self-protection, the research is clear: Persuasive messages that arouse moderate levels of fear in audience members are more effective than those that generate high levels of fear. This fact is especially true, moreover, when the speaker gives audience members a set of clear-cut steps they can take to reduce the fear the speaker has aroused.[19]

As you can see in Figure 13.3, the relationship between fear and persuasive effects is like the relationship between speech anxiety and performance, explained in Chapter 3. As the level of fear aroused in an audience begins to increase, so do persuasive effects. Too much fear, however, diminishes persuasive effects because it tends to elicit denial from audience members. In a sense, audience members respond to the high level of fear the speaker has aroused in them by saying, "That could never happen to me."

If employed in moderation, however, fear can be effective. Many public service campaigns use moderate levels of fear to encourage positive behaviors such as not smoking, practicing safe sex, and taking advantage of medications that control high blood pressure. The slogan "If not for yourself, then do it for the

FIGURE 13.3

The Relationship Between Fear Appeals and Persuasion. As the level of fear aroused in an audience begins to increase, so do persuasive effects. Too much fear, however, diminishes persuasive effects.

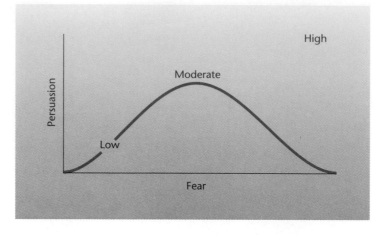

ones you love" is a good example. Produced by the American Heart Association, this persuasive message tells people with high blood pressure that they need to think about the feelings of the people they would leave behind if they failed to control their blood pressure. This message involves a mild but effective level of fear. Fear isn't an inherently unethical form of persuasion. Used moderately to achieve an ethical end, it is but one of the choices you have in deciding how to appeal to your audience.

Appealing to Primitive Beliefs

Emotional appeals such as fear frequently are combined with appeals to primitive beliefs. Primitive beliefs are basic, instilled since childhood. Research shows that the use of appeals that connect with primitive beliefs about reciprocity, liking, authority, social support, scarcity, and commitment is both widespread and effective in persuasive communication.[20]

Reciprocity   Reciprocity is best illustrated by that old saying, "You scratch my back, and I'll scratch yours." A reciprocity-based appeal can work in one of two ways in a persuasive speech. Candidates for political office often promise to give something in return for a person's vote. They may promise to reciprocate by proposing legislation, supporting a specific bill, or voicing a concern of their constituency.

Another common way reciprocity is used in a persuasive speech is when the speaker calls on the audience to reciprocate. During homecoming week, as a case in point, the school president may appeal to alumni for financial support. The appeal is usually couched in terms of "giving something back to the institution that gave you so much."

The reason reciprocity is so effective is because people are conditioned from an early age to return favors, gifts, and services. Reciprocity is a norm. Thus, when people receive a promise or are asked to return something received, the conditioned response is to reciprocate in kind.

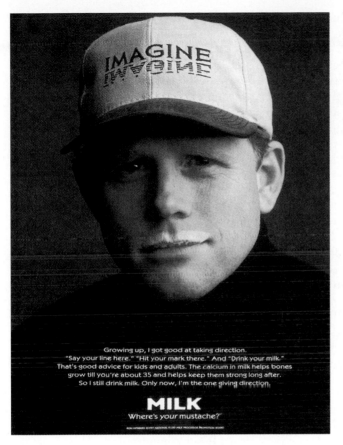

Growing up, I got good at taking direction.
"Say your line here." "Hit your mark there." And "Drink your milk."
That's good advice for kids and adults. The calcium in milk helps bones
grow till you're about 35 and helps keep them strong long after.
So I still drink milk. Only now, I'm the one giving direction.

MILK
Where's your mustache?

The "Got Milk?" campaign uses celebrities, such as actor-director Ron Howard, who are presumed to be well liked by potential consumers.

Liking   Liking is another primitive belief commonly used in persuasive campaigns. Politicians, for instance, enlist stars from film and music to speak persuasively on their behalf. The assumption is that if a star is well liked, the feeling may be generalized to the candidate the star endorses. Liking is a staple of advertisers, who employ well-known people as spokespersons for a product. It's not that the celebrity is an expert about the product, but that he or she is well liked by the public. Thus, if well-liked figure Michael Jordan eats Wheaties, or a celebrity like Ron Howard drinks milk, the hope is that the public will also like the product being pitched.

Authority   Authority-based appeals tap into another primitive belief. Research shows that some people are predisposed to comply with the requests of individuals and institutions perceived as authoritative. Examples of these authoritative sources range from members of law enforcement and the clergy to federal agencies such as the military. Thus, a speaker attempting to encourage a group of Catholics to voice their opposition to abortion might use the words of the Pope as an appeal. Similarly, a politician speaking to veterans might rely on an endorsement received from a military hero to win the audience's votes in the election.

Social Support   An appeal based on social support is nothing more than an appeal based on numbers. There's a tendency among people to think that if enough folks say something is so, then it must be so. Thus, product advertisers tout their product as "the number-one seller in its class" in an effort to convince consumers that their product must be the best. Research shows that when people are confronted with an appeal supported by large numbers, they are much more likely to be persuaded by the appeal, to jump on the bandwagon, so to speak. In a sense, they accept social support as a form of grounds for the argument.

Scarcity   The appeal to scarcity is based on the law of supply and demand. It is a maxim in economics that when demand exceeds supply, the value of the commodity increases. Thus, an appeal based on scarcity is also one based on relative value. As is the case with reciprocity, authority, and social support, people are conditioned to believe that something which is scarce is valuable enough to demand their attention. Persuasive speeches about the environment frequently use scarcity as the basis of appeal. For instance, the ecological benefit of the rain forests is made even more valuable when the speaker tells the audience that the world's rain forests are disappearing at an alarming rate.

Commitment   Commitment is one of the most powerful methods of persuasion. Evangelists, such as Billy Graham, for example, ask audience members to come forward and make a commitment to change. Similarly, when Jesse Jackson speaks to potential voters, he normally has voter registration forms available to be signed on the spot, thus asking his audience to make an immediate commitment to involvement in the political process. When people make even small commitments as a result of a persuasive message, the principle of psychological consistency comes into play. This principle tells us that we all feel pressure to keep our attitudes, beliefs, and values consistent with our commitments. Thus, if an appeal to commitment leads a person to write a letter, or to volunteer to serve, or to sign a petition, it increases the chances that the person's attitudes, beliefs, and values will reflect the commitment. Thus, in some cases action may actually precede changes in attitude, reversing the normal order of persuasive goals.

VIDEO FILE

If you have access to the videotape that accompanies this text, view segment 10. It shows Josette Parker's persuasive speech "Condemnation to Compassion."

To reiterate, the appeals you make in your persuasive message should reflect your goal and your audience. Not all audiences jump aboard after hearing an authority-based appeal. There also are people who steadfastly refuse to get on a bandwagon, no matter how many other people have already done so. Choosing the right form of appeal or appeals to flesh out your persuasive message, therefore, is part science and part art. In the box on pages 364–365 an outline of a persuasive speech by Josette Parker in which she uses a wide variety of appeals, including her own experience, evidence, and emotional appeal, to make her case.

PERSUASIVE SPEAKING IN PRACTICE

The last topic to discuss is, knowing what you now know, how to actually prepare your persuasive speech. We recommend three steps: (1) adapting your goals to your audience, (2) organizing your speech effectively, and (3) balancing the means of persuasion.

Evangelist Billy Graham uses public commitment as a way of gaining religious converts.

Adapting Your Goals to Your Audience

Speeches to reinforce or inoculate an audience presume that your audience members are either already supportive of your point of view or uninformed about the topic. These are friendly or neutral audiences. In such cases, you can expect your views to receive a fair hearing. You will want to build a strong case, of course, but you need not fear your audience will reject you and your message out of hand.

A speech to change attitudes, by definition, means your audience disagrees with you. This is termed a hostile audience. Although they may not be overtly hostile (booing and hissing), they are unlikely to be open to your point of view without a lot of work on your part. Such a speech requires you to begin with a common ground on which you and your audience can agree. After doing so, it is realistic only to try to move them slightly toward your position on the topic. Speaking to a group of gun owners about the need for gun control is a difficult task. You might begin by indicating you agree with the Second Amendment and do not seek to infringe on their right to bear arms. Rather, you want to see control of those kinds of weapons that are primarily used by gangs against law-abiding citizens. Perhaps you would simply argue for banning Teflon-coated bullets that can pierce police body armor. In any case, you would not expect a massive conversion from this type of audience.

Finally, speeches that seek to prompt people to act presume that your audience is prepared by prior messages to take action or that your topic is not inherently

Sample Persuasive Speech Outline

Title of speech.

CONDEMNATION TO COMPASSION

by Josette Parker

Specific purpose is to change audience attitudes about welfare recipients.

Specific Purpose: To persuade the audience that many factors contribute to poverty, and we should learn to treat the poor with respect and dignity.

Introduction

Speaker begins with a story of her own experience as a welfare recipient, enhancing her credibility.

I. **Open With Impact:** In April 1993 I lost my job when the company I worked for went bankrupt, had our car break down, and had no health insurance and a baby on the way.

   A. I was forced to take unemployment, WIC [Women, Infants and Children], and food stamps.

   B. I have never been treated with such disrespect.

   C. Are the poor not worthy of respect and dignity?

Thesis statement is clearly labeled.

II. **Focus on Thesis Statement:** We should consider all factors that contribute to poverty before we pass a harsh judgment on the poor.

Speaker shows the audience that they could find themselves in the same situation, citing one of her professors.

III. **Connect With the Audience:** Dr. George Wright of California State University–Chico states that all of us in the middle class are about two paychecks away from poverty or homelessness (personal communication, 1998).

Preview of main points is clear.

IV. **Preview:** Today I want to show you how the media propagate myths about welfare recipients, how we are not all given the same opportunities to succeed financially, and finally, how accepting the differences in our life circumstances can lead us to have compassion and understanding for the poor.

Body

Body of speech is labeled.

I. **Main Point:** The media show the average welfare queen as a Black, single woman with many children, who is too lazy to work.

Speaker refutes stereotype of welfare recipients.

   A. These are the facts (Chideya, 1995; Ellingson & Ferrini, 1997):

Speaker shows the facts don't fit the myths.

      1. Most welfare recipients work for a living.

      2. The majority are White and live in the suburbs.

      3. Seventy percent have two children or less, the same as the national average.

      4. Seventy percent leave the rolls within 2 years.

      5. The average AFDC payment is less than half the poverty level.

   B. So the average welfare recipient isn't who I thought it was.

(**Signpost:** But don't we live in the land of opportunity?)

II. **Main Point:** Our country has an enormous disparity in income (Naiman & Zepezauer, 1996).

   A. The top 1 percent owns 80 percent of our nation's wealth.

Notice how the speaker personalizes the figures on disparity in wealth.

      1. Unless you are making $2.3 million a year, you aren't in this group.

      2. That means 99 percent must share 20 percent of the wealth.

B. We have a large disparity, but what about tax dollars going to welfare?

Notice that this is a two-sided presentation, in which the speaker states and then answers the common arguments that are offered against welfare.

    1. Welfare is only 1 percent of the federal budget (Naiman & Zepezauer, 1996).

    2. We spend billions on subsidies and tax breaks for the rich.

    3. The military budget is $265 billion, larger than the next six largest military budgets in the world combined.

C. What about fraud?

    1. Any public system is susceptible to fraud.

    2. Millions are lost to tax fraud by the middle and upper class.

(**Signpost:** So, the average welfare recipient is not who I thought and there is great disparity, but you're thinking, I've overcome the odds and so can you!)

III. **Main Point:** The problem with this is that we are not all born with the same life chances.

A. We form templates of our lives built on foundations of family, morality, and education.

B. We impose our templates on those without foundations.

C. We think: If I can do it, so can you.

D. A child born in poverty does not have the same chance to succeed.

(**Signpost:** The more accepting we are of others' different life situations, the more compassion we can have; if we fail to see the whole picture, we can make blanket statements.)

Conclusion

Conclusion labeled.

I. **Summarize:** Our country was founded on the principles of life, liberty, and the pursuit of happiness.

Does this really summarize the points of the speech or make yet another point?

A. The system does not work and today's reform is punitive.

B. The poor have always been with us and probably always will be; what will we do?

C. Buddhists, Muslims, Christians, and Jews, all believe we should serve the poor.

II. **Close With Impact:** Reform begins in here, the heart, our attitudes and beliefs about each other.

How effectively does the speech conclude? Does the conclusion have the same impact as the opening?

A. We must sift through the myths, see the disparity, and accept the differences in life chances if we have compassion.

B. I am not asking to bring in the homeless, or to volunteer 20 hours at the local homeless shelter, although that would be great.

C. The next time you see your neighbor in need, speak to him or her with respect and dignity.

    1. This may be the only time someone treats that person with dignity.

    2. Let it come from you.

References

Note that the references do not include the personal communication from Dr. Wright. This is the correct format for APA style, where personal communications are cited only in the text itself.

Chideya, F. (1995). <u>Don't Believe the Hype.</u> New York: Plume.

Ellingson, L., & Ferrini, A. (1997). <u>Women's Health Issues.</u> Dubuque, IA: Kendall-Hunt.

Naiman, A., & Zepezauer, M. (1996). <u>Take the Rich Off Welfare.</u> Tucson, AZ: Odonian Press.

controversial. For example, prompting people to floss their teeth is not a topic that people are hostile to, though they may be uninformed about the benefits of acting. Such a speech needs to focus on the tangible benefits of action. In the case of an audience already primed by previous messages, your main task is to motivate them to act. People have heard for years about the benefits of wearing seat belts, yet a significant number still fail to do so. Rehashing arguments they have already heard is of little use with such people. You need to tell them something new that will get them to finally act. A dramatic story, for example, about how your own life was saved by wearing a seat belt might be the key ingredient in such a speech.

Organizing Your Persuasive Speech

In Chapter 8 we introduced a number of ways to organize a speech. Two organizational patterns described there are particularly suited to your persuasive speeches. The first is the problem–solution pattern, sometimes called stock issues. This pattern of organization analyzes a problem in terms of harm, significance, and cause and proposes a solution that is described, feasible, and advantageous. Many persuasive topics are about problems we face individually or as a society. By beginning with a discussion of the problem, the speaker heightens the audience's interest but avoids turning off a hostile audience with a solution they might initially reject. A speech on gun control that begins with a discussion of the growing gang problem is far more likely to receive a hearing from a pro-gun group than a speech that begins by calling for gun control.

The second pattern useful for persuasive speaking is Monroe's motivated sequence, a five-step organizational scheme including attention, need, satisfaction, visualization, and action. Because the final step is action, this pattern is particularly well suited to speeches calling for your audience to act. As should all good speeches, this type begins by capturing the audience's attention. Like the problem–solution pattern, this speech focuses on a problem (called a need) before proposing its solution (satisfaction). But this pattern goes further by asking the audience to visualize the satisfaction of the need and then calling on them to act.

Regardless of the organizational pattern you choose, there are some principles of organization you should follow. First, always put your best arguments and support either early or late in the speech. Do not hide them in the middle. Over the years, research has shown that in some cases people best remember what they hear first, whereas in other cases, what comes last is most memorable. Either way, the middle of the speech is not the place for your best material.

Second, with hostile or indifferent audiences, it is particularly important to have some of your best material early in the speech. Otherwise, they will tune you out before you get to the critical points you want to make.

Balancing the Means of Persuasion

Finally, although it might sometimes seem like we have treated ethos, logos, and pathos as separate means of persuasion, this is not really the case in practice. Your ethos will affect how your audience perceives the logos of your speech. If you have high credibility, the audience is more likely to accept your arguments. Similarly, if you have strong evidence and arguments in your speech, your credibility will grow in the audience's mind. And unless you touch the audience with pathos, it is unlikely that they will be motivated to act or believe in what they have heard. Although Carolynn McCarthy, profiled for you in Chapter 5, certainly had credibility and used strong logic in her speeches, were it not for the emotional appeal associated with the loss of her husband and injury to her son from a gun-wielding fanatic, it is unlikely she would have prevailed in getting elected to Congress. In short, a good persuasive speech relies on all three factors—speaker, message, and audience—for its success.

SUMMARY

Persuasive speaking begins with an assessment of the rhetorical situation, which includes the goal(s) the persuasive speech is designed to achieve. Four common goals of a persuasive speech are to reinforce existing beliefs and attitudes, to inoculate against counterpersuasion, to change attitudes, and to prompt the audience to act. The probability of a persuasive speech's achieving these goals requires a thorough understanding of the audience's cultural, demographic, and individual diversity. Finally, an assessment of the rhetorical situation demands that speakers examine the constraints they face, including ethical boundaries.

Opinion leadership is the hallmark of the successful persuasive speaker. The combination of similarity with an audience and credibility, including competence and character, enhance your chances of being perceived as an opinion leader. Aristotle proposed a three-part model of persuasion comprising ethos, logos, and pathos. *Ethos,* or perceived credibility, is essential if a speaker hopes to persuade an audience. *Logos,* or the words of the speech in the form of logical proof, also has been shown to affect a persuasive speaker's success. *Pathos,* or the emotions a speaker stirs in the audience, interacts with ethos and logos in the process of persuasion. *Elaboration likelihood* shows speakers the two potential paths an audience can take in response to a persuasive message. One is complex and requires critical thinking; the other is more simplistic and involves conditioned responses to certain kinds of appeals.

Research has shown that, properly used, evidence can greatly enhance a persuasive presentation. Three types of evidence commonly used are personal experience, or *first-order data;* expert testimony, or *second-order data;* and facts and statistics, or *third-order data.*

Two-sided messages are generally more effective than one-sided speeches. Two-sided messages also confer greater credibility on a speaker and can be used to inoculate an audience against counterpersuasion.

Sometimes speakers use appeals designed to produce conditioned rather than elaborated responses from an audience. These appeals are meant to trigger basic emotions such as fear and rely on primitive beliefs about such things as reciprocity, liking, authority, social support, scarcity, and commitment. Such appeals can be both effective and ethically used in constructing a persuasive speech.

Check Your Understanding: Exercises and Activities

1. Suppose you are giving a speech on the topic of capital punishment. How would you change your persuasive message to achieve each of the four persuasive goals: reinforcement, inoculation, attitude change, and action? Using the concept of the rhetorical situation, how would these goals differ depending on possible audiences for this topic and the constraints you would face in each situation?

2. On a topic of your choosing, construct examples of appeals based on the six primitive beliefs discussed in the chapter (reciprocity, liking, etc.).

3. Consider the following list of topics: (1) preventing AIDS, (2) preventing tooth decay, and (3) the importance of wearing seat belts. Construct a brief message based on a moderate-level "fear" appeal for each of these topics. At what level—low, moderate, or high—do you think your fear appeal would diminish the persuasive effects, causing audience members to reject your message? At what point do you think arguments based on fear on these topics would become unethical?

4. Follow up on the list of tips we gave for assessing and enhancing perceptions of your credibility. List the specific factors you believe make you credible about the topic of your persuasive speech. Then describe how you plan on using these specific factors so that they will sustain the perception of credibility as you deliver your speech.

5. Newspaper editorials constitute a persuasive message. To improve your ability in recognizing the types of appeals being used, select a recent column from a nationally syndicated writer such as George Will, William Safire, Molly Ivins, or Ellen Goodman. Mark what you consider to be appeals the columnist is using. Note whether these appeals are intended to affect your emotions or your primitive beliefs. Finally, label the emotion or belief the appeal is targeted at arousing.

Notes

1. Aristotle, *Rhetoric,* trans. W. Rhys Roberts (New York: Modern Library, 1954), 25.

2. William J. McGuire, "Inducing Resistance to Persuasion: Some Contemporary Approaches," in *Advances in Experimental and Social Psychology,* ed. L. Berkowitz (New York, Academic Press, 1964), 191–229.

3. M. Fishbein and I. Ajzen, *Belief, Attitude, Intention, and Behavior,* (Reading, Mass.: Addison-Wesley, 1975), 12–13.

4. "Trouble at the Top," *U.S. News and World Report,* 17 June 1991, 41–42.

5. M. Sherif and C. I. Hovland, *Social Judgment: Assimilation and Contrast Effects in Communication and Attitude Change* (New Haven: Yale University Press, 1961).

6. Everett M. Rogers, *Diffusion of Innovations*, 3rd ed. (New York: Free Press, 1983).

7. Aristotle, *Rhetoric*, 25.

8. Sarah Trenholm, *Persuasion and Social Influence* (Englewood Cliffs, N.J.: Prentice Hall, 1989).

9. Carl I. Hovland, Irving L. Janis, and Harold H. Kelly, *Communication and Persuasion* (New Haven: Yale University Press, 1953); James C. McCroskey, *An Introduction to Rhetorical Communication*, 5th ed. (Englewood Cliffs, N.J.: Prentice Hall, 1986); David K. Berlo, James B. Lemert, and Robert J. Mertz, "Dimensions for Evaluating the Acceptability of Message Sources," *Public Opinion Quarterly* (Winter 1969–1970), 33: 562–576; Kenneth E. Anderson: *Persuasion: Theory and Practice* (Boston: Allyn & Bacon, 1971). For a useful chart comparing various researchers' terms for these key components of credibility, see John R. Wenburg and William W. Wilmont, *The Personal Communication Process* (New York: Wiley, 1973), 145–147.

10. Richard E. Petty and John T. Cacioppo, *Communication and Persuasion: Central and Peripheral Routes to Attitude Changes* (New York: Springer-Verlag, 1986).

11. Irvin A. Horowitz and Kenneth S. Bordons, *Social Psychology* (Mountain View, Calif.: Mayfield, 1995), 287–288.

12. John C. Reinard, "The Empirical Study of the Persuasive Effects of Evidence: The Status After Fifty Years of Research," *Human Communication Research*, 15 (Fall 1988), 3–59.

13. Reinard, "The Empirical Study," 46.

14. This summary of findings is abstracted from Reinard's excellent book, *Foundations of Argument: Effective Communication for Critical Thinking* (Dubuque, Iowa: W. C. Brown, 1991), 125–127.

15. James C. McCroskey, *An Introduction to Rhetorical Communication*, 7th ed. (Needham Heights, Mass.: Allyn & Bacon, 1997).

16. Mike Allen, "Meta-Analysis Comparing the Persuasiveness of One-Sided and Two-Sided Messages," *Western Journal of Communication* 55 (1991): 390–404.

17. Aristotle, *Rhetoric*.

18. Aristotle, *Rhetoric*.

19. Irving Janis, "Effects of Fear-Arousal on Attitude Change: Recent Developments in Theory and Experimental Research," in *Advances in Experimental and Social Psychology*, vol. 3, ed. L. Berkowitz (New York: Academic Press, 1967), 166–224.

20. Robert Cialdini, *Influence: Science and Practice*, 2nd ed. (New York: HarperCollins, 1988).

CHAPTER 14

Republican Mary
Matalin and
Democrat James
Carville prove that
people can argue
about ideas and yet
respect each other's
opinions.

Thinking and Speaking Critically

OBJECTIVES

After reading this chapter, you should be able to:

- Explain the difference between argumentativeness and verbal aggressiveness.
- Analyze, construct, and evaluate arguments using the Toulmin model of reasoning.
- Differentiate among patterns of reasoning.
- Identify and refute common fallacies of argument.

KEY CONCEPTS

argumentativeness

authority warrant

backing

causal warrant

claim

comparison (analogy) warrant

critical thinking

fallacy

generalization warrant

grounds

inference

pseudoreasoning

qualifier

rebuttal

sign warrant

verbal aggressiveness

warrant

*It is better to debate
a question without
settling it than to settle
a question without
debating it.*

—JOSEPH JOUBERT

Sample Persuasive Message: The Case Against Firearms by Sarah Brady

Note the claims made in this persuasive message, the type of evidence offered in support of these claims, and the warrants, implied or stated, that link the grounds with the claims.

Grounds: Statistics, examples.

As America enters the next decade, it does so with an appalling legacy of gun violence. The 1980s were tragic years that saw nearly <u>a quarter of a million Americans die from handguns—four times as many as were killed in the Viet Nam War.</u> We began the decade by witnessing yet another President, <u>Ronald Reagan, become a victim of a would-be assassin's bullet.</u> That day <u>my husband Jim,</u> his press secretary, also became a statistic in America's handgun war.

Hyperbole.

<u>Gun violence is an epidemic</u> in this country. In too many cities, the news each night reports another death

Warrant: Drug trade causes gun violence.

by a gun. As dealers push out in search of new addicts, Smalltown, U.S.A., is introduced to the <u>mindless gun violence fostered by the drug trade.</u>

Warrant: Guns purchased for self-defense kill children.

And we are killing our future. <u>Every day a child in this country loses his or her life to a handgun.</u> Hundreds more are permanently injured, <u>often because a careless adult left within easy reach a loaded handgun purchased for self-defense.</u>

Claim: Assault weapons could turn streets into combat zones.

Despite the carnage, America stands poised to face an even greater escalation of bloodshed. The growing popularity of <u>military-style assault weapons could turn our streets into combat zones.</u> Assault weapons, designed solely to mow down human beings, are <u>turning up at an alarming rate in the hands of those most prone to violence</u>—drug dealers, gang members, hate groups and the mentally ill.

Grounds: Rate up among violence-prone.

Grounds: Examples of Stockton, Louisville, Colorado. Is this a hasty generalization?

The <u>Stockton, Calif., massacre of little children</u> was a warning to our policymakers. But Congress lacked the courage to do anything. During the year of inaction on Capitol Hill, we have seen too many other tragedies brought about by assault weapons. <u>In Louisville</u> an ex-employee of a printing plant went on a shooting spree with a Chinese-made semiautomatic version of the AK-47, gunning down 21 people, killing eight and himself. <u>Two Colorado women</u> were murdered and several others injured by a junkie using a stolen MAC-11 semiautomatic pistol. And Congress votes itself a pay raise.

The first week in April 1981 was a good time to be a Republican. Ronald Reagan had just been sworn in as president that January, after defeating Democrat Jimmy Carter. It was even better if you happened to hold an important post in the Reagan White House, as did Press Secretary James P. Brady. As a result, Brady was feeling good about himself and his boss, who had just delivered a speech to 3,500 labor leaders.

As usual, a throng of reporters and tourists awaited President Reagan and his entourage as they emerged from the building. As usual, the reporters present immediately began to shout, "Mr. President, Mr. President." And, as usual, Press Secretary Brady stepped ahead of the president to field the questions the reporters were yelling.

The *National Rifle Association*, meanwhile, breathes a sigh of relief, gratified that your attention is now elsewhere. The only cooling-off period the N.R.A. favors is a postponement of legislative action. It counts on public anger to fade before such outrage can be directed at legislators. The N.R.A. runs feel-good ads saying guns are not the problem and there is nothing we can do to prevent criminals from getting guns. <u>In fact, it has said that guns in the wrong hands are the "price we pay for freedom." I guess I'm just not willing to hand the next John Hinckley a deadly handgun.</u> Neither is the nation's law-enforcement community, the men and women who put their lives on the line for the rest of us every day.

> *Rebuttal to NRA.*

Two pieces of federal legislation can make a difference right now. <u>First, we must require a national waiting period</u> before the purchase of a handgun, to allow for a criminal-records check. Police know that waiting periods work. In the <u>20 years that New Jersey has required a background check, authorities have stopped more than 10,000 convicted felons from purchasing handguns.</u>

> *Claim: Waiting period needed.*
>
> *Grounds: N.J. example.*

<u>We must also stop the sale and domestic production</u> of semiautomatic <u>assault weapons.</u> These killing machines clearly have no legitimate sporting purpose, as President Bush recognized when he permanently banned their importation.

> *Claim: Must stop assault weapons.*

These public-safety measures are <u>supported by the vast majority of Americans—including gun owners.</u> In fact, these measures are so sensible that I never realized the campaign to pass them into law would be such an uphill battle. But it can be done.

> *Claim: Vast majority support. But where is the evidence? No grounds.*

<u>Jim Brady knows the importance of a waiting period. He knows the living hell of a gunshot wound.</u> Jim and I are not afraid to take on the N.R.A. leaders, and we will fight them everywhere we can. As Jim said in his congressional testimony, "<u>I don't question the rights of responsible gun owners. That's not the issue. The issue is whether the John Hinckleys of the world should be able to walk into gun stores and purchase handguns instantly.</u> Are you willing and ready to cast a vote for a commonsense public-safety bill endorsed by experts—law enforcement?"

> *Grounds: Testimony, personal experience.*
>
> *Refutes counterargument of "responsible gun owners."*

Are we as a nation going to accept America's bloodshed, or are we ready to stand up and do what is right? When are we going to say "Enough"? We can change the direction in which America is headed. We can prevent the 1990s from being bloodier than the past ten years. <u>If each of you picks up a pen and writes to your Senators and Representative tonight, you would be surprised at how quickly we could collect the votes we need to win the war for a safer America.</u>

> *Claim: Call for action.*

Let us enter a new decade committed to finding solutions to the problem of gun violence. Let your legislators know that voting with the gun lobby— and against public safety—is no longer acceptable. Let us send a signal to lawmakers that we demand action, not excuses.

What happened in the next two seconds was horrifying. John Hinckley, a disturbed young man, fired six shots from a .22 caliber automatic pistol in the direction of President Reagan, hitting the president, Secret Service Agent Tim McCarthy, and Brady. Reagan and McCarthy recovered completely. Brady, wounded in the head, was permanently disabled and would never completely recover his considerable talents as a communicator.

Fast-forward 12 years. Sarah Brady is testifying before Congress about the merits of a handgun-control bill that bears her husband's name see the box, "In Their Own Words: The Case Against Firearms." In a short time, the Brady Bill will become law, the culmination for Sarah and Jim Brady of a

BEWARE OF SPEAKERS BEARING GIFTS...

decade-long campaign to control the purchase of guns like the one that had
been used by John Hinckley. In the course of that campaign, Sarah Brady not
only became the founder of Handgun Control, Inc., a nationwide lobbying
group dedicated to changing handgun laws, but she also became a public
speaker of unquestionable skills. In the process, she had to learn to marshal
evidence and reason persuasively, if she was to achieve her goals. Sarah Brady
had a persuasive message that her audience could not ignore.

As with so many controversial issues, there are two sides to this argument.
Opponents of gun control have countered proponents such as Sarah Brady
with their own evidence and reasoning. In the box "In Their Own Words:
The Case for Firearms" on pages 376–377, J. Warren Cassidy, the executive
vice-president of the National Rifle Association, attempts to refute the case
for gun control. As we examine the nature of critical thinking and constructive argument in this chapter, we will refer back to both Brady's and Cassidy's
messages on gun control.

Although you may never find yourself thrust into the national limelight like
Sarah Brady or Warren Cassidy, you can still count on preparing and delivering
at least a few persuasive speeches over the course of your life. Furthermore, you
will be the audience for literally thousands of persuasive messages. As you read
this chapter, you will become more familiar with how to think and speak critically about important topics.

CRITICAL THINKING AND PUBLIC SPEAKING

Critical thinking is the process of making sound inferences based on accurate evidence and valid reasoning. Understanding how to think critically about arguments is the first step to constructing and communicating those arguments to an audience. As noted in Chapter 13, logical proof should be an ethical part of any persuasive message. To successfully persuade others of your side of a controversial issue, it is important to have well-constructed, sound arguments for your side. As the elaboration likelihood model introduced in the preceding chapter shows, you are more likely to induce a permanent change in attitude if you use sound evidence and reasoning.

Pseudoreasoning and Fallacies

As pointed out in Chapter 4, we spend more of our time listening to others than actually speaking. Understanding critical thinking is essential to differentiating messages that are logical from those that are not. Frequently, something sounds good on first hearing but proves to be illogical. **Pseudoreasoning** refers to an argument that appears sound at first glance but contains a fallacy of reasoning that renders it unsound. A **fallacy** is "an argument in which the reasons advanced for a claim fail to warrant acceptance of that claim."[1] Thus, one of the goals of this chapter is to help you recognize fallacies that are a sign of pseudoreasoning. Even if you agree with the conclusion of a speaker, you ought to do so based on sound logic, not just because he or she sounds good.

It is important to distinguish here between intentional and unintentional fallacies. Certainly not everyone who makes an error in reasoning is intending to deceive. On the other hand, someone who is seeking to "pull the wool over an audience's eyes" may indeed use fallacies intentionally. Either way, it is the consumer of communication—the audience—who must remain vigilant to avoid being misled, whether by accident or design, by pseudoreasoning.

Argumentativeness and Verbal Aggressiveness

In Chapter 6, we maintained that when listeners detect fallacious reasoning, they are ethically obligated to bring it to light. Simply remaining silent allows the speaker to mislead those who are not well trained in critical thinking. However, there is an important distinction between being argumentative and being verbally aggressive. In his book *Arguing Constructively*, Dominic A. Infante makes the distinction between these two personality traits.[2] **Argumentativeness** is the trait of arguing for and against the *positions* taken on controversial claims. For example, an argumentative person might say, "The idea of a flat tax sounds good, but it would lead to massive increases in the federal debt." **Verbal aggressiveness,** on the other hand, is the trait of attacking the *self-concept* of those with whom a person disagrees about controversial claims. A verbally aggressive person might say, "The flat tax sounds like something a bunch of rich freeloaders dreamed up while sailing their yachts." Argumentativeness is not only socially

Sample Persuasive Message: The Case For Firearms by J. Warren Cassidy

Use of comparison of First and Second Amendments.

The American people have a right "to keep and bear arms." <u>This right is protected by the Second Amendment to the Constitution, just as the right to publish editorial comment in this magazine is protected by the First Amendment.</u> Americans remain committed to the constitutional right to free speech even when their most powerful oracles have, at times, abused the First Amendment's inherent powers. Obviously the American people believe no democracy can survive without a free voice.

In the same light, the authors of the Bill of Rights knew that a democratic republic has a right—indeed, a need—to keep and bear arms. Millions of American citizens just as adamantly believe the Second Amendment is crucial to the maintenance of the democratic process. Many express this belief through membership in the National Rifle Association of America.

Red herring: What does where N.R.A. supporters live have to do with the issue at hand?

Our cause is neither trendy nor fashionable, but a basic American belief that spans generations. <u>The N.R.A.'s strength has never originated in Washington but instead has reached outward and upward from Biloxi, Albuquerque, Concord, Tampa, Topeka—from every point on the compass and from communities large and small.</u> Those who fail to grasp this widespread commitment will never understand the depth of political and philosophical dedication symbolized by the letters N.R.A.

Unsupported assertion: Which scholars?

<u>Scholars who have devoted careers to the study of the Second Amendment agree</u> in principle that the right to keep and bear arms is fundamental to our concept of democracy. No high-court decision has yet found grounds to challenge this basic freedom. Yet some who oppose this freedom want to waive the constitutionality of the "gun control" question for the sake of their particular—and sometimes peculiar—brand of social reform.

beneficial, it is the only way one can take the process of critical thinking into the public arena. Verbal aggressiveness, on the other hand, is a destructive and hostile trait that destroys personal relationships. Constructive argumentativeness is the best approach for the public speaker. Being able to disagree without being disagreeable fosters a positive communication transaction.

The authors were recently witnesses to the possibility that people can disagree without being disagreeable. Mary Matalin, former deputy campaign direc-

In doing so they seem ready, even eager, to disregard a constitutional right exercised by at least 70 million Americans who own firearms. Contrary to current antigun evangelism, these gun owners are not bad people. They are hardworking, law abiding, tax paying. They are safe, sane and courteous in their use of guns. They have never been, nor will they ever be, a threat to law-and-order.

History repeatedly warns us that human character cannot be scrubbed free of its defects through vain attempts to regulate inanimate objects such as guns. What has worked in the past, and what we see working now, are tough, N.R.A.-supported measures that punish the incorrigible minority who place themselves outside the law.

As a result of such measures, violent crimes with firearms, like assault and robbery, have stabilized or are actually declining. We see proof that levels of firearm ownership cannot be associated with levels of criminal violence, except for their deterrent value. On the other hand, tough laws designed to incarcerate violent offenders offer something gun control cannot: swift, sure justice meted out with no accompanying erosion of individual liberty.

Violent crime continues to rise in cities like New York and Washington even after severe firearm-control statutes were rushed into place. Criminals, understandably, have illegal ways of obtaining guns. Antigun laws—the waiting periods, background checks, handgun bans, et al.—only harass those who obey them. Why should an honest citizen be deprived of a firearm for sport or self-defense when, for a gangster, obtaining a gun is just a matter of showing up on the right street corner with enough money?

Antigun opinion steadfastly ignores these realities known to rank-and-file police officers—men and women who face crime firsthand, not police administrators who face mayors and editors. These law-enforcement professionals tell us that expecting firearm restrictions to act as crime-prevention measures is wishful thinking. They point out that proposed gun laws would not have stopped heinous crimes committed by the likes of John Hinckley Jr., Patrick Purdy, Laurie Dann or mentally disturbed, usually addicted killers. How can such crimes be used as examples of what gun control could prevent?

There are better ways to advance our society than to excuse criminal behavior. The N.R.A. initiated the first hunter-safety program, which has trained millions of young hunters. We are the shooting sports' leading safety organization, with more than 26,000 certified instructors training 750,000 students and trainees last year alone. Through 1989 there were 9,818 N.R.A. certified law-enforcement instructors teaching marksmanship to thousands of peace officers.

Frankly, we would rather keep investing N.R.A. resources in such worthwhile efforts instead of spending our time and members' money debunking the failed and flawed promises of gun prohibitionists.

Marginal notes:

Straw argument: gun-control advocates do not say gun owners are bad people.

Rebuttal to Sarah Brady's claim of epidemic.

Negative examples: where gun control failed.

Stereotypes: Police administrators as out of touch with rank-and-file police.

Effect-to-cause relationship questioned: Gun control would not have prevented crimes.

False dilemma: It's not either hunter safety or fighting gun control.

---

tor for George Bush and conservative talk-show host "debated" her husband, James Carville, who managed the 1992 presidential campaign of Bill Clinton and served as one of his chief defenders during the Lewinsky scandal. Despite their obvious political differences, they treated each other with good-humored respect. The audience, which was apparently deeply divided on partisan lines, nevertheless cheered both speakers and even gave them a standing ovation at the end of the evening. Learning to disagree about issues, while respecting the

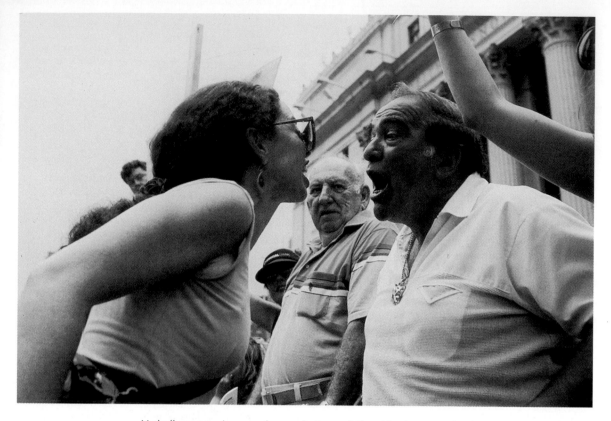

Verbally aggressive people can destroy relationships by engaging in personal attacks.

other side's right to believe as they do, is the hallmark of civility in argument. One can be argumentative without being verbally aggressive.

THE TOULMIN MODEL OF ARGUMENT

One way to become a better critical thinker and speaker is to use philosopher Stephen Toulmin's model of argument, depicted in Figure 14.1. Toulmin's model makes an excellent template to use in constructing and evaluating arguments. According to Toulmin, a sound argument involves *at least* a claim, grounds for making the claim, and a warrant that connects grounds and claim.[3]

A **claim** is a conclusion that a persuasive speaker wants an audience to reach as a result of a speech. Speakers can make claims about the facts as they see them, about basic human values, and about public policies. As you might imagine, it's not uncommon for a speaker to make claims about each of these during the course of a speech. The differences between these types of claims are discussed later in this chapter.

FIGURE 14.1
The Toulmin Model
of Argument

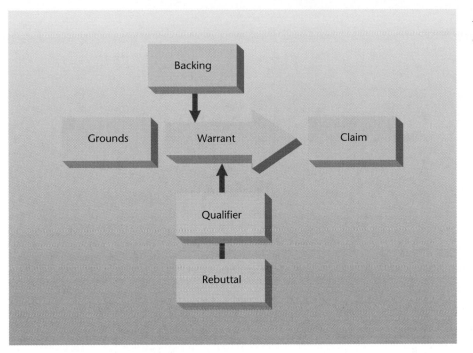

Just because someone asserts a claim, that doesn't constitute an argument for its truth. An argument also requires **grounds,** which are the evidence a speaker offers in support of a claim. This evidence can be based on personal experience, expert testimony, established fact, or statistics or other data.

Good speakers also connect the grounds they offer as evidence in support of their claims. Such a connection between grounds and claim is called a **warrant.** Although warrants can be implied, we think these connections between grounds and claim are best stated by the speaker.

This is not the complete model, however. Toulmin indicates that three additional parts of an argument *may* be present. In some cases, for example, the warrant may be one that is not obvious to audience members. In that case, a fourth element of Toulmin's model, backing, comes into play. **Backing** is support for the warrant. If an audience does not already believe in the warrant, the speaker will need to build additional argument and evidence to support it before attempting to convince the audience of the soundness of the whole argument. Knowing which warrants an audience will accept and which require additional backing is essential to effective speaking.

An additional component is the **rebuttal,** which represents an exception to or a refutation of the argument. It is usually preceded by the word "unless," indicating that the claim is true except when conditions stated in the rebuttal are present. As we discussed in Chapter 13, it is important in presenting a two-sided message to let the audience know if they may encounter exceptions or refutations of your argument. Finally, unless an argument is 100 percent

FIGURE 14.2
Analysis of an
Argument Using
Toulmin's Model

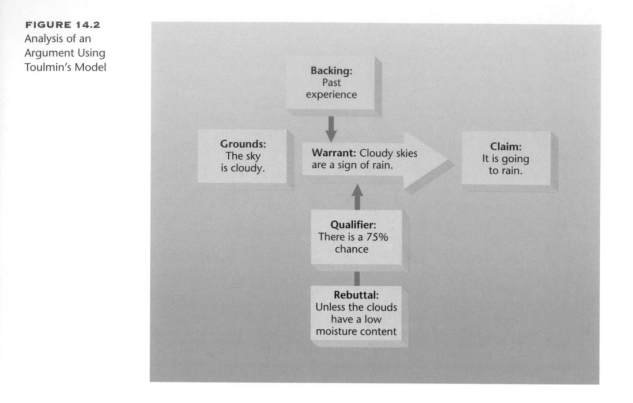

certain, it will need to have a **qualifier,** which is an indication of the level of probability of the claim.[4] Qualifiers may be a single word, such as "probably"; a brief phrase, such as "very likely"; or even a probability expressed as a percentage. In human affairs, it is rare to deal with absolute certainty. Acknowledging to an audience your degree of certainty helps you avoid appearing to take an extreme or unreasonable position.

How does this model of argument apply in actual practice? Let's begin with a simple case. Suppose you glance out the window and the sky is filled with clouds. You think to yourself, "It's going to rain," and you grab your umbrella. Although you may not realize it, your reasoning can be analyzed as an argument using Toulmin's model. Figure 14.2 shows how this analysis would look. Based on the *grounds* of a cloudy sky, you reason using the *warrant*, cloudy skies are a sign of rain, which is based on the *backing* of your past experience, that there is a 75 percent chance (*qualifier*) of the truth of the *claim* that it is going to rain, unless (*rebuttal*) the clouds have a low moisture content.

Now that you understand this basic version of Toulmin's model, let's look at the relationships among claims, grounds, and warrants in a more complicated situation. If you've read Sarah Brady's and J. Warren Cassidy's persuasive messages, note that both offer opposing claims on the issue of gun control—and both base these claims on reasoning and evidence.

VIDEO FILE

If you have access to the videotape that accompanies this text, view segment 11, which shows reasoning in action using the Toulmin model.

DILBERT reprinted by permission of United Feature Syndicate, Inc.

In the spirit of constructive argumentation, therefore, we will consider how to test arguments for their soundness. Using the Toulmin model, we will suggest appropriate tests for the grounds, claims, warrants, backing, qualifiers, and rebuttals of various types of arguments. Further, we will show how the failure to meet these tests can result in fallacies, turning what could be sound arguments into pseudoarguments.

FALLACIES ASSOCIATED WITH GROUNDS

All arguments are built on the grounds, or evidence, which the arguer points to in supporting the claim. If the grounds are either absent or defective, then the argument cannot be sound. In Chapter 7, we discussed various types of supporting material that might form the grounds of an argument, including examples, facts, statistics, expert opinion, explanations, descriptions, and narratives.

When you are examining the grounds of an argument, be sure that the examples are relevant, of sufficient quantity, and typical. Facts should come from a reliable source and be verifiable, recent, and consistent with other known facts. Statistics should be taken from a reliable and unbiased source, based on fair questions, and accurately collected. You should be told how the sample was selected to ensure that it was random and representative. Any differences should be greater than the margin of error, and the base of any percentages should be stated. Expert opinion depends on the source's expertise, reliability, and lack of bias. Explanations should be clear and accurate. Descriptions should be accurate and vivid. Narratives must have probability (coherence) and fidelity to the real world.

Grounds that fail one or more of these tests are likely to constitute a fallacy. In particular, there are four fallacies associated with grounds: unsupported assertion, distorted evidence, isolated examples, and misused statistics.

Unsupported Assertion

There are a number of ways in which the grounds, or evidence, in support of an argument can be defective. The most egregious case is the absence of any grounds to support a claim. The **unsupported assertion** is really the absence of any argument at all. Fans of the sitcom *Cheers* probably recognize this tendency in Cliff Claven, who is always spouting the most absurd facts as if they were gospel. An argument without grounds is no argument at all.

In his argument about firearms, J. Warren Cassidy claims, "Scholars who have devoted careers to the study of the Second Amendment agree in principle that the right to keep and bear arms is fundamental to our concept of democracy." What scholars? How many? The claim just sits there with no evidence to support it. This is not to say that it is untrue, merely that there are no grounds offered in the message to support it. Similarly, in her argument about handguns, Sarah Brady says, "These public-safety measures [meaning controls on guns] are supported by the vast majority of Americans—including gun owners." As with Cassidy's claim about scholars and the Second Amendment, there is no evidence to support Brady's claim; it is simply asserted.

Distorted Evidence

Less easily discovered is the argument that relies on distorted evidence to support its claim. **Distorted evidence** is significant omissions or changes in the grounds of an argument that alter its original intent.

A good example of distorted evidence is found on the movie advertisement page of your local newspaper. Frequently, a movie will tout itself as "daring," "enthralling," or "thumbs up" when a reading of the full review will reveal that these words were used in a different context. Perhaps the reviewers really said, "This movie was a daring attempt that missed the mark. The only thing that was enthralling about this movie was the credits that signaled it was ending. In deciding whether to rate this movie thumbs up or down, it took only about 10 minutes to see that this was thumbs way down!"

Isolated Examples

Another problem with grounds lies in the use of **isolated examples,** nontypical or nonrepresentative examples, to prove a general claim. Recall that to reason from examples requires that the instances be representative of the larger class—in a word, typical. It is almost always possible to find an isolated example to illustrate just about any claim. For example, we often hear about cases of welfare abuse. One radio commentator recently told the story of a man who reported to the police that his food stamps had been stolen from his car—a Mercedes. Of course, most people on welfare don't drive a Mercedes. Yet the image of welfare recipients living it up at the taxpayers' expense has been a staple of popular mythology for decades. The reality is that most people on welfare are children living in poverty. Isolated examples do not prove that everyone on welfare is lazy or abusing the system.

Misused Statistics

Statistics are often very helpful in giving us a general picture of a topic, something not provided by examples. However, to be useful, grounds must meet the basic tests outlined in Chapter 7. Let's now look at four of the most frequent cases of **misused statistics.**

Poor Sampling   Statistics based on self-selected or nonrandom samples are worse than useless—they're misleading. For instance, many television stations and newspapers now have call-in polls whereby you can express your opinion on the issues of the day by dialing one of two numbers, each representing one side of the issue. Of course, there is no guarantee that the station's audience represents the public at large or that members of the audience will call in proportion to their number in the general population.

Lack of Significant Differences   Often the difference between two candidates in a preference poll is less than the poll's margin of error. Thus, if candidate A leads B by three points, but the poll has a five-point margin of error, there is no statistical significance to that difference, a fact often ignored by political pundits.

Misuse of "Average"   People frequently cite the "average," or mean, to support a claim. They say such things as, "The average salary for college graduates is X." The intent is for the audience to infer that most college graduates make the salary mentioned. However, the average (or mean) is only one of three numbers that can be used to describe a collection of numbers like the salaries paid to college graduates. The other two are the median and the mode. Further, the average is frequently misleading because it is so easily distorted by extreme numbers.

As an example, consider the differences between the mean, the median, and the mode of houses selling at a range of prices:

$100,000
$100,000
$150,000
$250,000
$1,000,000
Mean = $320,000
Median = $150,000
Mode = $100,000

The *mean* is simply the arithmetic average: Add all the selling prices, and divide the total by the number of houses sold. The *median* is the midpoint in a series of numbers. Half of the houses sold for more and half for less than the median. Finally, the *mode* is simply the most frequently occurring number or value. In most cases, the median is more accurate than the mean. Certainly that is the case here because the mean would lead you to believe that most houses in the area described are more expensive than they are in actuality. The single home selling for $1 million not only inflates the "average" but misleads your thinking in the process.

Misuse of Percentages   Percentages are meaningful only if you know the base on which they are computed. Consider the confusion often present in political and commercial advertising. For example, although it is true that while Bill Clinton was governor, Arkansas led the nation in job creation in the year prior to his election as president, it is also true that Arkansas had one of the lowest job bases to begin with. If you start out at a very low level, even large percentage increases may not be very large in real terms.

FALLACIES ASSOCIATED WITH CLAIMS

There are three types of claims a person can make. A *claim of fact* is one that can in principle be verified by objective means. For example, J. Warren Cassidy claims that "the American people have a right 'to keep and bear arms.' This right is protected by the Second Amendment to the Constitution." This claim is easily verified by looking up the Second Amendment. Even if a claim of fact is not currently known to be true or false, as long as it is theoretically verifiable, it is still a factual claim. We don't know for sure if there is life on other planets, but theoretically the question could be answered empirically, if we had the means to directly observe radio signals from deep space, for example.

A *claim of value* makes judgments about good and bad, right and wrong. When Cassidy argues that "the Second Amendment is crucial to the maintenance of the democratic process," he has gone beyond mere fact to make a value judgment about the right to keep and bear arms.

A *claim of policy* offers a solution to some problem. Sarah Brady has a clear position on what should be done about gun violence: Pass a handgun waiting period and stop the sale of semiautomatic assault weapons. To convincingly prove a claim of policy, one must prove the stock issues that (1) there is a need for the policy, (2) the proposed policy would fulfill that need, and (3) the benefits of the proposed policy outweigh the costs. It seems clear that Cassidy disagrees with Brady on all three points. He argues that there is no need for the legislation she proposes, because tougher penalties for using a gun in committing a crime have worked. He argues that gun control won't work, using the examples of New York and Washington, cities with stiff gun-control laws and high crime rates. And he argues that to pass such laws would be unfair to law-abiding citizens.

Red Herring

Claims may be fallacious if they are irrelevant, the so-called red herring. Sometimes called a **smoke screen,** a **red herring** is an irrelevant issue introduced into a controversy to divert attention from the real controversy. Debates over public issues are well known for the use of red herrings to divert attention from the issues that concern most people. For example, Cassidy argues, "The N.R.A.'s strength has never originated in Washington but instead has reached outward and upward from Biloxi, Albuquerque, Concord, Tampa, Topeka—from every point on the compass and from communities large and small." Aside from taking advantage of the prevailing "anti-Washington" sentiment in the United States, what exactly does that have to do with whether we should pass the Brady Bill? It is a red herring, irrelevant to the issue at hand.

Arguing in a Circle

Another common fallacy is the use of a claim to prove its own truth, called arguing in a circle. **Arguing in a circle,** sometimes called **begging the question,** occurs when the argument actually proves nothing because the claim to be proved is used as the grounds or warrant for the argument. For example, consider the door-to-door evangelist who insists that you must believe in his or her version of the Bible. Why? you ask. The person immediately opens a Bible and quotes you scripture to support the claim. Basically the argument looks something like this:

Claim: My version of the Bible is the truth.

Grounds: Quotation from scripture.

Warrant: My version of the Bible is the truth.

In other words, the claim is also the warrant.

Of course, such clear-cut expressions of question-begging are rare. But many arguments, when distilled to their essence, do in fact beg the question.

FALLACIES ASSOCIATED WITH WARRANTS AND BACKING

Grounds do not directly prove a claim. There is a connection between the grounds and the claim, whether stated or unstated. You may recall that Toulmin calls this link the warrant. The warrant is the license that authorizes an arguer to move from grounds to a claim. Thus, if one were to argue, as in our earlier example, that it's going to rain because it is cloudy, the observation about clouds only proves it will rain given the warrant that clouds are a sign of rain. The process of moving from grounds, via a warrant, to a claim is called an **inference.**

Sometimes people confuse observed grounds with claims based on inference. To see how well you can distinguish between inferences and observations, try reading the story and answering the questions in the "Uncritical Inference Test" box nearby. This test was devised by William V. Haney, a former business professor who now heads his own consulting firm.

To his basic model of grounds-warrant-claim, recall that Toulmin adds backing, which is support for the warrant. In some cases a warrant is readily believed by an audience. In others, the warrant needs additional backing in the form of evidence before the audience will believe it is true. For example,

Uncritical Inference Test

INSTRUCTIONS

Read the following story. Assume that all the information presented in it is definitely accurate and true. Read it carefully because it has ambiguous parts designed to lead you astray. No need to memorize it, though. You can refer to it whenever you wish.

Next read the statements about the story and indicate whether you consider each statement true, false, or "?". "T" means that the statement is *definitely true* on the basis of the information presented in the story. "F" means that it is *definitely false*. "?" means that it may be either true or false and that you cannot be certain which on the basis of the information presented in the story. If any part of a statement is doubtful, make it "?". *Answer each statement in turn, and do not go back to change any answer later, and don't reread any statements after you have answered them. This will distort your score.*

To start with, here is a sample story with correct answers.

SAMPLE STORY

You arrive home late one evening and see that the lights are on in your living room. There is only one car parked in front of your house, and the words "Harold R. Jones, M.D." are spelled in small gold letters across one of the car's doors.

Statements About Sample Story

1. The car parked in front of your house has lettering on one of its doors. (T) F ?
   (This is a "definitely true" statement because it is directly corroborated by the story.)
2. Someone in your family is sick. T F (?)
   (This could be true, and then again it might not be. Perhaps Dr. Jones is paying a social call at your home, or perhaps he has gone to the house next door or across the street, or maybe someone else is using the car.)
3. No car is parked in front of your house. T (F) ?
   (A "definitely false" statement because the story directly contradicts it.)
4. The car parked in front of your house belongs to a woman named Johnson.
   T F (?)
   (May seem very likely false, but can you be sure? Perhaps the car has just been sold.)

So much for the sample. It should warn you of some of the kinds of traps to look for. Now begin the actual test. Remember, mark each statement *in order*—don't skip around or change answers later.

suppose your audience is unaware that the Supreme Court has upheld numerous gun-control laws over the years. They assume that the Second Amendment guarantees the unlimited right to bear arms. If you presented a warrant, therefore, that gun control was permissible under the Constitution, they would not believe it. Thus, you would need to present backing for that warrant. You might quote the Second Amendment, which begins "A well regulated militia. . . ." Similarly, you might cite a number of Supreme Court cases that have

THE STORY[1]

A businessman had just turned off the lights in the store when a man appeared and demanded money. The owner opened a cash register. The contents of the cash register were scooped up, and the man sped away. A member of the police force was notified promptly.

Statements About the Story

1. A man appeared after the owner had turned off his store lights.   T F ?
2. The robber was a *man*.   T F ?
3. The man who appeared did not demand money.   T F ?
4. The man who opened the cash register was the owner.   T F ?
5. The store owner scooped up the contents of the cash register and ran away.   T F ?
6. Someone opened a cash register.   T F ?
7. After the man who demanded the money scooped up the contents of the cash register, he ran away.   T F ?
8. While the cash register contained money, the story does *not* state *how much*.   T F ?
9. The robber demanded money of the owner.   T F ?
10. A businessman had just turned off the lights when a man appeared in the store.   T F ?
11. It was broad daylight when the man appeared.   T F ?
12. The man who appeared opened the cash register.   T F ?
13. No one demanded money.   T F ?
14. The story concerns a series of events in which only three persons are referred to: the owner of the store, a man who demanded money, and a member of the police force.   T F ?
15. The following events occurred: someone demanded money; a cash register was opened; its contents were scooped up; and a man dashed out of the store.   T F ?

Answers appear following the chapter notes, on pages 408–409.

Source: Excerpted with special permission from William V. Haney, *Communication and Interpersonal Relations*, 6th ed. (Homewood, IL: R. D. Irwin, Inc., 1992), 231–233, 241.

[1]The story and statements are a portion of the "Uncritical Inference Test," copyrighted 1955 and 1983 by William V. Haney.

permitted reasonable limits on gun ownership. Backing comes into play, therefore, when a warrant either is not known to the audience or is contrary to what they already believe.

Different types of warrants provide different ways of moving from grounds to claim and are associated with different patterns of reasoning. We introduce here the five most common types of warrants: generalization, comparison, causal, sign, and authority. In examining any argument, it is important to determine

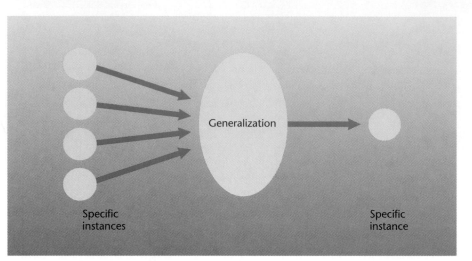

Generalization

Specific
instances

Specific
instance

whether the warrant and its accompanying backing are sound. We look at each type of warrant and suggest some of the common fallacies peculiar to each type of argument.

Generalization Warrants

A **generalization warrant** is a statement that either establishes a general rule or principle or applies an established rule or principle to a specific case. Warrants involving generalizations are used in two ways. Some warrants take specific instances and use them to establish generalizations. For example, suppose we want to generalize about college students. Based on our experience with the students in our public speaking class, we might generalize that "most college students are politically uninvolved." Other warrants take already existing generalizations and apply them to specific instances. For example, suppose we know from a previously established generalization that all college students must be high school graduates. Thus, we can conclude that any specific student in a college class is a high school graduate.

The relationship between a generalization-establishing warrant and a generalization-applying warrant looks like the diagram in Figure 14.3.

Establishing Generalizations A warrant that establishes a generalization uses specific instances, as represented in examples, statistics, narratives, and the like, to reach general conclusions. Consider Sarah Brady's argument. She uses specific examples and statistics to support her generalization that gun violence is an epidemic. She uses the examples of the Reagan assassination attempt, as well as the massacre of children on a schoolyard in Stockton, California, a Louisville shooting spree, and the murder of two Colorado women to support her generalization. She also cites statistics on the number of deaths from handgun violence. Warrants establishing generalizations are subject to tests of relevance, quantity, typicality, precision, and negative example. These tests can be expressed in the questions listed below.

Questions to Ask When Evaluating a Generalization

- Are the grounds relevant to the claim?
- Is there a sufficient quantity of grounds to establish the claim?
- Are the grounds typical of the larger population?
- Is overgeneralization avoided?
- Are there significant negative examples?

Let's apply these tests to Brady's generalization that gun violence is an epidemic. Clearly her examples are relevant. Is there a sufficient quantity of grounds to support the claim? She cites several examples, including her husband's wounds in the Reagan assassination attempt. In addition she cites statistics of 250,000 deaths from handguns in a decade. There seems to be plenty of evidence that a problem exists here.

Are the grounds typical? Certainly her examples are not. An attempted presidential assassination and the Stockton, California, schoolyard shooting were newsworthy precisely because they were not typical. However, Brady bolsters her specific examples with statistics. Thus, combining examples and statistics ensures that her grounds are not atypical.

Is overgeneralization avoided? Referring to gun violence as an "epidemic" suggests a level of urgency and danger on Brady's part. Is this really an epidemic, or is it a problem confined to certain areas of the country or certain populations? She never addresses that question.

Finally, are there negative examples? Brady claims that violence with firearms is widespread. But Cassidy presents evidence that violent crimes with firearms have stabilized or declined. These statistics constitute negative examples to refute Brady's claim of an epidemic.

The complete argument might look like the model in Figure 14.4. Based on the *grounds* of several examples and using the *warrant* that these examples are typical of gun violence, which is supported by the *backing* of statistics showing 250,000 deaths from handguns in the 1980s, Brady makes the *unqualified claim* that gun violence is an epidemic, unless violent crime has stabilized or declined, as Cassidy argues in *rebuttal*.

Hasty Generalization   The most common fallacy associated with warrants that generalize from specific instances to a general conclusion is known as **hasty generalization.** This occurs when there are too few instances to support a generalization or the instances are unrepresentative of the generalization. The key here is to limit generalizations to the extent justified by the grounds. For example, suppose you once purchased an American car. It gave you nothing but trouble. You decide American cars are unreliable and vow to purchase only foreign automobiles. You have engaged in hasty generalization. Maybe Fords are more reliable than Dodges.

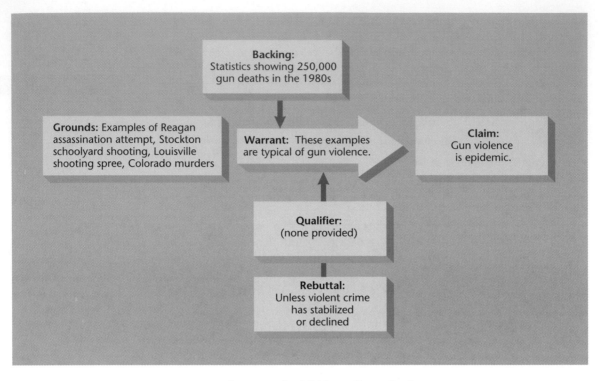

FIGURE 14.4   Argument Establishing a Generalization

Perhaps American manufacturers have improved their product. To reach a generalization from one or even a handful of instances is to form a hasty generalization.

Applying Generalizations   On the other hand, if we know a generalization is true, we can apply it to a specific instance and reach some valid conclusions about that specific instance. For example, we know that anyone born in the United States is, by definition, a U.S. citizen. Thus, if you show us your birth certificate, and it says you were born in Alaska, we know you are a U.S. citizen. Warrants applying generalizations are subject to tests of applicability to all cases, exceptions, backing, and classification.

Questions to Ask When Evaluating Applications of a Generalization

Tips and Tactics

- Does the generalization apply to all possible cases?
- Are there exceptions to the generalization? If so, does the specific case fall within one of the exceptions?
- Is the generalization well backed?
- Does the specific instance fall clearly within the category specified by the generalization?

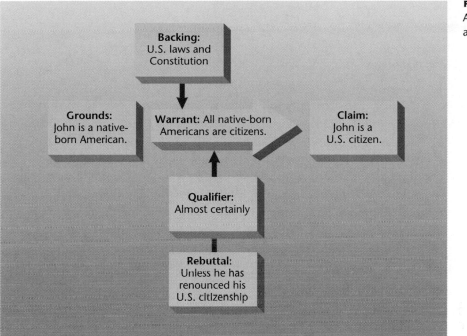

FIGURE 14.5
Argument Applying
a Generalization

Figure 14.5 illustrates an argument that applies a generalization. In this case, we know that the generalization *warrant*, all native-born Americans are citizens, is true because of the *backing* found in the U.S. laws and Constitution. Given the *grounds* that John is a native-born American, we can be almost certain (*qualifier*) that the *claim*, John is a U.S. citizen, is true. There is a possible *rebuttal*, however; the claim is true unless he has renounced his citizenship.

Stereotyping   The most common fallacy associated with warrants that apply established generalizations to specific instances is known as **stereotyping.** This fallacy assumes that what is considered to be true of a larger class is necessarily true of particular members of that class. Thus, although it may be true that professional basketball players are generally tall, you would be wrong to assume that Mugsy Bogues is tall just because he plays in the NBA. When you hear people talk about all people of any given race or group being the same, you can be fairly sure that the speakers are guilty of the stereotyping fallacy. "Everybody on welfare is lazy," "All college students are liberals," and "All politicians are crooks" are examples of stereotyping.

We must be cautious about applying generalizations. One of the authors recalls a lecture in which he was discussing the impact of proposed tuition increases on minority students. He argued that such students would be disproportionately hurt by the increased fees. After the class, he was approached by an African American student who pointed out that not all minority students are from poor families and not all poor students are from minority groups. Indeed, the student was right. There is always a danger in dealing with generalizations that one will stereotype a whole group when there are notable exceptions to such generalizations.

Not all NBA players fit the stereotype of being tall, as Mugsy Bogues (Golden State Warriors) proves.

False Dilemma   Another common fallacy associated with applying generalizations is the **false dilemma,** a generalization that implies there are only two choices when there are more than two. "America, love it or leave it," was a common false dilemma during the protests of the 1960s. Those who responded "America, change it or lose it" were probably just as guilty of either-or thinking. Thus, a true dilemma requires proof that there really are only two choices. Consider the following telephone call to a newspaper.

They should fight child abuse
I'd like to talk to the pro-lifers about abortion. They want to stop abortion so bad and they take their time to do it. Why don't they take the same painstaking time to help fight children being killed by dads and moms when they get a very light sentence?[5]

Of course, one can be both pro-life (or anti-abortion) and against children being killed by their parents. The key to a real dilemma is that there are in fact only two choices and that they are mutually exclusive. In this case, one could support both of these values without contradiction, and thus no real dilemma exists.

Comparison (Analogy) Warrants

An argument based on a **comparison (analogy) warrant** claims that two cases that are similar in some known respects are also similar in some unknown respects. These arguments are called comparisons or, more commonly, analogies. They are subject to tests of literalness versus figurativeness, similarity, and relevance.

Questions to Ask When Evaluating Comparisons or Analogies

Tips and Tactics

- **Are only literal analogies used for proof?**
- **Do the similarities outweigh the differences?**
- **Are the similarities more relevant than the differences to the claim being made?**

Let's begin with the difference between literal and figurative analogies. A *literal analogy* claims that two different instances are really similar. For example, prior to the 1991 war in the Persian Gulf, many proponents of using military force compared Saddam Hussein to Adolf Hitler. They argued that if Saddam's occupation of Kuwait was allowed to stand, he would continue to conquer his neighbors and expand his territory, just as Hitler had done in Europe. Opponents of military involvement, on the other hand, often argued that the Gulf War could become another Vietnam War, with the United States bogged down in a faraway foreign land, in a war that would be both unpopular at home and costly in terms of lives and money. Both sides were attempting to provide literal analogies to other wars in order to support their claims that the United States either should or should not fight in the Persian Gulf.

A *figurative analogy*, on the other hand, is a device of language that is used to enhance the persuasiveness of a speech. While a figurative analogy clearly seeks to establish some similarity between the two items being compared, no one could reasonably argue that they are really alike. For example, some people made the comparison of Saddam to a schoolyard bully. If the United States didn't stand up to him, he would be encouraged to become a bigger bully. No one believed, however, that Saddam was just a big bully using his fists to beat up little kids and steal their lunch money. A schoolyard bully might cost you a black eye and your lunch money. Saddam cost human lives and billions of dollars.

Although there is nothing wrong with figurative analogies as a persuasive device, if you rely on them to provide proof for a claim, you are on shaky ground. There is no logical force to such arguments.

Next, in a good analogy or comparison the similarities should outweigh the differences. If they do not, the analogy will not be very powerful. For example, when comparing Adolf Hitler and Saddam Hussein, there are clearly many similarities. Both were dictators, both engaged in atrocities against their neighbors and their own people, and both invaded neighboring nations. There are also important

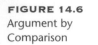

FIGURE 14.6
Argument by
Comparison

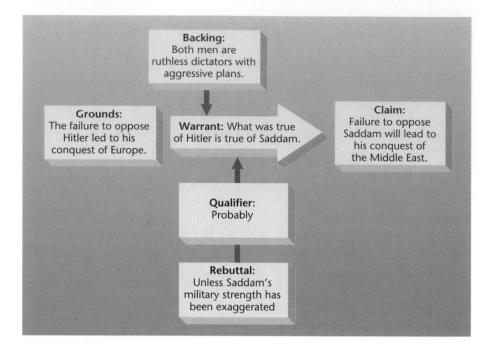

differences. For example, Hitler commanded one of the most powerful military machines in history, whereas Saddam's army proved to be technologically backward. Further, initially there was no united front against Hitler; in fact, the Soviet Union had signed a pact with him. With very few exceptions, there was an array of nations opposing Saddam that was almost unparalleled in recent history.

Finally, the similarities, rather than the differences, should be most relevant to the claim being made. In the comparison of Saddam and Hitler, whereas Hitler and his allies had the military might to make war on the world, Saddam was unable to launch a meaningful attack on even his closest enemy, Israel.

Figure 14.6 shows how the complete argument by comparison might evolve on this topic. Based on *grounds* that the failure to oppose Hitler led to his conquest of Europe, and using the *warrant* that what was true of Hitler is true of Saddam, probably (*qualifier*) the *claim* that the failure to oppose Saddam will lead to his conquest of the Middle East is true. *Backing* for the warrant comes from the common traits that both men are ruthless dictators with aggressive plans. The claim is true unless (*rebuttal*) Saddam's military strength has been exaggerated.

False Analogy   The most common fallacy associated with comparison warrants is the **false analogy.** This occurs when two things that are not really comparable are compared as if they were essentially the same. For example, we recall a letter written to a newspaper by a reader angered with newly enacted laws requiring motorcyclists to wear helmets. This reader complained that the legislature had become another Saddam Hussein, acting like a dictator in passing a mandatory helmet law.

FIGURE 14.7
Reasoning From
Cause to Effect

Of course, the differences in these two situations are dramatic. The legislature is an elected body. The law was passed based on safety concerns and is not unlike laws requiring motorists to wear seat belts. The key to the analogy is whether the legislature and Saddam are both dictators. In the case of Iraq, the people have no way, short of a coup or revolution, to remove the offending person, whereas the voters have an opportunity every two years to "throw the bums out."

Causal Warrants

Frequently we seek to determine either what has caused something or what effect a particular action will have. An argument based on a **causal warrant** claims that a cause will produce or has produced an effect. We can reason either from cause to effect or from effect to cause.

Reasoning from *cause to effect* involves predicting what will happen if some action is taken. For example, in recent years the ozone layer that protects the earth has developed "holes," or thin spots. Based on this fact, some experts predict that there will be many more deaths from skin cancer than if the ozone layer had not developed holes. Clearly this reasoning process moves from a cause (depletion of the ozone layer) to a predicted effect (skin cancer deaths) (Figure 14.7). Based on the *grounds* that the ozone hole allows more UV radiation to enter the atmosphere and using the *warrant*, UV radiation causes skin cancer, which has *backing* from scientific studies, most likely (*qualifier*) the *claim* is true that skin cancer death rates

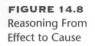

FIGURE 14.8
Reasoning From
Effect to Cause

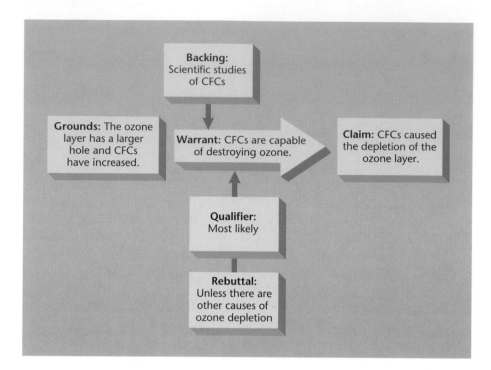

will increase, unless (*rebuttal*) people wear sunscreen and reduce their exposure to UV radiation.

On the other hand, one might ask why the ozone layer has been depleted. According to some experts, chlorine-containing chemicals, called CFCs (chlorofluorocarbons), are the principal culprit in destroying the ozone. These chemicals are found in auto air conditioners, refrigerators, and the like. In this instance, one is reasoning from *effect* (depletion of the ozone layer) *to cause* (CFCs) (Figure 14.8). This argument shows that based on the *grounds* that the ozone layer has a larger hole and CFCs have increased, using the *warrant* that CFCs are capable of destroying ozone, which has *backing* from scientific studies, most likely (*qualifier*) the *claim* is true that CFCs caused the depletion of the ozone layer, unless (*rebuttal*) there are other causes of ozone depletion.

Causal warrants are subject to tests of relatedness, other causes, other effects, and mistaking order in time for causality.

Tips and Tactics

Questions to Ask When Evaluating Causal Reasoning

- Is the cause related to the alleged effect?
- Are there other causes of the effect?
- Are there other effects from the same cause?
- Has time sequence been mistaken for cause (post hoc fallacy)?

Let's apply these tests to the argument about CFCs and the depletion of the ozone layer. First, is the depletion *related* to CFCs? Based on a considerable body of scientific study, this connection seems well established. Further, is the ozone depletion *related* to the increase in skin cancer? Again, scientific studies have established that ultraviolet radiation is a cause of skin cancer and that the ozone layer screens out ultraviolet radiation from the sun.

Are there *other causes* of the effect? Although CFCs cause ozone depletion, there are other causes as well. For example, the exhaust from shuttle rockets contributes to the breakdown of the ozone layer. Although this may not be the major cause of the problem, it means that eliminating CFCs alone may not be enough to end the problem.

How about *other effects* from the same cause? If CFCs are banned immediately, we may lose many of their benefits, such as air conditioning. Although some substitutes have been developed, they may not work in existing refrigeration units. So, although banning CFCs might seem like a simple solution, we need to consider other effects such a ban would cause.

Finally, we must be careful not to assume a causal relationship just because two events occur one after the other in *time*. We recall a letter to a local newspaper that attributed the end of the California drought to the prayers of particular ministers in a small foothill community. Although it is true that the ministers prayed and the rains came, that does not mean one event caused the other. Similarly, although skin cancer death rates are rising as the ozone is decreasing, that does not prove, in and of itself, that the ozone depletion is causing the death rates from skin cancer to rise. It might be the case, for example, that people are spending more time in the sun than they once did. One should always be particularly suspicious of claims of cause and effect based solely on time sequence.

Although the preceding discussion may suggest that causal arguments are difficult to make, they can, nevertheless, be successfully and persuasively made. For example, there is considerable scientific evidence to support the effects of tobacco on health, and few independent scientists dispute the harmfulness of the product. A speaker relying on such experts and scientific studies would be on solid ground. Often a speaker is best advised to make causal arguments when they can be buttressed by expert testimony and scientific studies, and clearly meet tests of relatedness, other causes and effects, and time order as outlined in this chapter.

Post Hoc   Warrants dealing with effect-to-cause reasoning frequently commit the fallacy of assuming that because one event preceded another, the first event must be the cause of the second event. Technically, this is known as the post hoc, **ergo propter hoc** fallacy ("after the fact, therefore because of the fact"). Cassidy argues that the passage of tough laws to punish those who use guns illegally has worked. "As a result of such measures, violent crimes with firearms, like assault and robbery, have stabilized or are actually declining." Of course, just because such laws were passed and crime stabilized or declined does not mean one event caused the other. For example, many demographers attribute the recent decline in violent crime to the fact that there are relatively fewer people in the most crime-prone age group (late teens to early 20s). This is a result of the delay of baby boomers in starting families until they reached their late 20s or early 30s. As these children begin to enter adolescence, some demographers predict that we will see crime once again rise. Just because one event—gun laws—was followed by another—reduced crime—in no way proves that the first event caused the other.

Slippery Slope   Warrants that reason from cause to effect are susceptible to the **slippery slope fallacy.** This fallacy involves assuming that just because one event occurs, it will automatically lead to a series of undesirable events, like a row of dominoes falling down automatically once you knock over the first one. In common language, this fallacy is sometimes expressed, "If you give them an inch, they'll take a mile."

How many times have you heard someone argue that allowing abortions will lead to infanticide? Or perhaps you've been told that if you don't get a college degree, you will end up homeless and broke. The slippery slope fallacy occurs when you assume that a series of events will result from one action without there being a relationship between the action and the projected events. Nevertheless, it is not necessarily a slippery slope to argue that one action will follow another if the relationship can be clearly demonstrated. For example, it can be mathematically demonstrated that to continue to charge items on a credit card without paying any more than the minimum monthly payment will lead to deeper and deeper debt. And, of course, the judicial system relies heavily on the role of precedents in making decisions. Much of the debate at the impeachment trial of President Clinton revolved around what precedents a vote for impeachment might set. So future effects are important, if they can be clearly shown by sound reasoning.

Sign Warrants

Perhaps you've heard someone say, "It's going to rain. I can feel it in my bones." Or you've read a newspaper article stating that the economy is in a recession, because the latest "leading economic indicators" are pointing downward. These are examples of reasoning from sign. A **sign warrant** is reasoning in which the presence of an observed phenomenon is used to indicate the presence of an unobserved phenomenon.

In sign reasoning, the warrant asserts that the grounds provide a reliable sign that the claim is true. Some signs are infallible; most are merely probable. The absence of brain waves is considered legally as an infallible sign of death. On the other hand, no one would claim that the rise or fall of stock prices is even close to an infallible sign of the state of the economy. Sign warrants are subject to tests of reliability and conflicting signs.

Tips and Tactics

Questions to Ask When Evaluating Sign Reasoning

- **Are the signs reliable indicators of the claim?**
- **Are there conflicting signs?**

FIGURE 14.9
Sign Reasoning

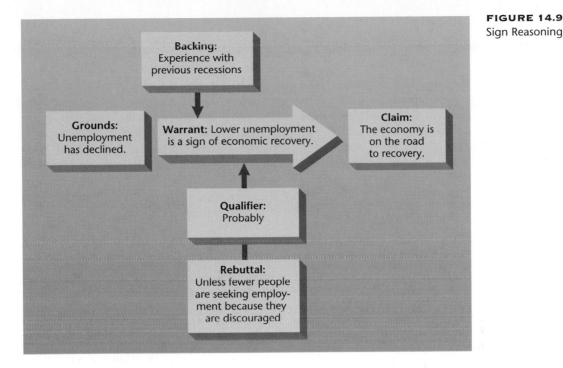

A detective examines a crime scene for signs of forced entry, struggle, and the like. Anyone who is a fan of Sherlock Holmes will recall that he often made a case based on the most obscure signs. One small sign would point him to the guilty subject every time.

Unfortunately, in real life, such reliable signs are harder to find. In testing sign reasoning, ask how reliable such signs have been in the past. For example, economists often make predictions about the future of the economy based on figures for unemployment, housing starts, and so on. A careful examination of their track record in making such predictions will suggest just how much confidence you should have in their reasoning.

The second test is to look for conflicting signs. Whereas one economist may point to decreased unemployment as a sign of economic upturn, another may conclude that there are fewer unemployed because the economy is so bad many workers have given up seeking jobs.

Unless a sign is infallible, most sign reasoning at best indicates the probability that a claim is true. For example, Figure 14.9 represents the argument about lower unemployment and the future of the economy. Based on the *grounds* that unemployment has declined, using the *warrant* that lower unemployment is a sign of economic recovery, based on the *backing* of experience with previous recessions, probably (*qualifier*) the *claim* is true that the economy is on the road to recovery, unless (*rebuttal*) fewer people are seeking employment because they are discouraged.

Mistaking Correlation for Cause   The most common fallacy associated with sign reasoning is **mistaking correlation for cause.** A correlation simply means two things occur in conjunction with each other, without regard to their cause. How often have you heard someone claim that one event caused another, just because they occurred in tandem? Historically, when the stock market was on the rise, so were women's hemlines. Although one may be a "sign" of the other, it is ludicrous to assume the stock market caused the hemlines to go up or vice versa. Just because one event signifies another does not mean they are causally related. For example, a recent news report noted that there is a higher-than-normal incidence of heart disease among bald men. However, this does not prove that baldness causes heart disease or that wearing a toupee will reduce the risk of heart attack. Although the two factors are correlated, the most likely explanation is that common underlying factors cause both baldness and heart disease.

Authority Warrants

Sometimes the link between grounds and claim comes from the authoritativeness of the source of the grounds. An **authority warrant** is used in reasoning in which the claim is believed because of the authority of the source. Recall from Chapter 13 that many people respond almost unthinkingly to authority figures. This is not reasoning, but an unthinking response. Just because Vanessa Williams drinks milk, for example, does not mean that every milk drinker is a potential Miss America. On the other hand, when an argument relies on the expertise of a respected authority, that can be a valid reason for acting. For example, if your doctor tells you that you need to lose weight, you are likely to trust her judgment and at least *try* to shed the unwanted pounds. The key to an authoritative argument is that the person is truly an expert in the area of concern. Further, it is important that the authority is relying on correct information. If your doctor is given the wrong test results, no matter how knowledgeable or reliable she is, her conclusions are suspect.

Authority warrants are subject to tests of whether the authority is truly an expert and whether the authority has accurate information.

Questions to Ask When Evaluating Authority Warrants

- **Is the authority truly an expert in the area under discussion?**
- **Is the authority acting on reliable information?**

An example of an argument from an authority warrant is found in Figure 14.10. Based on the *grounds* that your doctor tells you to lose weight, using the *warrant* that you have confidence in the doctor's expertise, based on the *backing* of training in medical school and years of experience, almost certainly (*qualifier*) the *claim* is true that I should lose weight, unless (*rebuttal*) I can't afford a weight-loss plan and I am unable to lose weight on my own.

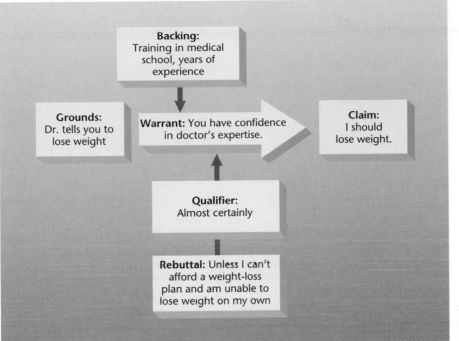

FIGURE 14.10
Argument Using an
Authoritative Warrant

Halo Effect One common fallacy associated with reasoning based on an authority warrant is called the **halo effect.** Just because you like or respect a person, you tend to believe whatever he or she says. Millions of people, for example, listen to radio talk-show host Rush Limbaugh. However, Limbaugh has apparently misstated a number of "facts," according to a recent report by the media watchdog group FAIR (Fairness and Accuracy in Reporting). For example, Limbaugh claimed that "if 4,000 votes . . . had gone the other way in Chicago—Richard Nixon would have been elected in 1960."[6] Yet FAIR points out that Kennedy won by a greater margin than all of Illinois's electoral votes, and thus the results in Chicago could not have changed the outcome of the election. And FAIR cites Limbaugh as ignoring the overwhelming medical evidence to the contrary when he stated, "It has not been proven that nicotine is addictive."[7]

However, not every Limbaugh listener accepts everything he says. It is a common misconception (one which we shared when writing the previous edition of this book) that "dittoheads," who call in to his show and say, "Mega dittos, Rush," mean that whatever he says, they believe. Actually, what "mega dittos" means is something far different, as explained in the nearby box "Speaking of . . . Dittoheads," which reprints an e-mail the authors received from one of the students using the previous edition of the book.

Ad Hominem The reverse of the halo effect is called argument **ad hominem,** meaning an argument "against the person." This fallacy says a claim must be false

Dittoheads

As we were in the process of revising this text, we received an e-mail from a student who was more expert on Rush Limbaugh than we were. So, in fairness to all the "dittoheads" out there, we are reprinting an excerpt from his e-mail. After noting that we had characterized Rush Limbaugh listeners as uncritically believing everything Rush said because when they called the show, they would say "mega dittos, Rush," Vance Lassey, a senior at the University of Kansas, pointed out our own fallacy:

I grew up on the seat of an International Harvester tractor . . . that . . . had only an AM radio, so I was stuck listening to talk radio or oldies, and sometimes oldies got . . . well, old. So . . . I was witness to the birth of the term "dittohead" and the use of the term "ditto" in his program.

The reason that his callers say "ditto" or "megadittos" is . . . to say basically, "I love your show, keep up the good work." Back in the 80's when his show was not syndicated all over the place, more and more people were catching on each day. Each time one of them got through to talk with him, they'd say stuff like "I love your show, you're the voice of America, I wish more people knew about you, blah blah blah" and it got really really repetitive—so finally, somebody got the idea to say "ditto." . . .

So, apologies to all the dittoheads out there. Just because you say "mega dittos, Rush" doesn't mean your critical thinking skills are suspended. Rather, it's just a time-saving way to say you love the show. And thanks to Vance for setting us straight.

because the person who said it is not credible, regardless of the argument itself. This should be distinguished from legitimate questions about the truthfulness or character of a source of evidence. Clearly, an admitted perjurer is not a reliable source of evidence in a civil or criminal trial. The ad hominem fallacy applies when the attack on character is not directly related to legitimate concerns about a person's reliability as a source of evidence, but is substituted for a rational consideration of the person's argument.

Ad hominem is often associated with name-calling. Name-calling occurs when a person or group of people are characterized by a term that is loaded with negative connotations. When a political candidate is characterized as a "bozo," "womanizer," or "wimp," these terms raise emotional feelings without providing rational grounds for rejecting the candidate. The use of negative terms for ethnic, religious, racial, and sexual groups is also a type of name-calling. Consider, for example, the use of terms such as "chick," "tomato," or "bimbo" to characterize a woman or terms such as "jock," "stud," or "hunk" to refer to a man. Sexist, racist, and bigoted language is an insidious form of name-calling that degrades entire groups of people. Just because you do not like someone or someone is called a derogatory name does not mean their arguments should be rejected out of hand. It is just as bad to reject everything Rush Limbaugh says as false as it is to assume everything he says is gospel.

FALLACIES ASSOCIATED WITH QUALIFIERS

Toulmin believes that arguers should qualify their claims. As we pointed out earlier in this chapter, a qualifier is an indication of the level of probability of a claim. Some arguments are virtually certain to be true, whereas others have a much lower degree of certainty. Depending on the nature of the argument, a qualifier can make a big difference. For example, in a criminal trial, the claim that the defendant is guilty must be true "beyond a reasonable doubt," a phrase that acts as the qualifier of the argument for guilt. Thus, a very high degree of certainty is required before a jury can convict someone of a criminal offense. On the other hand, in a civil case, the standard is "a preponderance of evidence." Thus, if it is more likely than not that the defendant wronged the plaintiff, the judgment should go to the plaintiff. That is why someone found not guilty in a criminal trial can still be sued in civil court. The level of proof that is required is different.

So, too, in your argumentation, you need to know what level of proof your audience will expect. Thus, as with virtually every other aspect of public speaking, the success of your reasoning depends on careful analysis of your audience. As a listener, you should also be clear about what level of proof you need before accepting a claim. Many of the fallacies of reasoning associated with qualifiers are a result of overstating or distorting the degree of certainty with which the arguer has supported his or her claim. Two common fallacies are the use of loaded language and hyperbole.

Loaded Language

Language that has strong emotional connotations is termed **loaded language.** Depending on the specific characteristics of your audience, what you might consider neutral language may in fact carry strong emotional connotations. Notice how Cassidy uses terms such as "antigun evangelism" and "gun prohibitionists" to characterize his opponents. Terms like evangelism and prohibition are "loaded" with connotations of extremism and closed-mindedness, thus overstating the claim against people who seek regulation, rather than outlawing, of guns.

Of course, effective persuasion often requires vivid, intense, and expressive language, as we discussed in Chapter 9. There is a fine but important line between language that is necessarily vivid and language that is so "loaded" that it distorts the reasoning being presented. There is no hard-and-fast rule that can be applied here. Speakers and listeners need to exercise their judgment in evaluating the use of language.

Hyperbole

Hyperbole is an exaggeration of a claim. Rather than properly qualifying or limiting the impact of a statement, the person engaged in hyperbole exaggerates the claim in question. Those who oppose Sarah Brady, for example, might well consider her use of the term "epidemic" as an exaggeration of the problem of gun violence. Other examples of hyperbole include the use of such terms as "superstar," "greatest ever," and "mega-hit." It often seems as if it is not enough any more to be a star, to be great, or to have a mere hit. Hyperbole ends up cheapening the currency of our language, inflating claims and devaluing more moderate language.

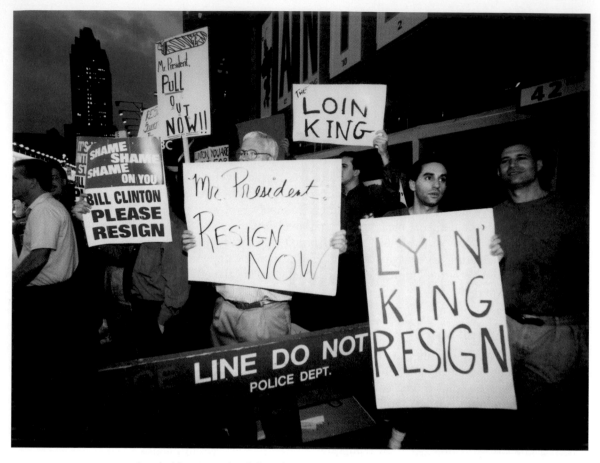

Loaded language is a fallacy because it inflames passions rather than appealing to reasoning.

FALLACIES ASSOCIATED WITH REBUTTALS

The rebuttal to an argument is an exception to or refutation of an argument. It too can be flawed. Fallacies of rebuttal can occur when a speaker misanalyzes an opponent's argument or sidesteps the other side of the issue completely.

Straw Person

The **straw person** fallacy occurs when someone attempts to refute a claim by misstating the argument being refuted. Rather than refuting the real argument, the other side constructs a person of straw, which is easy to knock down.

Sarah Brady favored a seven-day waiting period for the purchase of a handgun. J. Warren Cassidy's argument is based on defending "the right to keep and bear arms." But Brady never argued that there was no such right or that it should be abolished. She favored regulation, not "prohibition," of gun ownership. Thus, Cassidy's rebuttal attacks an argument that was never made. Be wary of rebuttals that seem too easy. It may be that the other side of the argument has been misstated just to make it easy to refute.

Ignoring the Issue

The fallacy of **ignoring the issue** occurs when the claim made by one side in an argument is ignored by the other. For example, imagine that you are speaking before a group about the effects of the depletion of the ozone layer on the environment. Skin cancer death rates will increase, you argue. We need to change over to safer refrigerants in our cars. Suppose someone attempts to rebut your argument by saying that the government has grown too big and bureaucratic and that it is time to get rid of government waste. This rebuttal is simply not responsive to the argument you have posed. In short, the issue you have presented has been ignored, and the rebuttalist has shifted ground to another issue entirely.

THE NON SEQUITUR: AN ARGUMENT THAT DOES NOT FOLLOW

Up until now, we've looked at each component of an argument as a separate source of fallacies. Of course, you also have to look at the argument as a whole. Even if the grounds are true, the warrant believable, and so on, if the argument doesn't hang together logically, it is still fallacious. Thus, the final fallacy of reasoning we examine is the non sequitur.

A **non sequitur** is an argument that does not follow from its premises. In Toulmin's terms, there is no logical connection between the claim and the grounds and warrant used to support the claim. Consider the example of a person who called in this opinion to a local newspaper:

> **No wonder welfare is so popular**
> I'd like to thank the person who dropped the two little black lab-mix puppies off at the golf course some time in the week of Jan. 28. What irresponsible person caused others to try to find homes for these dogs? It's amazing people don't take responsibility for their actions and cause other people to. No wonder everybody's on welfare.[8]

Aside from stereotyping people on welfare as irresponsible and hyperbolizing in claiming that "everybody's on welfare," this argument has absolutely no link between its grounds—the two dogs abandoned at the golf course—and its claim—that this irresponsibility is symptomatic of people on welfare.

We have discussed numerous fallacies in this chapter. To review them, see the box "Defects of Reasoning: The Fallacies."

Defects of Reasoning: The Fallacies

FALLACIES ASSOCIATED WITH GROUNDS

unsupported assertion: The absence of any argument at all.

distorted evidence: Significant omissions or changes in the grounds of an argument that alter its original intent.

isolated examples: Nontypical or nonrepresentative examples that are used to prove a general claim.

misused statistics: Statistics that involve errors such as poor sampling, lack of significant differences, misuse of average, or misuse of percentages.

FALLACIES ASSOCIATED WITH CLAIMS

red herring (smoke screen): An irrelevant issue introduced into a controversy to divert attention from the real controversy.

arguing in a circle (begging the question): An argument that proves nothing because the claim to be proved is used as the grounds or warrant for the argument.

FALLACIES ASSOCIATED WITH GENERALIZATION WARRANTS

hasty generalization: An argument that occurs when there are too few instances to support a generalization or the instances are unrepresentative of the generalization.

stereotyping: The assumption that what is considered to be true of a larger class is necessarily true of particular members of that class.

false dilemma: A generalization that implies there are only two choices when there are more than two.

FALLACY ASSOCIATED WITH COMPARISON (ANALOGY) WARRANTS

false analogy: The comparison of two different things that are not really comparable.

FALLACIES ASSOCIATED WITH CAUSAL WARRANTS

post hoc, ergo propter hoc ("after the fact, therefore because of the fact"): The assumption that because one

event preceded another, the first event must be the cause of the second event.

slippery slope: The assumption that just because one event occurs, it will automatically lead to a series of undesirable events even though there is no relationship between the action and the projected events.

FALLACY ASSOCIATED WITH SIGN WARRANTS

mistaking correlation for cause: The assumption that because one thing is the sign of another, they are causally related.

FALLACIES ASSOCIATED WITH AUTHORITY WARRANTS

halo effect: The assumption that just because you like or respect a person, whatever he or she says must be true.

ad hominem: The claim that something must be false because the person who said it is not credible, regardless of the argument itself.

FALLACIES ASSOCIATED WITH QUALIFIERS

loaded language: Language that has strong emotional connotations.

hyperbole: An exaggeration of a claim.

FALLACIES ASSOCIATED WITH REBUTTALS

straw person: An argument made in refutation that misstates the argument being refuted. Rather than refuting the real argument, the other side constructs a person of straw, which is easy to knock down.

ignoring the issue: An argument made in refutation that ignores the claim made by the other side.

ADDITIONAL FALLACY

non sequitur: An argument that does not follow from its premises.

SUMMARY

Reasoning and *critical thinking* are important both in constructing good arguments and in listening to the arguments of others. *Pseudoreasoning* involves arguments that may appear sound at first glance but ultimately contain a *fallacy* of reasoning. *Argumentativeness* is the trait of arguing for and against the positions taken on controversial claims. *Verbal aggressiveness* is the trait of attacking the self-concept of those with whom a person disagrees about controversial claims.

Grounds for an argument consist of evidence supporting a claim, such as examples, facts, statistics, expert opinion, explanation, description, and narratives. There are a number of sources of fallacious grounds, including unsupported assertions, distorted evidence, isolated examples, and misused statistics.

Claims may be of fact, value, or policy. Examples of fallacies associated with claims are the red herring (or smoke screen) and arguing in a circle (begging the question), when a claim is used to prove itself.

Warrants link grounds and claims by means of generalization, comparison, cause, sign, and authority. *Backing* is support for the warrant and is especially important in cases in which the audience is either unfamiliar with the warrant or unconvinced of its truth. Each type of argument is subject to special tests of reasoning.

Sources of defective *generalization warrants* include hasty generalization, stereotyping, and false dilemmas. A common source of defective *comparison warrants* is the false analogy. Defective *causation warrants* may occur due to the post hoc, ergo propter hoc and the slippery slope fallacies. A common source of defective *sign warrants* is mistaking correlation for cause. Common fallacies associated with *authority warrants* are the halo effect and the ad hominem fallacy.

Qualifiers are an indication of the level of probability of the claim. In using qualifiers, you should avoid fallacies such as loaded language and hyperbole. A *rebuttal* is an exception or refutation of an argument. A misguided rebuttal occurs when the argument refuted is not the real argument presented, but merely a straw person which is easy to knock down, or the issue is ignored. Finally, the non sequitur is an argument that does not follow from its premises.

Check Your Understanding: Exercises and Activities

1. Find a published argument, such as a letter to the editor, an advertisement, an editorial, or a political ad. Identify the claim being made and the grounds on which the claim is based. Is the warrant explicitly stated? If not, determine the implied warrant. What backing, if any, is offered for the warrant? Is the argument adequately qualified? Are there possible rebuttals to the argument?

2. Find an example of each of the following types of arguments in a publication: cause to effect, effect to cause, sign, comparison, establishing a generalization, applying a generalization, authority. Which of these arguments is the strongest, logically, and which is the weakest? Explain your answer in terms of the tests of reasoning outlined in this chapter.

3. Pick an advertisement from any print medium—for example, magazines, newspapers, or direct mail. In a brief paper, identify at least three fallacies used in the advertisement. Define each fallacy in your own words. Cite the specific example of each fallacy from the ad, and explain why the example meets the definition. Finally, highlight the fallacies on a copy of the ad and attach the copy to your paper.

4. Analyze the arguments for and against gun control as presented by Sarah Brady and J. Warren Cassidy in this chapter. Which argument is logically the strongest? Which contains the most fallacies? Which do you find most persuasive?

Notes

1. Brooke Noel Moore and Richard Parker, *Critical Thinking*, 5th ed. (Mountain View, Calif.: Mayfield, 1998), 476.

2. Dominic A. Infante, *Arguing Constructively* (Prospect Heights, Ill.: Waveland Press, 1988).

3. Stephen Toulmin, Richard Rieke, and Allan Janik, *An Introduction to Reasoning*, 2nd ed. (New York: Macmillan, 1984).

4. Toulmin originally termed this the *qualifier* but added the term *modality* in his later works. We prefer the simpler term, *qualifier*, which is what we will use in this book.

5. "Tell It to the ER," *Chico Enterprise Record*, 13 March 1992, 2A. Reprinted by permission.

6. "Facts and Fantasy," *Newsweek*, 11 July 1994, 6.

7. "Facts and Fantasy," 6.

8. "Tell It to the ER," *Chico Enterprise Record*, 16 February 1992, 2A. Reprinted by permission.

Answers to "Self-Assessment: Uncritical Inference Test," pages 386–387

1. ? Do you know that the "businessman" and the "owner" are one and the same?

2. ? Was there necessarily a robbery involved here? Perhaps the man was the rent collector—or the owner's son. Either might demand money.

3. F An easy one to keep up the test-taker's morale.

4. ? Was the owner a man?

5. ? May seem unlikely, but the story does not definitely preclude it.

6. T   The story says that the owner opened the cash register.

7. ?   We don't know who scooped up the contents of the cash register or that the man necessarily ran away.

8. ?   The dependent clause is doubtful—the cash register may or may not have contained money.

9. ?   Again, a robber?

10. ?   Could the man merely have appeared at a door or a window without actually entering the store?

11. ?   Stores generally keep lights on during the day.

12. ?   Could not the man who appeared have been the owner?

13. F   The story says that the man who appeared demanded money.

14. ?   Are the businessman and the owner one and the same—or two different people? The same goes for the owner and the man who appeared.

15. ?   "Dashed"? Could he not have "sped away" on roller skates or in a car? And do we know that he actually left the store? We don't even know that he entered it.

CHAPTER 15

A wedding toast is a common public speaking event that almost everyone faces at some time.

More Everyday Speaking

OBJECTIVES

After reading this chapter, you should be able to:

- Make an effective impromptu presentation.
- Lead or participate in a small group and a panel discussion.
- Present a speech of introduction.
- Present or accept an award.
- Make a speech of commemoration.
- Make a speech to entertain.
- Be interviewed on television.

KEY CONCEPTS

agenda	speech of acceptance
eulogy	speech of commemoration
group	speech of introduction
panel discussion	speech of recognition
reframing	speech to entertain

You've been giving your attention to a turkey stuffed with sage; you are now about to consider a sage stuffed with turkey.

—WILLIAM MAXWELL EVARTS (1818–1901), American statesman, speaking after a Thanksgiving dinner[1]

The Wedding Toast

Here are some tips offered by the Korbel Wedding Toast Hotline for nervous toasters:

1. Remember why you are being asked to give the toast.
2. Make sure your toast is something everyone can relate to.
3. Jokes, humor, and anecdotes are great ways to enliven a toast.
4. Try to know your material well enough so that you do not need your notecards.
5. Speak loudly enough so everyone can hear you.
6. Make your toast with your own personal style.
7. Remember, people will not be judging you as they might if you were giving a business presentation.
8. Toasts should be kept short and sweet.
9. When preparing your toast, sometimes it helps to look though old photographs or letters.
10. When delivering a wedding toast, make sure to stand and indicate the couple you are toasting.

Source: Adapted from Korbel Wedding Toast Hotline Web site, http://korbel.com/trade.html#source.

In Chapter 3 we mentioned that approximately 40 percent of all adults report that their greatest fear is giving a public speech. Perhaps it is not too surprising to learn, then, that fully 97 percent of Americans fear presenting a wedding toast! The reasons offered by the people surveyed include but are not limited to: (1) forgetting what to say, (2) being too emotional, (3) being boring, and (4) unintentionally saying something that is perceived as offensive. In response to this survey, Korbel Champagne Cellars, a California winery, has established a hot line for people to call to learn tips about the do's and don'ts of wedding toasting (see the box "The Wedding Toast"). In its first three years of operation the hotline has received 22,000 calls.[2]

This chapter focuses on both the predictable and occasionally special situations in which you will be required to speak over the course of your everyday life. These situations include impromptu speaking, sometimes leading group discussions, participating on informative panel discussions, saying thank you when you've been singled out for recognition, introducing someone who is being honored or who is the principal speaker of the occasion, and speaking to commemorate an occasion of celebration or solemnity. We begin by talking about reframing your perspective about speaking in situations both everyday and special.

REFRAMING: SPEAKING AS STORYTELLING

The late Senator Robert F. Kennedy was fond of paraphrasing Irish playwright George Bernard Shaw by saying, "Some people see things as they are and say: why? I dream things that never were and say: why not?"[3] This familiar quotation eloquently alludes to the importance of perspective in analyzing and responding to circumstance. This kind of behavior can be thought of in terms of **reframing**—revising your view of a situation or an event. Recall that the degree to which you are anxious about a speaking transaction depends on how you view it. As we said early on in this book, looking at a speech as a performance is likely to make you more anxious than looking at a speech as a natural but refined extension of your everyday communication skills.

One effective way to reframe your point of view about the kind of speaking this chapter describes is to think of it as a form of storytelling. Although you probably gave few "speeches" prior to taking this class, chances are good that you told innumerable stories. Good stories share a similar organizational sequence with good speeches. An involving story hooks an audience with its introduction, builds to a climax either humorous or dramatic, and concludes with a memorable resolution to the climax.

Rhetorical scholar Walter R. Fisher argues that storytelling is not only an effective way to involve an audience but also an effective way to share a message.[4] Former President Ronald Reagan frequently conveyed the point he was attempting to make through storytelling. Many pundits in the media, moreover, attribute much of his reputation as an effective communicator to his ability to weave an involving and convincing story.[5]

Storytelling needn't be long-winded nor overly complicated. To the contrary, many of the best stories are short and to the point. Effective stories or narratives share two common elements, as we first discussed in Chapter 7: *probability* and *fidelity*.

Probability

The property of storytelling termed probability is straightforward. Narrative probability is the internal coherence of the story. Coherence concerns the degree to which the structure of the story holds up in the eyes of an audience. Does the story make sense as told? Do the parts of the story hang together? Effective stories are logically consistent in structure, even if the content of the story requires that we suspend disbelief, as is the case with fairy tales and some science fiction. Did you know that Mark Twain, for example, was a gifted public speaker as well as writer? He could tell even the most improbable story in such a way that what he was suggesting seemed completely plausible. What's more, this was true whether he was talking about the exaggerated athleticism of a jumping frog in the gold fields of California or transporting a Connecticut man back into the time of King Arthur's court.

Fidelity

The second property of effective storytelling—fidelity—concerns truthfulness. We are predisposed to believe stories whose messages ring true with our own experience. Depending on the occasion, you probably share a lot in common with your audience, from being friends of the bride and groom at a wedding to sharing the sorrow of family members when giving a eulogy. You can draw on these commonalities to increase the narrative fidelity of your stories, whether they grow out of your individual experience or experiences with which most of your audience can relate.

It can be helpful to approach a speech task such as thanking people or making an introduction as a form of storytelling. Audiences relate well to recognition speeches and the like when they are told as a story. Remember, though, that to be effective your speech and the story it tells must meet the tests of probability and fidelity. This framework sets the stage for preparing to meet head-on the predictable situations in which you will be expected to speak both now and in your future. Because these situations vary tremendously in the degree to which you'll be able to prepare, let's look first at the type of speaking where you'll have little or no time to gather your thoughts and supporting material.

IMPROMPTU SPEECHES: SPEAKING WITHOUT ADVANCE NOTICE

There will be times in your life when you will be asked to speak without specific, advance notice. Recall from Chapter 2 that such unrehearsed speeches are called impromptu. You may be asked to make an unanticipated toast or say a few words at a wedding, bar or bat mitzvah, or christening. Or you may be asked to defend or argue against the position of a colleague at work. Finally, you simply may be asked to explain yourself to a superior or agency to which you are accountable.

First Things First: Anticipate the Occasion

If you read Stephen J. Covey's book *The Seven Habits of Highly Effective People*, you'll learn that being unprepared isn't one of them.[6] Frankly, there are situations where the probability of your being asked to speak ranges from low to high. No one knows better than you the chances that you'll be asked to say a few words at a social occasion or in a professional setting. Forewarned is forearmed. Thus, if there is even the slightest chance you'll be asked to speak, you should prepare in advance. Does this mean that you should write out a speech? Not really. What we are talking about here is anticipating what you might be asked to say based on the context in which you'll find yourself. This will, at the very least, enable you to mentally and visually rehearse your response. Should you not be asked to speak as you'd anticipated, you'll only be better prepared for the next time one of these occasions to speak pops up.

Tips for Impromptu Speaking

If you were to participate in impromptu speaking at a collegiate speech tournament, this is what would typically happen. You would be handed a slip of paper with three topics on it. The topics might be general and abstract, such as the quotation we cited from Robert F. Kennedy, or an issue widely reported in the media. You would be given two minutes to prepare and five minutes to speak on the one topic you selected.

If this sounds frightening, then consider this: There may be times during your life when you don't even get two minutes to prepare, much less choose your topic from a choice of three. To assist you in adapting to such truly impromptu situations, we offer the following guidelines.

Get Organized   The thing that impresses people the most about people who speak effectively off-the-cuff is the appearance of organization. Whether you are responding to the query of an instructor or speaking to an issue being debated at work, the first thing you want to do is get organized. One of the easiest and most effective patterns for organizing an impromptu speech is to (1) introduce the point(s) you want to make, (2) expand on the point(s) you make, (3) and conclude with a statement that summarizes the point(s) made. This harks back to the "tell 'em what you're going to tell 'em, tell 'em, and then tell 'em what you told 'em" sequence introduced in Chapter 8. Consider a classroom example, in which the instructor asks, "What's your take on the effects of rap lyrics on violence?" One student responds: "I have two points to make . . . about the effects of rap. First, the effects are exaggerated. Second, most people who think rap affects violence are clueless about modern music. So what I'm saying is they're making a mountain out of another molehill." Notice in this example that the first sentence not only previews the points being made but also restates in modified form the question asked. The two points are made and then summarized in the final sentence. Compare this response with another hypothetical but not atypical one from a student: "I don't know . . . I guess I disagree. It's just a bunch of people who are out of it coming down on alternative music. Get a life, you know?" This second response is both disorganized and equivocal, bringing us to our second guideline.

Take a Position   Few of us are favorably impressed with people who fail to take a stand, who equivocate even as they're trying to build a response to a query. When someone asks a speaker, "What's your opinion or your position?" we think the speaker is obligated to give it. On the other hand, if a speaker has not yet formulated a clear-cut opinion, an audience would much rather hear the person say "I'm ambivalent" or "I'll need more information than I've been given" than hem and haw in response to such a query.

Use Powerful Language   Powerful language goes hand in hand with the first two guidelines. Organization is key to appearing powerful. We expect powerful people to not equivocate, to take a stand even if it is clearly one of neutrality. For example, sometimes a person may say simply, "That is really none of my business. It is for the people directly affected to decide for themselves." Recall that powerful language avoids the use of unnecessary qualifiers and long questions. Powerful people say such things as "My opinion is firm" or "My experience leads me to the unequivocal belief. . . ." Powerful people do not say, "I could be wrong but I think . . ." or "I believe it's okay, do you?" Impromptu speaking is tough enough without undermining your authority with powerless language.

Hitchhike   It's sometimes effective to begin an impromptu message with what others already have said on the matter. This hitchhiking technique shows that you have been actively listening. It also acknowledges the contributions of others, even if you disagree with what they've said. For example, "Bill's point that this situation demands caution is well taken, but I must respectfully disagree for a couple of reasons." You also might say, "Let me summarize what's been said thus far, and then I'll add my two cents worth." Again, this kind of bridge tells your audience you are tuned in *and* organized.

Use Stories and Anecdotes   If you know a story or an anecdote that contains a lesson that is both relevant and straightforward, by all means use it as a basis for your impromptu speech. History is full of examples of stories and anecdotes about the famous and notorious. Organizational culture, moreover, often gives rise to stories about people and events that can be used to make one or more points in an impromptu speech. Some stories and anecdotes are so general they can be applied to almost any point you choose to make. The real power of Aesop's fables, for instance, is that each contains multiple lessons you can apply to life.

Invest in Reference Works   Impromptu speaking is a matter of when, not if. Thus, we recommend you purchase for your personal and permanent library at least two kinds of reference books, in addition to a standard book of quotations such as *Bartlett's*. First, look for one composed of contemporary quotes from well-known and widely recognized people. At the same time, invest in a book of anecdotes compiled from the lives of the famous and notorious. Then find and commit to memory quotes and anecdotes that can be applied generally to topics and issues you may be asked to speak about. Although these tips are meant to help you most with impromptu speaking situations, they can be easily generalized to everyday situations where you know for certain that you will be speaking, and situations where there is a high probability that you will be speaking.

LEADING AND PARTICIPATING IN SMALL GROUPS

Besides impromptu speaking, you will probably speak in numerous group discussions in both your educational and professional careers. A **group** consists of three or more individuals who are aware of each other's presence, share a mutually interdependent purpose, engage in communication transactions with one another, and identify with the group. As a leader of a group, you also are the chief spokesperson. As such, there are several important functions you will be asked to perform. Although we cannot introduce you to all of these functions here, we want to alert you to those most relevant to the main topic and scope of this book.

Leadership Functions

As you attempt to lead a group, there are a number of functions that you need to perform yourself or delegate to someone in the group: These include but are not limited to developing an agenda, keeping the discussion on track, asking questions to promote discussion, summarizing and transitioning to other points, and setting the agenda for the next meeting.

Developing an Agenda   A group without an agenda is one that will likely floun-der. The **agenda** defines the purpose and direction the group takes, the topics to be covered, and the goals to be achieved. A sound agenda is every bit as impor-tant to a group's success as sound organization is to a speech's success. For exam-ple, suppose you are dealing with the problem of crime on your campus. Each person in the group can be assigned to gather some information prior to the meeting. Then, you might meet with an agenda such as the following:

I. What is the crime rate on our campus? What specific crimes occur and how often?

II. What percentage of crime in our city is committed by college students? What types of crimes are committed against college students?

III. What steps have been taken on campus to reduce crime?

IV. How do our campus crime rates compare with national statistics?

V. What conclusions can we draw? Is crime "under control" on our campus? Do we need to make changes to reduce crime?

VI. Set agenda for next meeting.

Keeping the Discussion on Track   Although "off-topic" discussions can some-times be productive, more often than not they are a diversion from the real is-sues at hand. Particularly disruptive are "ain't it awful" tangents, where everybody in the group shares their complaints—about the task, the boss, or whatever. These complaints may have their place, but they are unlikely to help the group get the job done. Most group members are reluctant to criticize their peers as being off the subject, and it is usually the leader who has to bring the group back on track. A tactful suggestion that "maybe we're straying from the topic" or a question that refocuses the group on the subject is usually enough to get things back on task. Even a little humorous reminder that the group has wan-dered can do wonders.

Asking Questions to Promote Discussion   There are many types of questions a designated leader (or any member, for that matter) can ask. Four of the most im-portant types of questions are questions asking for information, those asking for interpretation, those asking for suggestions, and questions about procedure. A *question of information*, for example, might be to ask, "What is the average crime rate for colleges our size?" Such a question requires a factually based response. A *question of interpretation* might be, "Do students really feel safe on our campus?" This question is not one that can be answered simply by reading off statistics. It calls for group members to form conclusions based on the information they've gathered, as well as to add their own subjective interpretation of the informa-tion. The third type of question, *asking for suggestions*, might be, "What can we do to reduce crime on this campus?" This question calls for ideas from group members aimed at solving a problem the group has identified. Finally, a *proce-dural question* might be asked of the group, "Do we want to brainstorm possible solutions?" This question asks the group if they want to follow a certain proce-dure. All four types of questions are important if a group is to achieve its goals.

To be effective, small groups need leadership and active participation by all members.

Summarizing and Transitioning to Other Points   As we pointed out regarding your speeches, summaries and transitional devices such as signposts are highly functional. At some point it will become apparent that the group is moving in some direction. Although not everyone may agree on every point, as the leader you can try to summarize those points on which everyone agrees, thus defining which issues need further exploration. For example, you might say: "It seems that we all agree that there's a serious crime problem on our campus. Furthermore, it looks like assault and theft are the biggest problems. What we need to figure out is why these problems are getting worse and if there's anything we can do about them. Any ideas?"

Setting the Agenda for the Next Meeting   Assuming the group's task has not been completed, the next action is to agree on time and place and agenda items for the next meeting. Particularly important is making sure members know what their individual responsibilities are prior to the next meeting. One of the great advantages of groups is that tasks can be subdivided. But that only works if everyone does what is agreed upon.

Panel Discussions

A **panel discussion** is an extemporaneous group discussion held for the benefit of an audience. In a panel discussion, as in a speech, it is important that the group have a clear outline of the topics to be covered, and that members are adequately prepared. The advantage of a panel discussion is that it is a blend of preparation and spontaneity. Members should feel free to comment on one another's points, ask questions, and openly discuss points throughout the presentation.

A panel discussion requires a leader to act as the *moderator* of the presentation. The moderator calls on members and keeps the discussion on track. Members who want to comment on another member's statement should wait to be recognized by the moderator. A panel discussion is more formal than a normal private group discussion.

Most panel discussions also provide an opportunity for audience members to ask questions. This can occur as the group moves through its outline or be held as a *forum* period at the end of the panel presentation.

The outline for a panel discussion is similar to that of a speech; however, some modifications need to be made. The following would be an example of a panel discussion outline on the topic of secondhand smoke.

I. Introduction of topic and group members.

II. Is secondhand tobacco smoke harmful?

III. What is being done to limit exposure to secondhand smoke?

IV. What is causing these efforts to fall short?

V. Recommendations for new regulations on smoking in public places.

Ideally, each member should be able to offer comments on each of these topics, rather than having one member prepared on each topic. A panel discussion should be a true discussion, not a series of individual presentations.

SPEAKING ON SPECIAL OCCASIONS

Speaking at special occasions may be less common than speaking in groups, but it is still likely during the course of your life. At such times your job will be to emphasize the special nature of the occasion in thought, word, and deed. Most of the time, you will be able to prepare and practice in advance of such situations. Other times, you may be asked, in impromptu fashion, to "say a few words." The special occasions you can anticipate speaking at over the course of your life include: expressing thanks; introducing a speaker or an honored guest; speaking in recognition of a person, group, or organization; making a commemorative speech; and speaking to entertain people.

Speech of Acceptance

A **speech of acceptance** is a speech expressing thanks for an award or honor. Consider Emma Thompson's speech of acceptance at the 1993 Academy Awards ceremony. She said: "Ladies and gentlemen, I really don't know how to thank the Academy for this [holding the Oscar], but also for this view. It's overwhelming to see so many faces of people who have entertained me all my life. It takes my breath away."[7]

Emma Thompson's brief but eloquent thanks for her best actress Oscar is a model for a gracious speech of acceptance.

In connecting with her audience, Thompson combines the principles of reciprocity and liking to create a favorable impression. Not only does she thank the Academy for the award, but for her view as well. In the process she tells members of the audience they have been giving something to her she can't repay: a life's worth of entertainment. Research shows that we have a tough time not liking people who like us—for example, people who sincerely flatter us. Thompson's thank-you speech, then, is a model you may want to follow in patterning your own. In the span of three sentences it shows that a good speech of acceptance (1) is brief, (2) is genuine, (3) reciprocates for the award or praise given, and (4) attempts to engender liking. This is not to say that all speeches of acceptance must be as brief as this speech. Thompson's thank you at the Golden Globe Awards ceremony the same year was much longer, yet it did not exceed the audience's patience.

Speech of Introduction

A **speech of introduction** is a speech that briefly sets the stage for an upcoming speaker. Speeches of introduction are designed to meet two objectives. The first is to enlist the audience's attention and interest. The second objective is to reinforce or induce audience perceptions of credibility. Perhaps the most unusual speech of introduction we have heard recently was when James Carville and

Mary Matalin, a married couple who represent the liberal and conservative ends of the political spectrum, debated each other at our university. They were supposed to be introduced by a graduate of our university, political consultant Ed Rollins. However, he was unable to attend. So Carville, in what appeared to be an impromptu speech, introduced his own wife and adversary for the evening, praising her as "my best friend, and the best wife any man could have."[8] His introduction set the stage for a spirited and entertaining debate between the oddest of couples in contemporary American politics.

Although you may never introduce your own opponent in a debate, it is likely that at some time you will be called on to introduce a speaker to an audience. Usually, the audience is favorably disposed toward the speaker or they wouldn't be there. However, sometimes a speaker is not well known and needs a buildup of credibility before the speech. In any case, a good way to look at a speech of introduction is to remember the three basic principles of introducing any speech: open with impact, connect with the audience, and focus on the upcoming presentation.

Open With Impact   Your first task as an introducer is to build enthusiasm for the main speaker. A lukewarm or trite introduction is worse than none at all. Thus, look for a way to capture the audience's attention immediately. Sometimes humor, a brief anecdote, or a moving story will fill the bill.

Connect With the Audience   Why should the audience listen to the speaker? What's in it for them? Just as you must connect with the audience in your own speeches, the same is true in a speech of introduction. What special qualifications does the speaker have? Why is the topic of special concern to the audience? Answer these questions in terms the audience can relate to if you want them to be motivated to listen. Focus on the speaker's competence and character. Even if a speaker's credibility is established, you should reinforce the perception by mentioning one or two examples that clearly emphasize competence and character. If the speaker's credibility has yet to be established, mention at least one thing that addresses the speaker's competence on the topic and one that addresses the speaker's good character.

Focus on the Upcoming Presentation   Finally, it is the introducer's task to focus the audience's attention on the upcoming presentation. Make sure you know the speaker's topic, and coordinate your introduction with his or her speech. Nothing is worse than preparing an audience to hear a speech on one topic only to have the speaker announce that the topic has been changed. There are also some general guidelines that you should follow for a speech of introduction.

Guidelines for a Speech of Introduction

- *Be brief.* The audience came to hear the speaker, not the introducer. A 1- or 2-minute introduction is sufficient for most speech situations. For a particularly lengthy or formal speech situation, the introduction might be longer, but in no case should it exceed about 10 percent of the speaker's time (6 minutes out of an hour, for example).

- *Don't steal the speaker's thunder.* Although you want to prepare the audience for what is to come by focusing their attention on the topic, you should not discuss the substance of the speech topic. Again, the audience wants to hear the speaker's views on the topic, not yours. Your job is to create an appetite for the upcoming main course, not fill up the audience with hors d'oeuvres.

- *Be prepared: Work with the speaker in advance.* It is best to talk to the speaker or a representative about your role as introducer. Are there specific points to be stressed? Is there anything the speaker wants to avoid? Some speakers may even want to preview your introductory remarks or may provide written suggestions for you.

Speech of Recognition

The elements of a good speech of introduction also apply to speeches of recognition. A **speech of recognition** is a speech presenting an award or honor to an individual. Open your recognition speech by discussing the importance of the occasion, the award being made, or the special contribution made by the honoree. Provide examples or testimony from those who know the honoree to illustrate his or her merit. Also, consider couching your speech in the form of a story about the person.

Connect with your audience. Give them a personal glimpse, either from your own experience or from testimony of those who know the honoree. It is important for your audience to feel that the award is, in a sense, coming from them.

Unless the name of the honoree is known in advance, it should be saved until the end of the recognition speech. Not only will this build suspense, audience members will start to guess at the honoree with each new bit of information you provide. As you conclude, focus on the honoree by name. Usually a recognition speech ends with something like this, "And so it is my great pleasure to announce the winner of the lifetime achievement award, our own Taylor Smith!"

Speech of Commemoration

A **speech of commemoration** is a speech that calls attention to the stature of the person or people being honored, or emphasizes the significance of an occasion. There are several kinds of commemorative speeches. Some of these speeches focus on cause for celebration, for example, a national holiday or a 50th wedding anniversary. Remember it is the occasion or people who have given cause for celebration that should be the focus of your speech.

Another type of speech of commemoration is one given to memorialize a specific person (Martin Luther King, Jr.) or the people we associate with a special and solemn occasion (members of the armed forces on Memorial Day). Finally, a **eulogy** is a kind of commemorative speech about someone who has died that is usually given shortly after his or her death. For example, when Earl Spencer eulogized his sister, Diana, Princess of Wales, he spoke lovingly of her

Earl Spencer's moving eulogy for his sister, Diana, Princess of Wales, was seen throughout the world.

as "the very essence of compassion, of duty, of style, of beauty. All over the world she was a symbol of selfless humanity, a standard-bearer for the rights of the downtrodden, a very British girl who transcended nationality, someone with a natural nobility who was classless, who proved in the last year that she needed no royal title to continue to generate her particular brand of magic."[9]

In many ways, a speech of commemoration is like an extended recognition speech. With the obvious exception of a eulogy, the honoree may even be present and be asked to say a few words after the commemoration. Sometimes these speeches take a humorous form, such as a "roast." Although jokes and embarrassing incidents are recited, they are done in good fun and ultimately the honoree is praised for his or her accomplishments.

A speech of commemoration should, like any other speech, open with impact. Begin by calling attention to the stature of the person being honored or the occasion that necessitates the memorial.

As with any speech, it is important to connect with the audience. What ties the audience and the person, people, and occasion together? A eulogy often recounts the deceased's common ties to the audience. Family and friends are usually present, and recounting memorable events from the life of the deceased helps everyone cope with their loss.

For the honoree, focus on the best that person has accomplished. For a retiree, it might be his or her accomplishments in the workforce. For a public figure, it might be what he or she stood for. For a fallen hero, the heroic deeds that cost a life are a source of meaning.

The substance of a speech of commemoration is usually less structured than that of other speeches. Nevertheless, there should be a theme or an essential point that you want to share with the audience. For example, in Jeraline Singh's high school graduation speech (see the box "America!"), she emphasizes throughout her belief that living in the United States is a gift and should be viewed as such. As someone who immigrated from Fiji, her speech shares her experiences in a way that uplifted her classmates.

Finally, a speech of commemoration should close with impact, leaving a lasting impression. A verse of scripture might provide just the right note to close a eulogy. Jeraline Singh used an anonymous quote to close her graduation speech.

Speeches to Entertain[10]

Sometimes known as after-dinner speaking because it's frequently given following a meal, a speech to entertain is more than just a string of jokes or a comedy monologue. A **speech to entertain** is a speech that makes its point through the use of humor. Like all speeches, a speech to entertain should have a clear focus. Of course, many speeches contain humor as an element. What makes the speech to entertain different is that its primary purpose is to bring laughter to the audience, not to persuade or inform them, though that may occur along the way. A speech meant to entertain is ideally suited to the storytelling format of speaking. This type of speech also is every bit as taxing as persuasive or informative speaking.

Selecting a Topic   The first task is to select a topic for your speech to entertain. The best place to begin is with yourself. Have you had experiences that, at least looking back, were funny? A good topic needs to have the potential to develop into a full-blown speech, not just one or two good punch lines. It needs to be something your audience can relate to. Many of the funniest speeches are about the frustrations of everyday life. Avoid the temptation to adopt the latest *Saturday Night Live* routine. Work from your own experiences and from experiences shared by those in your audience.

Consider your audience's expectations for the speech. You probably don't want to repeat stories you know your audience has heard before. If you are speaking to a group of lawyers, you probably can count on their having heard every lawyer joke known to humankind. Pick something that can connect you, assuming you are not a lawyer, to them. For example, there are few people today, including lawyers, who have not shared the frustrations of dealing with computers that seem to know just when to crash and make your life miserable.

You must, of course, be sensitive to an audience's diversity in developing and delivering a speech to entertain. We live in an era in which a racial or ethnic joke that would have been accepted a few years ago can end a career or lead to the demise of a relationship, as was the case with Whoopi Goldberg and Ted Danson. It wasn't that long ago, you may recall, that Danson, with Goldberg's approval, donned blackface makeup to speak at a celebrity roast of Goldberg. The speech turned out to be an embarrassing disaster for both Danson and Goldberg, one we assume they would like all of us to permanently forget.

America! by Jeraline Singh

If you know anything about me, you would know that February 14, 1987, was a very special day for me. If you do not know why it is special, that's fine. It was the day that I came to America. And it will always be the greatest day of my life.

On my first day as a freshman, the one thing that I told everyone was how proud I am to be an American, and to this day, I am still saying it with the same passion if not more. I am hoping that all those hours I spent preaching sunk into some of you and today you sit in your chairs and are proud to be in America.

I have spent the majority of my life in America, but unlike many of you out there, I have spent some years away from America. Because of these experiences I truly can say that America is the greatest nation in the world. I know that I can give you all the reasons to be proud of being an American, but your mind is set. The teachers in this school learned the hard way; changing a teenager's mind is like changing the beginning of the world. So, I will not waste my time (or yours) telling you something that you already know—but will not admit because it is not popular belief.

For those of you out there who love America, but will not say so because you are afraid of being an outcast, let me tell you something. I have lived my life as an outcast, and I would rather live that way than not be able to express my true feelings for the greatest nation in the world. I want you to remember that the next time a war breaks in the Middle East or Bosnia, the next time a person comes into office when the people did not vote him in, or the next time you walk down the street and make it back home safe with all your limbs, that you are free in America.

So, you ask, what does being an American have to do with the rest of your lives? Whether it be in a four-year university, junior college, the armed forces, or the workforce, you will always be an American and because of that you are one of the few in the world who got to chose the path you take in life.

Prepare well for the rest of your life. Be confident enough for yourself so that you may someday help another get the confidence you have. I was lucky in high school because SIFE (Students in Free Enterprise) and Butte College Connection gave me that confidence I needed this past year. For the past three years, Upward Bound helped me as well (so that I knew what I wanted in life and helped me realize that the simple things in life are the ones worth fighting for the most). I remember that I learned who I really am by talking to Mr. Steve Ladrech. I know that all

of us out there thank the teachers who got us interested in computers; My teacher would be Mr. Michael Bertsch and the teachers of Chico High West. I recommend to all of you, if you have someone special who changed your life, tell them before it is too late.

Next year, when most of our support bonds will be gone, what can we do so that we move up instead of down in life? I would recommend you do something for someone else. Mentor a child in your college town, or help an organization like the American Red Cross or do something as simple as donating blood. Remember the younger generation will follow in our footsteps.

The transition that we had from our first day at Chico High School to our last day was a very hard one for our class. We lost idols, heroes, and a princess along with classmates who we adored and admired, went through major floods and El Nino, and we had our last laugh with Seinfeld and the gang. But through strong ties with Chico High we made it through, and we thank all the Gods for that, along with ourselves.

Class of 1998, be proud of Chico High, be proud of leaving Chico High with a diploma in your hand, and above all be very very proud of being an American because no doubt you are living in the greatest nation in the world. I leave you with an anonymous quote: "Life's battles don't always go to the stronger or faster man, but soon or late the man who wins is the man who thinks he can." Class of '98: Good luck in your future endeavors.

Ted Danson's attempt at humor at a roast for Whoopi Goldberg was an embarrassing disaster.

In developing the content of your speech to entertain, brainstorming is a useful technique. Recall from Chapter 2 that brainstorming involves a group of people getting together and rapidly firing off ideas. Someone keeps a list. No crit-icism or evaluation of the ideas is permitted—that comes later. The key to brain-storming is to hitchhike one idea on another. The wilder and crazier the ideas, at this point, the better. You can always tone them down later.

Once you have a list of ideas for jokes, write each one on a card or slip of pa-per. The next step is to sort them out and organize them into a speech.

Organization   A speech to entertain should resemble any other good speech in organization: Open with impact, connect with your audience, and provide a clear focus in your introduction. It is very important to capture your audience's attention almost immediately. Unless you are already a highly skilled and entertaining speaker, this is not the time for a three-minute story leading to one punch line. So, try to get a laugh in the first sentence or two. Sometimes just an outrageous statement will do this. When Mary Matalin spoke of her husband, James Carville, for example, she began by pointing out that he had served his country as a Marine, reaching the rank of corporal. This, she noted, "makes him the highest ranking military officer in the current administration." Even liberals in the audience saw the humor in her backhanded compliment to her husband, which simultaneously reminded everyone of the president's lack of military experience.

Another example of an attention-getting opening came when Russ Woody, who is an Emmy- and Golden Globe–winning comedy writer, spoke at our university commencement. He began by stating:

> Look . . . I write sitcoms for a living, so don't expect much. Which means . . . basically, I'm gonna tell a few jokes. Hit a few well-worn platitudes. And try to sell you a Dodge minivan.

Russ's full speech is reprinted in Appendix B, and his helpful hints for writing humorous introductions are found in Chapter 8, on page 221.

Although it is important to focus your audience's attention on the topic of your speech, a preview of points is rare in a speech to entertain. Part of humor is surprise, and telegraphing your jokes in a preview will undermine the audience's surprise.

The body of your speech can be organized in a number of ways. A simple chronological or narrative form works well when telling a story or describing a series of events. A topical arrangement allows you to organize your speech around major topics.

In concluding a speech to entertain, you normally would not summarize your points. You would, however, want to close with impact or, as the old adage goes, "Leave 'em laughing."

Sources of Humor   What are some sources of humor? We hesitate to try to define what is funny. After all, everyone's sense of humor is different, and what is funny to one person will leave another completely stone-faced. Some people love David Letterman and hate Jay Leno, others the reverse, and some people enjoy them both.

Nevertheless, a few traditional sources of humor deserve mention:

- *Exaggeration.* Exaggeration is a well-tested source of humor. Wits from Mark Twain to the present day have relied on exaggeration to make their point. Russ Woody, mentioned earlier, used exaggeration to describe his own graduation experience:

  > I will be brief . . . because I remember my own graduation . . . though not *too* clearly. We were over in Laxson Auditorium, and it was a comfy 105 degrees out . . . and just slightly less than double that in the auditorium.
  >
  > Anyway, the man who gave the commencement speech talked for close to 15 hours. He said we were all sailing ships out on the ocean of

life, and we were the beating hearts of an upwardly mobile nation, and we had a bunch of mountaintops to climb . . . And the only thing I *really* came away with, besides hathair, was something about a new technology in ventilation systems that was greatly improving the output of poultry in tested areas of Missouri.

- *Incongruity.* Something that doesn't fit in seems funny. Woody Allen once wore tennis shoes with a tuxedo (semiformal attire?). We frequently poke fun at politicians whose words and deeds don't match. When the State of California was sending out IOUs instead of checks, Jay Leno commented that the latest Southern California earthquake wasn't really an earthquake, just the governor bouncing more checks.

- *Attacking authority.* The attack on authority has been a staple of humor since anyone can remember. Will Rogers made fun of Congress, Jay Leno makes fun of politicians, and Chris Rock makes fun of everybody, himself included!

- *Puns.* Use at your own risk!

- *Sarcasm.* Used with care, sarcasm can be a good source of humor (particularly when directed against sources of authority). But be careful you don't create sympathy for your victim. Sarcasm that is too edgy or biting can seem mean-spirited and bitter rather than funny. One of Mary Matalin's charms is that she is able to poke fun at her husband and his Democratic friends and yet still appear a loving wife.

- *Irony.* Sometimes a powerful source of humor, irony can also make a serious point. The fact that Microsoft founder and billionaire Bill Gates had his presentation of Windows 98 marred by a computer failure was a source of material for late-night comedians for several days.

- *The rule of three.* Milton Berle once claimed that he could make an audience laugh at anything, if he preceded it with two funny jokes. Try it. Once you have people laughing, they often will continue to laugh even at a line that isn't funny.

- *Self-deprecating humor.* Often the safest humor is that directed at yourself. Not only do you avoid alienating anyone, you show that you are a regular person. When Hall-of-Fame quarterback Terry Bradshaw spoke at a "speechathon" along with such luminaries as former president Gerald Ford, former congressman Jack Kemp, and former senator Bill Bradley, he wondered out loud why he was there. Gazing out at an audience of prominent business leaders, he admitted: "I made my living, unlike you, by putting my hands under another man's butt."[11]

- *Delivery.* Humor depends on direct contact and immediacy with your audience. Thus, use of a manuscript or conspicuous notes will destroy the spontaneity of the experience. Even if you have memorized your speech, however, it is important that it sound fresh and spontaneous.

One of the authors, Michael Scott, is shown here interviewing Al Roker on CNBC television.

Use a lively and animated manner in presenting your speech. Timing in comedy is everything. Knowing when to pause, what word to punch, and the right tone of voice to use are not things you can learn from reading a book. Only by trying out your speech with friends and experimenting with different ways of delivering the same line can you tell what delivery is best.

Not everyone is comfortable with speaking to entertain. But done well and tastefully, it can be an enjoyable experience for both the speaker and the audience.

SPEAKING ON TELEVISION

Although you might not plan on being a television newscaster or celebrity, many people in ordinary life find themselves confronted with a television interview at some time or another. Not just business executives need to be able to handle a

Chatting It Up on TV: Paul Burnham Finney

Many executives turn into TV regulars and routinely go out on cross-country tours to promote a new product or service. But few of the veterans take their camera assignments casually.

"Steal the show," says Mariana Field Hoppin, president of MFH Travel Marketing Ltd. and a longtime spokeswoman for Avis Europe. "When you walk into the studio, win over the camera crew and interviewer, and you've got them in the palm of your hands."

It's important to do that. "The public is taking the lazy way out—getting their information on the tube," as one corporate communications director puts it.

"Smart executives have to be prepared for surprises on the road," he goes on to say. When the Tylenol-tampering scare struck Johnson & Johnson, C.E.O. James E. Burke signed up for a crash course at the Executive Television Workshop [ETW] before facing the public.

Screen test: Among the tips ETW feeds its corporate students:

- Get a good fix on the questions you'll be asked by contacting the TV or radio station. (Ask around if the direct approach doesn't work.)
- Tell your story, or somebody else will—and not always correctly.
- Memorize the basic points you want to make, and keep them uppermost in your mind.
- Stick to solid colors in dress—no loud patterns allowed. And wear contacts rather than glasses, if possible.
- Women: don't show up in a short skirt that rides above the knees.

- Park yourself in the front third of the chair. You'll look more alert and interested that way.
- Glance at 3-by-5 card notes during commercials or station breaks—never when on camera.
- Say it all in 45 seconds when answering an interviewer. "Short, clear answers," as TV commentator David Brinkley advises.
- Use anecdotes and "sparklers" to brighten your delivery.
- Don't repeat a negative statement—it only lends credence to it.

Digestible bits: "We stress the importance of establishing a conversational tone," says Executive Television Workshop marketing director Carol Heimann. "Executives get very techy in the way they talk. A reporter is only a conduit to the public. Break your explanations into digestible bits. Try to act as though you're in a living room, chatting with someone."

Ultimately, the impression you leave with your audience counts more than your words. Some 90% of what they remember is your "voice" and "nonverbal communications," according to studies. In short, body language matters as much as your thoughts.

"One of your biggest assets," says Heimann, "is a smile. It can change a million opinions. You can disarm your audience. If you're relaxed, you'll relax the people who are watching."

Source: Article appeared first in *Newsweek*'s 1990 Special Ad Section, "Management Digest." Reprinted by permission.

television interview; so do supervisors and line personnel who may be on the scene of a breaking news event. Unless you expect to be on television and have been given a list of questions you will be asked in advance, speaking on TV is a lot like impromptu speaking. You want to appear organized, come across as firm rather than indecisive, and use powerful language. Speaking on TV also demands nonverbal immediacy behaviors, so you'll want to look back at Chapter 10 for a discussion of effective delivery tips.

One question that always arises when being interviewed on television is where to look. Do you look at the camera or at the interviewer or from one to the other? One suggestion comes from Dorothy Sarnoff, who provides communication training to corporate executives. She suggests: "Focus on the left eye of the interviewer, then the right eye—and back to the left. Not a windshield-wiper effect, but slowly so your own eyes don't look dead."[12] Some other suggestions for talking on television are included in the box "Chatting It Up on TV: Paul Burnham Finney."

In conclusion, the best advice we can give is to be prepared and stick to your theme. Interviews are frequently videotaped and then edited for a sound bite. You want to make sure that whatever is left on the cutting-room floor, your essential message will reach the viewers.

SUMMARY

Public speaking is a fact of life. Over the course of yours, you can expect to speak on a number of predictable and sometimes special occasions. One way to approach these special speaking occasions is to treat them as opportunities for storytelling. Good stories are organized in a similar fashion to speeches and are characterized by probability and fidelity.

Storytelling can be used effectively in a variety of types of speaking as well as when leading or participating in *groups* and *panel discussions*. Storytelling also works well with impromptu speaking, speeches given without advance preparation. Effective impromptu speeches demand clear organization, taking a stand, and using powerful language.

Other types of speeches that can benefit from storytelling include *speeches of acceptance, speeches of introduction, speeches of recognition, speeches of commemoration,* and *speeches to entertain* an audience.

Although it once was a rarity, speaking on television is increasingly common. Rules for effective speaking on video include looking at the interviewer rather than the camera unless speaking directly to the viewers and preparing in advance when possible for the questions you'll be asked.

Check Your Understanding: Exercises and Activities

1. Your best friend is getting married, and you will be asked to say a few words at the wedding. Prepare your toast. Do the same thing for a wedding anniversary, a baptism, and a bar or bat mitzvah.

2. Think of a special award for one of your classmates. Write a speech of recognition for presenting the award.

3. Track down several quotations and anecdotes that are general enough to be used as an opening or a closing for a speech of acceptance or a speech of recognition. Three sources to which you can turn are:

    Clifton Fadiman, ed., *The Little Brown Book of Anecdotes* (Boston: Little, Brown, 1985).

    Edmund Fuller, ed., *2,500 Anecdotes for All Occasions* (New York: Avenel Books, 1980).

    James B. Simpson, ed., *Simpson's Contemporary Quotations: The Most Notable Quotes Since 1950* (Boston: Houghton Mifflin, 1988).

4. A speech of nomination can either make or break the nominee's chances for being elected to office. Speeches of nomination are more common than you may think. Social clubs such as fraternities and sororities, business and professional associations such as the Soroptomists, Rotary, or local Bar are all examples. On a separate sheet of paper, list and explain what you think are the essential characteristics of a speech of nomination. Then see if you can find a published example of a speech of nomination that conforms to your criteria. Note conforming examples on a copy of the speech with a highlighter and share your analysis with classmates.

Notes

1. Edmund Fuller, ed. *2,500 Anecdotes for All Occasions* (New York: Avenel Books, 1980), 135.

2. *News from Korbel.* (1998). [Online] Available: http://korbel.com/trade. html#source (28 September 1998).

3. Theodore H. White, *The Making of the President 1968* (New York: Atheneum, 1969), 171. Shaw's original lines appear in his play *Back to Methuselah*, Part I, Act I. The Serpent in the Garden of Eden says to Eve, "You see things; and you say 'Why?' But I dream things that never were; and I say 'Why not?'" See George Bernard Shaw, *The Complete Plays of Bernard Shaw* (London: Odhams Press Limited, 1934), 857.

4. Walter R. Fisher, *Human Communication as Narration* (Columbia: University of South Carolina Press, 1987).

5. Peggy Noonan, *What I Saw at the Revolution: A Political Life in the Reagan Era* (New York: Random House, 1990).

6. Stephen J. Covey, *The Seven Habits of Highly Effective People* (New York: Fireside Books/Simon & Shuster, 1989).

7. Anita Creamer, "One More Word on the Oscars," *Sacramento Bee*, 3 April 1993, Scene, 1.

8. Kevin Jeys, "Irreconcilable Differences," *Chico News and Review*, 8 October 1998, 29.

9. "I Stand Before You . . . ," *Newsweek*, 15 September 1997, 24.

10. Adapted from Jack Perella and Steven R. Brydon, "Speaking to Entertain," in *Intercollegiate Forensics: A Participant's Handbook*, ed. T. C. Winebrenner, 42–46. © 1992 Northern California Forensics Association.

11. Sam Stanton, "Clinton Remains Topic A at Cal Expo Speechathon," *Sacramento Bee*, 10 October 1998, A23.

12. Article appeared first in *Newsweek's* 1990 Special Ad Section, "Management Digest," Paul Burnham Finney, "The Business of Communicating," 16.

Student Speeches

These student speeches were transcribed from videotape. Because speaking extemporaneously often leads to unintended errors or misspoken words, we have edited and corrected the transcripts for you to read.

Speech of Self-Introduction:
Who Am I? *by Jonathan Studebaker*

This speech was delivered by Jonathan Studebaker, who is profiled in Chapter 2, page 28. If you have access to the videotape accompanying this text, you will find his speech in segment 12. In reading this speech, try to answer the following questions:

- How well does Jonathan open, focus, and connect with his audience?
- How does this speech of introduction differ from a more formal speech in terms of structure and use of supporting materials, such as evidence?
- Comment on Jonathan's use of rhetorical questions throughout his speech.
- What do you think is Jonathan's purpose in presenting this speech? In what ways is Jonathan using this opportunity to speak as an opinion leader on the issue of how we perceive persons with disabilities?
- If you have access to the videotape of this speech, compare the experience of seeing and hearing Jonathan with reading his speech.

Good morning!

Who am I? Why am I here? Seems like I've heard that before. For myself, I've been asked these and other questions. Two of them I'd like to answer for you today.

I've been asked: "Are you a midget?" "What do you have?" "What's your disability?" "Why are you small?" But I'd really like people to ask me: "What do you like to do?" "What's your favorite color?" So what I'll try to do is answer both of these today.

I'm a nice guy. Don't worry, I won't bite. I like to do many things, except water ski. I've gone to school. I've gone to elementary school, high school, and I graduated from Cal State Chico.

A lot of people ask, "So why are you here?" Well, I'm here because I want to educate others. I've coached football at Chico State University. I was the kicking coach for three years. And out of those three years I had two kickers make first team all-conference. So how do you coach football? You do it by simply telling people what to do. Well, how do you do that? You do it by doing a lot of the things that we all do—by studying, by reading, by listening to others. And that's what I've done throughout my life, and that is what has made me who I am.

Like I said, I'm a nice person. I'm cheerful, I'm energetic. Okay, so I have a disability. I was born with osteogenesis imperfecta, a disease which causes my bones to be fragile. Have you ever accidentally dropped a glass on the floor? What happens? It breaks. Well, my bones kind of break like glass, which is why I tell people, when you carry me, treat me like your best crystal.

I'm happy about being who I am. I wouldn't change a thing. I've done a lot of things in my life. Like I said, I've coached football, I graduated from college, things that people wouldn't think a person with my condition would do.

So who am I? Well, I'm Jonathan Studebaker, Jonathan Peter Charles Studebaker. Why such a long name? Well, my middle name is Charles, which came later. And Charles is kind of a symbol of a lot of things. My dad used to call me chicken when I was younger. And then it evolved to chicken Charles, and now Charles. Now, some of you might be offended by being called chicken. But, you know what, it doesn't matter to me. I like being who I am. I've been put here to educate others, not by teaching others, but by just being myself.

Thank you.

Informative Speech: Eating Disorders and Their Warning Signs *by Kelli Wells*

This speech by Kelli Wells concerns the dangers of eating disorders and how to spot them. If you have access to the videotape accompanying this text, you will find her speech in segment 12. After reading this speech, answer the following questions:

- How does Kelli use the message attributes of relative advantage, observability, and comprehensibility in her speech?

- Determine whether Kelli's speech primarily explains, instructs, demonstrates, or describes her topic.

- Discuss the relationship between informative and persuasive speaking illustrated in this speech.

- How appropriate and how effective do you think Kelli's use of personal experience is in motivating you to listen to her speech about eating disorders?

- As a result of learning the information presented in the speech, how likely is it that you would be able to identify a person suffering from anorexia or bulimia?

- In what ways did Kelli make the organization of her speech clear? How do you evaluate her use of previews, signposts, and summary?

I knew my best friend had a problem. Didn't she know what she was doing to herself? Her weight and food consumption had become an obsession with her. I could see how it was controlling her. But in her mind, it was all she could control. She couldn't eat anything without quickly running to the bathroom. I had to hear daily how fat she was and how her life would be so much better if she was thinner. As she got deeper and deeper into an eating disorder, bulimia nervosa, she was no longer the person I used to know. I know the signs of an eating disorder, and I was able to confront her about her problem. She was able to get help and now she's doing much better.

I've seen firsthand how an eating disorder can affect someone. That's why it's important that we all know about them and the warning signs of an eating disorder. You may be able to save a life. Knowing more about eating disorders will enable you to be more aware of what may be going on in the mind of even a friend or a family member.

Tonight, you will be informed of the main types of eating disorders, who are the most likely candidates, and the signs to look for.

The two main types of eating disorders are anorexia and bulimia nervosa. The fear of obesity and the pursuit of thinness represent the driving force in both these mental disorders.

In anorexia nervosa this fear is expressed through a number of symptoms, including the desire to maintain a very low body weight, body-image disturbance, and avoiding food altogether. There is intense fear of getting fat and an obsession with being thin. These are the two most cognitive features of anorexia.

Anorexic individuals also struggle with body-image disturbance. They have a distorted view in which they perceive their body to be fat, in spite of its thin appearance. They also suffer extreme dissatisfaction with the size or the shape of the body. Food avoidance is another problem. Anorexics will avoid food altogether and obtain only small amounts of diet food, such as salads or fruits.

Young women with bulimia nervosa share many of the same symptoms as anorexics. Most bulimic women are dissatisfied with their current body weight. Bulimics, however, are not as effective in dieting and usually weigh within the normal range. So they are able to avoid treatment for many years. But actually what they are doing to their bodies is completely destroying their systems. Bulimics binge-eat, which means they eat large amounts of food uncontrollably, and then force themselves to purge the calories consumed to avoid weight gain. For many bulimic individuals the act of eating is associated with the feeling of being out of control. They're able to regain control by purging.

Now that you are informed of the two main types of eating disorders, anorexia and bulimia nervosa, it's important to know who the most likely candidates are for having these disorders.

The most widespread group of people that are affected by these disorders are young women. Our society today believes that the thinner you are, the better your life will be. Young women begin to measure their self-esteem on their dieting success. They believe that eating is the cause and result of many of their problems. So they become trapped in a vicious cycle of rigid behavior focused on food. We're continually confronted in newspapers, magazines, and television with ads imploring and encouraging us to eat and prepare all kinds of food. At the same time, young women are encouraged and pressured to be thin and maintain perfect figures by fashion designers. This paradox is hard to manage and for most young women results in an eating disorder.

In doing my research, I found statistics for college populations from the book *Eating Disorders: Assessment and Treatment*, by Scholtz and Johnson. In 22 studies done across college campuses, an average of 7.6 percent of college women suffer from some type of eating disorder. As we can see, this is a problem that shouldn't be forgotten.

Now that I have informed you that young women are the most affected by these disorders, it is crucial to know the warning signs. In bulimia nervosa, the warning signs are dehydration, digestive disorders, severe dental problems, and muscle weaknesses. In anorexia, the symptoms are dry skin and hair, cold hands and feet, general weakness, and most importantly, extreme weight loss.

In conclusion, let me summarize the three main points I informed you about tonight. First, the two main types of eating disorders are bulimia and anorexia nervosa. Second, young women are the most likely candidates for having these disorders. And thirdly, the symptoms which I shared with you are important to know in helping a friend or even a family member.

My best friend felt what many women feel everywhere, that to be thin equals happiness. Eating disorders are vicious traps that, once you get into, are very hard to get out of. Hopefully now, by knowing more about them, you can help someone you care about.

Persuasive Speech: Fear Is Real Among Freshman Students *by Ryland Hill, Jr.*

This persuasive speech is by Ryland Hill, Jr., who after retiring from the navy, decided to go back to school at age "thirty-something." Although Ryland is in many respects dissimilar to his classmates, he focused his speech on something he believes he shared with all undergraduates—fear. If you have access to the videotape accompanying this text, you will find his speech in segment 12. After reading this speech, ask yourself the following questions:

- Which of the four possible goals of persuasive speaking discussed in Chapter 13 is Ryland fulfilling?
- Evaluate Ryland's use of logos, including his use of first-, second-, and third-order data.
- Identify the use of motivational appeals—including fear—in Ryland's speech.
- Explain how Ryland, who is older than most of his fellow students, bridges his dissimilarity to them and builds his credibility as a speaker.
- How well you think this speech connects to the interests of an audience of first-year college students? How could the connection between Ryland and his audience have been made stronger?
- Based on Ryland's speech, what change, if any, do you have in your attitudes toward college?

Eleanor Roosevelt once quoted an unknown author by saying, "You gain strength, courage and confidence by every experience in which you . . . stop to look fear in the face. . . . You must do the thing you think you cannot do."

Today, in the '90s, incoming college freshmen often report becoming anxious before entering college. The transition from high school to college brings fears to the surface. Likewise, students who return to college after many years of absence report similar fears.

College freshmen find it difficult to identify exactly where the problem lies. As a reentry student myself, I have experienced the same difficulty and would like to persuade you that it's essential to be aware of the subtle effect that fear has on each and every one of us in each class that we take.

Today we'll look at some reasons why the fear of failure, the fear of the unknown, and self-fulfilling prophecies have paralyzed freshman students from achieving their full potential. And finally we'll discuss three solutions that can eliminate harmful effects that fear can produce.

Freshman students develop fears that create doubt. A common fear is the fear of failure. Some students doubt their ability to succeed at the college level. These students have often received negative feedback throughout their elementary and high school years. They suffer from low self-esteem and are insecure about their new academic experience.

Students in their first year have the potential to do well in school, but usually they underachieve and they may be afraid of making mistakes. But in the counseling center at Berkeley's Writer's College, students are told that making mistakes is important. It is a way of learning about our strengths, and what works well for us, and what does not work. It's only when we do not learn from our mistakes and refuse to correct them that they become failures. People don't reach their full potential because [they fail to face up to] important challenges in life, as Robert Steinberg writes in 1986. It is also easier for students to spend a lot of energy and time dodging the system and their work as assigned due to the fear of failure.

Now that we understand why the fear of failure has such a crippling effect on students in their first year, let's examine another reason why fear plays such a pivotal role in the lack of a freshman's success.

Instead of high school counselors making students see that they have the potential to achieve, they make predictions which students feel are like a prophet predicting their very future. Well-meaning counselors sometimes steer students away from attending college. They advise the students to consider the workforce instead. In today's economy, jobs today call for more than just a high school diploma. The students receive a "can't do" message, further lowering their self-esteem. Often this leads to a cycle of low grades, fulfilling the prophecy of failure.

Robert Steinberg's book *Intelligence Applied* explains why intelligent people may fail. Steinberg has identified stumbling blocks that get in the way of even the brightest and the sharpest of freshman students, and prevent them from becoming academically successful. "It scarcely matters what talents people have if they are not motivated to use them," he writes.

First-semester students rely on the correctness of their college professors. Students are still immature and rely on others for their external rewards. But a lot of students say that immaturity has nothing to do with their grades here at

Chico State University. Steinberg states: "A lack of self-confidence gnaws away at a person's ability to get things done and this becomes a self-fulfilling prophecy." It's all in your mind.

Now that we understand how self-fulfilling prophecies can create fear in freshman students, let's take a brief look at the fear of the unknown and see how it can be a deterrent to our success as first-year students.

Any new experience that one knows little about can be real scary. On holidays and birthdays, for instance, we receive unknown gifts that are new and different, yet we don't fear those types of gifts, do we? Yet maybe it all lies in the way one packages things. An attractive package that we are expecting is the one that we look forward to receiving. College officials here at Chico State University should let freshman students know that there is a beauty and a joy in the gift called a college education.

Now that we can see how fear of the unknown can disguise itself as a problem, let's look at three solutions that can be very helpful in battling fears that we face on our college campuses.

First is to identify some traits that define a successful student. Successful students tend to be risk takers. Just enrolling in college is a risk to some. Yet they do it, and they take the first step toward success. Successful students also learn from their mistakes. Remember, it's not a failure if you're willing to correct your mistake and learn from it. They need to recognize their successes and overcome their failures as Professor Johnson, 1990, says.

The second solution is that we must look at college life as a challenge. When we view college life as a roller coaster with its ups and its downs, as long as we believe that life is going to return to the top again, we can rise to the challenge and we can persevere.

And lastly, we can envision our future. We must see ourselves as successful people. And even when things become blurry, and even when we're losing our focus, we can maintain the ability to fine-tune our lives and become even more goal directed.

We must have faith in ourselves and stay persistent, and stay willing to keep trying. When we don't succeed the first time, we can search for solutions until we are successful. It is difficult for many students to appreciate their own success. I'm going to repeat that. It is difficult for many college students to appreciate their own success. Successful students have learned to celebrate their victories, but most importantly, they have learned to overcome their college fears.

To summarize, today we have discussed reasons why fear is real among college freshmen, and we gave practical solutions to overcoming it. Successful freshman students are confident enough to believe in themselves. But most importantly, they expect their classmates to appreciate their abilities.

As Eleanor Roosevelt reminds us, while thinking about overcoming our college fears, "You gain strength, courage, and confidence by every experience in which you . . . stop to look fear in the face. . . . You must do the thing you think you cannot do. You must do the thing you think you cannot do." Thank you.

Public Speeches

Remarks, August 19, 1992, *by Mary Fisher*[1]

This speech was delivered by Mary Fisher at the 1992 Republican National convention in Houston, Texas, on Wednesday, August 19. As founder of the Family AIDS Network and a person who is HIV-positive, Fisher addressed a convention that was largely socially conservative about issues such as AIDS. As you read this speech, attempt to answer these questions:

- How well did Mary Fisher adapt to the rhetorical situation she faced as a speaker at the Republican National Convention?
- To what audience or audiences was this speech addressed?
- What do you see as Fisher's purpose or purposes in presenting this speech? What stages of opinion leadership do you see this speech addressing?
- How do you feel about the issue of AIDS after reading this speech? Have you changed your beliefs, attitudes, values, or behavioral intentions?

Thank you. Thank you.

Less than three months ago at Platform Hearings in Salt Lake City, I asked the Republican Party to lift the shroud of silence which has been draped over the issue of HIV and AIDS. I have come tonight to bring our silence to an end. I bear a message of challenge, not self-congratulation. I want your attention, not your applause.

I would never have asked to be HIV-positive, but I believe that in all things there is a purpose; and I stand before you and before the nation gladly. The reality of AIDS is brutally clear. Two hundred thousand Americans are dead or dying. A million more are infected. Worldwide, 40 million, 60 million, or 100 million infections will be counted in the coming few years. But despite science

---

[1] This text is from the Official Report of the Proceedings of the Thirty-Fifth Republican National Convention, published by the Republican National Committee.

and research, White House meetings, and congressional hearings; despite good intentions and bold initiatives, campaign slogans and hopeful promises, it is—despite it all—the epidemic which is winning tonight.

In the context of an election year, I ask you, here in this great hall, or listening in the quiet of your home, to recognize that the AIDS virus is not a political creature. It does not care whether you are Democratic or Republican; it does not ask whether you are black or white, male or female, gay or straight, young or old. Tonight, I represent an AIDS community whose members have been reluctantly drafted from every segment of American society.

Though I am white and a mother, I am one with a black infant struggling with tubes in a Philadelphia hospital.

Though I am female and contracted this disease in marriage and enjoy the warm support of my family, I am one with the lonely gay man sheltering a flickering candle from the cold wind of his family's rejection.

This is not a distant threat. It is a present danger. The rate of infection is increasing fastest among women and children. Largely unknown a decade ago, AIDS is the third leading killer of young adult Americans today. But it won't be third for long, because unlike other diseases, this one travels. Adolescents don't give each other cancer or heart disease because they believe they are in love, but HIV is different; and we have helped it along. We have killed each other with our ignorance, our prejudice, and our silence.

We may take refuge in our stereotypes, but we cannot hide there long, because HIV asks only one thing of those it attacks. Are you human? And this is the right question. Are you human? Because people with HIV have not entered some alien state of being. They are human. They have not earned cruelty, and they do not deserve meanness. They don't benefit from being isolated or treated as outcasts. Each of them is exactly what God made—a person, not evil, deserving of our judgment; not victims, longing for our pity—people, ready for support and worthy of compassion. (Applause.)

My call to you, my Party, is to take a public stand, no less compassionate than that of the President and Mrs. Bush. They have embraced me and my family in memorable ways. In the place of judgment, they have shown affection. In difficult moments, they have raised our spirits. In the darkest hours, I have seen them reaching out not only to me, but also to my parents, armed with that stunning grief and special grace that comes only to parents who have themselves leaned too long over the bedside of a dying child.

With the president's leadership, much good has been done. Much of the good has gone unheralded, and as the president has insisted, much remains to be done. But we do the president's cause no good if we praise the American family but ignore a virus that destroys it. (Applause.)

We must be consistent if we are to be believed. We cannot love justice and ignore prejudice, love our children and fear to teach them. Whatever our role as parent or policymaker, we must act as eloquently as we speak—else we have no integrity.

My call to the nation is a plea for awareness. If you believe you are safe, you are in danger. Because I was not hemophiliac, I was not at risk. Because I was not gay, I was not at risk. Because I did not inject drugs, I was not at risk.

My father has devoted much of his lifetime to guarding against another holocaust. He is part of the generation who heard Pastor Nemoeller come out of the Nazi death camps to say, "They came after the Jews and I was not a Jew, so, I did not protest. They came after the trade unionists, and I was not a trade unionist, so, I did not protest. Then they came after the Roman Catholics, and I was not a Roman Catholic, so, I did not protest. Then they came after me, and there was no one left to protest." (Applause.)

The lesson history teaches is this: If you believe you are safe, you are at risk. If you do not see this killer stalking your children, look again. There is no family or community, no race or religion, no place left in America that is safe. Until we genuinely embrace this message, we are a nation at risk. Tonight, HIV marches resolutely to AIDS in more than a million American homes. Littering its pathway with the bodies of the young men, young women, young parents, and young children. One of those families is mine. If it is true that HIV inevitably turns to AIDS, then my children will inevitably turn to orphans.

My family has been a rock of support. My 84-year-old father, who has pursued the healing of nations, will not accept the premise that he cannot heal his daughter. My mother refuses to be broken. She still calls at midnight to tell wonderful jokes that make me laugh. Sisters and friends, and my brother Phillip, whose birthday is today, all have helped carry me over the hardest places. I am blessed, richly and deeply blessed, to have such a family. (Applause.)

But not all of you have been so blessed. You are HIV-positive, but dare not say it. You have lost loved ones, but you dare not whisper the word AIDS—you weep silently. You grieve alone. I have a message for you. It is not you who should feel shame. It is we, we who tolerate ignorance and practice prejudice, we who have taught you to fear. We must lift our shroud of silence, making it safe for you to reach out for compassion. It is our task to seek safety for our children, not in quiet denial but in effective action.

Some day our children will be grown. My son Max, now 4, will take the measure of his mother; my son Zachary, now 2, will sort through his memories. I may not be here to hear their judgments, but I know already what I hope they are. I want my children to know that their mother was not a victim. She was a messenger. I do not want them to think, as I once did, that courage is the absence of fear. I want them to know that courage is the strength to act wisely when we are most afraid. I want them to have the courage to step forward when called by their nation or their party and give leadership, no matter what the personal cost. I ask no more of you than I ask of myself or my children. To the millions of you who are grieving, who are frightened, who have suffered the ravages of AIDS firsthand—have courage and you will find support. To the millions who are strong, I issue the plea—set aside prejudice and politics to make room for compassion and sound policy. (Applause.)

To my children, I make this pledge: "I will not give in, Zachary, because I draw my courage from you. Your silly giggle gives me hope; your gentle prayers give me strength; and you, my child, give me reason to say to America, 'You are at risk.' And I will not rest, Max, until I have done all I can to make your world safe. I will seek a place where intimacy is not the prelude to suffering. I will not hurry to leave you, my children, but when I go, I pray that you will not suffer shame on my account." To all within the sound of my voice, I appeal: "Learn with me the lessons of history and of grace, so my children will not be afraid to say the word AIDS when I am gone. Then, their children and yours may not need to whisper it at all." God bless the children, God bless us all, and good night.

Commencement Address *by Russ Woody*

This speech was delivered by our friend and former student Russ Woody, who is profiled in Chapter 8 on page 221. It was delivered to the graduating class of 1998 at California State University, Chico, on May 23, 1998, and is reprinted with his permission.

After you read this speech, answer these questions:

- How does Russ Woody capture the audience's attention at the outset of his speech?
- As a graduate of the same university, what does Russ do to connect with his audience?
- Despite his career as a writer of comedy, what serious messages are embedded in Russ's speech?
- How does Russ use historical examples and quotations to make his point?
- Consider Russ's use of language. How does his choice of words and phrases enhance the speech?

Look . . . I write sitcoms for a living, so don't expect much. Which means . . . basically, I'm gonna tell a few jokes. Hit a few well-worn platitudes. And try to sell you a Dodge minivan.

I will be brief . . . because I remember my own graduation . . . though not *too* clearly. We were over in Laxson Auditorium, and it was a comfy 105 degrees out . . . and just slightly less than double that in the auditorium.

Anyway, the man who gave the commencement speech talked for close to 15 hours. He said we were all sailing ships out on the ocean of life, and we were the beating hearts of an upwardly mobile nation, and we had a bunch of mountaintops to climb . . . And the only thing I *really* came away with, besides hathair, was something about a new technology in ventilation systems that was greatly improving the output of poultry in tested areas of Missouri.

It was on that day, I made a solemn vow to myself that I would never graduate again. And that's a vow I've kept.

Let me first just say—you are so fortunate to have gone to school here in Chico. I know it's been a lot of hard work, but come on—it's Chico.

And I hope you look back on your days and years here with great fondness, as I do. And—well, except for the memories of Marge—that meter maid with the big hair. I know this is an old issue for me, but I still have nightmares—I'm dead and buried and Marge is writing a ticket because time has run out on my headstone. I mean, come on, the woman was writing tickets when I was a freshman. Don't these people eventually have to retire?

I won't pretend today to impart great wisdom . . . I mean, the only valid advice I have to offer is . . . never take a job working with Cybill Shepard. That and the toilet seat thing, you know, putting it down when you're finished—helps the marriage.

Oh, wait a minute . . . Don't die without reading *Catch 22*.

When you leave Chico, you will be entering a professional world that is being changed by technology at a stunning rate. It is a rate of change that no generation before you has faced.

And that daunting task is made more difficult by the fact that it requires you to focus on specialized and compartmentalized professions. And therein lies the dichotomy that will often be your obstacle: *Focus* . . .

Because the problems of the next millennium will need to be solved by those of you who see *more* than a *singular perspective*.

The solutions to the hurtles you'll face . . . will call for new and different ways of thinking. New and different ways of thinking that, *yes*, require the narrow vision of a microscope, but as well, the panoramic view of a fish-eye lens.

And *that* will be your challenge. To look *outside* your *field of expertise* to find solutions . . . to see the possibilities of lateral options . . .

Remember to . . . look for answers in unexpected places. In fact, *expect* to find ideas in unexpected places.

After all, spaghetti came from China.

In 1872 our own Leland Stanford—governor of California—was at the track and had an argument with a friend about "whether horses touch the ground with one foot when they're galloping." The bet was settled by a man named Edward Mybridge, who lined up a series of cameras with strings attached to the shutters . . . and then made a horse run through the strings. What they ended up with was a series of photographs . . . that presaged the *motion picture camera*.

Although the troubling part for me is . . . he was governor of California . . . Did he have *nothing* going on in his life?

In the 1870s artists were being replaced by photographers. Photographs were *better* than paintings because . . . they were more true to the subject . . . more accurate. . . . They captured every detail. So, a few people like Monet, Renoir, Pissaro started painting *without* detail. Their alternative was called Impressionism.

The man who came up with roll-on deodorant got the idea from a ball-point pen.

When management at the El Cortez Hotel in San Diego were stumped trying to figure out a way to add more elevators to the hotel without shutting the place down or disrupting the guests, a janitor overheard the conversation and asked why they just didn't build the elevators on the *outside* of the hotel.

The El Cortez became then the *forerunner* of an architectural feature that has been *emulated throughout the world*.

And . . . in the 1820s an Englishman named Charles Babbage put together an odd-looking contraption made up of cogs and gears: It was the *computer*. An acquaintance of his, Ada Byron, then came up with a way to program it. She got the idea from . . . the *weaving loom*. It seems a hundred years earlier a French weaver had come up with a device that helped him weave patterns on his loom. It was called a *punch card*.

And most of these ideas came about amidst the ever-present backdrop of pessimism—the ever-present backdrop of narrow vision.

- Like Charles Duell, from the U.S. Patents Office, who said that everything that *can* be invented *has* been invented. He said that in 1899.
- Or the Hewlett-Packard exec who told Steve Jobs to take a hike because he had not yet finished college.
- Or the brain surgeon at Decca Records who turned down the Beatles in 1962 because . . . "groups with guitars were on their way out."

Of course, no discussion of lateral thinking would be complete without referencing one of the greatest thinkers of our time—Steven Wright—who said . . . "I put spot remover on my dog. Now he's gone."

He also pondered . . . "How much deeper *would* the ocean be, if sponges didn't live there?"

And he once "went to a general store, but they wouldn't let him buy anything specific."

Beethoven poured cold water over his head to stimulate his brain while he was composing.

Charles Dickens only faced *north* when he wrote . . . and Victor Hugo wrote naked. Which . . . I don't know . . . maybe that points more to their *emotional problems* than their genius . . . But, sometimes, great ideas come from people with emotional problems. *And I say that with a good deal of pride.*

Then again . . .

. . . Caligula made his horse a senator.

In the next few years especially, you will get a good deal of advice from a great many people . . .

I remember, when I graduated from here, my mother took me aside and said . . . "Russ, you go to school to learn of a great many things that will become clear to you *only* when your life has been sealed from the hardships of someone else's life who is facing both insurmountable odds and relative ease . . . "

And I thought about that . . . and I had *no idea* what it meant. It is only now, in retrospect, that the meaning of what she had to say is clear to me. She was insane. But we're not here to talk about my problems. We're here to talk about your problems.

So . . . how will you *know* what is good advice and what is bad? You'll know because the *good* advice will agree with what is in your heart. The late Joseph Campbell, who taught Comparative Mythology at Sarah Lawrence, said the end result of all his studies . . . the answer to man's eternal question about life that he sought to find in mythology . . . is . . . *Follow your Bliss.*

In a series of interviews with journalist Bill Moyers a couple of years before he died . . . (Uh, *Campbell* died, not Moyers—Moyers is still alive, but almost exclusively on PBS) . . . Anyway, Campbell said . . . that the work and the lifestyle that brings you joy . . . *that* is your bliss.

When Moyers asked Campbell if following your bliss wasn't more a journey to save yourself than a journey to save the world, Campbell said that, in saving yourself, "you save the world." He said . . . "The influence of a vital person . . . vitalizes. The world without spirit is a wasteland."

I would add to Campbell's thoughts by saying that, while you are pursuing your bliss, your success . . .

Remember to pursue, as well, the success of *those around you.*

Pursue the success of your *colleagues,* certainly . . .

And Pursue the success of your *loved ones* . . . without whom, there is no end to your means.

And as you gain that success and the respect of others in your chosen field both above and below you, . . . remember to repay that respect, but repay just a little more to those—*below* you. That is the mark of a good person. A successful person.

And, while you're in the process of being nice to others . . . remember to be nice to yourself. Because you *will* screw up. You *will* stumble, you *will* fall. *And then you will forget to extend kindness to yourself . . .*

My wife and I have a little boy named Henry . . . which is a *good* thing. (The fact that I know every single stinking word of *Dumbo* isn't so great . . .) But I have also become reacquainted with the work of Dr. Seuss . . . and he had something worthwhile to say on the subject . . .

He said . . .

I'm sorry to say so
But, sadly, it's true
That Bang-ups
And Hang-ups
Can happen to you

I'm afraid that *some* times
You'll play lonely games too.
Games you can't win
'cause you'll play against you.
But on you will go
though the weather be foul.
On you will go
though your enemies prowl.
On you will go
though the Hakken-Kraks howl.
On-ward up many

A frightening creek,

though your arms may get sore

And your sneakers may leak.

And . . . for some of you, there will come a time when you stumble or fall *because* you have chosen *kindness* or *decency* or *honor* above a particular boost to your own career. If that happens, *then* you will truly be successful.

Because . . . when you *do* meet your professional goals, and you have done so within the boundaries of *decency* and *kindness* and *honor,* you will know not only success . . . but bliss.

So be sure when you step.

Step with care and great tact

And remember that Life's

A Great Balancing Act.

Just never forget to be dexterous and deft.

And never mix up your right foot with your left.

And will you succeed?

Yes! You will, indeed!

(98 and 3/4 percent guaranteed.)

To the class of 1998 . . .

Thank you . . .

Good luck . . .

God bless you.

Glossary

abstract A summary of an article or a report

active listening Listening that involves conscious and responsive participation in the communication transaction.

active mindfulness The degree to which speakers and audiences are consciously aware of the transactions between them.

ad hominem The claim that something must be false because the person who said it is not credible, regardless of the argument itself.

agenda Something that defines the purpose and direction a group takes, the topics to be covered, and the goals to be achieved.

anxiety Feelings of fear and uncertainty usually accompanied by physical symptoms such as butterflies in the stomach, perspiring, and unsteadiness.

appreciative listening Listening that involves obtaining sensory stimulation or enjoyment from others

arguing in a circle (begging the question) An argument that proves nothing because the claim to be proved is used as the grounds or warrant for the argument.

argumentativeness The trait of arguing for and against the positions taken on controversial claims.

attitude A learned predisposition to respond in a consistently favorable or unfavorable manner with respect to a given object.

audience The individuals who share and listen to a public speech.

audience diversity The cultural, demographic, and individual characteristics that differ among audience members.

audio aids Presentational aids that use sound only, such as tape recordings.

audiovisual aids Presentational aids that combine sound and sight, such as films, videotapes, filmstrips, and slide/tape presentations.

authority warrant Reasoning in which the claim is believed because of the authority of the source.

backing Support for a warrant.

bar chart A chart that uses bars or columns to represent various quantities.

behavioral intention A person's subjective belief that he or she will engage in a specific behavior.

belief An assertion about the properties or characteristics of an object.

Boolean operators Terms, such as *and, or,* and *not,* used to narrow or broaden a computerized search of two or more related terms.

brainstorming A creative process used for generating a large number of ideas.

call and response pattern A pattern of organization in which a call by the speaker is followed by a response from the audience.

canons of rhetoric Classic laws of invention, arrangement, style, delivery, and memory, refined by the Romans.

categorical imperative Immanuel Kant's ethical principle that one should act only in a way that one would will to be a universal law.

categorical pattern A pattern of organization based on natural divisions in the subject matter.

causal pattern A pattern of organization that moves from cause to effect or from effect to cause.

causal warrant An argument that claims a cause will produce or has produced an effect.

CD-ROM Compact disc-read only memory, used for storage and retrieval of data.

channel The physical medium through which communication occurs.

chat lines Real-time discussions with other computer users on topics of common interest.

claim A conclusion that persuasive speakers want their audience to reach as a result of their speech.

comparison (analogy) warrant A statement that two cases that are similar in some known respects are also similar in some unknown respects.

compatibility The perception that a message is consistent with existing belief systems.

competence-enhancing language Words that emphasize rather than undermine audience perceptions of a speaker's competence.

comprehensibility The perception that a message is not too difficult or complex to understand.

comprehension The act of understanding what has been communicated.

connotative meanings The secondary meanings of words, often with a strong emotional, personal, and subjective component.

constraint A limitation on one's choices in a rhetorical situation.

constructive self-talk The use of positive coping statements instead of negative self-talk.

content (of messages) The essential meaning of what a speaker wants to convey.

context Information that surrounds an event and contributes to the meaning of that event.

coping skills Mental and physical techniques used to control arousal and anxiety in the course of speaking in public.

credibility The degree to which an audience trusts and believes in a speaker.

critical listening Listening for the purpose of making reasoned judgments about speakers and the credibility of their messages.

critical thinking The process of making sound inferences based on accurate evidence and valid reasoning.

cross cue–checking Gauging what a person says verbally against the nonverbal behaviors that make up metacommunication.

cultural diversity Differences among people in terms of language, beliefs, and customs.

cultural relativism The notion that the criteria for ethical behavior in one culture should not necessarily be applied to other cultures.

culture A learned system of language, beliefs, customs, and values with which specific people identify.

decoding The process by which a code is translated back into ideas.

deficiency needs Basic human needs, which must be satisfied before higher-order needs can be met. They include needs for food, water, air, physical safety, belongingness and love, and self-esteem and social esteem.

delivery The nonverbal behaviors by which speakers convey their message to an audience.

demographic diversity Differences among people in terms of demographics.

demographics Basic and vital data regarding any population.

denotative meanings The generally agreed upon meanings of words, which are usually found in the dictionary.

description A word picture of something.

distorted evidence Significant omissions or changes in the grounds of an argument that alter its original intent.

elaboration likelihood model A model of persuasion designed to explain why audience members will use an elaborated thinking process in some situations and not in others.

e-mail Electronic mail; a message sent electronically from one computer, over the network, to one or more other computers.

emblem A nonverbal behavior that can be directly translated into words and phrases and may replace them.

encoding The process by which ideas are translated into a code that can be understood by the receiver.

environment Our physical surroundings as we speak and the physical distance separating us from our audience.

ethical relativism A philosophy based on the belief that there are no universal ethical principles.

ethics A system of principles of right and wrong that govern human conduct.

ethos The degree to which an audience perceives a speaker as credible.

eulogy A kind of commemorative speech about someone who has died that is usually given shortly after his or her death.

example A specific instance that represents some larger class.

expert opinion A quotation from someone with special credentials in the subject matter.

explanation An account, an interpretation, or a meaning given to something.

extemporaneous delivery A mode of presentation that combines careful preparation with spontaneous speaking. The speaker generally uses brief notes rather than a full manuscript or an outline.

extended narrative A pattern of organization in which the entire body of the speech is the telling of a story.

fact Something that is verifiable as true.

fallacy An argument in which the reasons advanced for a claim fail to warrant acceptance of that claim.

false analogy The comparison of two different things that are not really comparable.

false dilemma A generalization that implies there are only two choices when there are more than two.

feedback Audience member responses, both verbal and nonverbal, to a speaker.

first-order data Evidence based on personal experience.

flip chart A series of drawings, charts, or graphs, usually attached at the top by a binding and supported on an easel.

flow chart A chart that uses boxes and arrows to represent the relationship of steps in a process.

formal outline A detailed outline used in speech preparation, but not, in most cases, in the actual presentation.

ganas A desire to succeed regardless of the odds against it.

generalization warrant A statement that either establishes a general rule or principle or applies an established rule or principle to a specific case.

general purpose The primary function of a speech. The three commonly agreed upon general purposes are to inform, to persuade, and to entertain.

good reasons Statements, based on moral principles, offered in support of propositions concerning what we should believe or how we should act.

goodwill The perception by the audience that a speaker cares about their needs and concerns.

grounds The evidence a speaker offers in support of a claim.

group Three or more individuals who are aware of each other's presence, share a mutually interdependent purpose, engage in communication transactions with one another, and identify with the group.

growth needs Higher-order human needs, which can be satisfied only after deficiency needs have been met. They include self-actualization (the process of fully realizing one's potential), knowledge and understanding, and aesthetic needs.

halo effect The assumption that just because you like or respect a person, whatever he or she says must be true.

hasty generalization An argument based on too few instances to support a generalization or on instances that are unrepresentative of the generalization.

hyperbole An exaggeration of a claim.

ignoring the issue An argument made in refutation that ignores the claim made by the other side.

illustrators Nonverbal behaviors that accompany speech and "show" what is being talked about.

impromptu delivery A spontaneous, unrehearsed mode of presenting a speech.

inclusive language Language that helps people believe that they not only have a stake in matters of societal importance but also have power in this regard.

incremental goals Steps one must complete to accomplish a long-term goal.

index A listing of sources of information, usually in newspapers, journals, and magazines, alphabetically by topic.

inference The process of moving from a ground, via a warrant, to a claim.

informative speaking The process by which an audience gains new information or a new perspective on old information from a speaker.

interdependence A relationship in which things have a reciprocal influence on each other.

Internet A collection of computer networks connecting computers around the world.

Internet service provider (ISP) A commercially available way to connect to the Internet.

invention The creative process by which the substance of a speech is generated.

isolated examples Nontypical or nonrepresentative examples that are used to prove a general claim.

key term A word or phrase used in library catalogs and indexes to identify a subject.

language intensity The degree to which words and phrases deviate from neutral.

line graph A graph in which numerical data are shown as a series of points connected by a line; often used to show changes over time.

linguistic relativity hypothesis The idea that what we perceive is influenced by the language in which we think and speak.

listening The process of receiving, attending to, and assigning meaning to aural as well as visual and tactile stimuli.

loaded language Language that has strong emotional connotations.

logos The proof a speaker offers to an audience through the words of his or her message.

long-term goals Those ends that one can hope to achieve only over an extended period of time.

main points The key ideas that support the thesis statement of a speech.

manuscript delivery A mode of presentation that involves writing out a speech completely and reading it to the audience.

marginalizing language Language that diminishes people's importance and makes them appear to be less powerful, less significant, and less worthwhile than they are.

memorized delivery A mode of presentation in which a speech is written out and committed to memory before being presented to the audience without the use of notes.

message The meaning produced by communicators.

metacommunication The message about the message; generally conveyed nonverbally.

mistaking correlation for cause The assumption that because one thing is the sign of another they are causally related.

misused statistics Statistics that involve errors such as poor sampling, lack of significant differences, misuse of average, or misuse of percentages.

Monroe's motivated sequence A five-step organizational scheme, developed by speech professor Alan Monroe, including (1) attention, (2) need, (3) satisfaction, (4) visualization, and (5) action.

narrative An extended story that is fully developed, with characters, scene, action, and plot.

narrative fidelity The degree to which a narrative rings true to real-life experience.

narrative probability The internal coherence or believability of a narrative.

negative self-talk A self-defeating pattern of intrapersonal communication, including self-criticizing, self-pressuring, and catastrophizing statements.

non sequitur An argument that does not follow from its premises.

nonverbal behavior A wordless system of communicating that also is continuous, uses multiple channels simultaneously, and is spontaneous.

novelty The quality of being new and stimulating.

observability The degree to which information can be seen.

online catalog A computerized listing of library holdings.

opinion leader A person who routinely uses principles of persuasion to shape people's beliefs about ideas, products, practices, and each other.

organizational chart A chart that represents the structure of an organization, using boxes and lines to convey hierarchy and lines of authority.

overhead transparency A plastic sheet that can be drawn on or used in a photocopier to produce an image that can be projected on a screen for an audience to see.

panel discussion An extemporaneous group discussion held for the benefit of an audience.

pathos The emotional states in an audience that a speaker can arouse and use to achieve persuasive goals.

perception The process by which we give meaning to our experiences.

persuasion The process by which a speaker influences what audience members think or do.

physiological arousal The physical changes that occur when a person is aroused, such as increased pulse, greater alertness, and more energy.

pie chart A circular chart that divides a whole into several parts, each represented by a slice of the circle proportional to its share of the whole.

pinpoint concentration Listening that focuses on specific details.

plagiarism Stealing the ideas of others and presenting them as one's own.

post hoc, ergo propter hoc ("after the fact, therefore because of the fact") The assumption that because one event preceded another, the first event must be the cause of the second event.

presentational aids Visual, audio, and audiovisual devices that can add an important dimension to a speech.

preview A forecast of the main points of a speech.

primary sources Original sources of information.

proactive delivery Delivery in which the speaker takes the initiative and anticipates and controls for as many variables as possible, rather than merely reacting to them.

problem–solution pattern A pattern of organization that analyzes a problem in terms of (1) harm, (2) significance, and (3) cause and proposes a solution that is (1) described, (2) feasible, and (3) advantageous.

pseudoreasoning An argument that appears sound at first glance but contains a fallacy of reasoning that renders it unsound.

qualifier An indication of the level of probability of a claim.

rebuttal An exception to or a refutation of an argument.

red herring (smoke screen) An irrelevant issue introduced into a controversy to divert attention from the real controversy.

reframing Revising one's view of a situation or an event, usually in a positive direction.

refutational pattern A pattern of organization that involves (1) stating the argument to be refuted, (2) stating the objection to the argument, (3) proving the objection to the argument, and (4) presenting the impact of the refutation.

regulators Gestures that influence the amount and type of feedback a speaker receives from the audience.

relational component (of messages) The collective impact of the verbal and nonverbal components of a message as it is conveyed.

relative advantage The perception that a message is beneficial.

research The process of gathering supporting materials for a speech.

retention The act of storing what was communicated in either short- or long-term memory.

rhetorical question A question that the audience isn't expected to answer out loud.

rhetorical situation A natural context of persons, events, objects, relations, and an exigence (goal) which strongly invites utterance.

secondary sources Information sources that rely on other (primary) sources rather than gathering information firsthand.

second-order data Evidence based on expert testimony.

selective attention Making a conscious choice to focus on some people and some messages, rather than others.

self-adapting behaviors Distracting touching behaviors that speakers engage in unconsciously.

self-talk (sometimes referred to as **intrapersonal communication**) Communicating silently with oneself.

sensorial involvement A process that involves listening with all the senses, not simply the sense of hearing.

sexist language Language, such as *housewife* and *fireman*, that stereotypes gender roles.

short-term goals Those ends one can accomplish in the near future.

signposts Transitional statements that bridge main points.

sign warrant Reasoning in which the presence of an observed phenomenon is used to indicate the presence of an unobserved phenomenon.

situational ethics The philosophy that there are overriding ethical maxims, but that sometimes it is necessary to set them aside in particular situations to fulfill a higher law or principle.

slippery slope The assumption that just because one event occurs, it will automatically lead to a series of undesirable events, even though there is no relationship between the action and the projected events.

source credibility The audience's perception of the believability of the speaker.

spatial pattern A pattern of organization based on physical space or geography.

speaker's notes Brief notes with key words, usually written on cards, used by a speaker when presenting a speech.

specific purpose The goal or objective a speaker hopes to achieve in speaking to a particular audience.

speech anxiety Feelings of discomfort that people experience before, during, and after speaking in public.

speech of acceptance A speech expressing thanks for an award or honor.

speech of commemoration A speech that calls attention to the stature of the person or people being honored, or emphasizes the significance of an occasion.

speech to entertain A speech that makes its point through the use of humor.

speech of introduction A speech that briefly sets the stage for an upcoming speaker.

speech of recognition A speech presenting an award or honor to an individual.

spiral pattern A pattern of organization that employs repetition of points, with the points growing in intensity as the speech builds to its conclusion.

star pattern A pattern of organization in which all of the points are of equal importance and can be presented in any order to support the common theme.

statistics Numerical summaries of data, such as percentages, ratios, and averages, that are classified in a meaningful way.

stereotyping The assumption that what is considered to be true of a larger class is necessarily true of particular members of that class.

straw person An argument made in refutation that misstates the argument being refuted. Rather than refuting the real argument, the other side constructs a person of straw, which is easy to knock down.

subpoint An idea that supports a main point.

supporting point An idea that supports a subpoint.

symbol Something that stands for or suggests something else by reason of relationship or association.

system A collection of interdependent parts arranged so that a change in one produces corresponding changes in the remaining parts.

thesis statement A single declarative sentence that focuses the audience's attention on the central point of a speech.

third-order data Evidence based on facts and statistics.

time pattern A pattern of organization based on chronology or a sequence of events.

totalizing language Language that defines people exclusively on the basis of a single attribute, such as race, ethnicity, biological sex, or ability.

transaction A simultaneous exchange of verbal and nonverbal messages between two or more people.

trialability The opportunity to experiment with an idea, a product, or a practice without penalty.

trustworthiness The perception by the audience that they can rely on a speaker's word.

usenet groups Electronic "newsletter" to which subscribers can contribute.

universalism The philosophy that there are ethical standards that apply to all situations regardless of the individual, group, or culture.

unsupported assertion The absence of any argument at all.

utilitarianism The philosophy based on the principle that the aim of any action should be to provide the greatest amount of happiness for the greatest number of people.

values More general than attitudes, enduring beliefs that hold that some ways of behaving and some goals are preferable to others.

verbal aggressiveness The trait of attacking the self-concept of those with whom a person disagrees about controversial claims.

verbal immediacy The use of language that promotes the perception of closeness between speaker and audience.

verbal qualifiers Words and phrases that erode the impact of what a speaker says in a speech.

visual aids Presentational media that convey a message visually.

visual imagery The process of mentally seeing (imagining) oneself confidently and successfully performing an action or a series of actions.

warrant The connection between grounds and claim.

wave pattern A pattern of organization in which the basic theme, often represented by a phrase, is repeated again and again, much like a wave cresting, receding, and then cresting again.

Web browser A program that allows the user to search for and reach World Wide Web sites from his or her own computer.

wide-band concentration Listening that focuses on patterns rather than details.

World Wide Web A collection of thousands of sites where "server" computers can allow you to access text, graphics, audio, and even video on your "client" computer.

zone of interaction The area in which speakers can easily make eye contact with audience members.

Credits

Photos

Part 1 p. 1T, © Kevin Horan/Stock Boston; p. 1B, © Bob Daemmrich/The Image Works **Chapter 1** p. 2, Courtesy Chico Enterprise-Record, photo by Fred Arn; p. 4L, Courtesy Cara Cupp; p. 4M, Courtesy Randy Larson; p. 4R, Courtesy Doug Pete; p. 6, Courtesy Keith Hawkins; p 12, © Brad Markel/Liaison Agency, Inc.; p. 18, *Waterfall*, 1961, © 1999 M.C. Escher/Cordon Art-Baarn-Holland. All Rights Reserved. **Chapter 2** p. 24, © J. Marshall/The Image Works; p. 27, © Bob Daemmrich/The Image Works; p. 28, Courtesy Jonathan Studebaker, photo by Mary Calvert; p. 44, © Kevin Horan/Stock Boston; p. 46, © David Young-Wolff/PhotoEdit **Chapter 3** p. 52, © Alán Gallegos/AG Photograph; p. 60, © Peter MacDiarmid/Camera Press/Retna, Ltd.; p. 68, © Reuters/Corbis-Bettmann; p. 70, © Joel Gordon; p. 71, © Ben Davidson/Photo 20-20 **Chapter 4** p. 76, © Steve Woit/Index Stock Imagery, p. 85, © David Maung/Impact Visuals; p. 86, © Charles Gupton/Tony Stone Images; p. 96, © Steve Skjold/PhotoEdit; p. 101, © Bob Daemmrich/Stock Boston **Part 2** p. 105T, © Reuters/Mike Theiler/Archive Photos; p. 105B, © Michael Newman/PhotoEdit **Chapter 5** p. 106, © Loren Santow/Impact Visuals; p. 109, Courtesy Carolyn McCarthy; p. 115, Courtesy Tomoko Mukawa; p. 120, © Billy E. Barnes/Jeroboam; p. 130, © Andrew Kent/Retna, Ltd.; p. 131, © Joel Gordon; p. 132, © Corbis/Bettmann-UPI **Chapter 6** p. 136, ©

Reuters/Corbis-Bettmann; p. 138, © 1982 Paramount/MP & TV Photo Archive; p. 140, © Gamma Presse Images/Liaison Agency, Inc.; p. 148, © AP/Wide World Photos; p. 152, © Corbis/Bettmann-UPI; p. 157, © Reuters/Mike Theiler/Archive Photos; p. 158, © Karen Borchers **Part 3** p. 163T, © David Young-Wolff/PhotoEdit; p. 163B, © L.S. Stepanowicz/Index Stock Imagery **Chapter 7** p. 164, © Cindy Charles/PhotoEdit; p. 171, © Gary A. Conner/PhotoEdit; p. 173, © Vic Bider/PhotoEdit; p. 175, Everett Collection; p. 180, © David Young-Wolff/Photo Edit; p. 190, Courtesy Rick Rigsby **Chapter 8** p. 202, © Ron Chapple/FPG International; p. 204, © Michael Newman/PhotoEdit; p. 212, © L.S. Stepanowicz/Index Stock Imagery; p. 221, Courtesy Russ Woody; p. 224, © AP/Wide World Photos; p. 230, © Bob Daemmrich/Stock Boston **Chapter 9** p. 234, © Bob Daemmrich/Stock Boston; p. 237, © The Granger Collection, New York; p. 240, © 1995 New Line/R. Torres/MP & TV Photo Archive; p. 241, Collection of Millicent Rogers Museum; p. 244, © Terry Ashe/Liaison Agency, Inc.; p. 246, Courtesy Hal Riney & Partners, Inc.; p. 249, © AP/Wide World Photos **Chapter 10** p. 260, © Syracuse Newspapers/Dick Blume/The Image Works; p. 262, © Mark Peterson/SABA; p. 266, © Myrleen Ferguson Cate/PhotoEdit; p. 273TL, © Tom McCarthy/Index Stock Imagery; p. 273TR, ©

Jeff Greenberg/Index Stock Imagery; p. 273B, © Robert W. Ginn/Index Stock Imagery; p. 279, © AP/Wide World Photos; p. 282, © Martin Simon/SABA **Chapter 11** p. 292, © Liaison Agency, Inc., p. 296, © David Young-Wolff/PhotoEdit; p. 302, © Jeff Greenberg/PhotoEdit; p. 312, © David J. Sams/Stock Boston **Part 4** p. 315T, © Stanley Rowin/Index Stock Imagery; p. 315B, © Bob Daemmrich/The Image Works **Chapter 12** p. 316, © Anne Chadwick Williams/Sacramento Bee; p. 319, © Sam Forencich; p. 325, © David Shopper/Stock Boston; p. 326, © Yvonne Hemsey/Liaison Agency, Inc.; p. 330, © ABC/The Everett Collection **Chapter 13** p. 338, © Bob Daemmrich/The Image Works; p. 340, © Robert Giroux/Liaison Agency, Inc.; p. 342, © Bob Daemmrich/The Image Works; p. 359, © Joel Gordon; p. 361, © Michael Newman/PhotoEdit; p. 363, © AP/Wide World Photos **Chapter 14** p. 370, © David Kennerly/Liaison Agency, Inc.; p. 372, © Reuters/Mike Theiler/Archive Photos; p. 376, © AP/Wide World Photos; p. 378, © Robert Brenner/PhotoEdit; p. 392, © Reuters/Ron Schwane/Archive Photos; p. 404, © Jeff Christensen/Liaison Agency, Inc. **Chapter 15** p. 410, © Telegraph Colour Library/FPG International; p. 418, © Stanley Rowin/Index Stock Imagery; p. 420, © Corbis/Reuters; p. 423, © AP/Wide World Photos; p. 425, Courtesy Jeraline Singh; p. 426, © Corbis/Reuters; p. 429, Courtesy Mike Scott

Figures

Figure 1.1 Based on Abraham Maslow, *Motivation and Personality*, 2nd ed. (New York: Harper & Row, 1970). Adapted with permission from Michael D. Scott and William G. Powers, *Interpersonal Communication: A Question of Needs* (Boston: Houghton Mifflin, 1978), 10. Figure 11.2 U.S. Bureau of the Census, *Statistical Abstract of the United States: 1995*, 115th edition. (Washington, D.C., 1995), 298. Figure 11.3 U.S. Bureau of the Census, *Statistical Abstract of the United States: 1995*, 115th edition. (Washington, D.C., 1995), 568. Figure 11.4 U.S. Bureau of the Census, *Statistical Abstract of the United States: 1995*, 115th edition. (Washington, D.C., 1995), 250 and 106. Figure 14.1 *An Introduction to Reasoning*, Second Edition, by Stephen Toulmin, Richard Rieke, and Allan Janik. Copyright © 1984. Adapted by permission of Prentice-Hall, Inc. Upper Saddle River, NJ.

Text

Chapter 3 p. 56, From James C. McCroskey, *An Introduction to Rhetorical Communication, 7th Edition*, Allyn & Bacon, 1997. Reprinted with permission from the author. **Chapter 4** p. 84, Reprinted with the permission of Simon & Schuster from *Scuse Me While I Kiss This Guy* by Gavin Edwards. Copyright © 1995 by Gavin Edwards. p. 90, From Lawrence R. Wheeless, "An Investigation of Receiver Apprehension and Social Context Dimensions of Communication Apprehension," *The Speech Teacher* 24 (1975):261-268. Copyright © 1975 by National Communication Association. Reprinted by permission of the publisher.

Chapter 5 p. 109, Reprinted with permission from Congresswoman Carolyn McCarthy. p. 116, From William Gudykunst, *Bridging Differences, 2nd Edition*. Copyright © 1994 by Sage Publications, Inc. Reprinted by permission of the publisher. **Chapter 6** p. 146, Credo for a Free and Responsible Society reprinted by permission of the National Communication Association. **Chapter 7** p. 184, Netscape Communications Corporation has not authorized, sponsored, or endorsed, or approved this publication and is not responsible for its content. Netscape and the Netscape Communications Corporate Logos, are trademarks and trade names of Netscape Communications Corporation. All other product names and/or logos are trademarks of their respective owners. **Chapter 8** From E. Hughes, J. Silverman, and D.R. Wienbroer, *Rules of Thumb*, McGraw-Hill, 1990, p. 99. Reprinted with permission of the publisher. **Chapter 9** p. 253, From *Twentieth Century Selling*. © Dr. Loretta Malandro. Taught in her program "Speak With Impact," offered by Malandro Communication Inc., Scottsdale, Arizona. p. 256, From John D. O'Connor, "Cops Hold Cabbie in Hit-Run Death," *San Francisco Examiner*, 12 August, 1994, p. A4. Reprinted by permission of the publisher. **Chapter 10** p. 262, 263, From Diana Griego Erwin, "Signs Were There; Facts Were Missing," *Sacramento Bee*, December 17, 1995, A2. Reprinted with permission from the publisher. **Chapter 13** p. 354, From Richard E. Petty and John T. Cacioppo, "The Elaboration Likelihood Model of Persuasion," in *Advances in Experimental and Social Psychology*, Vol. 19, ed. Leonard

Berkowitz, Academic Press, 1986. Reprinted by permission of the authors. **Chapter 14** pp. 373-376, From Sarah Brady and J. Warren Cassidy, "The Case for Firearms . . . And the Case Against Them," *Time Magazine*, January 29, 1990. Copyright © 1990 Time Inc. Reprinted by permission. p. 380, From Stephen Tuolmin, Richard Rieke, and Allan Janik, *An Introduction to Reasoning, 2nd Edition*, Prentice-Hall, Inc., 1984. Copyright © 1984 Prentice-Hall, Inc. Adapted by permission of Prentice-Hall, Inc., Upper Saddle River, NJ. p. 386, Excerpted with special permission for William V. Haney, *Communication and Interpersonal Relations*, 6th Ed., R.D. Irwin, Inc., 1992, 231-233, 241. The story and statements are a portion of the "Uncritical Inference Test," copyright 1955 and 1983 by William V. Haney. p. 392 From "Tell It to the ER," *Chico Enterprise Record*, 13 March 1992, 2A. Reprinted by permission. p. 405 From "Tell It to the ER," *Chico Enterprise Record*, 16 February 1992, 2A. Reprinted by permission. **Chapter 15** pp. 424, 426-428, Adapted from Jack Perella and Steven R. Brydon, "Speaking to Entertain," in *Intercollegiate Forensics: A Participant's Handbook*, ed. T.C. Winebrenner, 42-46. Copyright © 1992 Northern California Forensics Association. With permission. p. 430, Article first appeared in *Newsweek's* 1990 Special Ad Section, "Management Digest." Reprinted by permission. **Appendix B** p. 439, Reprinted with permission from the Republican National Committee. p. 442, Reprinted with permission from Russ Woody.

Index